PHP 5

Your visual blueprint™ for creating open source, server-side content

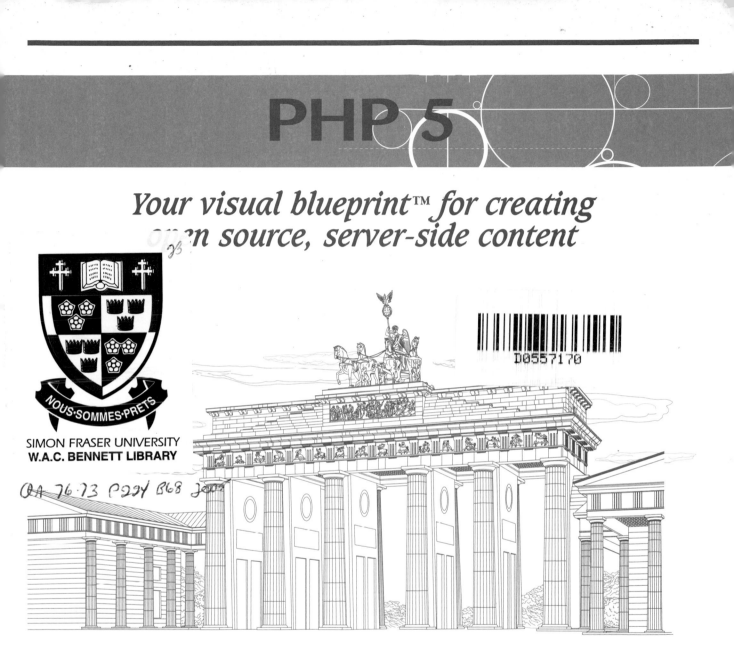

D0557170

by Toby Joe Boudreaux

WILEY

Wiley Publishing, Inc.

PHP 5: Your visual blueprint™ for creating open source, server-side content

Published by
Wiley Publishing, Inc.
111 River Street
Hoboken, NJ 07030-5774

Published simultaneously in Canada

Copyright © 2005 by Wiley Publishing, Inc., Indianapolis, Indiana

Library of Congress Control Number: 2005921025

ISBN-13: 978-0-7645-8332-2
ISBN-10: 0-7645-8332-8

Manufactured in the United States of America

10 9 8 7 6 5 4 3 2 1

1K/RV/QU/QV/IN

Trademark Acknowledgments

Contact Us

For general information on our other products and services please contact our Customer Care Department within the U.S. at 800-762-2974, outside the U.S. at 317-572-3993 or fax 317-572-4002.

For technical support please visit www.wiley.com/techsupport.

Berlin's Brandenburg Gate

Berlin's Brandenburg Gate, designed by Karl Gotthard Langhans and completed in 1791, has witnessed a turbulent history. Through it, Napoleon marched victorious in 1806. Around it, the Berlin Wall grew up to divide a city and a nation. Before it, President Reagan made an impassioned plea for unity in 1987. Reopened in 1989 after the fall of the Wall, it now stands as a monument to freedom, its magnificent sculptures and reliefs restored. Learn more about the Brandenburg Gate and other Berlin landmarks in *Frommer's Germany,* available wherever books are sold or at www.frommers.com.

WILEY

Sales

Contact Wiley
at (800) 762-2974
or (317) 572-4002.

PRAISE FOR VISUAL BOOKS...

"This is absolutely the best computer-related book I have ever bought. Thank you so much for this fantastic text. Simply the best computer book series I have ever seen. I will look for, recommend, and purchase more of the same."

—David E. Prince (NeoNome.com)

"I have several of your Visual books and they are the best I have ever used."

—Stanley Clark (Crawfordville, FL)

"I just want to let you know that I really enjoy all your books. I'm a strong visual learner. You really know how to get people addicted to learning! I'm a very satisfied Visual customer. Keep up the excellent work!"

—Helen Lee (Calgary, Alberta, Canada)

"I have several books from the Visual series and have always found them to be valuable resources."

—Stephen P. Miller (Ballston Spa, NY)

"This book is PERFECT for me - it's highly visual and gets right to the point. What I like most about it is that each page presents a new task that you can try verbatim or, alternatively, take the ideas and build your own examples. Also, this book isn't bogged down with trying to 'tell all' – it gets right to the point. This is an EXCELLENT, EXCELLENT, EXCELLENT book and I look forward purchasing other books in the series."

—Tom Dierickx (Malta, IL)

"I have quite a few of your Visual books and have been very pleased with all of them. I love the way the lessons are presented!"

—Mary Jane Newman (Yorba Linda, CA)

"I am an avid fan of your Visual books. If I need to learn anything, I just buy one of your books and learn the topic in no time. Wonders! I have even trained my friends to give me Visual books as gifts."

—Illona Bergstrom (Aventura, FL)

"I just had to let you and your company know how great I think your books are. I just purchased my third Visual book (my first two are dog-eared now!) and, once again, your product has surpassed my expectations. The expertise, thought, and effort that go into each book are obvious, and I sincerely appreciate your efforts."

—Tracey Moore (Memphis, TN)

"Compliments to the chef!! Your books are extraordinary! Or, simply put, extra-ordinary, meaning way above the rest! THANK YOU THANK YOU THANK YOU! I buy them for friends, family, and colleagues."

—Christine J. Manfrin (Castle Rock, CO)

"I write to extend my thanks and appreciation for your books. They are clear, easy to follow, and straight to the point. Keep up the good work! I bought several of your books and they are just right! No regrets! I will always buy your books because they are the best."

—Seward Kollie (Dakar, Senegal)

"I am an avid purchaser and reader of the Visual series, and they are the greatest computer books I've seen. Thank you very much for the hard work, effort, and dedication that you put into this series."

—Alex Diaz (Las Vegas, NV)

Credits

Project Editor
Sarah Hellert

Acquisitions Editor
Jody Lefevere

Project Development Manager
Lindsay Sandman

Copy Editor
Kim Heusel

Technical Editor
Namir Shammas

Editorial Assistant
Adrienne D. Porter

Editorial Manager
Robyn Siesky

Media Development Manager
Kit Malone

Special Help
Windows screen shots provided by
Namir Shammas and Joseph Shammas

Manufacturing
Allan Conley
Linda Cook
Paul Gilchrist
Jennifer Guynn

Book Design
Kathryn Rickard

Production Coordinator
Maridee V. Ennis

Layout
Sean Decker
Jennifer Heleine
Amanda Spagnuolo

Screen Artist
Jill A. Proll

Cover Illustration
Shelley Norris

Proofreader
Nancy L. Reinhardt

Quality Control
Brian H. Walls

Indexer
Richard T. Evans

**Vice President and Executive
Group Publisher**
Richard Swadley

Vice President and Publisher
Barry Pruett

Composition Services Director
Debbie Stailey

About the Author

Toby Boudreaux has been involved in Web development since 1998. His experience includes working as a Designer for Nerve.com, Design Technologist for The Chopping Block, Web Developer for Threespot Media, and Director of Engineering for EVB and Horn Group.

He has expertise in LAMP development, Java programming, Flash application development, standards-compliant markup, accessibility, and usability.

He lives in Brooklyn, New York, with his wife Michele and three chubby cats.

Author's Acknowledgments

I owe a great deal to my dear friend Chandler McWilliams for recommending me to the Acquisition Editors at Wiley; to both Adrienne Porter and Jody Lefevere for coordinating the project; to Copy Editor Kim Heusel and Project Editor Sarah Hellert for their continual guidance and patience; to Namir Shammas for his excellent feedback and technical prowess. I could not have undertaken such a project without the support of my wife, Michele, and her willingness to postpone and reschedule plans, to bring me tea, and to act as a test subject for introductory topics.

TABLE OF CONTENTS

TABLE OF CONTENTS

TABLE OF CONTENTS

HOW TO USE THIS VISUAL BLUEPRINT BOOK

PHP 5: Your visual blueprint for creating open source, server-side content uses clear, descriptive examples to show you how to use the newest version of PHP to develop portable, powerful Web applications. If you are already familiar with PHP, you can use this book as a quick reference for many PHP tasks.

Who Needs This Book

This book is for the experienced computer user who wants to find out more about PHP. It is also for more experienced PHP users who want to expand their knowledge of the different features that PHP has to offer.

Book Organization

PHP 5: Your visual blueprint for creating open source, server-side content has 12 chapters.

Chapter 1, Getting Started with PHP, covers the installation and configuration of PHP on Windows and Mac OS X platforms.

Chapter 2, PHP Language Basics, introduces readers to the basic syntax of PHP including the use of variables, operators, and procedural functions.

Chapter 3, Working with Arrays, covers the use of arrays in PHP and teaches readers to create, manipulate, and print the contents of arrays.

Chapter 4, Working with Text, teaches readers to process and manipulate textual data.

Chapter 5, Working with Filesystem and I/O, covers creating, opening, reading from and writing to files on your Web server.

Chapter 6, Working with Forms, covers the use of HTML forms to capture, validate, and process user data.

Chapter 7, Using Cookies and Sessions, teaches readers to use cookies and sessions to persist data across HTTP requests.

Chapter 8, Introduction to Objects, introduces readers to the core concepts of Object-Oriented Programming (OOP) and covers the support for OOP in PHP5.

Chapter 9, Introduction to Databases, covers the use and design of relational databases including the use of Structured Query Language (SQL).

Chapter 10, Using Databases, covers popular relational database systems such as SQLite and MySQL as well as the new MySQLi interface.

Chapter 11, Debugging and Errors, introduces readers to methods of gracefully handling errors reported by PHP processor during execution.

Chapter 12, Working with XML, covers the XML support in PHP including DOM, SAX, and XSLT support.

What You Need to Use This Book

The use of PHP requires a computer for which the reader has the ability to install and configure software. PHP and MySQL are available for all popular operating systems and require very little in the way of resources.

To write PHP scripts, you need a text editor, such as BBEdit or TextPad. Transferring files to a remote Web server requires the use of an FTP program such as CuteFTP for Windows or Transmit for Mac OS X.

WINDOWS REQUIREMENTS

Windows 98, 2000, NT, ME, or XP

MAC REQUIREMENTS

Mac OS X

Operating System Differences

When developing PHP applications for multiple operating systems, the only special considerations are when using file handling mechanisms and other file IO operations. PHP is quite portable across platforms and can be developed in a platform-agnostic fashion.

The Conventions in This Book

A number of styles have been used throughout *PHP 5: Your visual blueprint for creating open source, server-side content* to designate different types of information.

Courier Font

Indicates the use of PHP such as tags or attributes, scripting language code such as statements, operators, or functions, and code such as objects, methods, or properties.

Italics

Indicates a new term.

An Apply It section takes the code from the preceding task one step further. Apply It sections allow you to take full advantage of PHP.

Extra

An Extra section provides additional information about the preceding task. Extra sections contain the inside information to make working with PHP easier and more efficient.

What's on the Web Site

The Web site www.wiley.com/go/php5visual contains the sample files that you can use to work with the tasks in *PHP 5: Your visual blueprint for creating open source, server-side content*.

Introduction to PHP

PHP is a scripting language used primarily on Web servers running the Apache HTTP server software. While uses for PHP are many, the core functionality is to provide a language and framework for the development of Web applications. As of November 2004, the reported usage of PHP was at nearly 18 million domains. Combined with Linux, the Apache HTTP server, and the MySQL database system, PHP provides functionality to the great portion of the servers on the World Wide Web.

History

PHP/FI

The name PHP is a recursive acronym meaning "PHP: Hypertext Preprocessor." The roots of PHP are in the Perl language, most notably in a set of Perl scripts created by Rasmus Lerdorf in 1995 for use in developing his own personal Web site. The toolset he created was called PHP/FI, or "Personal Home Page/Forms Interpreter," and allowed users to easily manage submitted forms and perform logging and tracking functions. The initial version of PHP was an interpreted scripting language that could be embedded into HTML pages and a parser that processed the embedded scripts on each page request. By adhering to the standard HTTP request-response cycle the scripts could be easily developed, debugged, deployed, and maintained.

PHP 3

The popularity of the PHP module and the enthusiasm of the Open Source community lead to PHP being rewritten as an Apache module with robust capabilities and enhancements. The first version of PHP written as an Apache module and resembling the language we use today was PHP 3. The PHP 3 project was created by Andi Gutmans and Zeev Suraski in 1997. The most important change to the PHP effort in version 3 was an architecture that allowed developers to easily contribute to and extend PHP.

PHP 3 continued the notion of using embedded scripts, or *scriptlets*, in an HTML document. By passing documents with a `.php` extension through the PHP preprocessor before allowing Apache to serve them, each embedded scriptlet could be parsed and executed and any relevant output substituted in its place. Simple tasks such as variable substitution or more complex actions such as database connectivity were suddenly available to users with a knowledge of HTML and access to the PHP documentation. Because of the interpreted nature of PHP, compiling scripts was not a requirement. Much like the way that browsers render HTML each time a page is viewed, the PHP module for Apache would render server-side scripts. The change-and-refresh development cycle was familiar to HTML developers, and PHP quickly developed a following among programmers and markup specialists alike. At its peak, it is estimated that PHP 3 was installed on 10 percent of the Web servers on the Internet.

PHP 4

Each version of PHP seems to not only add functionality but also optimize the existing code base. Much like the development of PHP 3, the next version, PHP 4, was in large part rewritten to take into account new features and optimizations.

The central goals in the PHP 4 project were to optimize the code base to allow for more efficiency in large and complex applications and to facilitate modularity and portability in both the underlying language implementation and the interpreted scripting language used by Web developers. An important addition to PHP 4 was limited support for object-oriented programming (OOP) using classes. Though incomplete in comparison to other languages, the support for OOP in PHP 4 allowed developers with little experience in other languages to begin to understand the importance and power of OOP.

PHP 5

Object-oriented programming is a central feature in the newest version of PHP, which is PHP 5. Though still in its early releases, PHP 5 has been praised as a mature language for Web programming, comparable in many ways to Java and the Microsoft C# language. Though different from both in many ways, PHP 5 has already proven to be an excellent object-oriented language for Web development whose benefits in many ways outshine those of the aforementioned languages.

Open Source

The licensing of PHP is undoubtedly one of the core attractions. PHP is open source and free software, which means that there is no cost for installation or usage and that any skilled developer can contribute to the project. Because the source code from which PHP is compiled is open, a community of peers comprised of people from all over the world can review the source, helping to identify inefficiencies, stability issues, and security risks. Along with locating these problems, any developer may help repair the code base.

Cross-Platform

PHP is a cross-platform language, meaning that both the engine and the code can be used on nearly every major operating system. The majority of the code written in PHP is portable from Unix to Windows to Mac OS X, for example. The cross-platform nature makes it easy for developers working on different operating systems and server configurations to share their code, creating a rich code base available by way of open-source projects and community Web sites.

Database Interaction

Another great strength of PHP is the ease with which a developer can create scripts that interact with databases. Database-driven Web sites are in high demand and the robust database libraries available for PHP allow developers to create sites quickly and efficiently, giving them the luxury of concentrating not on database connectivity implementation, but on the ways in which databases can be used with their sites.

Development Tools

Aside from a Web server with a build of PHP, the only additional tool you need to develop PHP applications is a text editor. There are no special integrated development environments (IDEs) or compilers required, though there are many available. Anyone can open a standard text file and begin writing PHP code. The low overhead and accessible learning curve are big attractions for developers looking for the path of least resistance in generating dynamic, server-side content.

Install Apache on Windows

In order to use PHP, you must have Web server software installed and configured to use PHP. The most popular Web server software is the Apache HTTPD server. Check the Apache Web site, www.apache.org, for the most recent stable release.

The Apache HTTPD Web server is extremely reliable and robust. Apache is the most popular Web server on the Internet and is used on small, low-traffic sites as well as on extremely large, load-balanced commercial sites.

The Apache Web server for Windows installation process is fairly simple. Like most Windows installers, the Apache Web server installer is an executable "wizard" installer that takes you through the license acceptance and installation process. The Apache Web server can be installed on computers running any version of Windows, from Windows 95 through 98, 2000, Me, and XP.

The first screen of the installation wizard gives an overview of the software to be installed. The second screen is a standard End User License Agreement (EULA) stating the rights and restrictions for the software. You must consent to the license in order to proceed to the next step of the installation process.

After agreeing to the EULA, you are presented with a screen asking you to specify your Network Domain, Server Name, and the e-mail address of the administrator for the computer. The administrator will most likely be yourself, and you can use your own e-mail address. For development on a local computer, this is not as important as when hosting a production server. This dialog box will also present the option to install Apache for all users or only for your account. Generally it is best to install for all users, especially if you are the sole user of the computer.

You can choose the type of installation you want to perform during the install process, allowing for a custom configuration. You can always modify the configuration of Apache after installation, if need be.

Install Apache on Windows

① Begin the installation process by double-clicking the icon for the Apache Web server installation program.

The Installation Wizard appears.

② Click Next to continue on to the first step of the installer.

③ When presented with the license agreement, read the license and select the I accept option to accept the terms.

④ Click Next to continue.

⑤ View the contents of the Read This First window and then click Next to continue.

6 In the Server Information window, type your network domain.

Note: You can use the default, localhost, if no other is available.

7 Type the name of your server here.

8 Type an administrator e-mail address, such as administrator@localhost.

● Leave the recommended installation option selected.

9 Click Next to continue.

10 When the Setup Type window appears, select the default Typical installation.

11 Click Next to continue.

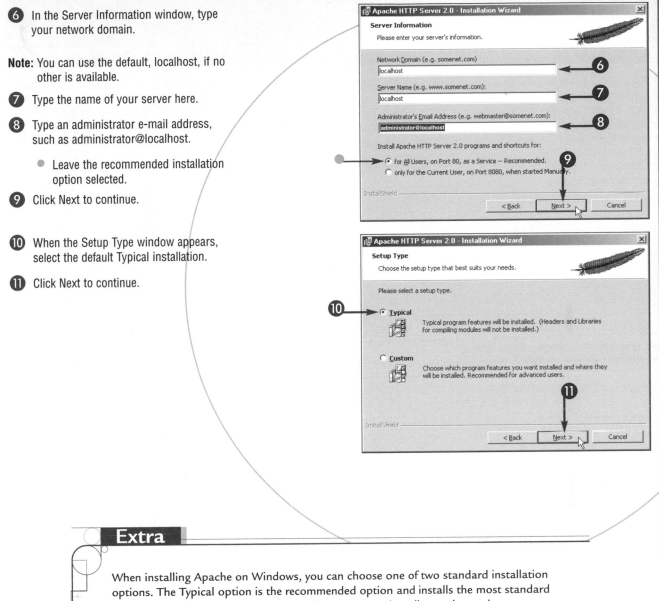

continued →

Extra

When installing Apache on Windows, you can choose one of two standard installation options. The Typical option is the recommended option and installs the most standard extensions and configuration options. The Custom option allows advanced system administrators and developers to select which modules they want to install.

Because Apache is an open-source project, there are no telephone hotlines or commercial support Web sites to which you can go for customer or technical support. There are a number of community sites on the Web whose members can provide assistance, but discretion should be used when communicating potentially sensitive information or taking advice. Most members of the open-source community are extremely helpful and kind, but all advice should be checked against manuals and documentation before committing changes to your server software.

The default destination for the installation is C:\Program Files\Apache Group\Apache2. You can specify another destination during the installation process, but it is recommended that you accept the default value for ease of maintenance and future updates to the Apache software. When browsing the Apache installation directory, you will find documentation as well as several standard modules that are used to add functionality to Apache.

The installation wizard displays a screen stating the default installation location of the Apache Web server software. You can choose to leave the default location as your target location, or change the location to another directory on your computer. Typically, it is best to install in the default location so that there is consistency across similar machines on which Apache is installed. You can change the installation directory by clicking Browse in the dialog box.

After choosing the location in which you want to install the Apache Web server, the wizard presents a final confirmation screen that allows you to go back and change any settings of which you are unsure. When you are confident in your choices for installation parameters, you can click Install to begin the automated installation process. If you decide against installing the Apache Web server at this point, you can click Cancel to abandon the process.

After the installation process is complete the wizard displays a screen noting that a successful installation operation has occurred. You can click Finish to end the wizard and resume normal computing.

To confirm that the Apache Web server has been installed and that it is running properly, you can use your Web browser to view a page. By default, Apache installs a welcome page in the main Web directory from which it serves files. You can view this page using the local *loopback address* http://127.0.0.1/. The loopback address is a special address each computer uses to identify itself to local applications. If the Apache installation process was successful, the default Apache welcome page appears.

Install Apache on Windows *(continued)*

The Destination Folder window appears.

- It is recommended that you use the default folder for the installation directory.

- Alternately, you can click Change and browse to another folder.

⑫ Click Next to continue.

The Ready to Install the Program window appears.

⑬ View the information and click Install to continue.

The installer sets up the Apache files.

⑭ Click Finish to conclude the installation process.

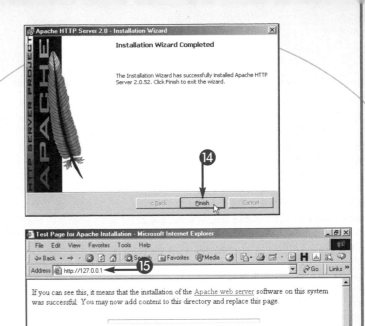

⑮ You can test the installation by opening a Web browser and going to the location: http://127.0.0.1/.

If your browser does not load the page, try the installation again.

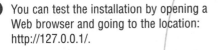
Extra

You can start and stop Apache using the command prompt. In the command prompt window, change to the directory in which Apache was installed, usually C:\Program Files\Apache Group\ Apache2. Type `apache` to start the Web server. You can use the same command to stop Apache by passing arguments. To stop Apache, type `apache -k shutdown`.

When installing Apache Web server on a computer running a Windows operating system, a folder containing shortcut commands for the Apache Web server is typically added to the Programs folder on the Start menu. This folder allows quick access to common Apache tools and commands.

The installation program installs a README file in the Apache installation folder that contains information specific to the release of Apache you installed. The README file is an important part of the application package because it provides succinct notes about changes in the software as well as any special configuration advice or compatibility notes. While not required, it is a good idea to read this file.

Install Internet Information Services on Windows

T he Microsoft Internet Information Server (IIS) is Web server software that allows you to host multiple Web sites on the Internet or on a network such as a corporate Intranet using a standard Windows computer. With the IIS and accompanying tools, you can host and manage even the busiest Web sites. Though PHP is used more often with the Apache Web server than with Internet Information Services, IIS can be used with PHP quite well in both development and production.

You can install IIS from the Windows XP CD-ROM with which you installed Windows. First, use the Start menu to begin adding the program. Click Start, Control Panel, and then Add or Remove Programs. From the Add or Remove

Programs menu, click Add/Remove Windows Components. Find the option for Internet Information Services (IIS), select it, and then click Details.

In the Internet Information Services (IIS) window that appears, check the boxes for SMTP Service and World Wide Web Service, and then click OK. In the Windows Component selection, make sure that the Internet Information Services (IIS) box is checked and then click OK. The components you selected will be installed.

After IIS is installed, it is a good idea to restart your computer. The Internet Information Services automatically starts each time you restart your computer. When IIS is installed and running, you can install PHP.

Install Internet Information Services on Windows

1. Insert the Windows CD-ROM.

2. In the Control Panel, select Add/Remove Programs.

3. Click Add/Remove Windows Components to display the Windows Components Wizard.

4. Click Internet Information Services (IIS) (☐ changes to ☑).

5. Click Details to display the IIS window.

6. Click beside each IIS component you want to install (☐ changes to ☑).

7. Click OK to confirm your configuration.

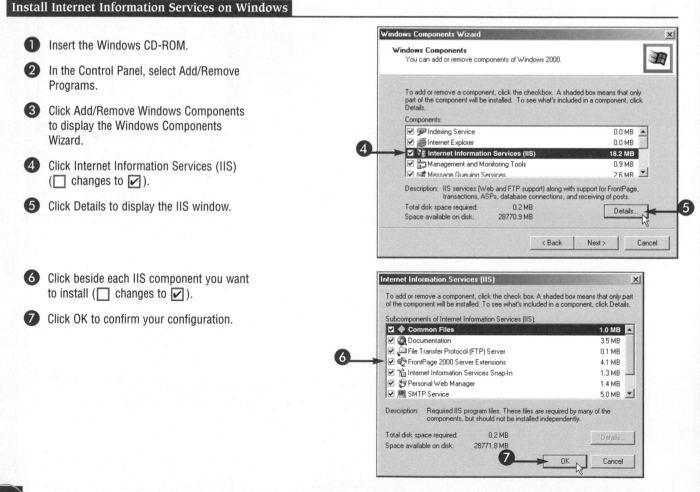

⑧ In the Windows Components Wizard, click Next to install the IIS package you have configured.

Windows Components Wizard

Windows Components
You can add or remove components of Windows 2000.

To add or remove a component, click the checkbox. A shaded box means that only part of the component will be installed. To see what's included in a component, click Details.

Components:

☑ 🔎 Indexing Service	0.0 MB	▲
☑ 🧭 Internet Explorer	0.0 MB	
☑ 📧 Internet Information Services (IIS)	18.2 MB	
☑ 📇 Management and Monitoring Tools	0.9 MB	
☑ 📨 Message Queuing Services	2.6 MB	▼

Description: IIS services (Web and FTP support) along with support for FrontPage, transactions, ASPs, database connections, and receiving posts.

Total disk space required: 0.2 MB
Space available on disk: 28770.9 MB

[Details...]

[< Back] [Next >] [Cancel]

⑨ When the completion dialog box appears, click Finish.

The Internet Information Services is installed.

Windows Components Wizard

Completing the Windows Components Wizard

You have successfully completed the Windows Components Wizard.

To close this wizard, click Finish.

Microsoft **Windows** 2000

[< Back] [Finish]

Extra

Before attempting to install IIS, you should log on to the computer with an Administrator account, because a standard user account is restricted from making machine-wide changes such as installing a Web server. This restriction is in large part in order to enforce security on the machine, but also helps ensure that applications are not accidentally installed or uninstalled. Logging on with an Administrator account ensures that you have proper permissions for executing installers. Take care when acting as an Administrator, because damage can be done to settings or questionable software can be installed.

After IIS is installed, the Internet Information Services window provides tools that allow you to administer your IIS Web sites. You can select the Administrative Tools option in the Control Panel to reveal the Internet Information Services window.

Add a Virtual Directory to Internet Information Services

The default installation of Internet Information Services (IIS) creates a number of directories that can be used to serve Web pages, including PHP scripts. These directories are stored in the `C:\Inetpub\wwwroot` folder. Only pages stored in this directory, or a subdirectory, can be served by IIS. This is a security feature that allows a computer to act as a Web server without compromising all files on the server. You can create a virtual directory to serve pages that are not contained within the document root as if they are.

You can use the Virtual Directory Creation Wizard to create and properly configure a virtual directory from which PHP pages can be served. You must give the virtual directory an alias, which is a name by which users will access pages in the directory.

From the Start menu, navigate to the Programs directory, select Administrative Tools, and then click Internet Services Manager. Expand the server name. Right-click the Default Web Site entry, point to New, and click Virtual Directory. Type the name of the alias you want to use in the Virtual Directory Creation Wizard. Click Browse to locate the directory you want to use as the directory for your alias. On the last screen, click Finish to complete the wizard.

Virtual directories allow IIS to serve files from directories in locations other than the main Web root. For example, a folder that stores XML data for your site might be used as the location for a virtual directory with the alias 'xml.' This allows users to access the XML data using the path /xml/ relative to the Web root.

Add a Virtual Directory to Internet Information Services

① Use the Start menu to access the Control Panel, and then choose Administrative Tools.

② Double-click Internet Services Manager to display the IIS window.

③ Click the plus sign (+) to display a list of Web sites currently running on the Web server.

④ Click the Web site to which you want to add a virtual directory.

⑤ Click Action.

⑥ Click New.

⑦ Click Virtual Directory.

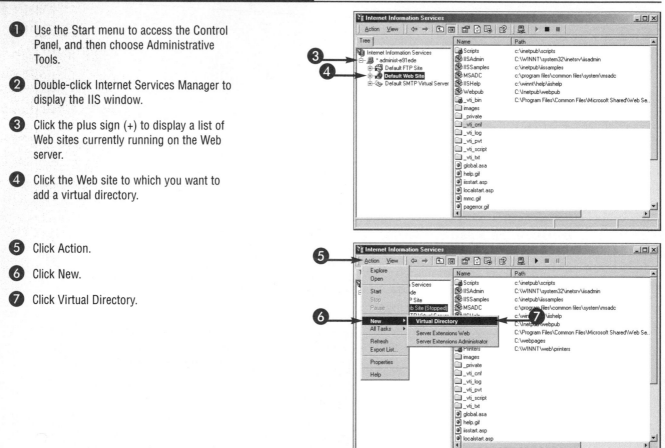

The Virtual Directory Creation Wizard appears.

8 Click Next to continue.

The Virtual Directory Alias window appears.

9 Type an alias for the new virtual directory.

10 Click Next to continue.

Virtual Directory Creation Wizard

Welcome to the Virtual Directory Creation Wizard

This wizard will help you create a new virtual directory on this web site.

Click Next to continue.

8

< Back | Next > | Cancel

Virtual Directory Creation Wizard

Virtual Directory Alias
You must give the virtual directory a short name, or alias, for quick reference.

Type the alias you want to use to gain access to this Web virtual directory. Use the same naming conventions that you would for naming a directory.

Alias:
PHPVB **9**

10

< Back | Next > | Cancel

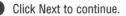

Extra

You can also use Windows Explorer to add a virtual directory to the Internet Information Services. The first step is to select the directory you want to use as the target of your virtual directory. Click the File menu and choose Properties. In the Properties dialog box, click the Web Sharing tab and select the "Share this folder" option. In the Edit Alias dialog box that appears next, specify the alias you want to use for your virtual directory. Select the access and application permissions to use for the virtual directory and click OK. Click OK in the Properties dialog box, and the virtual directory is added to IIS.

To remove a virtual directory from IIS, open the Internet Information Services window and select the virtual directory you want to remove. Click the Delete button (☒) and choose Yes in the confirmation dialog box that appears. Removing a virtual directory immediately prevents users from accessing the content in the target directory.

continued →

Add a Virtual Directory to Internet Information Services (continued)

You must specify the location of the directory you want to add as a virtual directory. The access permissions for the directory must also be specified. The access permissions determine how the pages in the directory — whether plain HTML or dynamic pages like PHP — can be utilized.

The Read permission allows users viewing your site to access the Web pages with their Web browsers. This access permission must be set for a directory from which you want to serve Web content. Without the Read permission, no content in the directory will be accessible.

The Run scripts permission allows scripts to run in the directory. Execution of PHP and other dynamic content is dependent upon this access permission being set. By default, the Run scripts permission is turned on.

The Execute permission allows scripts and applications to be executed. This option should be set for any special executable applications installed on your Web server.

The Write permission allows files to be dynamically created in the directory targeted by your virtual directory. If you have scripts that need to create files dynamically, such as image-generation scripts, this permission must be turned on.

The Browse permission allows users to view a listing of files in the directory targeted by your virtual directory. When turned on, a user has access to all files and subdirectories in the directory. When a user specifies the path to the virtual directory but not a specific file, a listing of all contents of the directory is presented.

Because virtual directories function to provide access to files in various locations on your Web server, you should be careful to remove any sensitive content from the target directory before setting permissions allowing for the virtual directory to be used. Security through obscurity is a poor security policy and hoping that users will not find content in directories is not sufficient.

Add a Virtual Directory to Internet Information Services (continued)

The Web Site Content Directory window appears.

⑪ Type the path to the directory you want to add as a virtual directory.

● Alternately, you can click Browse to locate your target folder.

⑫ Click Next to continue.

The Access Permissions window appears.

⑬ Select the access permissions you want to allow (☐ changes to ☑).

⑭ Click Next to continue.

A message appears alerting you that you have successfully created a Virtual Directory.

⑮ Click Finish to close the installer.

● The virtual directory, with the alias you specified in Step 9, is added to IIS and appears in the directory listing.

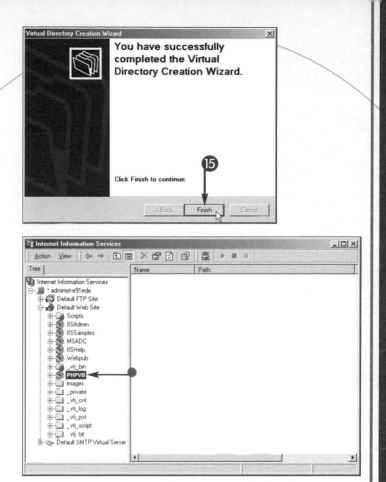

Extra

You can change the execute permissions for a virtual directory in IIS after the directory has been created. To change the execute permissions, repeat Steps 1 and 2 from this task to open the Internet Information Services window. Select the virtual directory you want to change. Click the Properties button (🖳) to open the Properties dialog box. Select the option in the Execute Permissions area that you want to use. The Scripts and Executables option allows files in the directory to be accessed and executed. The Scripts only option allows only scripts to be run. The None option allows access to static files, such as HTML files and images, but no access to scripts or executables.

Set File and Folder Permissions on Windows

You can set file and folder permissions to allow or restrict access to files by certain users or groups of users. The Internet Information Services application serves files and executes scripts according to these permissions. The types of permissions that can be set for files and folders depend on the operating system and file system installed on the Web server. For example, setting permissions on a Linux server is much different than performing the same operations on a Windows XP server.

When IIS is installed on your Windows server, a user account is created called IUSR_(computername), where (computername) is the name of the computer on which the user account is installed. For example, a computer called WEBDEV would have an account named IUSR_WEBDEV. This account is part of the Everyone group. If you deny the Everyone group access to resources such as files and

folders, you can use the IUSR account to allow users you specify to access information in the restricted resource.

You can set permissions for single users or groups to specify how either can access files and folders. Full Control allows users to modify, add, move and delete files. Additionally, these users can change permissions. The Modify option allows users to modify, add, move, and delete files. Read & Execute allows users to run applications and scripts, such as PHP scripts. Read allows users to display files, and Write allows users to modify files.

Windows file and folder permissions work with the access permissions set in Internet Information Services. Access permissions set for a folder in IIS apply to all users who access the folder. Windows folder permissions apply only to users and groups you specify. When Windows file and folder permissions and IIS access permissions differ for the same resource, the Web server uses the most restrictive permissions.

Set File and Folder Permissions on Windows

① Click the file or folder for which you want to change permissions.

② Click File.

③ Click Properties to display the Properties dialog box.

④ Click the Security tab.

● The users who have permission to the file or folder you chose in Step 1 appear here.

● Their current level of permission appears here.

⑤ Click Add.

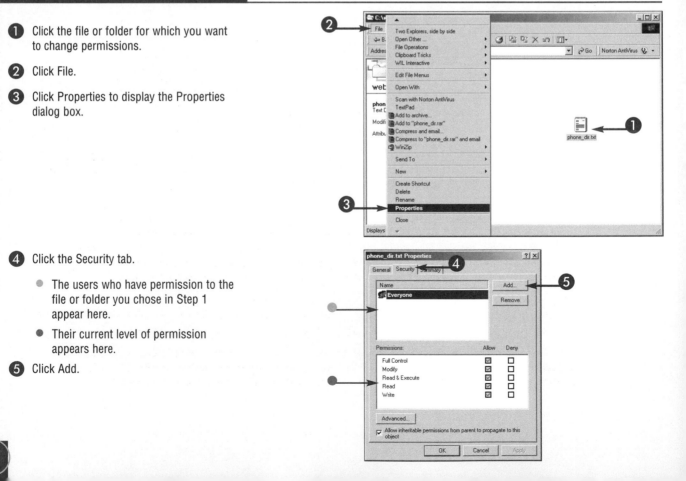

The Select Users or Groups dialog box appears.

⑥ Click a user or group to which you want to grant access to the file or folder.

⑦ Click Add.

Repeat Steps 6 and 7 for each user or group to which you want to grant access.

⑧ Click OK.

⑨ In the Properties dialog box, click a user or group to view their permissions.

⑩ Click an option to allow or deny a given permission.

⑪ Click OK to confirm your changes.

Windows sets the permissions.

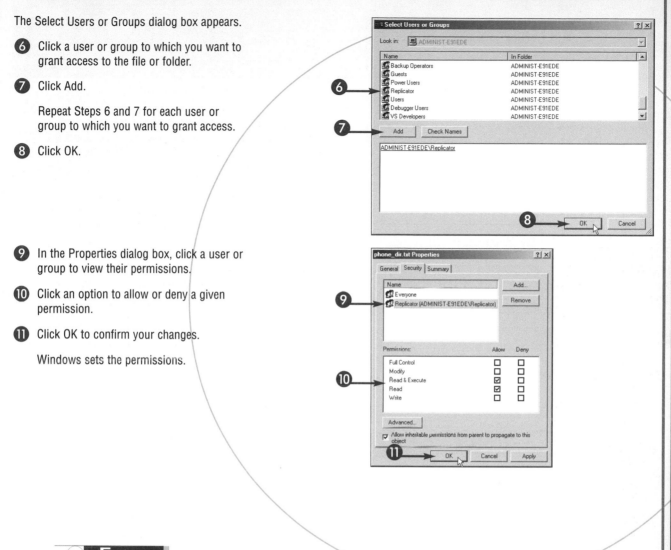

Extra

Take great care when setting file and folder permissions on a Web server. This is true on both Internet and intranet sites. To gain a full understanding of file and folder permissions and the implications of any changes you are considering, you should refer to the operating system and Web server documentation. Incorrectly setting permissions on a Web server can leave the server open to serious security problems as well as data fidelity problems such as corrupted or deleted data.

When moving PHP scripts and associated files between Web servers, you must be careful to ensure that the permissions on the final server match those on the initial server. The permissions are not transferred, and are often reset when files are uploaded through FTP or similar protocols.

If you want to revoke access to a file for a given user or group you can remove the user or group. Repeat Steps 1 to 4 of this task to display the Security tab of the Properties dialog box. Click the user or group that you no longer want to be able to access the file or folder and then click Remove.

Install PHP on Windows

In order to create and process PHP scripts on your Windows computer, you must install PHP. You can use the recent Windows versions of PHP on all modern Windows operating systems.

You can download a recent version of PHP for Windows from the PHP Web site at www.php.net.

The PHP installer is a standard Windows installation program that guides you through the installation process, including analyzing the current status of your system to determine the presence of required applications.

The computer on which you install PHP does not need to be connected to the Internet. You can use a standalone computer running Web server software such as the Apache HTTPD server or Internet Information Services to develop

your PHP pages. In fact, local development is often required as errors and vulnerabilities are never exposed to the outside world. Because of the portable, cross-platform nature of the majority of the PHP language, you will most likely be able to simply copy the files to your Web server for deployment.

Like most Windows installation programs, the PHP installer provides you with a copy of the license under which you can use the software. After accepting the license, you can choose the type of installation you want to perform. The Standard option is recommended for most users, but the Advanced option allows experienced users to specify options when performing the installation.

Install PHP on Windows

 Double-click the icon for the PHP installation program to start installing the program.

A welcome dialog box appears.

 Click Next to continue.

❸ In the next window, read the license agreement and click I Agree to continue the installation.

The Installation Type window appears.

❹ Select the type of installation you want to perform (○ changes to ⊙).

 Click Next to continue.

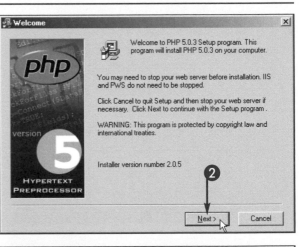

The Choose Destination Location window appears.

- It is recommended that you use the default folder.
- Alternately, you can click Browse to locate another folder.

⑥ Click Next to continue.

⑦ Type the name of the outgoing mail (SMTP) server.

Note: You can use the default, localhost, if no other is available.

⑧ Type the e-mail address you want displayed in outgoing mail messages.

⑨ Click Next to continue.

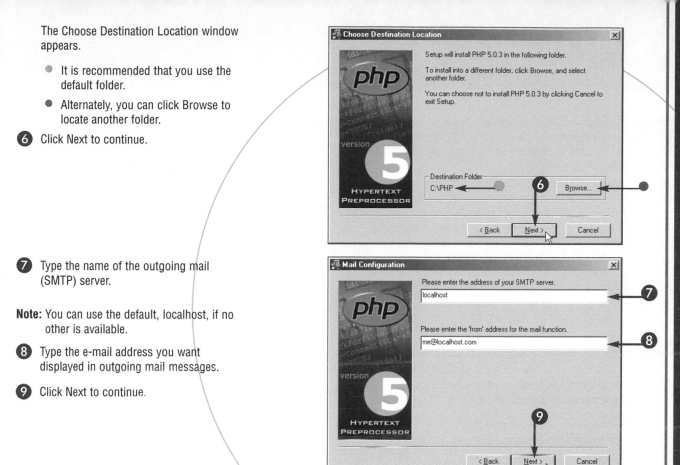

Extra

The most recent release of PHP is always available from the PHP Web site at www.php.net. Older versions of PHP are also available from the official site. Installing versions of PHP other than the newest release is helpful because many Web hosts do not immediately upgrade to new releases for fear of causing interruptions or introducing bugs into the sites they host for their clients. When working on a project that runs on an older version of PHP, you should develop the site using the same version.

While the differences in minor versions, such as PHP 4.3.2 and PHP 4.3.3, can be mild, it is best practice to develop your applications on a local development machine that matches the production server or servers in all respects. For PHP development, matching hardware is not important, though the local and production server should be roughly equivalent so that effects of load and heavy memory use can be taken into consideration. More important is that all software and permissions are matched. Ideally, the process of making a development version of your application available on the Internet should consist of nothing more than uploading files to your Web server.

continued →

The installer will prompt you for the location in which you want to install PHP. The default installation is `C:\PHP`. You can specify a different location, but the default option is recommended.

When installing PHP you can specify the name of the mail server the computer will use to send e-mail messages. This setting is important if you want to include the option of sending e-mail from your PHP scripts. You can specify any server running the Simple Mail Transfer Protocol (SMTP). Generally, the default value of "localhost" will suffice.

You should specify the e-mail address from which you want to send outgoing e-mail addresses when no additional mail

headers are used. Most often, this address is an alias for the system administrator or for the Web developer in charge of the server.

The installer application can automatically set certain configuration options for a given Web server. When prompted to choose the Web server with which you intend to use PHP, choose the version of IIS or Apache you have installed and configured.

After specifying all configuration options, you can finalize the installation by clicking Finish. When the installation is complete, you can configure PHP using the PHP configuration file as well as the Apache configuration file.

Install PHP on Windows (continued)

 Select the type of Web server you want to be configured to use with PHP.

If your Web server does not appear in the list, you can select None to configure the server manually.

⑪ Click Next to continue.

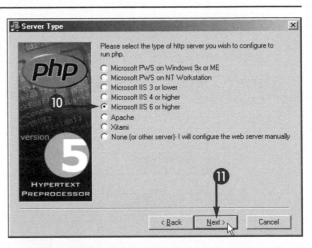

A dialog box appears indicating that you are ready to install PHP.

 Click Next to install PHP on your computer.

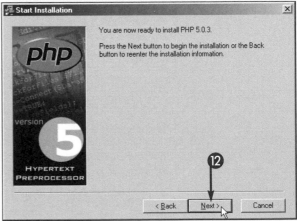

13 A dialog box appears telling you to configure Apache's httpd.conf file. Click OK to continue.

Note: Follow Steps 15 to 18 to configure Apache's httpd.conf file.

14 Click OK to close the next dialog box.

PHP is installed.

CONFIGURE APACHE'S HTTPD.CONF FILE

15 Open your httpd.conf file in a text editor. The httpd.conf is located in the conf directory of your Apache install directory.

16 Add a `ScriptAlias` directive mapping your PHP directory to the PHP interpreter at `c:/php/`.

17 Use an `AddType` directive to map the type `application/x-httpd-php` to the file extensions you want PHP to parse.

18 Add an Action directive mapping the `application/x-httpd-php` application type to the PHP executable.

Save the file and restart your computer to see the changes take effect.

Apache Configuration

Sorry, the software to automatically configure the Apache httpd.conf file has not yet been written. You will have to configure Apache manually. See the install.txt file for more details.

OK — 13

Installation complete

PHP 5.0.3 has been successfully installed.

Press the OK button to exit this installation.

NT users may need to set appropriate permissions for the various php files and directories. Usually IUSR_MachineName (or the user your web server runs as) will need read access to php.ini, read write access to the uploadtmp and session directories, and execute access for php-cgi.exe and php5ts.dll.

OK — 14

httpd.conf - Notepad

File Edit Format Help

```
# machine you can setup VirtualHost containers for them. Most configurations
# use only name-based virtual hosts so the server doesn't need to worry about
# IP addresses. This is indicated by the asterisks in the directives below.
#
# Please see the documentation at
# <URL:http://httpd.apache.org/docs-2.0/vhosts/>
# for further details before you try to setup virtual hosts.
#
# You may use the command line option '-S' to verify your virtual host
# configuration.
#
# Use name-based virtual hosting.
#
#NameVirtualHost *:80
#
# VirtualHost example:
# Almost any Apache directive may go into a VirtualHost container.
# The first VirtualHost section is used for requests without a known
# server name.
#
#<VirtualHost *:80>
#    ServerAdmin webmaster@dummy-host.example.com
#    DocumentRoot /www/docs/dummy-host.example.com
#    ServerName dummy-host.example.com
#    ErrorLog logs/dummy-host.example.com-error_log
#    CustomLog logs/dummy-host.example.com-access_log common
#</VirtualHost>
ScriptAlias /php/ "c:/php/"
AddType application/x-httpd-php .html .php .phtml
Action application/x-httpd-php "/php/php-cgi.exe"|
```

16 — ScriptAlias line
17 18 — AddType / Action lines

Extra

PHP should be installed only on the hard drive of the Web server machine. You should not install PHP on a network drive or on removable media such as an external FireWire drive. While it is technically possible to perform such an installation, the performance of the Web server will often be less than ideal and may become unavailable.

When specifying the e-mail address you want to display on outgoing e-mail messages, you may want to use an e-mail address set up for only this purpose. This is especially true on servers that send a lot of mail as bounced messages and can quickly fill the space allocated to a typical e-mail address.

If the computer stops responding before the installation of PHP is complete, there may be a problem with the system hardware, network connection, or the PHP installer itself. In such cases, you should close all open programs and restart the computer before attempting to reinstall the program.

Install Apache
on OS X

Mac OS X comes configured with proven versions of Apache and PHP installed by default. Both applications are configured with safety and efficiency in mind, and you will most likely want to update the version or enable additional options for each before beginning development.

Because Mac OS X is a Unix-based operating system, you can install software much the same as on other Unix and Linux systems, using the a shell session and the `configure`, `make`, `make install` sequence.

The first step in installing Apache is to download the most recent production version of Apache from the Apache Group Web site. Currently, the most recent major version is Apache 2. Unzip the archive containing the Apache source to a folder on your computer.

You will need to have administrative permissions to install software on the machine. If you are currently logged into the machine with a restricted user account, you can log off and back on as an administrator using the commands under the Apple menu.

Open the Terminal application in your Applications/Utilities folder. Use the `cd` command to change to the directory in which you unzipped the Apache source.

You can configure Apache using the configure script in the source folder. To `configure` Apache 2 for PHP 5 support, you can use the `--enable-mods-shared=ALL` configure directive. After the configure command runs, you can type `make` and press Enter to make the installable application.

If `make` executes successfully, type `make install` to install Apache 2 to your system.

Install Apache on OS X

1 Change directories to the location of your install using the `cd` command.

2 Unarchive the Apache source archive using the `tar -xzf filename` command.

```
● ● ●              Terminal — tcsh — 102x30
[tj-ibook:~] tobyboud% cd /src         ◄——— ①
[tj-ibook:/src] tobyboud% tar -xzf httpd-2.0.52.tar.gz  ◄——— ②
[tj-ibook:/src] tobyboud% 
```

3 Set installation options using the configure script in the Apache source directory.

- Pass any options, or flags, to the configure script according to your anticipated PHP use and the server on which it is being installed.

```
● ● ●              Terminal — tcsh — 102x30
[tj-ibook:/src] tobyboud% cd httpd-2.0.52/
[tj-ibook:/src/httpd-2.0.52] tobyboud% ./configure --enable-mods-shared=ALL  ◄———
                                                                        ③
```

④ Type `make` to make the installer.

⑤ After the installer is made, type `make install` to install Apache on your server.

④

```
○ ○ ○                Terminal — tcsh — 102x30
[tj-ibook:/src/httpd-2.0.52] tobyboud% make --silent
[tj-ibook:/src/httpd-2.0.52] tobyboud% make install --silent
[tj-ibook:/src/httpd-2.0.52] tobyboud%
```

⑤

⑥ Change directories to the bin directory of the install location. Type `apachectl start` to start Apache.

```
○ ○ ○                Terminal — tcsh — 102x30
[tj-ibook:/src/httpd-2.0.52] tobyboud% cd /usr/local/apache/bin/        ⑥
[tj-ibook:local/apache/bin] tobyboud% apachectl start
```

Extra

You can choose to install either Apache 1.3 or Apache 2 on your OS X machine. Either will work with PHP 5 and Apache 1.3 comes preinstalled. The choice between Apache 1.3 and Apache 2 depends primarily on which version of Apache is running on your production server as well as any special constraints or parameters in your project specifications.

Generally, it is a good idea to install both versions of Apache on your development machine and switch versions according to your current development needs. You can switch versions by stopping the current version and starting the alternate version. To stop Apache, the `apachectl` command is used. Because each installed version has its own `apachectl` command, you should be careful to specify the full path to the `apachectl` version you want to use. For example, you might have Apache 1.3 installed in `/usr/local/apache`, in which case you could start the server using `/usr/local/apache/bin/apachectl start`.

For an Apache 2 install located at `/usr/local/apache2` you can use the `/usr/local/apache2/bin/apachectl start` command.

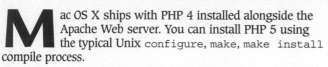

Mac OS X ships with PHP 4 installed alongside the Apache Web server. You can install PHP 5 using the typical Unix `configure`, `make`, `make install` compile process.

The first step in installing PHP is to download the most recent production version of PHP from the PHP Web site. At the time of this writing, the most recent version of PHP is version 5.0.3. Unzip the archive containing the PHP source to a folder on your computer.

You must have administrative permissions to install software on the machine. If you are currently logged on with a restricted user account, log out and back on as an administrator using the commands under the Apple menu.

Open the Terminal application in your Applications/Utilities folder. Use the `cd` command to change to the directory in which you unzipped the PHP source.

You can configure PHP with any number of configuration options. To configure PHP before compiling, you can use the configure script in the source folder. After the configure command runs, you can type `make` to make the installable application.

The `make` command compiles PHP for use on the server. When using the `make` command, you will see a number of messages scroll past in the Terminal window. If any errors are reported, take note and check your configuration options to ensure that libraries on which your configuration depends are installed properly.

If `make` executes successfully, type `make install` to install PHP on your system. You will need to restart Apache before using PHP.

Install PHP on OS X

1 Change directories to the location of your install using the `cd` command.

2 Unarchive the PHP download archive using the `tar -xzvf filename` command.

3 Set installation options using the `configure` script in the PHP source directory.

- Pass any options, or flags, to the `configure` script according to your anticipated PHP use and the server on which it is being installed.

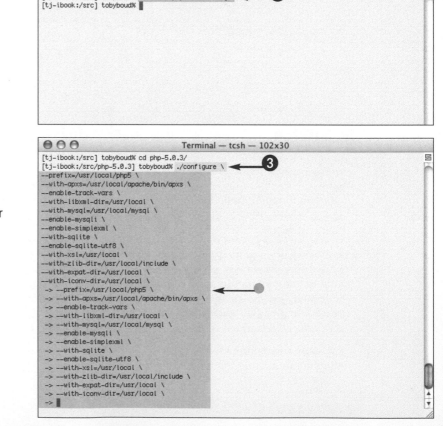

4 Type `make` to make the installer.

5 After the installer is made, type `make install` to install PHP on your server.

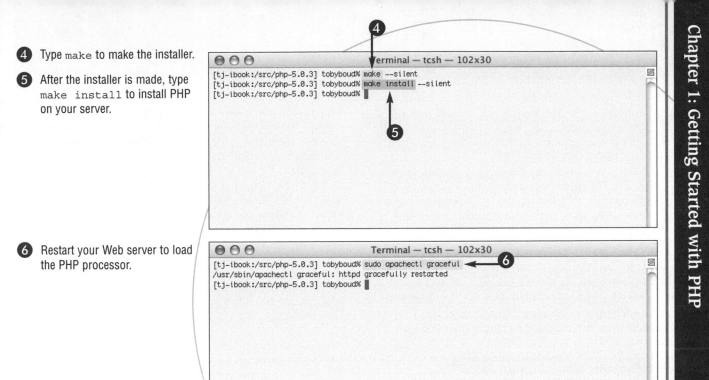

```
[tj-ibook:/src/php-5.0.3] tobyboud% make --silent
[tj-ibook:/src/php-5.0.3] tobyboud% make install --silent
[tj-ibook:/src/php-5.0.3] tobyboud%
```

6 Restart your Web server to load the PHP processor.

```
[tj-ibook:/src/php-5.0.3] tobyboud% sudo apachectl graceful
/usr/sbin/apachectl graceful: httpd gracefully restarted
[tj-ibook:/src/php-5.0.3] tobyboud%
```

Extra

OS X comes with a version of PHP pre-installed. At the time of this writing, the version of PHP included on the OS X client install is PHP 4. You can install both versions of PHP as long as the location of the install is different. For example, you can install PHP 5 into the `/usr/local/php5` directory. Note that you can have both PHP 4 and PHP 5 installed on your machine, but only one may be run per instance of Apache at a given time. In fact, you can have as many versions of PHP installed on your computer as you want as long as there are no library conflicts. Often, a development machine will have at least two or three minor versions of the latest major version release to accommodate any number of projects that may be in development. You can specify which version of PHP is loaded by the Apache Web server using the Apache configuration file, usually found at `/usr/local/apache/conf/httpd.conf`.

Set File and Folder Permissions on OS X

You can use the Terminal to set file and folder permissions on OS X. You can also use the Get Info option in the Finder to view and modify permission information about files and folders.

Because OS X is a Unix-based operating system, you can set folder and file permissions using the chmod, chown, and chgrp commands. In order to change the permissions of a file or folder, you must have user or group ownership permissions. If your account does not have permissions to modify a file, you can use the su command to switch to a user account with adequate permissions. For example, you might switch to a user named 'admin' using the command su admin. When prompted for a password, you must type the password of the account to which you are switching. You can perform a quick action as another user using the sudo command. For example, to change ownership of

the file 'test.php' to the user 'toby' you might use a command such as sudo chown toby test.php.

Another method of altering file and folder permissions is to use the OS X Finder. You can use the Finder to change permissions by opening the Get Info palette for a given file or folder. Right-click the target file or folder in the Finder and choose Get Info from the menu. Alternately, you can press the Apple key and the I key in combination to open the Get Info palette.

When the Get Info palette is open, you see a section called Ownership & Permissions. There are select boxes in this section. If you have permission to modify the ownership and permissions properties of the currently selected file, you can use the select boxes to change these properties. Otherwise, the menu is dimmed and unusable.

Set File and Folder Permissions on OS X

① Open the Terminal application from the Applications/Utilities folder.

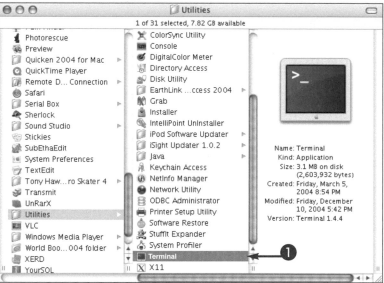

② Change directories to the directory in which your file exists using the cd command.

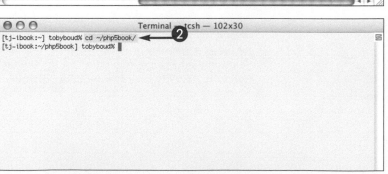

③ Type `ls -la` to see the current permission information for your file.

```
    ● ● ●                  Terminal — tcsh — 102x30
[tj-ibook:~] tobyboud% cd ~/php5book/
[tj-ibook:~/php5book] tobyboud% ls -la  ◄━━━━━③
total 0
drwxr-xr-x   3 tobyboud  tobyboud   102 27 Jan 21:52 .
drwxr-xr-x  45 tobyboud  tobyboud  1530 27 Jan 21:52 ..
-rw-r--r--   1 tobyboud  tobyboud     0 27 Jan 21:52 testfile.txt
[tj-ibook:~/php5book] tobyboud% ▊
```

④ Change the permissions of the file using the `chmod` command.

```
    ● ● ●                  Terminal — tcsh — 102x30
[tj-ibook:~/php5book] tobyboud% chmod 777 testfile.txt  ◄━━━━━④
[tj-ibook:~/php5book] tobyboud% ls -la
total 0
drwxr-xr-x   3 tobyboud  tobyboud   102 27 Jan 21:52 .
drwxr-xr-x  45 tobyboud  tobyboud  1530 27 Jan 21:52 ..
-rwxrwxrwx   1 tobyboud  tobyboud     0 27 Jan 21:52 testfile.txt
[tj-ibook:~/php5book] tobyboud% ▊
```

Extra

You can recursively set ownership and permission privileges for a directory by specifying a special flag for the `chmod` command. The `-R` flag tells the `chmod` command to apply the changes not only to the directory in question but to move through the directory setting the same permissions on each file therein. Because this option is recursive, the permissions of items in subfolders will be set as well as those in the main folder.

The Details section of the Get Info palette gives detailed permissions information for a given file. You can set your own permissions level, the owner of the file, access level of the owner, the group ownership and accompanying group access, and the level of permissions applicable to other users.

Configure PHP

PHP configuration is managed by modifying the contents of a configuration file, usually named `php.ini`. The configuration file is a plain text file that controls how PHP processes scripts and is read by the Web server when PHP is started.

You can edit the `php.ini` file using a standard text editor, such as Notepad on a Windows system, and vi or emacs on a Unix or Linux system. The Mac OS X application TextEdit is a useful text editor when developing on your Apple.

The format of the `php.ini` file is a standard configuration style in which each new line represents a directive. Comments are delimited using a semicolon (`;`) and entire lines can be commented out by placing a semicolon at the beginning of each line.

Directives are set using the name of the directive, followed by an equals sign (`=`) with the directive value. Most often, possible values are listed in comments in the `php.ini` file.

To set a directive, simply change the value to a recognized value other than the current setting and save the file. The next request to PHP is processed according to the changed configuration.

The most common changes made to a new installation of PHP is to set the appropriate level of error reporting for the server, based on its use and availability. For local development servers, you generally want very verbose error reporting. You can change the error reporting values using the `error_reporting` directive. For example, you can turn on all error reporting using the lines:

```
error_reporting = E_ALL

display_errors = On
```

Or, for a production server, where you want no errors displayed, you can set the error reporting level with the line:

```
display_errors = Off
```

Configure PHP

① Locate and open your `php.ini` file in a text editor.

② Find the Error handling and logging section.

③ Locate the `error_reporting` directive. Uncomment the line `error_reporting = E_ALL` if it is currently commented.

④ Locate the `display_errors` directive.

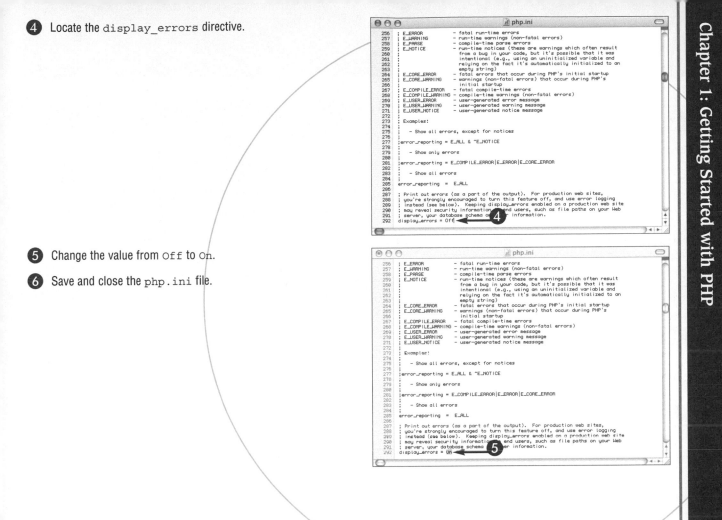

⑤ Change the value from `Off` to `On`.

⑥ Save and close the `php.ini` file.

Extra

On computers running a version of the Windows operating system, the `php.ini` file is typically located in the main Windows directory, such as `C:\WINNT` or `C:\WINDOWS`. On Unix systems, the location of the `php.ini` file can vary, but the file is often found in the `/usr/local/lib` directory. You can locate the file on a Unix system using the command-line locate tool. To locate all files whose path contains the string `php.ini` you can type `locate php.ini` and press Enter.

The `php.ini` configuration file can be used to manage which modules are enabled for your PHP installation. You can also use the configuration file to manage module-specific settings, such as the default host for MySQL connections, or session management options such as the location of session files and the name of the session identifier to be used in tracking user sessions.

You can read about all of the configuration options available in the php.ini file on the PHP Web site at www.php.net/manual/en/configuration.php.

Verify Installation

After the Web server software and a version of PHP are installed and the Web server is configured to process PHP files, you can verify the status of the installation and check the current configuration settings using a PHP script.

The phpinfo function is a globally accessible function that is a useful utility when learning about the configuration of a given PHP installation. The phpinfo function accepts no arguments and returns no result, acting instead as a utility function that gathers information about the current configuration of your Web server and displays it as an easy-to-understand HTML page.

You can use the phpinfo function by creating a new PHP script in your Web server document root. You can open a

block of PHP code by typing the <?php opening PHP processing instruction delimiter. On a new line, call the phpinfo function by typing phpinfo();.

You can close the PHP processing block by typing the closing processing instruction delimiter, ?>.

After you save the PHP script to your Web server, you can connect to the server using a standard Web browser. In the location bar, type the path to your server followed by the name of the phpinfo script you created.

When the page loads, you see a screen presenting detailed information not only about PHP but also about your Web server software and configuration.

Verify Installation

① Create a new PHP script using a text editor.

② Create a PHP processing block using the PHP processing instruction delimiters <?php and ?>.

③ Inside the PHP processing block, type phpinfo();.

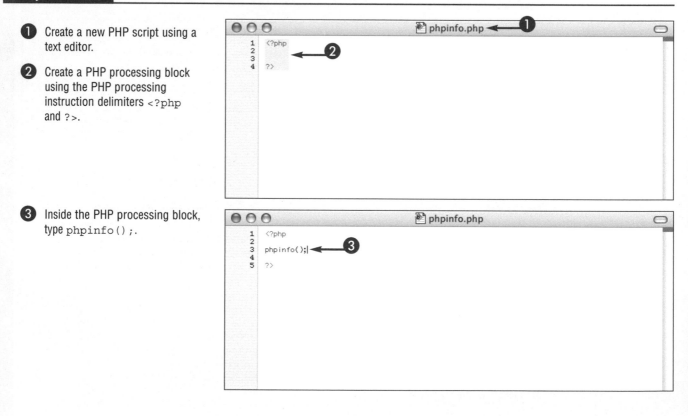

④ Save or upload the file to your Web server.

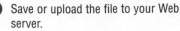

Save: BBEdit

Save As: phpinfo.php ◄━━━━④

Where: 🗁 TEST

☐ Save as Stationery   (Options...)

(Cancel) (Save)

⑤ View the script in your Web browser.

Detailed configuration information about your installation of PHP is displayed.

○○○   @ phpinfo()

Back Forward Stop Refresh Home AutoFill Print Mail   e

Address: @ http://127.0.0.1:9003/ch01/task11/Code/phpinfo.php   › go

PHP Version 5.0.2 ◄━━⑤   php

System	Darwin tj-iBook.local 7.7.0 Darwin Kernel Version 7.7.0: Sun Nov 7 16:06:51 PST 2004; root:xnu/xnu-517.9.5.obj~1/RELEASE_PPC Power Macintosh
Build Date	Dec 4 2004 13:38:54
Configure Command	'./configure' '--enable-xslt' '--with-xslt-sablot' '--with-apxs=/usr/sbin/apxs' '--with-gd' '--with-zlib' '--with-mysql=/Library/MySQL'
Server API	Apache
Virtual Directory Support	disabled
Configuration File (php.ini) Path	/usr/local/lib/php.ini
PHP API	20031224
PHP Extension	20040412

🌐 Internet zone

Extra

If the Web server and PHP information is not displayed when you view the phpinfo script in your Web browser, the Web server may have a configuration error. You can review the topics in this book related to the installation and configuration of not only PHP but of your Web server to help determine the error. You can also review the manual and various README files that were included in the distributions of PHP and of your Web server software to determine if there are special considerations, options, or steps that you may have missed when installing and configuring your software.

It is considered a security risk to host a phpinfo script on your Web server for any longer than absolutely necessary. This is mostly due to the level of detailed information provided by the script. While "security through obscurity" is not in and of itself an acceptable security model, taking steps to obscure details from outsiders is a helpful part of a larger security model.

If you want to limit the information the phpinfo script displays, you can pass one of the following PHP constant values to the phpinfo function: INFO_GENERAL, INFO_CREDITS, INFO_CONFIGURATION, INFO_ENVIRONMENT, INFO_MODULES, INFO_VARIABLES, or INFO_LICENSE. These options are useful if you want to provide only a specific group of configuration settings to other developers without making available all of the information about your server.

Upload Pages to a Web Server

You can upload your scripts to a Web server different than the local server on which you develop. In most cases, the final production server on which you deploy your sites is hosted and maintained by a hosting company. You can use the File Transfer Protocol (FTP) to transfer your files to your external server.

Before you can transfer files to your remote Web server, you need to install an FTP client application. Due to the ubiquity of the File Transfer Protocol there are many available FTP client applications for every major operating system. When you choose an FTP client, install it according to the instructions provided by the software publisher.

The first step in transferring files or folders to your remote server is to create a connection to the server. You can use an FTP program to transfer files from a machine running one operating system to a machine running a different operating system. For example, you can transfer files from

your Mac OS X computer to a Red Hat Linux Web server running your production site.

To create a connection with a remote FTP server, you must have certain information. The address of the server, either as a legitimate domain name or an IP address, allows your client application to locate the server on the Internet or intranet. You must also have a valid username and password for an account set up on the remote server in order to successfully establish a connection. Most FTP programs will allow you to save connection information for ease of reuse when connecting in the future. You should be aware that saving account information to a computer accessible by people other than yourself poses a significant security risk. If you use a computer accessible by others, be sure not to save connection information but instead type the address, username, and password each time a connection is necessary.

Upload Pages to a Web Server

① Open your FTP client application.

● Most FTP applications will open a display showing saved connections when first started.

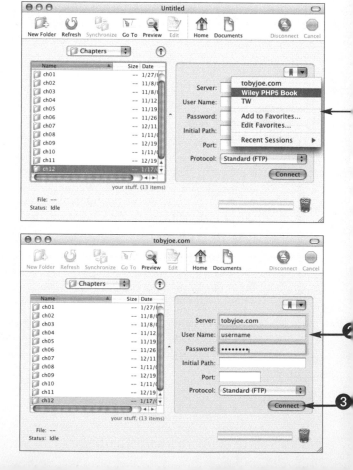

② Create a new connection by specifying the address of your server, your username, and your password.

③ Click Connect to open a connection.

- When your connection is established, a listing of files on the remote server appears.

④ Navigate to the folder representing your Web server document root.

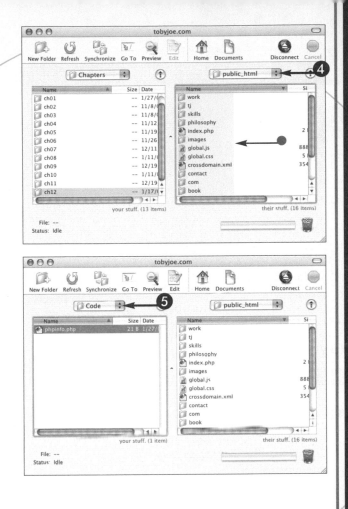

⑤ Using the local view of your files, navigate to the directory on your local machine in which your PHP scripts are saved.

continued →

Extra

Web hosting companies manage the hardware and software required to serve Web pages to people on the Internet. While it is possible to serve Web sites from machines on your own home Internet connection, for anything beyond the most trivial applications it is best to use a hosting company. Web hosts often provide nearly 100 percent uptime and help keep checks on security. You can also access support services if you need software installed or have questions about configuration options.

There are many available FTP applications for most popular operating systems. For Mac OS X, the Transmit client is a popular choice. For Windows, the CuteFTP program is a light and reliable FTP client. For Linux running the X Windows windowing system, you can use the AxY FTP program.

After you establish a connection to your remote Web server, you can read, write, and delete information from the server. You can transfer entire directories, single files, or file archives. Most FTP clients also allow you to select any number of individual files and directories and upload them in one operation.

You must browse to the location on the remote server to which you want to transfer your files. When you initially connect to the FTP server, the working directory is set to the default directory associated with your account. If you upload files without changing to the proper location on the remote server, the files may not be visible to your Web server software. The directory to which you should upload your files changes on a server-by-server basis. You can ask the server administrator for the location of the Web server document root, which is the directory from which files are served to Web browsers. In some cases, your host may have a configuration that restricts the location from which

PHP files may be served. You can check with your host for any specific rules for the particular server.

In some cases, FTP servers are configured to terminate a connection if no activity occurs for a given interval. This helps free unused resources for other users who may need to connect to the FTP server to manage their sites or files. If your session is dropped after an idle connection, you can simply reconnect.

A connection to an FTP server is temporary and volatile. That is, it is not a permanent and persistent connection. If you change files on your local development machine after uploading files to the remote server, you must connect and upload the new versions to the Web server to see changes take effect. Most FTP applications present a dialog box when an attempt to overwrite a file is made. You can choose to overwrite or cancel the upload. This safety mechanism helps prevent unwanted file overwrites.

Upload Pages to a Web Server (continued)

6 Drag a file from the local view to the remote view to upload it.

The progress is indicated in most FTP client applications.

7 Upload a directory by clicking the directory in your local view and dragging it to the remote view.

The progress is indicated in most FTP client applications.

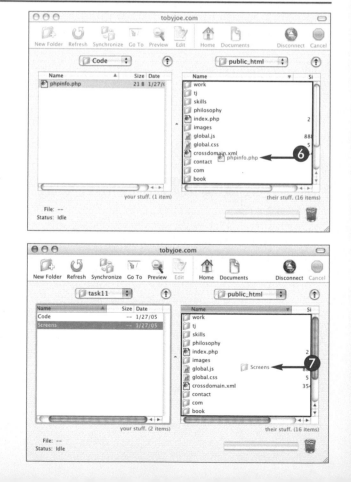

8 Disconnect from the FTP server either manually or by closing the FTP client application.

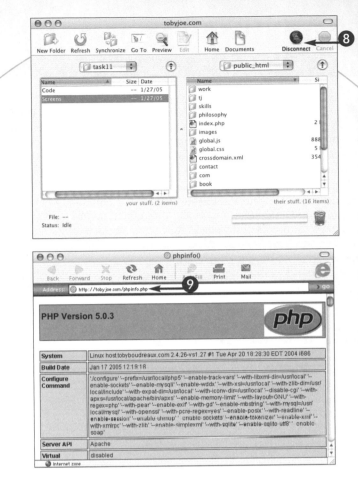

9 View your uploaded files in your Web server by typing the path to the newly uploaded file into a Web browser.

If the file is not displayed or if there is an error, check the location of the file on the remote server.

Extra

An important consideration when uploading files to a server is that any file in the document root of the server is most likely accessible to anyone with the ability to send HTTP requests to your server. Because the Web root is the directory from which files are meant to be served to your visitors, you should always keep sensitive information in a location outside of the Web root. PHP and similar languages can almost always access necessary files from locations outside of the Web root, but Web servers such as the Apache HTTPD server will never serve files protected in this manner.

PHP best practice where sensitive information is concerned is to keep files containing information such as database usernames and passwords in a special directory outside of the Web root. You can use the `require`, `require_once`, `include`, and `include_once` functions to access files located in any directory on your computer to which PHP and Apache have the appropriate permissions.

TYPE THIS:

```
$dbfile = $_SERVER['DOCUMENT_ROOT']
. '../secure/db.php';
require_once($dbfile) or die('Error
accessing required files.');
```

→

RESULT:

The file located in a directory called 'secure' outside of the Web root is included into the script.

Insert PHP Code into a Page

You can transform static HTML documents into dynamic, functional pages by adding PHP code. You can add PHP to pages you already have on your site or to entirely new projects quite easily.

Adding code to a page is done by first inserting the PHP processing instruction delimiters to the document. The opening delimiter is `<?php` and the closing delimiter is `?>`. The server treats any content within these delimiters as PHP. You can have many sets of delimiters in a single page, as long as you open and close them in order without nesting them.

When the server receives a request for a page with an extension mapped to the PHP engine, it forwards the page through the PHP preprocessor before sending any output to the browser. The preprocessor finds any blocks of code inside the processing instruction delimiters and runs it. The results of any output statements, such as print or echo, are added to the processed page at the point of the processing instructions. For example, you can use PHP to set the title of your page by adding an echo statement inside processing instructions between the `<title>` and `</title>` tags.

As long as your PHP code is placed in the proper delimiters, it is never sent as part of the response to the browser, even if there is an error in the processing. Not all code within the PHP block sends output. You must explicitly instruct the preprocessor to add content to the output stream sent to the browser.

Insert PHP Code into a Page

① Open the PHP block by typing the `<?php` opening delimiter.

② Close the PHP block by typing the `?>` closing delimiter.

③ Type a PHP `echo` statement within the delimiters.

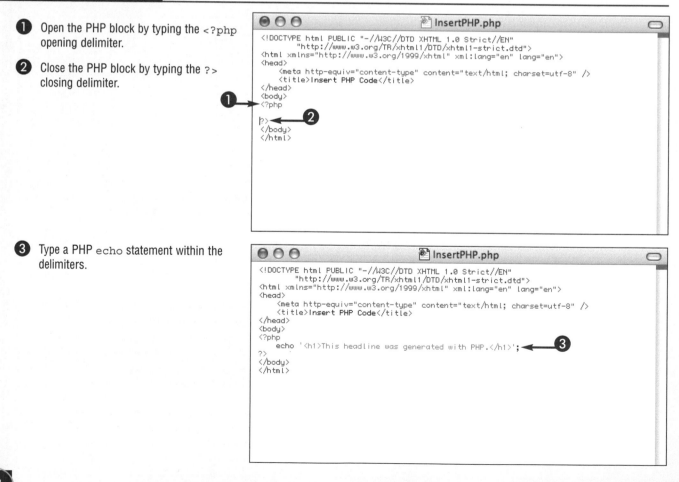

④ Save the PHP document to the Web server with a .php extension.

Save: BBEdit

Save As: InsertPHP.php ← ④

Where: 📁 Code

☐ Save as Stationery   (Options...)

(Cancel) (Save)

⑤ View the script in a Web browser.

The page is returned as a normal HTML document with the results of the PHP code in place of the code block.

Insert PHP Code

Back Forward Stop Refresh Home │ AutoFill Print Mail

Address: http://127.0.0.1 :9003/ch02/task1/Code/InsertPHP.php   › go

This headline was generated with PHP.

⑤

Extra

If you do not want to type <?php and ?> for every code block you create, you can choose to use other delimiters. For example, you can turn on the short_open_tag directive in your PHP settings and use <? and ?> as the delimiters. While this saves a few keystrokes and generally makes the code look cleaner when there are multiple blocks in the same document, it can cause problems when using XML or mixing in other processing instructions.

Example:
```
<?
echo 'This text was generated by PHP.'
?>
```

You can also use the ASP style delimiters <% and %> by turning on the asp_tags directive.

Example:
```
<%
echo 'This text was generated by PHP.'
%>
```

Finally, you can place your code inside <script> tags with a language attribute set to php.

Example:
```
<script language="php">
echo 'This text was generated by PHP.'
</script>
```

Generally, it is best to use the standard opening and closing delimiters unless there is an explicit need to do otherwise.

Add Comments

Adding comments to your code is an excellent practice. Comments allow you to add descriptive text to your scripts that is not sent to the browser when a user views the page. You can leave notes for yourself or other developers that can only be seen by those with access to the raw scripts on the server.

Commenting code is an important step in professional development because the purpose and function of a script is not always easy to infer. Without comments, the only means of understanding unclear code is to infer the meaning of variable and function names or to modify the code to see the results. By adding clear and descriptive comments, you can eliminate the need for dangerous and time-consuming reverse engineering practices.

You can place comments almost anywhere within your code. Like the PHP code in which they exist, comments are

delimited special characters. Single-line comments are delimited on only one side — that is, they have only an opening delimiter. The most common delimiter for single-line comments consists of two forward slashes. Anything between // and the end of the line is not processed by the Web server or written to the output stream.

Multiline comments require both opening and closing delimiters. To begin a multiline comment, you can add a forward slash followed by an asterisk /*. The comment continues, regardless of line breaks, until you end it with an asterisk followed by a forward slash */.

Any characters are allowed in single-line comments. Multiline comments can contain any characters or code except for other multiline comment delimiters. Nesting multiline comments results in a PHP processing error.

Add Comments

① Begin a single-line comment by typing //.

② Type a comment.

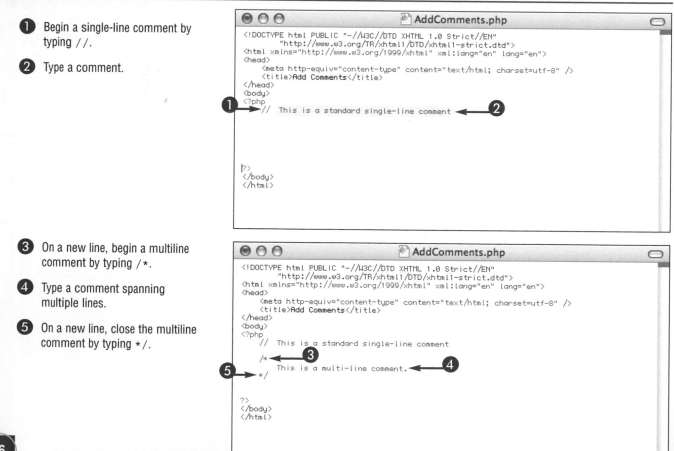

③ On a new line, begin a multiline comment by typing /*.

④ Type a comment spanning multiple lines.

⑤ On a new line, close the multiline comment by typing */.

6 Add a line of PHP code outside of the commented lines.

```
<!DOCTYPE html PUBLIC "-//W3C//DTD XHTML 1.0 Strict//EN"
        "http://www.w3.org/TR/xhtml1/DTD/xhtml1-strict.dtd">
<html xmlns="http://www.w3.org/1999/xhtml" xml:lang="en" lang="en">
<head>
    <meta http-equiv="content-type" content="text/html; charset=utf-8" />
    <title>Add Comments</title>
</head>
<body>
<?php
    // This is a standard single-line comment

    /*
        This is a multi-line comment.
    */

    echo 'This text will be processed by the PHP processor.';    ← 6
?>
</body>
</html>
```

7 View the script in a Web browser.

The page is returned with all noncommented code processed.

Address: http://127.0.0.1:9003/ch02/task2/Code/AddComments.php

This text will be processed by the PHP processor. ← 7

Extra

As an alternative to the double slash, you can begin a single-line comment with a hash mark, #. You may like this method better because it consists of one character instead of two, and may be more visually appealing. There is no alternate method of delimiting multiline comments.

No matter which style of commenting you choose, try to remain consistent both in style and in content. It is always a good idea to add author and modification date information to your comments in addition to descriptions of the code body.

Example:
```
<?php
# Author: Toby Boudreaux
# Email: php5book@tobyjoe.com
# Date: 2004.10.15
# Description: Example script illustrating alternate comment styles.
echo 'This text is generated by a well-commented PHP script.';
?>
```

Create a Numeric Variable

Y ou can use variables to store values generated by your scripts or to point to objects or functions within your script. You can think of variables as empty containers to be filled with values or references to things. Variables in PHP function as those in algebra. When a variable is created and assigned a value, it can be used in place of the value it represents. PHP 5 allows you to create variables that are dynamic and changeable or those that are static and unchangeable.

You can create a variable by typing a name beginning with a dollar sign ($). The second character must be a letter or underscore (_). The rest of the name may contain letters, numbers, and the underscore character.

Variable names are case-sensitive, so you should be careful to follow a capitalization convention consistently. PHP will not treat $container the same as $CONTAINER. Single-word

variable names are usually lowercase. The most common convention for variable names consisting of multiple words is to capitalize the first letter of all but the first word. An example is $myVariable. Another convention is to keep all letters lowercase and use an underscore character (_) to separate each word, such as $my_variable.

To assign a value to a variable, use the assignment operator (=) followed by the value you want to assign. It is not necessary to assign a value to a variable at the time you create it unless you are defining a constant. See more about constants in the task "Using PHP Constants."

A numeric variable can store any numeric value, positive or negative. To assign a negative numeric variable, place the minus sign (-) between the assignment operator and the value, such as $myVariable = -400.

Create a Numeric Variable

① Create a variable by typing the dollar sign ($) followed by a variable name.

● The second character must be either an underscore (_) or a letter.

② Type the assignment operator (=).

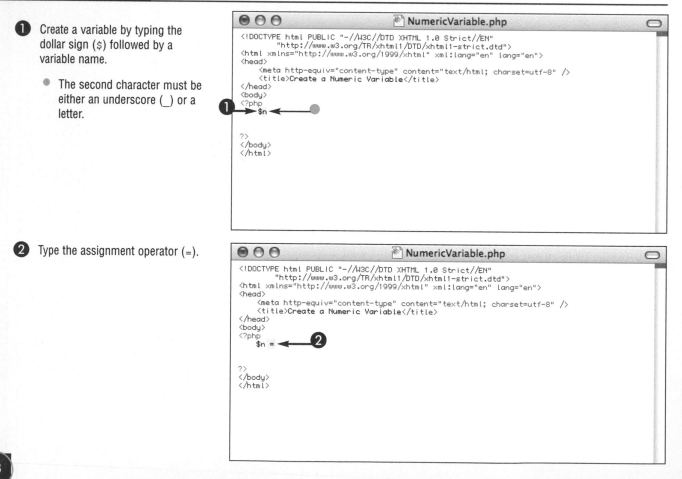

③ Type a value you want to assign to the variable, followed by a semicolon (;).

④ Use the echo function to write the value of the variable to the output stream.

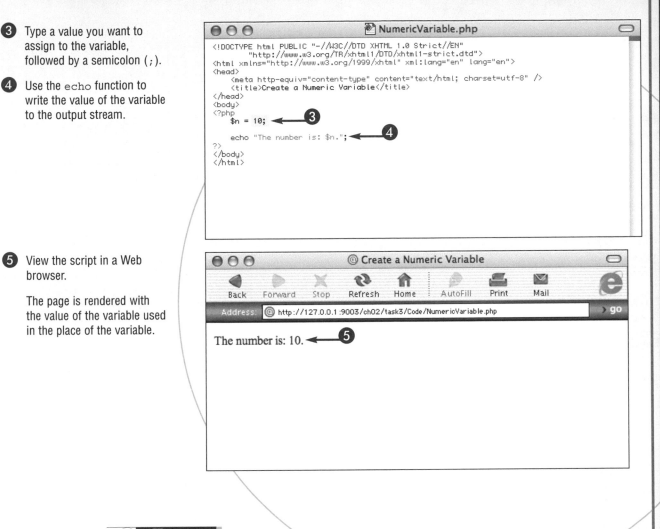

```
NumericVariable.php

<!DOCTYPE html PUBLIC "-//W3C//DTD XHTML 1.0 Strict//EN"
        "http://www.w3.org/TR/xhtml1/DTD/xhtml1-strict.dtd">
<html xmlns="http://www.w3.org/1999/xhtml" xml:lang="en" lang="en">
<head>
    <meta http-equiv="content-type" content="text/html; charset=utf-8" />
    <title>Create a Numeric Variable</title>
</head>
<body>
<?php
    $n = 10;          ←③

    echo "The number is: $n.";   ←④
?>
</body>
</html>
```

⑤ View the script in a Web browser.

The page is rendered with the value of the variable used in the place of the variable.

Create a Numeric Variable

Back Forward Stop Refresh Home AutoFill Print Mail

Address: http://127.0.0.1:9003/ch02/task3/Code/NumericVariable.php   go

The number is: 10. ←⑤

Extra

You can use the inval() and floatval() functions to convert string variables into integer or floating point numbers. See the task "Create a String Variable" for more information on string variables. These functions are particularly useful when processing information submitted from a form. For the most part, PHP is great at handling the types of variable and dealing with interactions between different types. Occasionally you may run into a situation in which PHP is not treating your variables the way you anticipated and these functions can help coax PHP to perform the correct behavior.

You can also use the strval() function to convert an integer or floating point number into a string.

Variable type becomes particularly important when performing comparison operations between variables. See the task "Using Operators" for more information on comparisons.

Create a String Variable

A string is a series of characters treated as a single piece of data. The PHP processor treats string variables as distinct instances. There are no inherent types for words or sentences. String variables allow you to use perform functions to add, extract, and exchange characters.

You can create a string variable by following the same steps outlined in the task "Create a Numeric Variable." The main difference between a statement creating a numeric variable and one creating a string variable is that the value on the right side of the assignment operator (=) is wrapped in either single (') or double (") quotes.

If your string value contains quotes, you can either choose the opposite quote type to delimit your string or *escape* the internal quotes. For example, if you mark your string with double quotes any double quote characters inside the string value must be immediately preceded by a backslash character.

The choice to use single or double quotes is yours, as long as the opening and closing quotes are the same. Functionally, the difference between the two is that double-quoted strings are *interpolated*. Interpolation is the process of finding special segments of a string that match control characters or variable names and replacing them with the associated values.

With single-quoted strings, this interpolation will not happen. PHP assigns the entire string, including the names of any variables, without substitution. Because single-quoted strings are not interpolated, they are slightly faster for PHP to process.

Create a String Variable

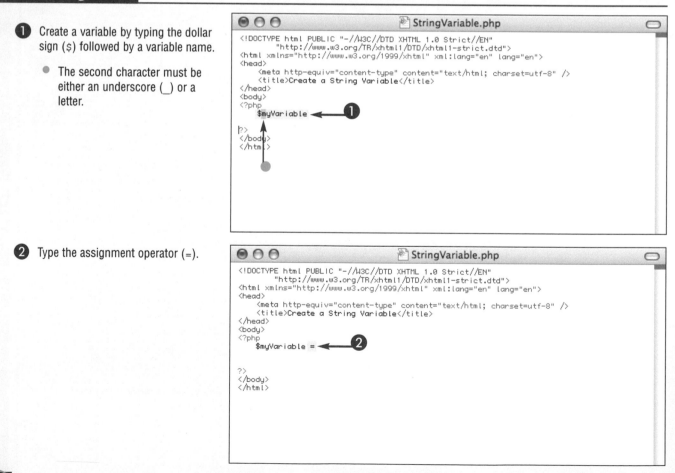

① Create a variable by typing the dollar sign ($) followed by a variable name.

● The second character must be either an underscore (_) or a letter.

② Type the assignment operator (=).

3 Type a value you want to assign to the variable, followed by a semicolon (;).

4 Use the `echo` function to write the value of the variable to the output stream.

```
StringVariable.php
<!DOCTYPE html PUBLIC "-//W3C//DTD XHTML 1.0 Strict//EN"
        "http://www.w3.org/TR/xhtml1/DTD/xhtml1-strict.dtd">
<html xmlns="http://www.w3.org/1999/xhtml" xml:lang="en" lang="en">
<head>
    <meta http-equiv="content-type" content="text/html; charset=utf-8" />
    <title>Create a String Variable</title>
</head>
<body>
<?php
    $myVariable = 'This is a single quoted string.';      3

    echo "$myVariable<br />";      4
?>
</body>
</html>
```

5 View the script in a Web browser.

The page is rendered with the value of the variable used in the place of the variable.

```
Create a String Variable
Address: http://127.0.0.1:9003/ch02/task4/Code/StringVariable.php    go

This is a single quoted string.    5
```

Extra

Double-quoted strings allow the use of control characters that are significant to the PHP processor. These are the most common control characters:

CONTROL SEQUENCE	DESCRIPTION
\n	Create a new line
\r	Carriage return
\t	Tab character
\\	Backslash character
\"	Double quotation mark
\$	Dollar sign
\012	Octal ASCII value
\x0A	Hex ASCII value

You can also define a string using the special *heredoc* syntax. Strings defined using the heredoc syntax behave exactly like double-quoted strings with the exception that double quote characters do not need to be escaped. This allows you to have assignment statements with many quotes that are clear to read and easy to maintain. To begin a heredoc string

assignment, type <<< followed by an identifier for the string. To close the string type the identifier followed by a semicolon. The closing identifier *must* begin in the first column and the line cannot contain any other characters except the semicolon. This means that the closing identifier cannot be indented. Heredoc syntax is useful if you need to create a variable containing a large chunk of HTML.

TYPE THIS:

```
$myVariable = <<<EOD
This is text contained in the variable
Double quotes " can be used without \\
backslashes
EOD;
echo $myVariable;
```

RESULTS:

The variable is printed and the formatting is kept intact.

Create a Constant

You can create a variable in PHP that cannot be changed after the initial assignment. This type of variable is known as a *constant*. Constants are globally accessible. Because their *scope* is global, you can access them from any function or object in your script. A common use for constants is to represent mathematically constant values such as PI.

You create constant variables differently than other variable assignments. Instead of using the assignment operator (`=`) you use the `define()` function. The function accepts two arguments. The first must be a string and represents the name by which you want to access your constant. Constants are named according to the same rules as other variables except that they do not begin with the dollar sign (`$`) character.

The second argument for the `define()` function is the value of your constant. This may be a string or numbers and may be set explicitly or as the result of a function or equation. After it is assigned, a constant variable may not be modified.

You can use constant variables the same as you do mutable variables. Whenever the PHP processor encounters the name of a constant variable it substitutes the associated value.

The PHP language includes many predefined constants that you can use in your scripts. It is a good idea to familiarize yourself with the predefined constants so you do not try to use the same names.

Create a Constant

① Begin the declaration by typing `define(`.

② Type the name of the constant, making sure to contain the name in single or double quotes.

③ Type a comma (`,`) followed by the value you want the constant to represent.

④ End the declaration with a closing parenthesis (`)`) and a semicolon.

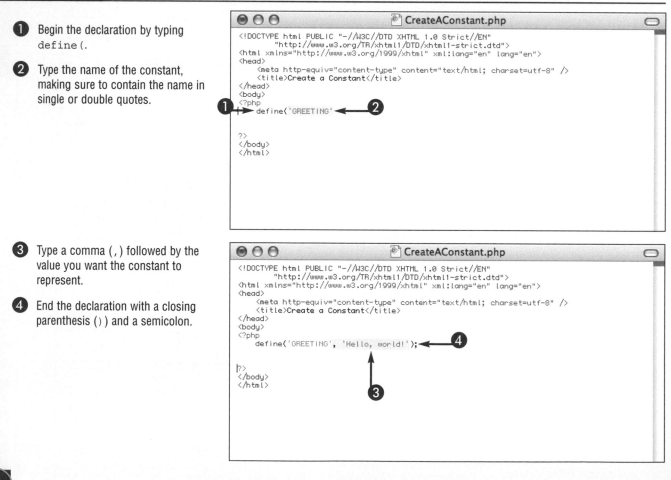

5 Create an echo statement to use the constant variable.

6 Repeat Steps 1 to 4 to create any additional constants.

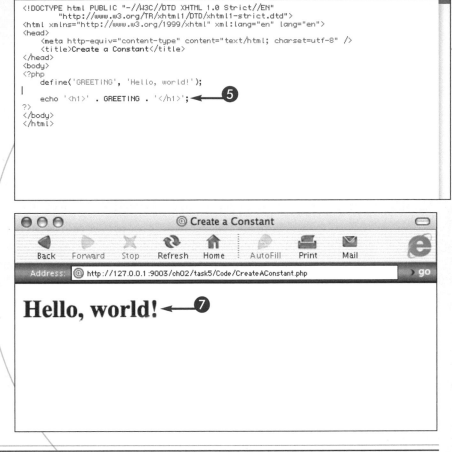

```
<!DOCTYPE html PUBLIC "-//W3C//DTD XHTML 1.0 Strict//EN"
        "http://www.w3.org/TR/xhtml1/DTD/xhtml1-strict.dtd">
<html xmlns="http://www.w3.org/1999/xhtml" xml:lang="en" lang="en">
<head>
    <meta http-equiv="content-type" content="text/html; charset=utf-8" />
    <title>Create a Constant</title>
</head>
<body>
<?php
    define('GREETING', 'Hello, world!');

    echo '<h1>' . GREETING . '</h1>';
?>
</body>
</html>
```

7 View the script in a Web browser.

The page is rendered with the value of the constant variable used in the place of the variable.

Address: http://127.0.0.1:9003/ch02/task5/Code/CreateAConstant.php

Hello, world!

Extra

You can check to see if a constant name is in use by passing the name as a string argument to the define() function. If you pass the name of a currently defined constant variable, the function returns 1. Otherwise, the function returns 0.

TYPE THIS:

```
define('GREETING', 'Hello, world!');
if(defined('GREETING')){
  echo GREETING;
}else{
  echo 'No greeting today';
}
```

RESULTS:

The value of the GREETING constant is written to the output stream. If you delete the first line, the constant is not defined. This results in "No greeting today" being printed.

You can look up the value of a constant dynamically with the constant() function. The function accepts a single string argument representing the name of the constant to be found. This function is useful if you have the name of a constant stored and need to find the value for that constant in the given script.

Example:

```
define('GREETING', 'Hello, world!');
$greetingKey = 'GREETING';
if(defined($greetingKey)){
  echo constant($greetingKey);
}else{
  echo "There is no constant named
$greetingKey.";
}
```

Using Operators

You use operators to manipulate values and values. In PHP, the operators allow you to concatenate strings, execute arithmetic operations, assign values to variables, compare values, and perform Boolean operations.

Operators are used with one or more values called *operands*. The most common operators are the arithmetic operators: + (addition), - (subtraction), * (multiplication), and / (division). These operators behave just as they do in common mathematics; the operator is placed between the two operands to perform a calculation:

```
1 + 2
```

As in algebra, you can use operators to manipulate values stored in variables. The above example can be written to use variables by replacing one or both of the numbers with a defined variable name.

Operators have what is called *precedence* or *order of operations*. Precedence determines which operators are executed first when statements consisting of multiple operations are processed. Take, for example, the statement:

```
1 * 3 - 2
```

The multiplication (*) operator takes precedence and is executed first. The value resulting from that operation is then used as the first value of the subtraction operation.

You can break from the default order of precedence and control the way PHP evaluates expressions using parenthesis (()). Operations enclosed in parentheses are always evaluated first. Nested parentheses are evaluated from inside to outside.

Arithmetic Operators

Arithmetic operators are used to perform mathematical operations.

+ (Addition)

Calculates the sum of two values.

```
echo 1 + 2;
```

Displays 3

- (Subtraction)

Calculates the difference between two values.

```
echo 3 - 2;
```

Displays 1

* (Multiplication)

Multiplies two values.

```
echo 1 * 3;
```

Displays 3

/ (Division)

Divides the first value by the second.

```
echo 3 / 1;
```

Displays 3

% (Modulus)

Calculates the remainder of the division of the first value by the second.

```
echo 3%2;
```

Displays 1

String Concatenation Operators

The concatenation operator is used to combine values to create a string. The concatenation operator is useful when combining strings with values from constants and arrays.

. (Concatenation)

```
define("USERNAME", "Jon");

$message = "The current user is: ".USERNAME;
echo $message;
```

Displays "The current user is: Jon"

Increment and Decrement Operators

The increment and decrement operators are useful shortcuts to two common programming tasks, incrementing and decrementing a numerical value.

++$value (Preincrement)

Adds 1 to a value before the value is used in the expression in which it is contained.

```
$value =  1;

echo ++$value;
```

Displays 2

--$value (Predecrement)

Subtracts 1 from a value before the value is used in the expression in which it is contained.

```
$value =  2;

echo --$value;
```

Displays 1

$value++ (Postincrement)

Adds 1 to a value after the value is used in the expression in which it is contained.

```
$value =  1;

echo $value++;

echo "<br />";

echo $value;
```

Displays

1

2

$value-- (Postdecrement)

Subtracts 1 from a value after the value is used in the expression in which it is contained.

```
$value =  2;

echo $value--;

echo "<br />";

echo $value;
```

Displays

2

1

Assignment Operators

The assignment operator (=) is used to assign a value to a variable. The assignment operator can also be combined with other mathematical operators to quickly and succinctly change the value of a variable. For example, the expression: `$x = $x + 2;` can be rewritten as `$x += 2`.

= (Assignment)

Sets the value of the first operand to the value of the second.

```
$x = 1;
echo $x;
```

Displays 1

+= (Addition-Assignment)

Sets the value of the first operand to its value plus the second value.

```
$x = 1;
$x += 2;
echo $x;
```

Displays 3

-= (Subtraction-Assignment)

Sets the value of the first operand to its value minus the second value.

```
$x = 3;
$x -= 2;
echo $x;
```

Displays 1

*= (Multiplication-Assignment)

Sets the value of the first operand to its value multiplied by the second value.

```
$x = 2;
$x *= 2;
echo $x;
```

Displays 4

continued →

Assignment Operators *(continued)*

/= (Division-Assignment)

Sets the value of the first operand to its value divided by the second value.

```
$x = 4;
$x /= 2;
echo $x;
```

Displays 2

.= (Concatenation-Assignment)

Sets the value of the first operand to a string containing its value with the second value appended at the end.

```
$x = "The time is ";
$x .= "now";
echo $x;
```

Displays "The time is now";

%= (Modulo-Assignment)

Sets the value of the first operand to the remainder of its value divided by the second value.

```
$x = 3;
$x %= 2;
echo $x;
```

Displays 1

Logical Operators

Logical operators are used to perform Boolean operations to determine the truth or falsity of statements in your script.

And

Checks if all values are true.

```
$x = 5;
$y = 2;
if (($x == 5) and ($y == 2)) echo "True";
```

Displays "True"

&&

Checks if all values are true. Same as and.

```
$x = 5;
$y = 2;
if (($x == 5) && ($y == 2)) echo "True";
```

Displays "True"

Or

Checks if any values are true.

```
$x = 5;
$y = 2;
if (($x == 5) or ($y == 9)) echo "True";
```

Displays "True"

||

Checks if any values are true. Same as or.

```
$x = 5;
$y = 2;
if (($x == 5) || ($y == 9)) echo "True";
```

Displays "True"

Logical Operators *(continued)*

Xor

Checks if only one value is `true`.

```
$x = 5;
$y = 2;
if (($x == 5) xor ($y == 7)) echo "True";
```

Displays "True"

!

Checks if a statement is not true.

```
$x = 9;
if (!($x == 5)) echo "True";
```

Displays "True"

Comparison Operators

Comparison operators compare values and return Boolean `true` or `false` values depending on the result.

== (Equal to)

Checks if the first operand is equal to the second.

```
$x = 5;
$y = "5";
if ($x == $y) echo "$x is equal to $y";
```

Displays "5 is equal to 5"

< (Less than)

Checks if the first operand is less than the second.

```
$x = 5;
$y = 10;
if ($x < $y) echo "$x is less than $y";
```

Displays "5 is less than 10"

=== (Identical to)

Checks if the first operand has the same value and type as the second.

```
$x = 5;
$y = 5;
if ($x == $y) echo "$x is identical to $y";
```

Displays "5 is identical to 5"

> (Greater than)

Checks if the first operand is greater than the second.

```
$x = 10;
$y = 5;
if ($x > $y) echo "$x is greater than $y";
```

Displays "10 is greater than 5"

!= (Not equal to)

Checks if the first operand is not equal to the second.

```
$x = 5;
$y = 3;
if ($x != $y) echo "$x is not equal to $y";
```

Displays "5 is not equal to 3"

<= (Less than or equal to)

Checks if the first operand is less than or equal to the second.

```
$x = 5;
$y = 5;
if ($x <= $y) echo "$x is less than or equal to $y";
```

Displays "5 is less than or equal to 5"

!== (Not identical to)

Checks if the first operand is not identical to the second.

```
$x = 5;
$y = "5";
if ($x !== $y) echo "$x is not identical to $y";
```

Displays "5 is not identical to 5"

>= (Greater than or equal to)

Checks if the first operand is greater than or equal to the second.

```
$x = 19;
$y = 5;
if ($x >= $y) echo "$x is greater than or equal to $y";
```

Displays "19 is greater than or equal to 5"

Perform a
Numeric Calculation

You can use numeric operators to perform mathematical calculations. Numeric operations consist of operators and operands. Operators determine the function of the operation while operands represent the values. You can use literal values such as 3.14 and -400 or variables representing values.

PHP includes several operators with which you are already familiar. Basic arithmetic operators include those such as addition (+), subtraction (-), multiplication (*), division (/) and modulus (%). These operators are used the same in PHP as they are in basic mathematics. Additional operators exist for functionality such as comparison, assignment, and logical functionality. There are also operators for incrementing and decrementing values. For more information about operators, see the task "Using Operators."

You can use variables to perform algebraic operations on dynamic expressions. The assignment operator (=) allows you to assign the result of a calculation to a variable for later use. You can use the variable representing the value of one operation as an operand in other operations. If you abstract your operations using variables instead of static values, you can write robust, dynamic operations that are easy to reuse in different contexts or scripts.

Perform a Numeric Calculation

① Begin the statement by typing the name of a variable to represent your initial value.

② Type the assignment operator (=) followed by the value with which you want to begin.

③ Type the name of the variable to represent the result of the calculation.

④ Type the assignment operator (=) followed by the body of the equation.

Note: All common arithmetic functionality is allowed in PHP using common operators.

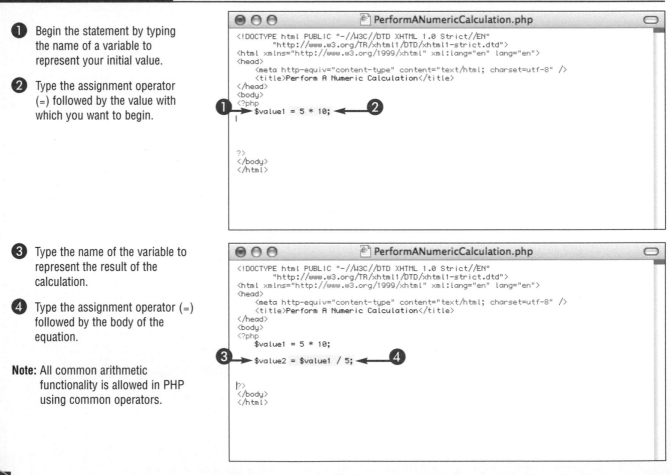

⑤ Create an echo statement to use the variable representing the result of your calculations.

⑥ Repeat Steps 1 to 5 to perform any additional numerical calculations.

```
PerformANumericCalculation.php

<!DOCTYPE html PUBLIC "-//W3C//DTD XHTML 1.0 Strict//EN"
        "http://www.w3.org/TR/xhtml1/DTD/xhtml1-strict.dtd">
<html xmlns="http://www.w3.org/1999/xhtml" xml:lang="en" lang="en">
<head>
    <meta http-equiv="content-type" content="text/html; charset=utf-8" />
    <title>Perform A Numeric Calculation</title>
</head>
<body>
<?php
    $value1 = 5 * 10;

    $value2 = $value1 / 5;

    echo "The result of the complex operation is: $value2.";      ⑤
?>
</body>
</html>
```

⑦ View the script in a Web browser.

The results of the numeric calculations appear.

```
@ Perform A Numeric Calculation

Back  Forward  Stop  Refresh  Home  AutoFill  Print  Mail

Address: @ http://127.0.0.1:9003/ch02/task7/Code/PerformANumericCalculation.php    ▸ go

The result of the complex operation is: 10. ◀─⑦
```

Extra

Complex operations with several operands are evaluated according to *operator precedence*. You can change the order of operations by enclosing suboperations in parentheses. Any operations inside parentheses are evaluated first. For example, in the equation a += (b-a)*c;, the calculation in parentheses is performed first and its value is used as the first operand in the multiplication sequence. This is because the multiplication operator (*) has precedence over the subtraction operator and is processed first. Without the parentheses, the operation a += b-a * c; would be evaluated as a += b-(a * c);, which would add an entirely different value to a than the initial example.

TYPE THIS:
```
$a = 10;
$b = 20;
$c = 0.5;

echo $a += ($b - $a) * $c;
```

RESULTS:

The value of $a is output as 15.

TYPE THIS:
```
$a = 10;
$b = 20;
$c = 0.5;

echo $a += $b - ($a * $c);
```

RESULTS:

The value of $a is output as 25.

Control Program Flow Using Conditional Statements

You can control the flow of your PHP scripts by using *conditional statements*. Conditional statements are constructs that contain code that is processed when a given condition is met. You can create forks in your program by inserting a point at which a test is run. Depending on the outcome of the test, your script performs different operations or functions.

The most common conditionals are the `if` and `if...else` statements. The `if` statement processes any code immediately following the condition on which to test. If the condition evaluates to `true`, the code is processed. The `if...else` statement adds the ability to specify code that runs when the condition evaluates to false.

You can create a conditional statement by typing the `if` keyword followed by parentheses (`()`) containing the expression you want to evaluate. The code you want to process when the condition is met should be enclosed in braces (`{}`). While braces are not required for a simple,

single-line conditional statement, use them so that all of your conditional statements are clear and consistent.

If you want to add an alternate block of code to be evaluated when the condition is false, you can add an `else` statement. Using an `else` statement ensures that at least one block of code is executed no matter what the outcome of the condition.

You can perform simple conditional assignments using the *ternary operator* (`?`). This is useful when you want to perform a simple task, such as an assignment, based on a conditional test. The primary benefit over an `if...else` statement is clarity. Ternary conditionals are most often used in assignments. For example, you may assign a greeting with a statement such as `$greeting = $morning ? 'Good morning!' : 'Hello!';`. If the `$morning` variable has a value of `true`, the `$greeting` variable is assigned the string 'Good Morning!' Otherwise, the `$greeting` is assigned 'Hello!'

Control Program Flow Using Conditional Statements

① Create a set of variables to use in the conditional test.

② Type `if()`.

③ Define your condition between the parentheses.

④ Add the block of code you want to process if the condition evaluates to `true`.

- Enclose the block of code in curly braces (`{}`).

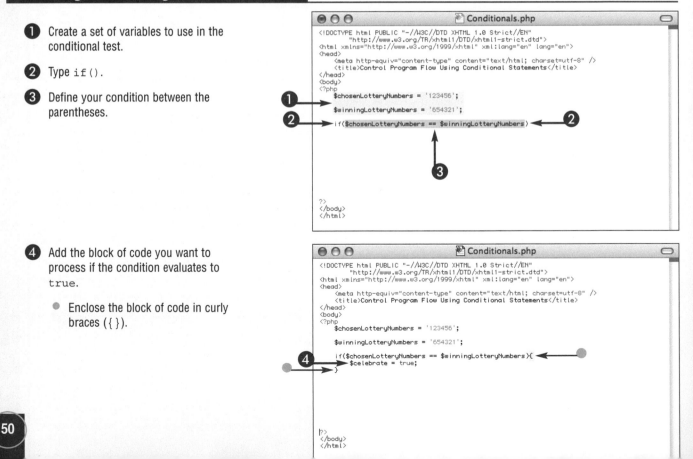

5 To add an alternate block of code, add the else keyword.

6 Type the block of code you want to process if the condition evaluates to false.

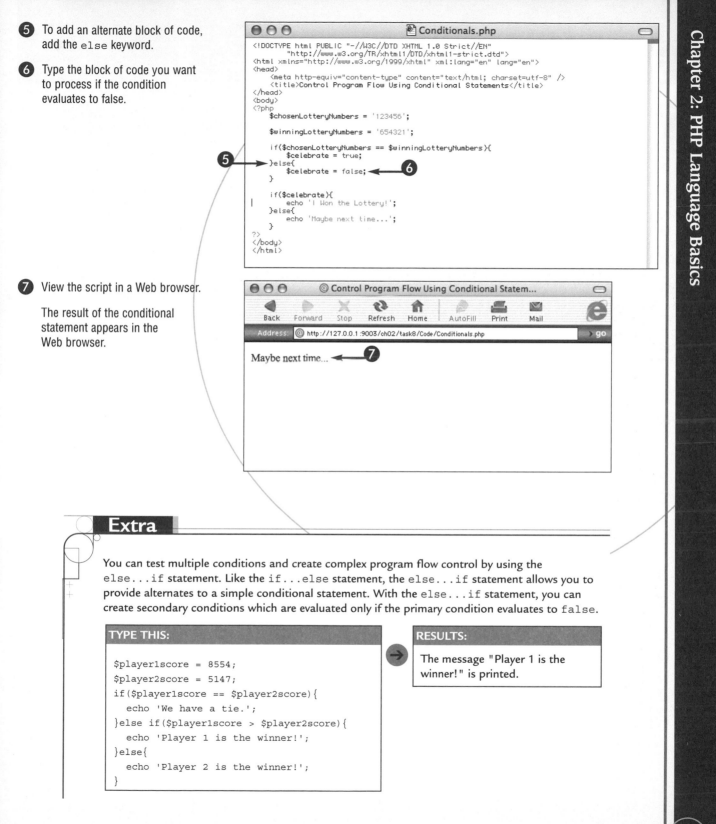

```
Conditionals.php
<!DOCTYPE html PUBLIC "-//W3C//DTD XHTML 1.0 Strict//EN"
        "http://www.w3.org/TR/xhtml1/DTD/xhtml1-strict.dtd">
<html xmlns="http://www.w3.org/1999/xhtml" xml:lang="en" lang="en">
<head>
    <meta http-equiv="content-type" content="text/html; charset=utf-8" />
    <title>Control Program Flow Using Conditional Statements</title>
</head>
<body>
<?php
    $chosenLotteryNumbers = '123456';

    $winningLotteryNumbers = '654321';

    if($chosenLotteryNumbers == $winningLotteryNumbers){
        $celebrate = true;
    }else{
        $celebrate = false;
    }

    if($celebrate){
        echo 'I Won the Lottery!';
    }else{
        echo 'Maybe next time...';
    }
?>
</body>
</html>
```

7 View the script in a Web browser.

The result of the conditional statement appears in the Web browser.

Control Program Flow Using Conditional Statem...

Back Forward Stop Refresh Home AutoFill Print Mail

Address: http://127.0.0.1:9003/ch02/task8/Code/Conditionals.php go

Maybe next time...

Extra

You can test multiple conditions and create complex program flow control by using the else...if statement. Like the if...else statement, the else...if statement allows you to provide alternates to a simple conditional statement. With the else...if statement, you can create secondary conditions which are evaluated only if the primary condition evaluates to false.

TYPE THIS:

```
$player1score = 8554;
$player2score = 5147;
if($player1score == $player2score){
  echo 'We have a tie.';
}else if($player1score > $player2score){
  echo 'Player 1 is the winner!';
}else{
  echo 'Player 2 is the winner!';
}
```

RESULTS:

The message "Player 1 is the winner!" is printed.

Using the Switch Statement

The `switch` statement allows you to control the flow of your program by testing a single value against many possible matches, or *cases*. When a matching case is found, any code immediately following the case is evaluated. Evaluation continues until a `break` statement is found. Usually, each case has a `break` statement as the last line of its body, telling the `switch` statement to break from the search for matches. A great benefit of `switch` statements is the ability to group possible matches with a single block of actions. You can group possible matches by stacking cases and omitting `break` statements and executable code from all but the last `case` in the group.

With the `switch` statement, you can handle complex conditions more elegantly than other conditional statements allow. A `switch` statement is more efficient than other equivalent conditional statements. This is because it is faster to evaluate a single condition against many values than to process many conditional tests.

Another benefit of `switch` statements is that the list of cases can grow over time, making your code easy to manage. Long `if...else` statements are difficult to maintain and understand, but `switch` statements are clear and extensible.

You can create a switch statement by typing the `switch` keyword followed by an expression or variable in parentheses and a set of braces (`{}`). Add any number of case statements to the body of the expression.

Using the Switch Statement

1 Create a variable to use in the switch statement.

2 Open the switch statement using the variable.

```
SwitchStatement.php
<!DOCTYPE html PUBLIC "-//W3C//DTD XHTML 1.0 Strict//EN"
    "http://www.w3.org/TR/xhtml1/DTD/xhtml1-strict.dtd">
<html xmlns="http://www.w3.org/1999/xhtml" xml:lang="en" lang="en">
<head>
    <meta http-equiv="content-type" content="text/html; charset=utf-8" />
    <title>Using the Switch Statement</title>
</head>
<body>
<?php
    $state = 'CA';

    switch($state){


    }
?>
</body>
</html>
```

3 Add a case statement by typing the `case` keyword followed by a possible value and a colon (`:`).

4 Type the code to execute in this case, and use the `break` statement to stop evaluating further cases.

```
SwitchStatement.php
<!DOCTYPE html PUBLIC "-//W3C//DTD XHTML 1.0 Strict//EN"
    "http://www.w3.org/TR/xhtml1/DTD/xhtml1-strict.dtd">
<html xmlns="http://www.w3.org/1999/xhtml" xml:lang="en" lang="en">
<head>
    <meta http-equiv="content-type" content="text/html; charset=utf-8" />
    <title>Using the Switch Statement</title>
</head>
<body>
<?php
    $state = 'CA';

    switch($state){
    case 'AL':
        echo 'You are in Alabama.';
        break;



    }
?>
</body>
</html>
```

5 Repeat Step 3 for any further cases.

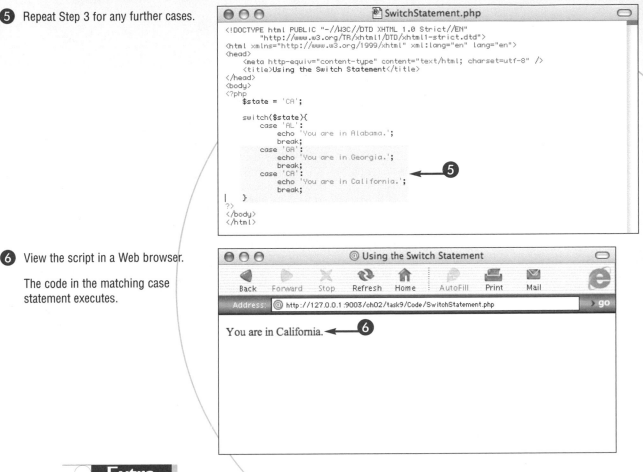

6 View the script in a Web browser.

The code in the matching case statement executes.

Extra

You can define code to be executed when no matching case statement is found. To catch unmatched cases, you can use the default statement. The default statement is much like a standard case statement. Instead of typing case followed by a value, you type default. When used, the default statement should represent the last case in the switch. You can combine the default statement with other case statements by omitting the break statement from any cases immediately preceding the default.

TYPE THIS:

```
$animal = 'Fish';

case($animal){
  case 'Chicken':
    echo 'Cluck cluck.<br />';
    break;
  case 'Pig':
    echo 'Oink, oink.<br />';
    break;
  default:
    echo 'Unknown animal.<br />';
}
```

RESULTS:

The $animal variable does not match any of the given cases so the code inside the default statement is evaluated.

Using While Loops

Loops are control structures that allow you to perform a repetitive task until a given condition is met. You can leverage the power of loops to make your code easier to comprehend and maintain than a series of duplicate statements would allow. For example, if you need to call a function hundreds or thousands of times, a simple loop can allow this in as little as three lines of code. Although there are a few types of loop structures in PHP, the most elegant and simple is the while loop.

A while loop begins with an opening statement consisting of the while keyword and the definition of the condition to be met in order for the body of the loop to be processed. The condition is placed inside a set of parentheses and can be a variable, operation, or a call to a function that returns a value. If you want to execute a loop ten times, your opening statement might be defined as: while ($count <= 10). If the condition does not contain or evaluate to

a Boolean value of true or false, the loop may run forever or may never execute at all. Because the loop condition must evaluate to true for the loop to continue, it is possible to create an endless loop by beginning the block with while(true){.

After you write the opening statement, you must define the body of the loop. This consists of any operations or actions to be completed every time the loop iterates and until the condition is met. You define your statement body in curly braces {} immediately after the opening statement. Most often, the body of your loop contains statements that modify the condition defined in the opening statement. Using the prior example, you may increment your variable $count each time the loop body is processed. When the $count variable has been incremented ten times, the loop condition evaluates to false and the loop exits.

Using While Loops

1. Create a counter variable and set the value to 0.

2. Define the opening statement of a while loop.

3. Add code to the body of the loop.

4. Increment the counter variable to track the number of times the loop has iterated.

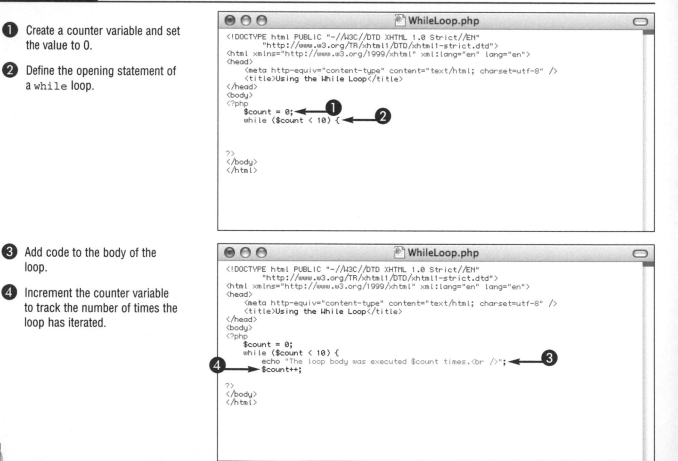

```
<!DOCTYPE html PUBLIC "-//W3C//DTD XHTML 1.0 Strict//EN"
    "http://www.w3.org/TR/xhtml1/DTD/xhtml1-strict.dtd">
<html xmlns="http://www.w3.org/1999/xhtml" xml:lang="en" lang="en">
<head>
    <meta http-equiv="content-type" content="text/html; charset=utf-8" />
    <title>Using the While Loop</title>
</head>
<body>
<?php
    $count = 0;
    while ($count < 10) {


?>
</body>
</html>
```

```
<!DOCTYPE html PUBLIC "-//W3C//DTD XHTML 1.0 Strict//EN"
    "http://www.w3.org/TR/xhtml1/DTD/xhtml1-strict.dtd">
<html xmlns="http://www.w3.org/1999/xhtml" xml:lang="en" lang="en">
<head>
    <meta http-equiv="content-type" content="text/html; charset=utf-8" />
    <title>Using the While Loop</title>
</head>
<body>
<?php
    $count = 0;
    while ($count < 10) {
        echo "The loop body was executed $count times.<br />";
        $count++;

?>
</body>
</html>
```

⑤ Close the statement body with a curly brace (}).

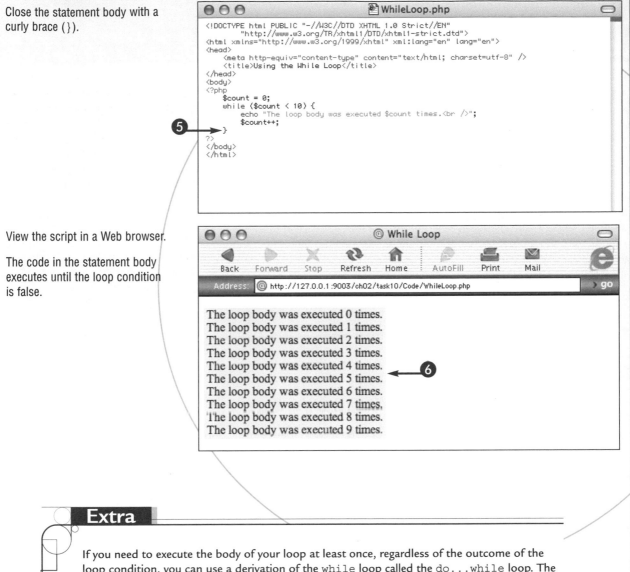

```
WhileLoop.php

<!DOCTYPE html PUBLIC "-//W3C//DTD XHTML 1.0 Strict//EN"
        "http://www.w3.org/TR/xhtml1/DTD/xhtml1-strict.dtd">
<html xmlns="http://www.w3.org/1999/xhtml" xml:lang="en" lang="en">
<head>
    <meta http-equiv="content-type" content="text/html; charset=utf-8" />
    <title>Using the While Loop</title>
</head>
<body>
<?php
    $count = 0;
    while ($count < 10) {
        echo "The loop body was executed $count times.<br />";
        $count++;
⑤→  }
?>
</body>
</html>
```

⑥ View the script in a Web browser.

The code in the statement body executes until the loop condition is false.

While Loop

Back Forward Stop Refresh Home AutoFill Print Mail

Address: http://127.0.0.1:9003/ch02/task10/Code/WhileLoop.php go

The loop body was executed 0 times.
The loop body was executed 1 times.
The loop body was executed 2 times.
The loop body was executed 3 times.
The loop body was executed 4 times.
The loop body was executed 5 times. ←⑥
The loop body was executed 6 times.
The loop body was executed 7 times.
The loop body was executed 8 times.
The loop body was executed 9 times.

Extra

If you need to execute the body of your loop at least once, regardless of the outcome of the loop condition, you can use a derivation of the while loop called the do...while loop. The do...while loop is different in that it executes the body of your loop first, then checks the condition to determine whether it should execute again. Like the while loop, the do...while loop continues to execute until the condition evaluates to false.

TYPE THIS:

```
do {
  echo 'The loop body was
executed.<br />';
} while (false);
```

→

RESULTS:

The browser displays: "The loop body was executed." Notice that, although the condition is false, the loop body is executed once. If this were written as a while loop, the body never executes and the browser displays nothing.

Using For Loops

The most common type of loop used in many programming languages is the `for` loop. The `for` loop groups the main control features of loops and provides a concise way to perform repetitive actions.

The simplest loop structure is the `while` loop. It is often used along with a counter variable, a looping condition that PHP evaluates before each loop cycle, and a statement within the loop body that increments or decrements the counter variable. See "Using While Loops" for more. The `for` loop consolidates these steps into a simpler structure.

You can create a `for` loop by first initializing a counter variable. This is normally a simple value assignment. See "Create a Numeric Variable" for more. Next, you must create a looping condition. The condition is in the same form as in an `if` or `while` statement — any single statement that evaluates to a Boolean `true` or `false` will suffice. Finally, add a statement that increments the counter variable at the

beginning of each loop cycle. Counter variables are most often incremented using the `++` operator. See "Using Operators" for more.

Each of the three elements that makes up the opening statement of the `for` loop is placed in parentheses and separated with semicolons. For example, a loop that runs 100 times might begin with a statement such as: `for ($i=0;$i<100;$i++)`.

Like other loop structures and conditional statements, the code that makes up the body of the loop is enclosed in braces (`{}`) immediately after the opening statement. You can have as many statements as you want in the loop body. The `for` loop helps ensure that you do not forget to increment your counters. Leaving out this step in a `while` loop results in a loop that never terminates, effectively locking your program.

Using For Loops

1. Type `for(`.

2. Initialize a counter variable with a value of `0`.

3. Terminate this statement with a semicolon (`;`).

4. Create the looping condition followed by `;`.

5. Type the name of your variable along with the increment operator `++`.

6. Close the opening statement by typing `) {`.

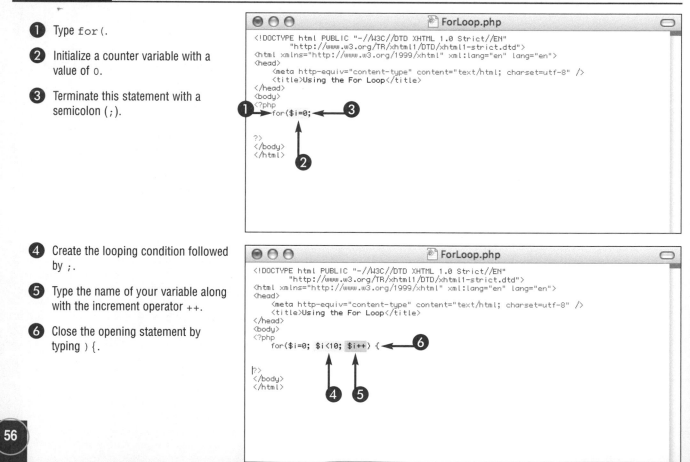

7 Add code to the loop body
followed by }.

```
ForLoop.php
<!DOCTYPE html PUBLIC "-//W3C//DTD XHTML 1.0 Strict//EN"
        "http://www.w3.org/TR/xhtml1/DTD/xhtml1-strict.dtd">
<html xmlns="http://www.w3.org/1999/xhtml" xml:lang="en" lang="en">
<head>
    <meta http-equiv="content-type" content="text/html; charset=utf-8" />
    <title>Using the For Loop</title>
</head>
<body>
<?php
    for($i=0; $i<10; $i++) {
        echo "The loop body was executed $i times.<br />";  ◄── 7
    }
?>
</body>
</html>
```

8 View the script in a Web browser.

The code in the statement body
executes until the loop condition
is false.

```
Using the For Loop
Back   Forward   Stop   Refresh   Home   AutoFill   Print   Mail
Address: http://127.0.0.1:9003/ch02/task11/Code/ForLoop.php    go

The loop body was executed 0 times.
The loop body was executed 1 times.
The loop body was executed 2 times.
The loop body was executed 3 times.
The loop body was executed 4 times.     ◄── 8
The loop body was executed 5 times.
The loop body was executed 6 times.
The loop body was executed 7 times.
The loop body was executed 8 times.
The loop body was executed 9 times.
```

Extra

You can terminate a loop explicitly with the break statement. For example, you may be using
your loop to scan an array for values. When the desired value is found, you can use the break
statement to stop the loop. This provides a way of optimizing your loops.

TYPE THIS:

```
$desired = 10;
for($i=0; $i<100; $i++){
  echo "The loop is on iteration:
$i.<br />";
  if($i == $desired){
    echo "Found $desired!";
    break;
  }
}
```

RESULTS:

The browser displays the iteration
message ten times, followed by the
"Found 10" message. If you choose
not to use the break statement,
the iteration message appears an
additional 90 times.

Create a Function

Y ou can organize and streamline your code using functions. Functions are a way to group related actions together. They provide a way to repeatedly execute them without retyping code. For example, you might need to display a message if a user enters invalid data in a form. Rather than retype the lines of code to check each form element, you can use a single function to do the work for you. By consolidating your code into functions, your scripts become easier to for you to write, understand, reuse, and debug.

You use the `function` keyword to create a new function. After the keyword, you type the name of the function. Function names cannot begin with a number and can only contain letters, numbers, and the underscore (_) character. It is a good practice to give functions simple and descriptive names. You can capitalize the first letter of each word to make the name easier to read, for example `validateUserInfo`. Choosing a consistent naming pattern is an important step in writing clear and manageable code.

The function name is followed by a set of parentheses. The body of the function follows the opening statement and is enclosed inside braces {}. Commonly, the body of a function is indented. This makes your code easier to read.

When you run the script, the statements inside the function body do not execute automatically. To execute a function, you write the name of the function followed by parentheses. For example, if you create a function named `validateUserInfo`, you execute the function by typing `validateUserInfo()`.

Create a Function

① Create a new function by typing the `function` keyword.

② Type the name of the function followed by parentheses (`()`) and an opening brace (`{`).

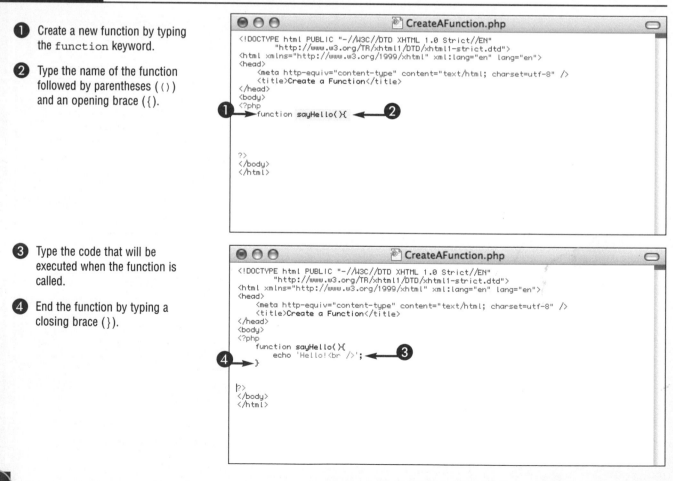

③ Type the code that will be executed when the function is called.

④ End the function by typing a closing brace (`}`).

⑤ Call the function by typing the function name followed by parentheses (( )).

Note: The parentheses tell PHP to execute the function.

⑥ View the script in a Web browser.

The code in the function is executed and the results are displayed in the browser.

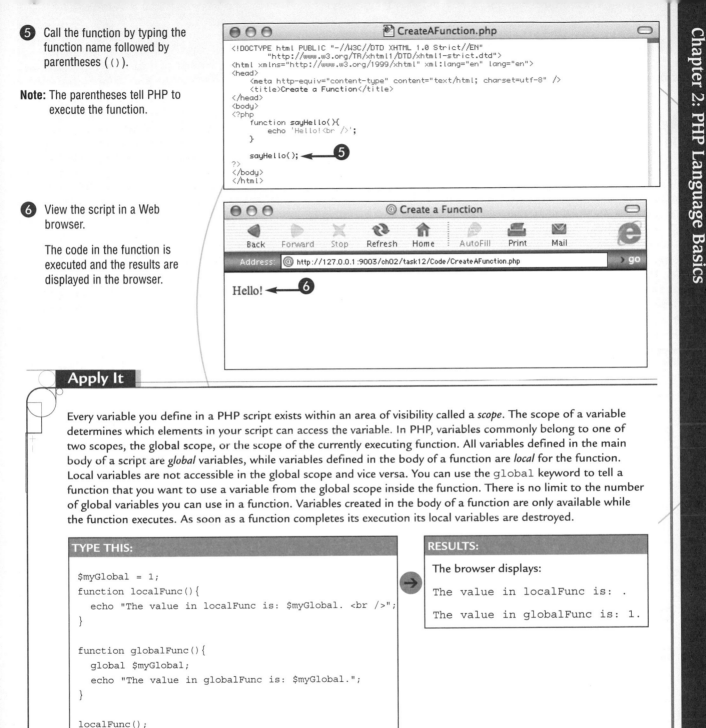

```
CreateAFunction.php

<!DOCTYPE html PUBLIC "-//W3C//DTD XHTML 1.0 Strict//EN"
        "http://www.w3.org/TR/xhtml1/DTD/xhtml1-strict.dtd">
<html xmlns="http://www.w3.org/1999/xhtml" xml:lang="en" lang="en">
<head>
    <meta http-equiv="content-type" content="text/html; charset=utf-8" />
    <title>Create a Function</title>
</head>
<body>
<?php
    function sayHello(){
        echo 'Hello!<br />';
    }

    sayHello();           ⑤
?>
</body>
</html>
```

```
Create a Function

Address: http://127.0.0.1:9003/ch02/task12/Code/CreateAFunction.php

Hello!  ⑥
```

Apply It

Every variable you define in a PHP script exists within an area of visibility called a *scope*. The scope of a variable determines which elements in your script can access the variable. In PHP, variables commonly belong to one of two scopes, the global scope, or the scope of the currently executing function. All variables defined in the main body of a script are *global* variables, while variables defined in the body of a function are *local* for the function. Local variables are not accessible in the global scope and vice versa. You can use the `global` keyword to tell a function that you want to use a variable from the global scope inside the function. There is no limit to the number of global variables you can use in a function. Variables created in the body of a function are only available while the function executes. As soon as a function completes its execution its local variables are destroyed.

TYPE THIS:

```
$myGlobal = 1;
function localFunc(){
    echo "The value in localFunc is: $myGlobal. <br />";
}

function globalFunc(){
    global $myGlobal;
    echo "The value in globalFunc is: $myGlobal.";
}

localFunc();
globalFunc();
```

RESULTS:

The browser displays:

```
The value in localFunc is: .

The value in globalFunc is: 1.
```

When `localFunc` executes, the value is not found because the variable does not exist in the local scope. The correct value is printed when `globalFunc` is called because the `global` keyword is used to declare a variable as global.

Return a Value from a Function

You can use functions to encapsulate series of statements that are related. Functions allow portability and clarity in your code. You can think of functions as a way of telling PHP to do a complex series of actions with a single, clear statement. Sometimes, you need PHP to tell you something about the series of actions undertaken when a function is called. This is called *returning a value* from a function.

You can specify the value to be returned using the `return` keyword. When a return statement is executed, the function terminates and returns the value immediately following the `return` keyword. Keeping this in mind, you may return a value early in the function call if no further code evaluation is necessary.

Often, you will want to know simply whether or not a function executes successfully. For these situations you simply return `true` or `false` by adding `return true;` or `return false;` at the appropriate point in your function body. You can then use the function call as a value the same way you do a variable. A conditional test for whether a function executes properly may be `if(todayIsTuesday())`. As long as your `todayIsTuesday` function is set to return `true` on Tuesday and `false` on all other days, your program operates properly.

You can use the value returned from a function in an assignment operation by calling the function after the assignment operator. For example, you may have a function that generates a random password called `makePassword`. You can store the password created in a variable by typing `$password = makePassword();`

Return a Value from a Function

① Create a new function by typing the `function` keyword.

② Type the name of the function followed by parentheses (`()`) and an opening brace (`{`).

③ Type `return` followed by the value you wish to return.

④ End the function by typing a closing brace (`{`).

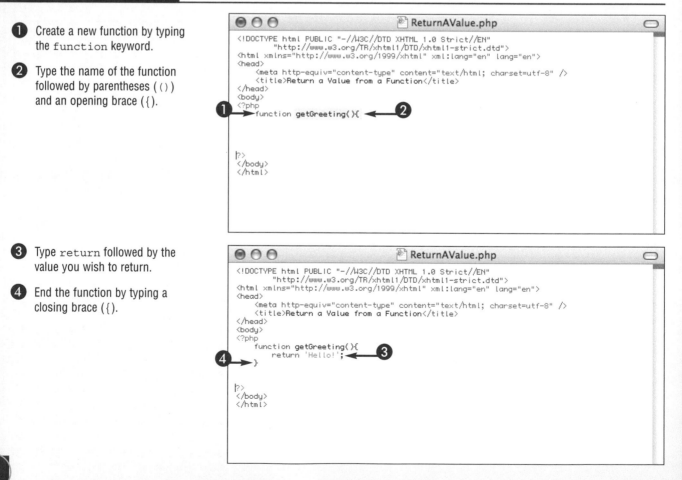

5 Call the function by typing the function name followed by parentheses (( )).

Note: The parentheses tell PHP to execute the function.

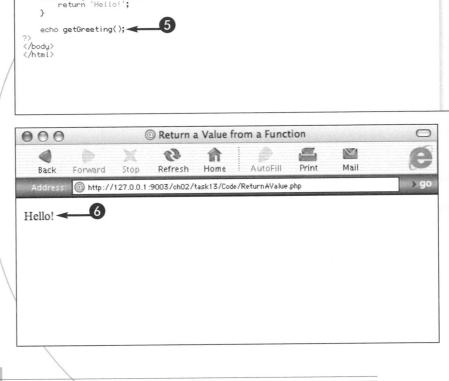

```
ReturnAValue.php

<!DOCTYPE html PUBLIC "-//W3C//DTD XHTML 1.0 Strict//EN"
        "http://www.w3.org/TR/xhtml1/DTD/xhtml1-strict.dtd">
<html xmlns="http://www.w3.org/1999/xhtml" xml:lang="en" lang="en">
<head>
    <meta http-equiv="content-type" content="text/html; charset=utf-8" />
    <title>Return a Value from a Function</title>
</head>
<body>
<?php
    function getGreeting(){
        return 'Hello!';
    }

    echo getGreeting();          5
?>
</body>
</html>
```

6 View the script in a Web browser.

The code in the function executes and returns the value specified by the return statement.

```
Return a Value from a Function

Back  Forward  Stop  Refresh  Home  AutoFill  Print  Mail

Address:  http://127.0.0.1:9003/ch02/task13/Code/ReturnAValue.php      go

Hello!     6
```

Apply It

A function can have many return statements. It is important to note that only one ever executes, as any return statement terminates execution of the function.

TYPE THIS:

```
$temperature = 80;
function coatNeeded(){
  global $temperature;
  if($temperature < 60){
    return true;
  }else{
    return false;
  }
}

if(coatNeeded()){
  echo "A coat is needed.";
}else{
  echo "No coat is needed.";
}
```

RESULTS:

The browser displays:

```
No coat is needed.
```

Pass Arguments to a Function

You can transform a static function that operates on static values into a dynamic function by passing *arguments* to it. By abstracting the values used inside a function into arguments, you can separate the functionality from the content, making your scripts more dynamic and useful.

To define a function that accepts arguments, type the function keyword followed by the name of the function you want to create. As with other function definitions, the next step is to type a set of parentheses. The difference between a dynamic and static function definition is that the parentheses in a dynamic function definition list the names of any arguments the function accepts. For example, you can create a function to get the area of a square by typing

function getArea($sideA, $sideB). You can access the values passed to the function inside the function body by using the $sideA and $sideB variable names. To call the function, you can type getArea(10, 20);. The value of $sideA is set to 10 and the value of $sideB is set to 20.

You can define your function to accept any number of arguments. As long as you list the name used for each argument in the function declaration, the values you pass are accessible inside the body of the function. As with many languages, PHP requires that you pass arguments in the order set in the function declaration. If you define your function to accept arguments $a and $b, each time you call your function the first argument is assigned to $a and the second to $b.

Pass Arguments to a Function

① Create a new function by typing the function keyword.

② Type the name of the function followed by parentheses (()) and an opening brace ({).

③ Inside the parentheses, list your arguments.

Note: Multiple arguments should be separated by commas.

④ Type the code to use the arguments inside the body of the function.

⑤ End the function by typing a closing brace (}).

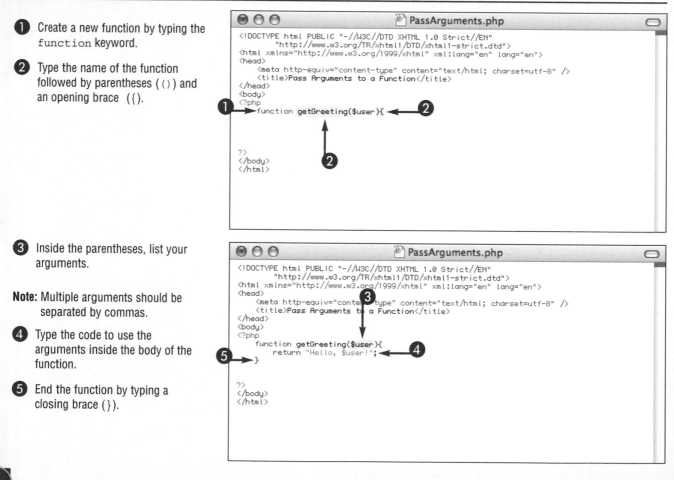

6 Call the function by typing the function name followed by your argument values in parentheses (( )).

Note: The order of the values should match the function definition.

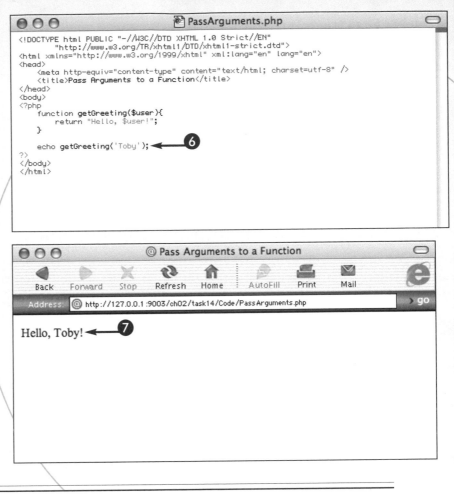

```
PassArguments.php

<!DOCTYPE html PUBLIC "-//W3C//DTD XHTML 1.0 Strict//EN"
        "http://www.w3.org/TR/xhtml1/DTD/xhtml1-strict.dtd">
<html xmlns="http://www.w3.org/1999/xhtml" xml:lang="en" lang="en">
<head>
    <meta http-equiv="content-type" content="text/html; charset=utf-8" />
    <title>Pass Arguments to a Function</title>
</head>
<body>
<?php
    function getGreeting($user){
        return "Hello, $user!";
    }

    echo getGreeting('Toby');          6
?>
</body>
</html>
```

7 View the script in a Web browser.

The code in the function executes, using the arguments as values in the function body.

```
Pass Arguments to a Function

Back  Forward  Stop  Refresh  Home  AutoFill  Print  Mail

Address: http://127.0.0.1:9003/ch02/task14/Code/PassArguments.php    go

Hello, Toby!        7
```

Apply It

While PHP does not allow you to pass more arguments than are specified in the function definition, it does allow you to set default values for optional arguments. You set a default value by adding an assignment operator and value to the variable name in the function declaration. It is good practice to set default values for any arguments that are usually set to the same value. In specific circumstances you can override the default value, but most of the time you can simply omit the value.

It is important to note that if you omit an optional value, it must be the last value you pass to a function. Otherwise, the function simply uses the next value passed as the value you wished to omit. For example, if your function accepts three values and you pass two, the third uses its default value. There is no way to pass only the first and third, and omit the second.

TYPE THIS:

```
function welcomeUser($user, $greeting=
'Hello,'){
  echo "$greeting $user.";
}


welcomeUser('Chandler');
welcomeUser('Aaron', 'Good to see you, ');
```

→ **RESULTS:**

The browser displays:

Hello, Chandler.

Good to see you, Aaron.

Pass Arguments by Reference

By default, when you pass a variable as an argument to a function, PHP passes only the value, not the variable itself. This is an important distinction if you need to create a function that modifies a variable instead of simply acting on the value represented by that variable. By prefixing a variable name with an ampersand (&) before the dollar sign ($), you can tell PHP to pass a reference to the variable itself.

When a variable is passed as a reference and the function modifies the argument, the original variable is modified. You can create a series of functions that modify a variable, passing it to each function, without having to worry about reassigning the value of the variable to reflect a value returned from your functions.

Most often, you pass by value, not by reference. The exception is when passing objects to functions. When you pass an object to a function, PHP automatically passes the object to your function by reference. This is in part due to the overhead of determining and copying complex values and states of objects. It is also because passing an object seems more natural to programmers familiar with other object oriented programming languages.

Keep in mind that you most likely define the arguments your function accepts using generic names. These names are often different than the names of the objects or variables you pass to your function. Even though the names do not match, passing by reference ensures that the value represented by your argument points directly to the original variable or object.

Pass Arguments by Reference

① Create a new function by typing the `function` keyword.

② Type the name of the function followed by parentheses (()) and an opening brace ({).

③ Inside the parentheses, type the names of any arguments you wish to pass, prefaced by an ampersand (&).

Note: Multiple arguments should be separated by commas.

④ Type the code to use the arguments inside the body of the function.

⑤ Type a closing brace (}) to end the function.

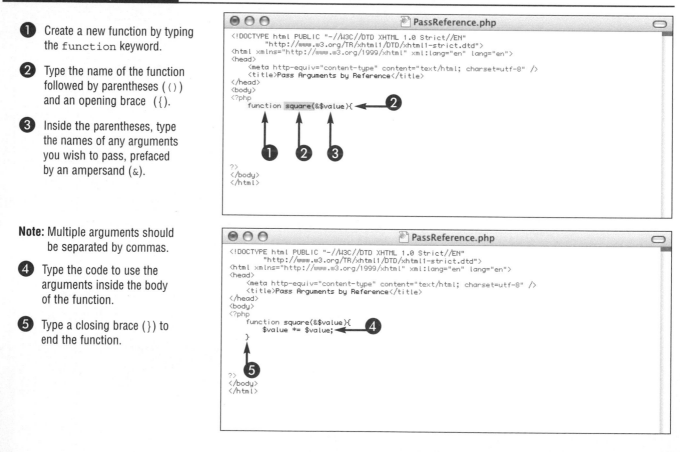

64

6 Call the function by typing the function name followed by your argument values in parentheses (()).

```
000                    PassReference.php
<!DOCTYPE html PUBLIC "-//W3C//DTD XHTML 1.0 Strict//EN"
        "http://www.w3.org/TR/xhtml1/DTD/xhtml1-strict.dtd">
<html xmlns="http://www.w3.org/1999/xhtml" xml:lang="en" lang="en">
<head>
    <meta http-equiv="content-type" content="text/html; charset=utf-8" />
    <title>Pass Arguments by Reference</title>
</head>
<body>
<?php
    function square(&$value){
        $value *= $value;
    }

    $n = 10;

    square($n);          ← 6

    echo "$n<br />";
?>
</body>
</html>
```

7 View the script in a Web browser.

The code in the function executes, modifying the original object.

```
000              @ Pass Arguments by Reference
 Back  Forward  Stop  Refresh  Home  AutoFill  Print  Mail
 Address: @ http://127.0.0.1:9003/ch02/task15/Code/PassReference.php    > go

100 ← 7
```

Extra

You can set up your function to always accept an argument as a reference. This ensures that your function acts predictably whether or not the function is called with ampersand-prefixed variables. For any variable you want to accept exclusively by reference, place an ampersand before the name in the function declaration.

TYPE THIS:

```
function square(&$value){
 $value *= $value;
}

$original = 5;
echo "The original value is:
$original.<br />";
square($original);
echo "The squared value is:
$original.";
```

RESULTS:

Even though you did not pass $original by reference, the function was defined to accept it by reference. The browser displays:

The original value is: 5.

The squared value is: 25.

Write a Recursive Function

For a function to be called in PHP, you must type the name of the function followed by a set of parentheses containing zero or more arguments you want to pass. To call a function a number of times, you can use a looping structure such as a while or for loop. In some cases, you may wish to define a function that is inherently called until a given condition is met. This allows you to treat a function as a single operation. When a function calls itself, it is called a *recursive function*.

Recursive functions are most often used in mathematical statements where operations need to be performed on a variable until a desired result is achieved. While you can create a function with an internal loop that calls another function until a condition is fulfilled, you complicate your code and break from the portability functions provide.

An example of an operation that needs to call itself is finding the factorial of a number. A factorial is the product of all positive integers less than or equal to a given number. To find the factorial of an argument $n, you can write a function that multiplies $n times the factorial of $n-1. As you can see, this requires finding the factorial of the number $n minus 1.

By using a recursive function, you can have a function call itself repeatedly with an argument that is changed by each call. This encapsulates the functionality of using a loop structure and multiple functions and allows you to perform this complex operation by calling a single function.

Write a Recursive Function

① Create a new function by typing the function keyword.

② Type the name of the function followed by parentheses (()) and an opening brace ({).

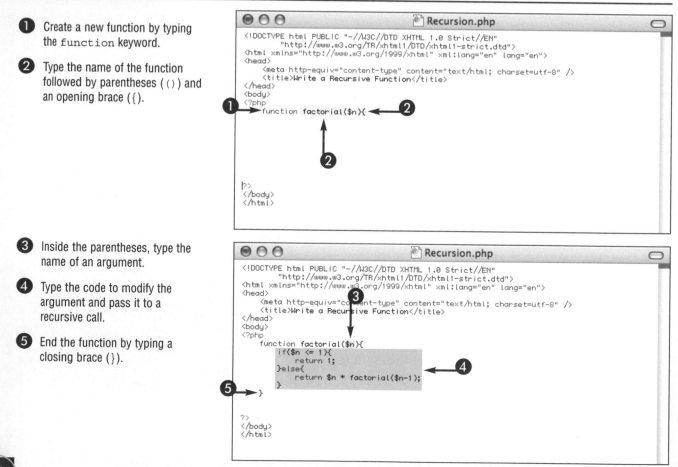

③ Inside the parentheses, type the name of an argument.

④ Type the code to modify the argument and pass it to a recursive call.

⑤ End the function by typing a closing brace (}).

6 Call the function by typing the function name followed by your argument values in parentheses (()).

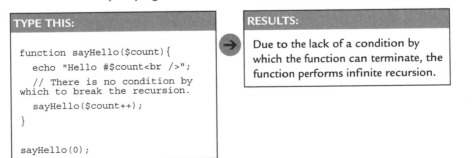

```php
<!DOCTYPE html PUBLIC "-//W3C//DTD XHTML 1.0 Strict//EN"
        "http://www.w3.org/TR/xhtml1/DTD/xhtml1-strict.dtd">
<html xmlns="http://www.w3.org/1999/xhtml" xml:lang="en" lang="en">
<head>
    <meta http-equiv="content-type" content="text/html; charset=utf-8" />
    <title>Write a Recursive Function</title>
</head>
<body>
<?php
    function factorial($n){
        if($n <= 1){
            return 1;
        }else{
            return $n * factorial($n-1);
        }
    }

    echo factorial(5);          6
?>
</body>
</html>
```

7 View the script in a Web browser.

The code in the function executes recursively.

Address: http://127.0.0.1:9003/ch02/task16/Code/Recursion.php

120 ◄── 7

Extra

It is important to consider the consequences of not having a built-in condition that results in the function returning a value and terminating. A recursive function that never terminates is said to perform infinite recursion. If a function call results in infinite recursion your program times out or crashes.

TYPE THIS:

```php
function sayHello($count){
  echo "Hello #$count<br />";
  // There is no condition by
which to break the recursion.
  sayHello($count++);
}


sayHello(0);
```

RESULTS:

Due to the lack of a condition by which the function can terminate, the function performs infinite recursion.

Using Dynamic Variables

PHP allows you to reference variables with variable names. When a variable is referenced by a dynamic variable name it is called a *variable variable* or a *dynamic variable*. Dynamic variables enable you to create highly flexible operations without creating complex conditional statements. Dynamic variables are not a distinct type of variable, but rather a functional type. Normal variables are referenced by a name made up of a dollar sign ($) followed by a literal string. An example of a normal variable is $myVariable. A dynamic variable is made up of a dollar sign plus the full name of a different variable representing a string literal.

You can use dynamic variables to find other variables in your script or to call functions dynamically. This is particularly useful when your variables are created dynamically at run-time instead of at the time you write

your PHP. For example, you may have a form processing script that takes any number of form values and validates them. If you do not know the exact list of form values, but you know that they share a common naming scheme, you can perform operations on them using dynamic variables.

Given a list of variables following a naming pattern such as 'message_1' and 'message_2' you can perform operations on the variables using a loop such as a do...while loop. By combining the 'message_' prefix with a number in each cycle of the loop, you can dynamically generate a name to use in referencing your form values. To check for variables matching each generated name, you can use the dollar sign operator ($) twice. An example might be $$name where $name is equal to 'message_2'. This tells PHP to look for a variable called $message_2.

Using Dynamic Variables

① Create a variable and assign it a simple string literal value.

② Create a second variable whose name is the value of the first variable.

③ Type the assignment operator followed by a value for the second variable.

④ Type the echo keyword followed by a dollar sign ($).

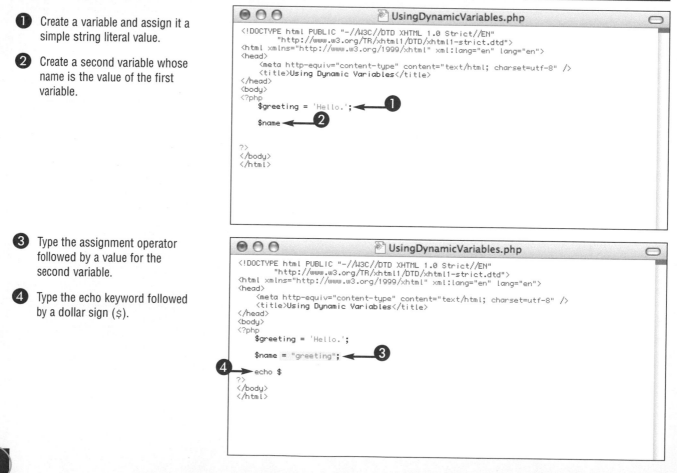

5 Type another dollar sign ($) plus the name of the first variable.

```
UsingDynamicVariables.php
<!DOCTYPE html PUBLIC "-//W3C//DTD XHTML 1.0 Strict//EN"
        "http://www.w3.org/TR/xhtml1/DTD/xhtml1-strict.dtd">
<html xmlns="http://www.w3.org/1999/xhtml" xml:lang="en" lang="en">
<head>
    <meta http-equiv="content-type" content="text/html; charset=utf-8" />
    <title>Using Dynamic Variables</title>
</head>
<body>
<?php
    $greeting = 'Hello.';

    $name = "greeting";

    echo $$name;          5
?>
</body>
</html>
```

6 View the script in a Web browser.

The value of the first variable determines the name of the second value, and the value of the second variable is printed.

```
Using Dynamic Variables
Back  Forward  Stop  Refresh  Home  AutoFill  Print  Mail
Address: http://127.0.0.1:9003/ch02/task17/Code/UsingDynamicVariables.php        go

Hello.   6
```

Extra

PHP allows you to perform variable function calls. A dynamic function call is performed in exactly the same way as a dynamic variable lookup. By storing the name of a function in a variable you can call a function dynamically. All that is required is to type the name of the variable representing the name of the function followed by parentheses. Be sure to pass along any arguments your function is expecting.

TYPE THIS:

```
function sayHello(){
  echo 'Hello. <br />';
}
function sayGoodbye(){
  echo 'Hello.<br />';
}

$funcName = 'sayHello';
$funcName();
$funcName = 'sayGoodbye';
$funcName();
```

RESULTS:

The browser displays:

Hello.

Goodbye.

Work with
Data Types

Unlike some programming languages, PHP does not require you to declare the type of value a variable represents. The data type of a variable is determined by the value it represents. The type changes whenever the value is modified. This is referred to as *dynamic typing* and is considered a convenient benefit of PHP. You can create a variable that may hold a number at one point, a Boolean value at another, and a string at yet another.

While dynamic typing is very convenient, it is often important to know the type of data a variable holds. Though PHP, like many scripting languages, performs automatic type conversion to accommodate operations performed on different types of operands, there are times when your intention is not the outcome of these automatic conversions.

PHP provides functions for getting and setting the type represented by a variable. To check the type of a variable, you can use the gettype function. This function accepts

the variable as an argument and will return a string representing the type. Possible return values include "boolean," "integer," "double," "string," "array," "object," "resource," "NULL," "user function," and "unknown type."

You can also test the type of a variable using built-in functions such as is_array(), is_bool(), is_float(), is_int(), is_null(), is_numeric(), is_object(), is_resource(), is_scalar(), and is_string(). Each of these accepts your variable as an argument and returns true if the variable matches the type specified in the function name or false if it does not.

You can attempt to change the type of a variable using the settype function. This function accepts two arguments: your variable and a string representing the name of the type you want the variable to become. If the operation is successful, settype returns true. Otherwise, it returns false.

Work with Data Types

① Type the name of a variable and assign a numeric value.

② Type the echo keyword followed by a call to gettype.

```
<!DOCTYPE html PUBLIC "-//W3C//DTD XHTML 1.0 Strict//EN"
    "http://www.w3.org/TR/xhtml1/DTD/xhtml1-strict.dtd">
<html xmlns="http://www.w3.org/1999/xhtml" xml:lang="en" lang="en">
<head>
    <meta http-equiv="content-type" content="text/html; charset=utf-8" />
    <title>Work with Data Types</title>
</head>
<body>
<?php
    $v = 125;
    echo gettype($v) . '<br />';


?>
</body>
</html>
```

③ Type a new assignment statement for the variable, assigning a string value.

④ Type the echo keyword followed by a call to gettype.

```
<!DOCTYPE html PUBLIC "-//W3C//DTD XHTML 1.0 Strict//EN"
    "http://www.w3.org/TR/xhtml1/DTD/xhtml1-strict.dtd">
<html xmlns="http://www.w3.org/1999/xhtml" xml:lang="en" lang="en">
<head>
    <meta http-equiv="content-type" content="text/html; charset=utf-8" />
    <title>Work with Data Types</title>
</head>
<body>
<?php
    $v = 125;
    echo gettype($v) . '<br />';

    $v = 'A string';
    echo gettype($v) . '<br />';


?>
</body>
</html>
```

⑤ Using `settype`, attempt to change the type of the variable to "integer."

⑥ Echo the output of the `settype` operation.

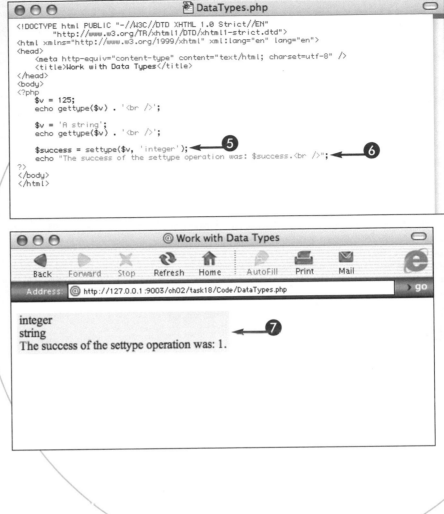

```
DataTypes.php

<!DOCTYPE html PUBLIC "-//W3C//DTD XHTML 1.0 Strict//EN"
    "http://www.w3.org/TR/xhtml1/DTD/xhtml1-strict.dtd">
<html xmlns="http://www.w3.org/1999/xhtml" xml:lang="en" lang="en">
<head>
    <meta http-equiv="content-type" content="text/html; charset=utf-8" />
    <title>Work with Data Types</title>
</head>
<body>
<?php
    $v = 125;
    echo gettype($v) . '<br />';

    $v = 'A string';
    echo gettype($v) . '<br />';

    $success = settype($v, 'integer');           ⑤
    echo "The success of the settype operation was: $success.<br />";    ⑥
?>
</body>
</html>
```

⑦ View the script in a Web browser.

The one (1) is the numerical value of a Boolean true value.

The code in the function executes, showing the various values for the variable as well as the result from the `settype` operation.

```
Work with Data Types

Address: http://127.0.0.1:9003/ch02/task18/Code/DataTypes.php

integer
string                    ⑦
The success of the settype operation was: 1.
```

Extra

As in many other languages, PHP also allows for type *casting*. Casting performs the same function as the `settype` function, but because it is not a function, it does not return a Boolean representing the success. To cast a variable to a different type, prefix the variable name with the name of the desired type in parentheses. This only casts the variable for a single assignment.

TYPE THIS:

```
$myNumber = 3.14;

echo "The floating point value
is: $myNumber. <br />";


$myInteger = (integer)$myNumber;

echo "The integer value is:
$myInteger. <br />";
```

RESULTS:

The floating point number is converted to an integer for the second statement. The browser displays:

The floating point value is: 3.14.

The integer value is 3.

Get Information About a Variable

PHP provides a number of functions you can use to determine information about a variable. The majority of the functions are used to test the type of data a variable represents. You can also determine whether a variable has been assigned a value.

To check the type of a variable, you can use the `gettype` function. You can also test the type of a variable using any of several functions such as `is_array()`, `is_bool()`, `is_float()`, `is_int()`, `is_null()`, `is_numeric()`, `is_object()`, `is_resource()`, `is_scalar()`, and `is_string()`. Each of these accepts your variable as an argument and returns `true` if the variable matches the type specified in the function name or `false` if it does not. For more on types, see the task "Work with Data Types."

You can determine whether a variable has been initialized using the `isset()` function. This function is often used

before trying to access the value of a variable, as PHP is often configured to throw an error if you access an undeclared variable. The `isset()` function returns `true` if the variable has been initialized and `false` if it has not.

Testing whether a variable is an instance of a given class can be accomplished three ways. The first is the `is_a()` function. This function accepts two arguments: the variable in question and a string representing the class name against which the PHP processor should test. The second is the `instanceof` operator. The `instanceof` operator requires two operands. The first is the object in question and the second is a pointer to the class. The third method of determining the class of a variable is to use the `get_class()` function, which returns the name of the class associated with a variable. If the variable is not an instance of a class, this function returns `false`.

Get Information About a Variable

① Begin a conditional `if...else` statement.

② For the condition, type `isset()` with a variable name.

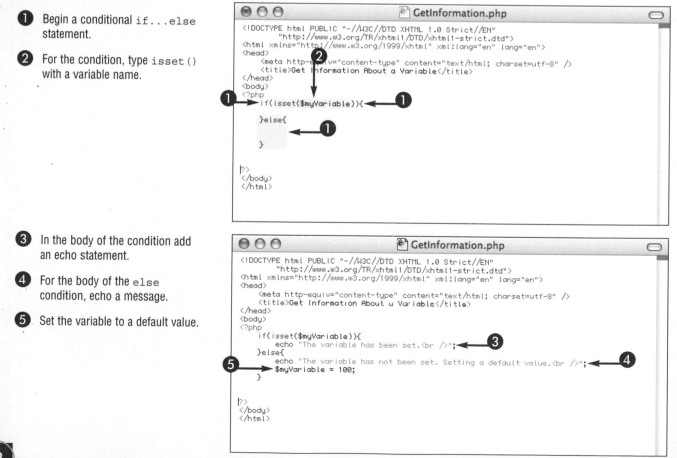

③ In the body of the condition add an echo statement.

④ For the body of the `else` condition, echo a message.

⑤ Set the variable to a default value.

6 Use the variable in an operation.

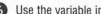

GetInformation.php

```
<!DOCTYPE html PUBLIC "-//W3C//DTD XHTML 1.0 Strict//EN"
        "http://www.w3.org/TR/xhtml1/DTD/xhtml1-strict.dtd">
<html xmlns="http://www.w3.org/1999/xhtml" xml:lang="en" lang="en">
<head>
    <meta http-equiv="content-type" content="text/html; charset=utf-8" />
    <title>Get Information About a Variable</title>
</head>
<body>
<?php
    if(isset($myVariable)){
        echo "The variable has been set.<br />";
    }else{
        echo "The variable has not been set. Setting a default value.<br />";
        $myVariable = 100;
    }

    echo $myVariable/2;          ◄———  6
?>
</body>
</html>
```

7 View the script in a Web browser.

Because the variable is not set, the `else` code block is processed.

@ Get Information About a Variable

| Back | Forward | Stop | Refresh | Home | AutoFill | Print | Mail |

Address: @ http://127.0.0.1:9003/ch02/task19/Code/GetInformation.php › go

The variable has not been set. Setting a default value.   ◄——— 7
50

Extra

Functions that provide information about variables are very useful for both normal program execution and debugging. Often, it is useful to get an exact picture of the state of a given variable or object. For some variable types, this can be accomplished by simply echoing the variable to the browser. For others, such as arrays, PHP provides functions for printing detailed information. You can use the `print_r` function to write detailed information about a variable to the output stream. The `print_r` function accepts the variable you want to print as an argument.

TYPE THIS:

```
$myArray = array(3.14, 'Toby',
'Michele');
echo '<pre>';
print_r($myArray);
echo '</pre>';
```

RESULTS:

The browser displays:

Array

(

  [0] => 3.14

  [1] => 'Toby'

  [2] => 'Michele'

)

Using PHP Constants

PHP provides many built-in constants representing information about the server, the scripting environment, and your PHP configuration. You can use these constants to gather information to perform conditional operations, log the context in which your scripts run, and to debug your scripts as they execute. Examples of constants are PHP_VERSION and PHP_OS representing the version of PHP and the operating system on which it is running.

These values are available within any scope of your application. Though constant variables cannot be changed, PHP provides a set of built-in "magic constants" that are always referenced by the same name but whose values change based on the context in which they are used. For example, the __LINE__ constant is a magic constant representing the number of the line of code currently being executed. The __FILE__ constant represents the full path to the currently executing file. If called from within an included file, it gives the full path to the included file.

You cannot use the name of a predefined constant for your own constants. Trying to assign a new value to a defined constant results in an error.

Using PHP Constants

1 Create a statement to echo a constant variable.

- Like all constants, no dollar sign is needed to access a system constant.

2 Repeat Step 1 for any system constants you want to access.

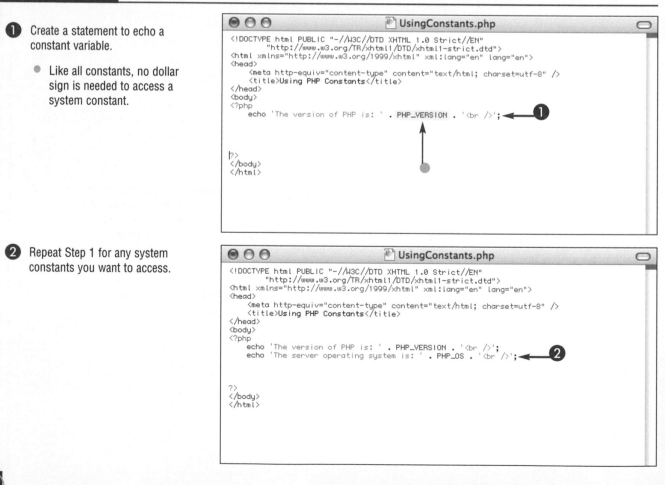

3 Type code to use a magic constant.

```
000                    UsingConstants.php
<!DOCTYPE html PUBLIC "-//W3C//DTD XHTML 1.0 Strict//EN"
        "http://www.w3.org/TR/xhtml1/DTD/xhtml1-strict.dtd">
<html xmlns="http://www.w3.org/1999/xhtml" xml:lang="en" lang="en">
<head>
    <meta http-equiv="content-type" content="text/html; charset=utf-8" />
    <title>Using PHP Constants</title>
</head>
<body>
<?php
    echo 'The version of PHP is: ' . PHP_VERSION . '<br />';
    echo 'The server operating system is: ' . PHP_OS . '<br />';

    echo 'File: ' . __FILE__ . ' on line: ' . __LINE__ . '<br />';
    echo 'File: ' . __FILE__ . ' on line: ' . __LINE__ . '<br />';
?>
</body>
</html>
```
← **3**

4 View the script in a Web browser.

The value of the first variable is used to determine the name of the second value, and the value of the second variable is printed.

```
000                    @ Using PHP Constants
Back  Forward  Stop  Refresh  Home  AutoFill  Print  Mail        e
Address: @ http://127.0.0.1:9003/ch02/task20/Code/UsingConstants.php    › go

The version of PHP is: 5.0.0
The server operating system is: Darwin
File: /Users/tobyboudreaux/Jobs/PHP5/Draft/Chapters/ch02/task20/Code/
UsingConstants.php on line: 13
File: /Users/tobyboudreaux/Jobs/PHP5/Draft/Chapters/ch02/task20/Code/
UsingConstants.php on line: 14
```
← **4**

Extra

You can create your own debugging function that utilizes magic constants to display information about your script. The __LINE__, __FILE__, __FUNCTION__, __CLASS__, and __METHOD__ constants represent useful information about the current script and the context in which it runs.

TYPE THIS:

```
function logInfo($message){
  sprintf("File:
%s\r\nLine:%d\r\nMessage:%s",
__FILE__, __LINE__, $message);
}
logInfo('Testing the logInfo
function.');
```

RESULTS:

The browser displays:

File: test.php

Line: 4

Message: Testing the logInfo function.

Include
a File

Y ou can use the `include` and `require` statements to bring content from separate files into your script. The code in the included files is evaluated when the file is processed. Grouping code that is repeated across several PHP scripts into included files enhances portability and scalability as well as clarity.

You can create a file that checks to see if a user has logged on to your site with a valid account. If not, the file can redirect the user to a log-on page. By using the `require` or `require_once` function, you can include this file at the beginning of each page you want to hide from unauthorized users.

The `include` and `require` functions accept a single argument representing the path to the file you want to include. This path must be a string and is relative to the

drive from which your application is being served. This is an important distinction for those accustomed to files being relative to the root of a Web application.

The `include` directive attempts to include and evaluate the file at the point in your script at which it is called. Any errors encountered while trying to find the file are not considered *fatal* — that is, they will not terminate execution of your program. You can use the `include` directive for trivial includes — those upon which the security and functionality of your script do not depend.

The require statement functions the same as the include statement except that any errors in the inclusion are considered fatal. If your script cannot find the file you want to include, the application terminates with an error.

Include a File

① Create a basic PHP script that prints a message to the screen.

② Save the script and note the location to which it is saved.

③ In a new script, type `include();`.

④ Inside the parentheses, type the path to the first script as a string.

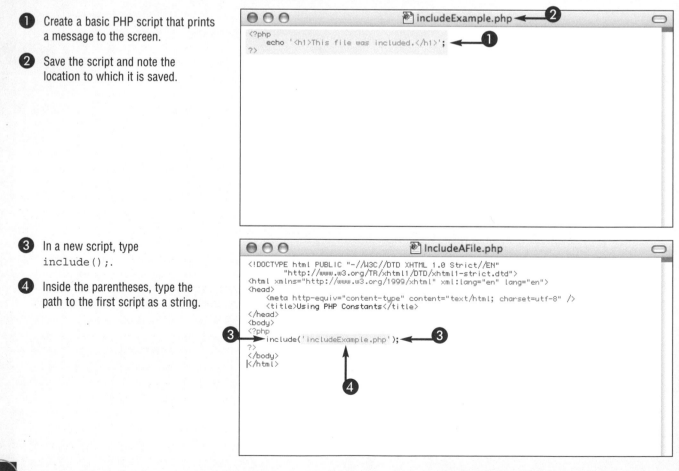

5 Save the second script.

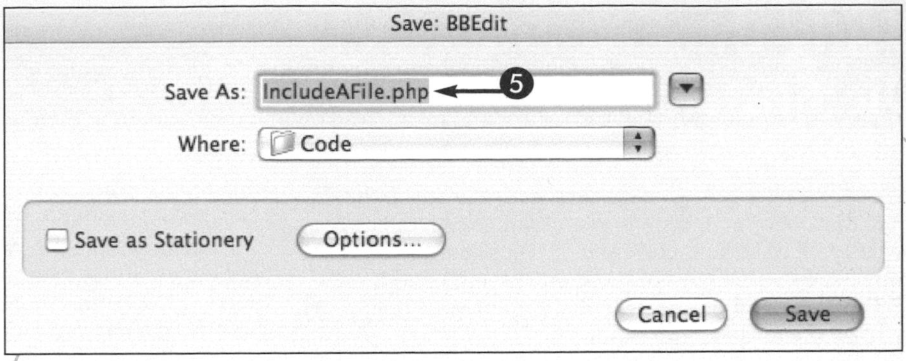

Save: BBEdit

Save As: IncludeAFile.php ◄── **5**

Where: Code

☐ Save as Stationery   Options...

Cancel   Save

6 View the script in a Web browser.

The contents of the first PHP script are included and evaluated as though they were written in the second file.

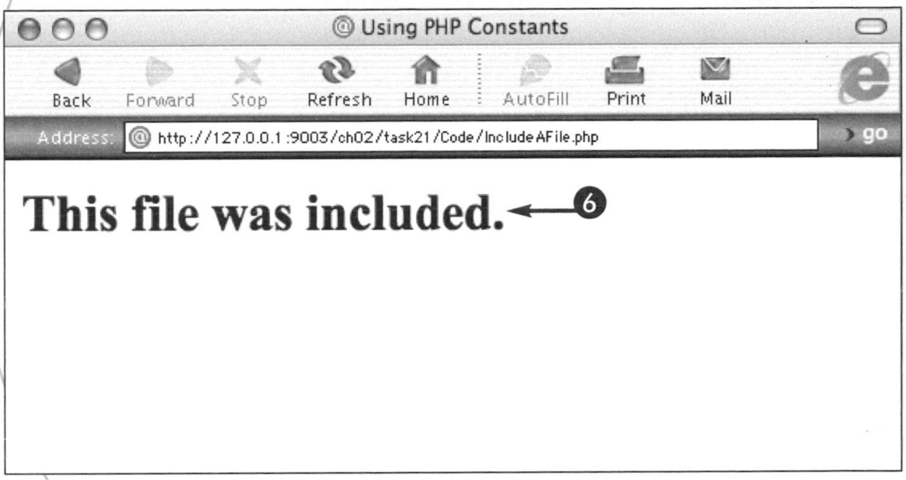

Using PHP Constants

Back Forward Stop Refresh Home AutoFill Print Mail

Address: http://127.0.0.1:9003/ch02/task21/Code/IncludeAFile.php

This file was included. ◄── **6**

Extra

Some files you may want to include are functional. That is, they are more than simple libraries of code, such as function definitions. If you have a script the inclusion of which is necessary for your application to function but that should only be included once, you can use the require_once statement. This is an enhanced version of the require statement. It includes the file only once per script, no matter how many times the file is requested.

TYPE THIS:

```
require_once('my_include.php');
include('my_include.php');
require ('my_include.php');
```

→

RESULTS:

The code in the my_include.php file is included and executed only once.

Using the Exit and Die Statements

I n some cases you may want your script to terminate execution before all code is processed. Often, this is for security or efficiency purposes. PHP provides two mechanisms by which you can end processing of your script. The exit and die statements both provide the ability to stop execution immediately.

The exit statement is used to gracefully terminate execution after certain actions. For example, you can redirect users to another page by setting a location header using the header function. After calling the header function, it is good practice to call exit so that your script ends immediately. You can also use exit to end your script conditionally. If a given condition is met and processing is no longer necessary, using exit increases the efficiency of your script.

You can use the die statement to immediately terminate execution and send a message to the output stream. The die statement is used mostly in debugging and in handling fatal errors. If, for example, you cannot perform a core function like connecting to a database server, you can use the die statement to end your script and write a message to the output stream immediately.

Essentially, exit and die are equivalent statements. As with many other constructs and tools that are equivalents, it is important to choose one style and maintain it consistently throughout your scripting. Consistency enhances clarity and ensures that other developers can use your code without the need for excess commenting.

Using the Exit and Die Statements

① Create a variable and set its value to false.

② Begin an if...else statement.

③ For the condition, test whether your variable is true.

④ Add any code you want to execute to the body of the if statement.

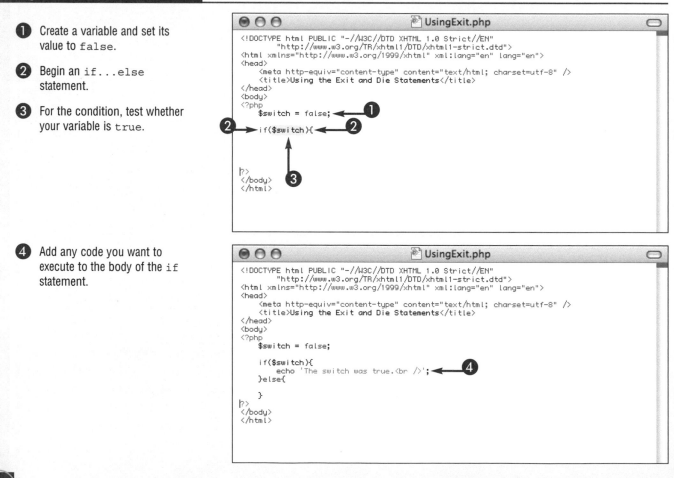

5 In the body of the else statement, type `die()`, passing a message you want to send the user as an argument.

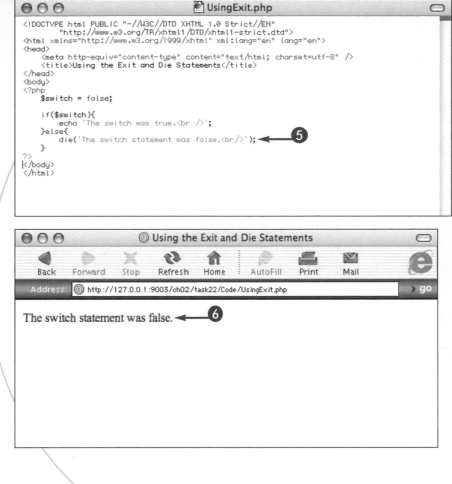

```
UsingExit.php

<!DOCTYPE html PUBLIC "-//W3C//DTD XHTML 1.0 Strict//EN"
        "http://www.w3.org/TR/xhtml1/DTD/xhtml1-strict.dtd">
<html xmlns="http://www.w3.org/1999/xhtml" xml:lang="en" lang="en">
<head>
    <meta http-equiv="content-type" content="text/html; charset=utf-8" />
    <title>Using the Exit and Die Statements</title>
</head>
<body>
<?php
    $switch = false;

    if($switch){
        echo 'The switch was true.<br />';
    }else{
        die('The switch statement was false.<br/>');  ←──── 5
    }
?>
</body>
</html>
```

6 View the script in a Web browser.

The contents of the first PHP script are included and evaluated as though they were written in the second file.

```
@ Using the Exit and Die Statements

Back   Forward   Stop   Refresh   Home   AutoFill   Print   Mail

Address: @ http://127.0.0.1:9003/ch02/task22/Code/UsingExit.php      › go

The switch statement was false. ←──── 6
```

Extra

You can call functions from within your `exit` and `die` statements. This is commonly used to set up a custom debugging message using built-in debugging functions. For example, you might use the `mysql_error()` function to find any errors associated with database connections or queries. Any function that returns a string value can be called from within your `exit` and `die` statements.

TYPE THIS:

```
//  This example assumes you have
an active database connection
$query = 'SELECT * FROM mytable';

$result = mysql_query($query);

if(!$result){

   die('There was an error in the
database query: <br />' .
mysql_query());

}else{

   // use the result of your query
here.

}
```

RESULTS:

→ The browser displays the custom error message with the result of the `mysql_error()` function on a new line.

Work with Dates and Times

PHP provides several useful functions for determining and handling date and time information. You can find the current date or time according to several standards, convert the date or time information into various readable formats, and perform mathematical operations on the information gathered.

The current date and time are dependent on the server on which your script is running. This means that the value returned by the date and time functions may not necessarily match the local time of users viewing your scripts. Luckily, if you know the time zone from which a user is viewing your site, you can use the functions provided by PHP to convert the server time into a local time for the user.

To access the current date, use the `date()` function. This function accepts two arguments. The first is the format string you want PHP to use in converting the date into a readable string. The second, optional parameter is a timestamp you want to use as an alternate to the server date.

You can find the current time using the `time()` function. This returns the number of seconds since January 1, 1970, also known as a *Unix timestamp*. This is not exactly analogous to the `date()` function. There is a function that operates much like the `date()` function called `strftime()`.

The `mktime()` function allows you to generate a Unix timestamp for a given date and time. The result of a `mktime()` statement can be used as the second argument for the `date()` or the `strftime()` functions.

Work with Dates and Times

① Type the name of a variable followed by the assignment operator.

② On the right side of the assignment operator, type `mktime()` and pass it a month, day, and year.

③ Create an `echo` statement to print the resulting Unix timestamp.

④ Type `date(`, a format string, and the name of your timestamp variable.

⑤ Close the date function by typing `)`.

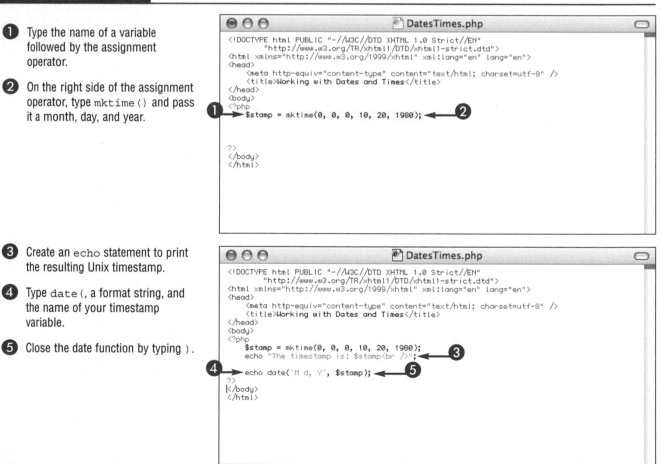

6 Repeat Steps 3 to 5 for any additional formats you want to use.

```
DatesTimes.php
<!DOCTYPE html PUBLIC "-//W3C//DTD XHTML 1.0 Strict//EN"
        "http://www.w3.org/TR/xhtml1/DTD/xhtml1-strict.dtd">
<html xmlns="http://www.w3.org/1999/xhtml" xml:lang="en" lang="en">
<head>
    <meta http-equiv="content-type" content="text/html; charset=utf-8" />
    <title>Working with Dates and Times</title>
</head>
<body>
<?php
    $stamp = mktime(0, 0, 0, 10, 20, 1980);
    echo "The timestamp is: $stamp<br />";

    echo date('M d, Y', $stamp);

    echo '<br />';

    echo date('m/d/y', $stamp);
?>
</body>
</html>
```

7 View the script in a Web browser.

The timestamp is printed using the format string specified in each date() function call.

```
@ Working with Dates and Times
Address: http://127.0.0.1:9003/ch02/task23/Code/DatesTimes.php

The timestamp is: 340873200
Oct 20, 1980
10/20/80
```

Extra

PHP provides an extremely useful function called strtotime. This function accepts nearly any English textual date and time description and uses it to generate a Unix timestamp. When passed a string representing a date or time, strtotime() attempts to create a valid timestamp from the value. If the function cannot find an appropriate timestamp, it returns negative one (-1).

TYPE THIS:

```
echo strtotime("now");
echo '<br />';
echo strtotime("next Tuesday");
echo '<br />';
echo strtotime("29 Feb 2001");
```

RESULTS:

The browser displays the timestamps for the date strings passed to strtotime(). For those PHP cannot use to generate a valid timestamp, such as the last call, the browser displays (-1).

Introduction to Arrays

Like most programming languages, PHP provides special data types representing groups, or *collections* of values. The most important collection in PHP is the array.

Values

You can think of an array as a list. Arrays provide a way of referring to a list of values with a single variable. This is useful when you wish to process an entire group of items in the same fashion or according to the same algorithm.

Values in an array can be of any data type. This means that you can use arrays to store numbers, strings, object and function pointers, and other arrays. Unlike some languages, an array in

PHP can store values of mixed types. You can have a single array that stores numbers, strings, and objects.

When an array value is set to another array the main array is called a *multidimensional array*. Multidimensional arrays are useful for representing complex data types such as lists of lists. PHP provides many useful functions for dealing with multidimensional arrays.

Keys

Values in arrays are accessed by way of *keys*. Keys are similar to variable names in that they are the name you use to find a specific value. A key may not be used for multiple values in the same array. There are two methods of storing and accessing values in arrays, which are differentiated by the type of keys you use. The simpler of the two uses numerical keys. This provides a convenient way of accessing values in your array in order. By using a loop structure you can iterate through the array, incrementing an index variable with each pass. This allows you to access each array item in order.

The second type of array is called an *associative array*. As the name implies, associative arrays are those that use a meaningful key for each stored value. For example, you may have keys with names such as 'name,' 'address,' and 'state.' By using meaningful, or associative, keys for each value you transform simple lists into descriptive objects. Unlike their numeric counterparts, associative arrays do not allow for numerically sorted values.

Simple lists, such as a grocery list, are best represented by a numerically indexed array. A collection of named values, such as a user's personal information, is best represented using an associative array.

Mutable

Unlike languages such as Java and C++, PHP does not require arrays to be declared as containing a static number of elements. Arrays may grow or shrink dynamically with no repercussions. Arrays in PHP are *mutable* in all cases.

Another distinguishing feature of arrays in PHP is that they are untyped, which means that you can store values of any type in your arrays and a single array may contain many types of data. For example, you may have an array called $person that includes string elements for a person's name, an array of other, similar arrays for the person's family, and a numeric value representing their ages. Typed arrays are convenient in many cases, but a thread running throughout the history of PHP is convenience and ease of use, and untyped arrays make development and modifications much easier than their strict counterparts.

Functionality

PHP provides several functions for performing operations on arrays. You can add, remove, insert, search, sort, and count array values using built-in functions. There are functions to print arrays to the output stream for debugging and other utility applications.

Some of the most useful array-handling functions are listed in the table that follows:

FUNCTION	DESCRIPTION
array_keys	Return all keys in an array as an array
array_push	Add a value to the end of an array
array_pop	Remove a value from the end of an array
array_merge	Combine two or more arrays into a single array
array_reverse	Reverse the order of elements in an array
array_search	Return the key for a given value in an array, if the value exists
array_values	Return all values in an array as an array
in_array	Return a Boolean true or false signifying whether a value is in an array
sort	Sort an array
rsort	Reverse sort an array
usort	Sort an array using a custom function
natsort	Sort an array using a "natural order" algorithm

Many functions in PHP return arrays as a result of their operations. For example, you can read the entire contents of a file, line by line, into an array with the file function. This is quite useful when handling tab- or comma-delimited files where each line is recognized as a new entry.

Array handling is certainly a strong point in PHP, and the functions provided as part of the standard framework are used more frequently than functions dealing with other data types. This is in part because arrays are very useful in representing aggregate data and also because the functions themselves are clear and easy to use.

Create
an Array

You can use the `array` function to create an array. The `array` function accepts zero or more arguments. Any arguments passed to the `array` function are set as the initial content of the array. The return type for the `array` function is an array.

Unlike languages such as Java and C++, you do not need to tell PHP the size of your array. The PHP processor allocates and deallocates memory as needed, so the size of your array can change during processing with no problems. There is no need to specify the type of values stored in your array. You can store any number of data types as values.

Though there are two types of arrays, you do not need to specify which you plan to use. The simplest type of array is numerically indexed. Values stored in a numerically indexed array are modified, added, and retrieved using a numeric index such as 0 or 120.

To create an array you first type the name of a variable you want to use to represent your array. Any standard PHP variable will work. The array name is followed by the

assignment operator (=) and the `array` function call. You can set initial array values by passing them to the `array` function as comma-separated arguments. For example, you can create an array with three default values using `$fruit = array('apple', 'orange', 'banana')`.

You can access values in an array by passing the value key to the array with square brackets. To access the 'orange' value in the `$fruit` array, you can type `$fruit[1]`. It is important to note that numeric keys in arrays are *zero-indexed*, meaning that they always begin with zero. Therefore, though the 'orange' value is the second value, the key is actually 1.

You can change or add a value at a given index in a similar fashion. To change the second value in the `$fruit` array from 'orange' to 'pineapple' you can type `$fruit[1] = 'pineapple';`. To add a value to the `$fruit` array, you can use the next available index. In this case, the next available index is 3, or the fourth slot. By typing `$fruit[3] = 'lemon';`, you can add an item to the fourth slot. For more, see "Add and Remove Elements from an Array."

Create an Array

① Type the name of a variable you want to use to represent your array, followed by the assignment operator (=).

② Type `array()`, passing any default values as comma-separated arguments.

③ Create a variable to represent the value at a given index in your array.

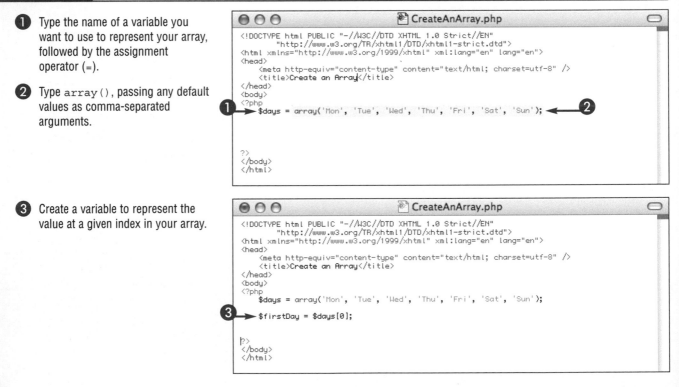

④ Use the `echo` statement to write the value of your variable to the output stream.

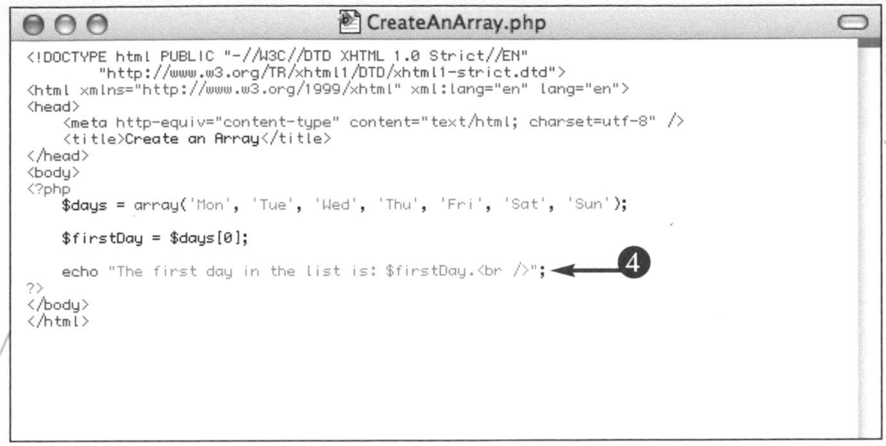

```
<!DOCTYPE html PUBLIC "-//W3C//DTD XHTML 1.0 Strict//EN"
        "http://www.w3.org/TR/xhtml1/DTD/xhtml1-strict.dtd">
<html xmlns="http://www.w3.org/1999/xhtml" xml:lang="en" lang="en">
<head>
    <meta http-equiv="content-type" content="text/html; charset=utf-8" />
    <title>Create an Array</title>
</head>
<body>
<?php
    $days = array('Mon', 'Tue', 'Wed', 'Thu', 'Fri', 'Sat', 'Sun');

    $firstDay = $days[0];

    echo "The first day in the list is: $firstDay.<br />";    ◄── ④
?>
</body>
</html>
```

⑤ View the script in a Web browser.

The value stored at the given index in your array appears.

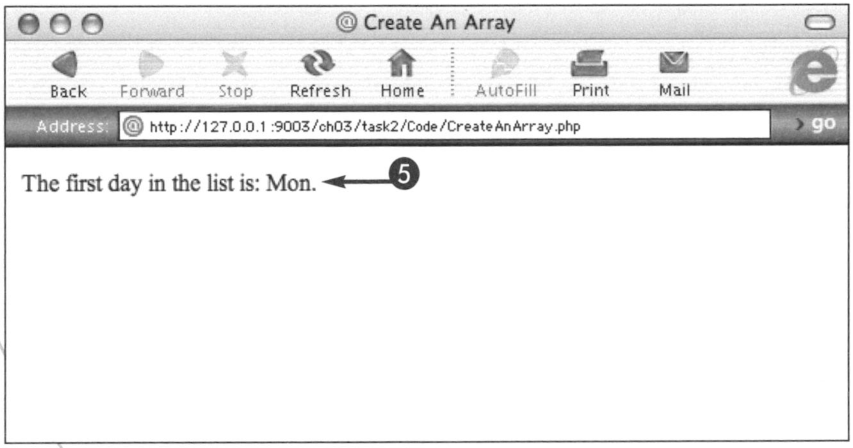

Address: http://127.0.0.1:9003/ch03/task2/Code/CreateAnArray.php

The first day in the list is: Mon. ◄── ⑤

Extra

You can use the `print_r` statement to print a description of an array. This is useful during the debugging stage when you want to double-check the values making up your array. To use this function, type `print_r()`, passing the variable representing your array as an argument.

TYPE THIS:

```
$myArray = array('Aaron', 'David', 'Jeffrey', 'Caleb');

print_r($myArray);
```

RESULTS:

The browser displays the structure of your array including all values.

```
Array
(
    [0] => 'Aaron'
    [1] => 'David'
    [2] => 'Jeffrey'
    [3] => 'Caleb'
)
```

Create an Associative Array

You can create arrays that use named keys instead of numbers. An array that uses strings as keys is known as an *associative array*. The advantage to using an associative array over a numerically indexed array is that the keys are meaningful for the values. For example, you can represent the name value in a `$person` array more clearly using `$person['name']` than a numeric key such as `$person[5]`.

Creating an associative array is identical to creating a standard array. You use the `array` function, passing in any values you want to set as the initial values. In order to assign default associative values, you must pass the arguments using a special syntax. First, type the name of the variable you want to use to represent the array. Follow it with the assignment operator (`=`) and a call to the `array` function. Each value you want to pass should be formatted as `key=>value`. That is, the string key you want to use,

followed by the `=>` operator, followed by the value. For example, to create an array of siblings, you can use `$siblings = array("olderbrother"=>"Rob", "youngerbrother"=>"Ryan");`. This allows you to access the "Rob" value with `$siblings["olderbrother"]`.

While any string can be used as a key, it is good practice to follow the same format you use for naming variables. Avoid spaces and punctuation, using only letters, numbers, and the underscore character. The names of keys used in arrays should be clear and concise. The names of array element keys are as important as the names of variables and functions because much of the clarity of code is what can be inferred from names.

Associate arrays are often returned from various built-in PHP functions. This is especially true when working with databases and form submissions.

Create an Associative Array

① Type the name of a variable you want to use to represent your array followed by the assignment operator (`=`).

② Type `array()`, passing any default values as comma-separated arguments.

③ Create a variable to represent the value at a given key in your array.

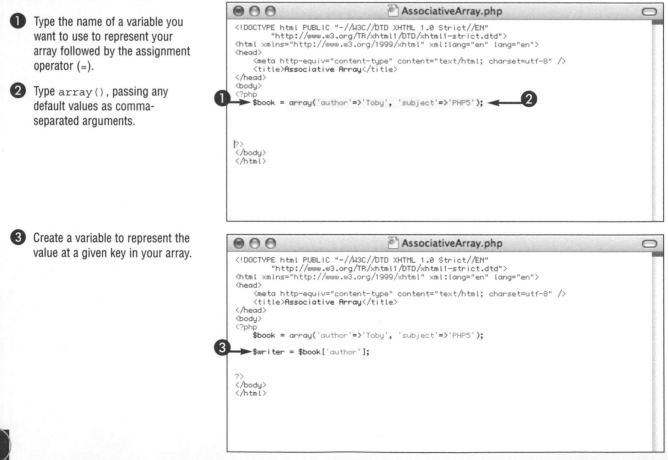

④ Use the `echo` statement to write the value of your variable to the output stream.

```
                                    AssociativeArray.php
<!DOCTYPE html PUBLIC "-//W3C//DTD XHTML 1.0 Strict//EN"
        "http://www.w3.org/TR/xhtml1/DTD/xhtml1-strict.dtd">
<html xmlns="http://www.w3.org/1999/xhtml" xml:lang="en" lang="en">
<head>
    <meta http-equiv="content-type" content="text/html; charset=utf-8" />
    <title>Associative Array</title>
</head>
<body>
<?php
    $book = array('author'=>'Toby', 'subject'=>'PHP5');

    $writer = $book['author'];

    echo "The author of the book is $writer.<br />";          ◄————④
?>
</body>
</html>
```

⑤ View the script in a Web browser.

The value stored for the given key in your array appears.

```
                                    @ Associative Array
  Back   Forward   Stop   Refresh   Home   AutoFill   Print   Mail

  Address:  @ http://127.0.0.1:9003/ch03/task3/Code/AssociativeArray.php          ▸ go


  The author of the book is Toby.  ◄————⑤
```

Extra

You can loop through the elements of an associative array using the `foreach` loop. Much like the `for` and `while` loop used for numerically indexed arrays, the `foreach` loop allows you to select an element on each pass and perform operations on it. The `foreach` loop has two possible definitions. The first follows the structure `foreach($array as $value)`. This selects each element and assigns it to the `$value` variable. The second form is `foreach($array as $key=>$value)` and extracts two variables on each pass of the loop: one for the key and one for the value. For more information about the `foreach` structure, see the task "Using the Foreach Statement."

TYPE THIS:

```
$myArray = array('mom'=>'Beverly',
'sister'=>'Shelly', 'nephew'=>'Noah',
'wife'=>'Michele');

foreach($myArray as $key=>$value){
  echo "The key:$key has the
value:$value<br />";
}
```

→

RESULTS:

The browser displays the key and value for each element in your array.

The key:'mom' has the value:'Beverly'

The key:'sister' has the value:'Shelly'

The key:'nephew' has the value:'Noah'

The key:'wife' has the value:'Michele'

Create a
Multidimensional Array

A multidimensional array is an array in which each element is itself an array. They are especially useful when handling information that might be well represented using a grid or table.

You can create a multidimensional array by setting the value of an element to an array. This can be done by passing arrays to the `array` function on the right side of an assignment operation or by explicitly setting an array as a value for a given key or index in your main array. For an array called `$multi` you can add an element at the first index by typing `$multi[0] = array('apples','oranges');`. Alternately, you can make the same assignment by typing `$multi = array(array('apples', 'oranges'));`.

You can think of the primary array elements as rows in a grid. Each contains another array whose elements can be

seen as cells in columns. When storing tabular data in multidimensional arrays, it is important to maintain parallel integrity; that is, be sure that the same number of cells is present in each element array. Otherwise, the logic you use in performing operations on your multidimensional array may fail.

Multidimensional arrays may consist of numeric or associative arrays, or a mixture thereof.

Accessing elements in multidimensional arrays is similar to accessing elements in single-dimensional arrays. The square brackets are used to pass the index or key of an element you want to retrieve. For a multidimensional array named `$table` you would select the first element using `$table[0]`. Keeping in mind that the element retrieved is itself an array, you can select its first item using `$table[0][0]`.

Create a Multidimensional Array

① Type the name of a variable you want to use to represent your array followed by the assignment operator (=).

② Type `array()`, passing any default values as comma-separated arguments or leaving the argument list empty to create an empty array as shown here.

③ Add an array to the first index using square brackets.

④ Repeat Step 3 for each array you want to store.

Note: Remember to use a unique index in each assignment operation to prevent overwriting previous entries.

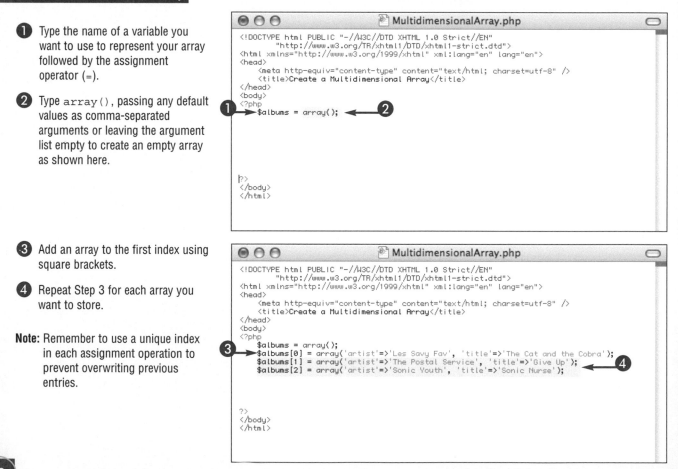

5 Select a value from the multidimensional array.

6 Use the echo statement to print the value to the output stream.

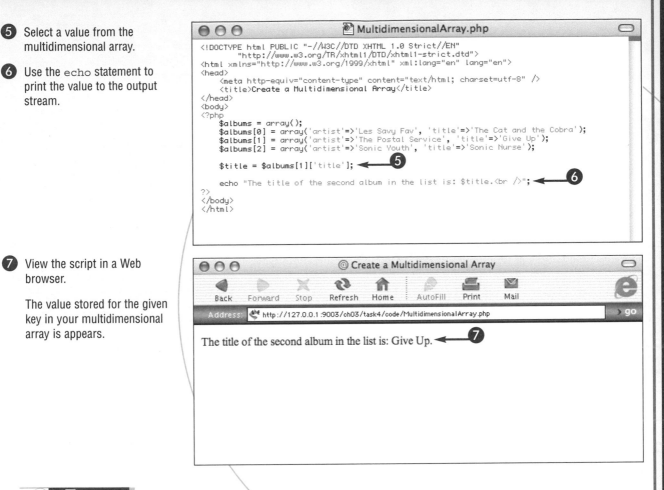

```
MultidimensionalArray.php

<!DOCTYPE html PUBLIC "-//W3C//DTD XHTML 1.0 Strict//EN"
        "http://www.w3.org/TR/xhtml1/DTD/xhtml1-strict.dtd">
<html xmlns="http://www.w3.org/1999/xhtml" xml:lang="en" lang="en">
<head>
    <meta http-equiv="content-type" content="text/html; charset=utf-8" />
    <title>Create a Multidimensional Array</title>
</head>
<body>
<?php
    $albums = array();
    $albums[0] = array('artist'=>'Les Savy Fav', 'title'=>'The Cat and the Cobra');
    $albums[1] = array('artist'=>'The Postal Service', 'title'=>'Give Up');
    $albums[2] = array('artist'=>'Sonic Youth', 'title'=>'Sonic Nurse');

    $title = $albums[1]['title'];          ← 5

    echo "The title of the second album in the list is: $title.<br />";   ← 6
?>
</body>
</html>
```

7 View the script in a Web browser.

The value stored for the given key in your multidimensional array is appears.

```
@ Create a Multidimensional Array

Back  Forward  Stop  Refresh  Home  AutoFill  Print  Mail

Address: http://127.0.0.1:9003/ch03/task4/code/MultidimensionalArray.php    › go

The title of the second album in the list is: Give Up.    ← 7
```

Extra

Multidimensional arrays are often imagined as tabular data. You can clearly display the values in multidimensional arrays using an HTML table. This approach is useful not only in development but in production as well. To build a table with your multidimensional array, you loop through each element in the main array, treating each as a row. Then, loop through the items in the element, treating each as a table cell. As long as your elements contain the same number of items, you have a nice, clear grid to use in examining your array.

TYPE THIS:

```
$people = array();
$people[0] = array('Toby', 'Joe', 'Boudreaux');
$people[1] = array('Michele', 'Lynn', 'Howley');
$people[2] = array('Chandler', 'Bryson', 'McWilliams');

echo '<table border="1">';
echo'<tr><th>First</th><th>Middle</th><th>Last</th></tr>';
foreach($people as $person){
    echo '<tr>';
    foreach($person as $name){
        echo "<td>$name</td>";
    }
    echo '</tr>';
}
echo '</table>';
```

RESULTS:

→ A table appears in the browser showing the first, middle, and last name of each person.

Change the Current Array Element

You can use a *pointer* to move through an array. This allows you to access elements sequentially, moving forward and backward. Pointers are internal to arrays and are, for all intents and purposes, transparent to you. Instead of accessing a pointer directly, you can use the next, prev, reset, and end functions to move the pointer to various locations within your array.

The reset function sets the internal pointer to the first item in the array. This function does not return a value and is, instead, treated as a pure utility function. You can call reset at any time you want to jump back to the first item in an array while using pointers.

You can move the pointer forward one item using the next function. Each time you call next the pointer moves forward one item unless there are no more items in the array. If there is a next item, next returns the item. If the

pointer is at the last element of the array when next is called, it returns false.

The prev function operates the same as the next function except that it moves the pointer back one position. If the pointer is already at the first element in the array, prev returns false.

You can access the element at the current pointer position by using the current function. The return value is either the current element or, if the internal pointer has been set beyond the bounds of the array, false.

If you want to iterate backward through your array, you can call end, which sets the pointer to the last element of the array. Like the other functions, the end function returns the last element. When the pointer is at the last element, you can use the prev function to move backward through the array.

Change the Current Array Element

① Type the name of a variable you want to use to represent your array, followed by the assignment operator (=).

② Type array(), passing any default values as comma-separated arguments.

③ Call the reset function to explicitly set the pointer to the first item.

④ Using the next function, move the pointer forward.

⑤ Echo the result of the next operation.

⑥ Repeat Steps 4 and 5 to move the pointer forward as many times as you want.

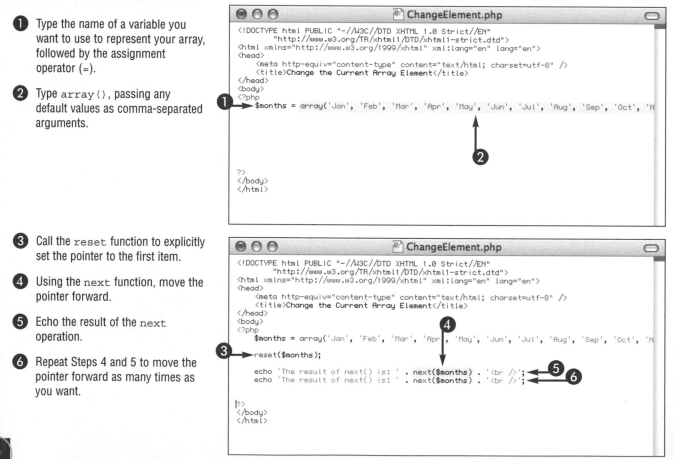

7 Using the `prev` function, move the pointer backward.

8 Echo the result of the `prev` operation.

9 Repeat Steps 7 and 8 to move the pointer backward as many times as you want.

ChangeElement.php

```
<!DOCTYPE html PUBLIC "-//W3C//DTD XHTML 1.0 Strict//EN"
        "http://www.w3.org/TR/xhtml1/DTD/xhtml1-strict.dtd">
<html xmlns="http://www.w3.org/1999/xhtml" xml:lang="en" lang="en">
<head>
    <meta http-equiv="content-type" content="text/html; charset=utf-8" />
    <title>Change the Current Array Element</title>
</head>
<body>
<?php
    $months = array('Jan', 'Feb', 'Mar', 'Apr', 'May', 'Jun', 'Jul', 'Aug', 'Sep', 'Oct', 'N

    reset($months);

    echo 'The result of next() is: ' . next($months) . '<br />';
    echo 'The result of next() is: ' . next($months) . '<br />';

    echo 'The result of prev() is: ' . prev($months) . '<br />';
?>
</body>
</html>
```

8 → (arrow pointing to `prev($months)`)

8 (arrow) **7** (arrow)

10 View the script in a Web browser.

The results of the pointer operations appear.

@ Change the Current Array Element

Back | Forward | Stop | Refresh | Home | AutoFill | Print | Mail

Address: http://127.0.0.1:9003/ch03/task5/code/ChangeElement.php → go

The result of next() is: Feb
The result of next() is: Mar ← **10**
The result of prev() is: Feb

Extra

The `next` and `prev` functions return false when the internal array pointer is at the end or beginning of your array. You can take advantage of this by using the `while` loop to iterate over the values in your array until a boundary is reached.

TYPE THIS:

```
$pets = array('Schmitty', 'Pookum', 'Tucker');
reset($pets);
echo "The current pet is: " . current($pets) . "<br />";
while($pet = next($pets)){
  echo "The current pet name is: $pet.<br />";
}
```

→

RESULTS:

The browser displays each pet name on a new line. When the internal pointer reaches the end of the array, the `next` function returns `false`, ending the `while` loop.

Add and Remove Elements from an Array

Arrays in PHP are highly dynamic. You can add and remove elements using the built-in `array_push`, `array_pop`, `array_shift`, and `array_unshift` functions. You can also add items by index using square brackets.

Adding an item to the end of an array is a common operation you can perform with the `array_push` function. The function accepts two or more arguments. The first is the variable used to represent your array. The additional arguments represent values you want to add to the end of the array. Each time you call `array_push`, the size of your array grows by the number of items passed as secondary arguments.

You can add an element to the beginning of your array using the `array_shift` function. Much like `array_push`, the `array_shift` function accepts two or more arguments.

The first is the target array to which you want to prepend values. The secondary arguments represent the values you want added at the beginning of the array.

To remove an element from the end of an array, you can use `array_pop`. The function accepts a single argument representing the array from which you want to remove an item and returns the value removed from the end of the array. The target array is modified on each successful call to `array_pop`, resulting in a size one less than before the value was removed. If there are no more items in your array, `array_pop` returns false.

You can remove the first element in your array using the `array_unshift` function. This function operates exactly as `array_pop` but targets and returns the first item in the array instead of the last.

Add and Remove Elements from an Array

① Type the name of a variable you want to use to represent your array, followed by the assignment operator (=).

② Type `array()`, passing any default values as comma-separated arguments.

③ Add an element to your array using the `array_push` function.

④ Use the `print_r` function to display the structure and contents of your array.

⑤ Remove an element from the end of your array using `array_pop`.

⑥ Use the `print_r` function to display the modified array.

7 Add an element to the beginning of your array using `array_unshift`.

8 Use `print_r` to display the modified array.

9 Remove the first item in your array by calling `array_shift`.

10 Use `print_r` to display the modified array.

11 View the script in a Web browser.

The results of the array modification statements appear.

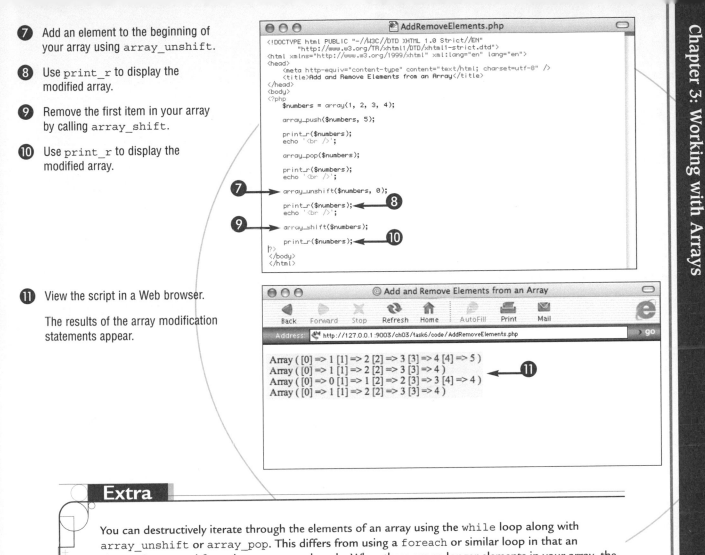

Extra

You can destructively iterate through the elements of an array using the `while` loop along with `array_unshift` or `array_pop`. This differs from using a `foreach` or similar loop in that an element is removed from the array on each cycle. When there are no longer elements in your array, the `while` loop exits. You can iterate forward using `array_unshift` or backward using `array_pop`.

TYPE THIS:

```
$pets = array('Schmitty', 'Pookum', 'Tucker');

while($pet = array_unshift($pets)){
   echo "The current pet name is: $pet.<br />";
}
```

RESULTS:

The browser displays each pet name on a new line. Each pet name is listed in the original order.

TYPE THIS:

```
$pets = array('Schmitty', 'Pookum', 'Tucker');

while($pet = array_pop($pets)){
   echo "The current pet name is: $pet.<br />";
}
```

RESULTS:

The browser displays each pet name on a new line. Each pet name is listed in the order opposite that in which it was added.

Replace Elements in an Array

Y ou can modify existing array contents using the built-in `array_splice` function. Though mostly used to replace elements in an array with an array of alternative elements, the `array_splice` function can also be used to remove and add elements at the beginning, middle, or end of an array.

The `array_splice` function accepts two required and two optional arguments and returns all items extracted from the original array. The required arguments are the target array and the numeric array offset at which the splice operation should begin. If called with only these two arguments, the function removes all elements from the offset position to the end of the array, returning them as an array.

You can limit the number of items removed by passing a third argument representing the number of items to be removed after the offset. If the third argument is positive,

the elements removed will be `$array[offset]` through `$array[number]`. If the third argument is negative, the elements removed will be those from `$array[offset]` through `$array[length - number]`.

The fourth argument is an optional array of values you want to place into the target array after the removal based on the first three arguments has completed. To remove all items after a given index and add an array of items, you must pass the size of the fourth argument as the third argument. For example, you might type `array_splice($people, 3, count($newPeople), $newPeople);`. This removes all elements after the fourth item (index 3), then appends all elements in the `$newPeople` array.

It is important to note that `array_splice` modifies the array you pass as the first argument.

Replace Elements in an Array

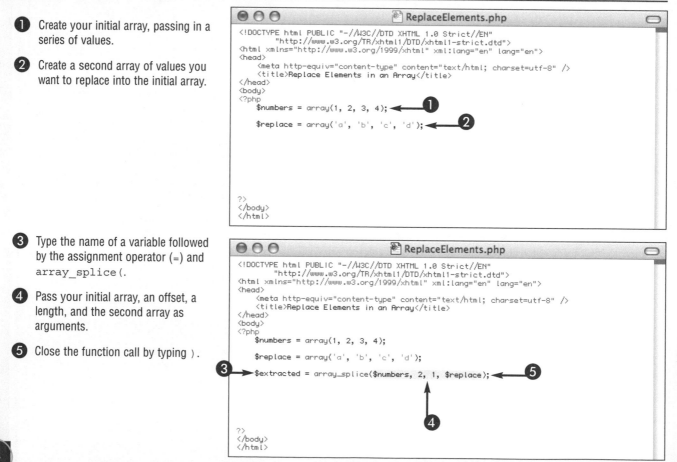

① Create your initial array, passing in a series of values.

② Create a second array of values you want to replace into the initial array.

③ Type the name of a variable followed by the assignment operator (=) and `array_splice(`.

④ Pass your initial array, an offset, a length, and the second array as arguments.

⑤ Close the function call by typing `)`.

6 Use the `print_r` function to view the returned values.

7 Use `print_r` to display the modified initial array.

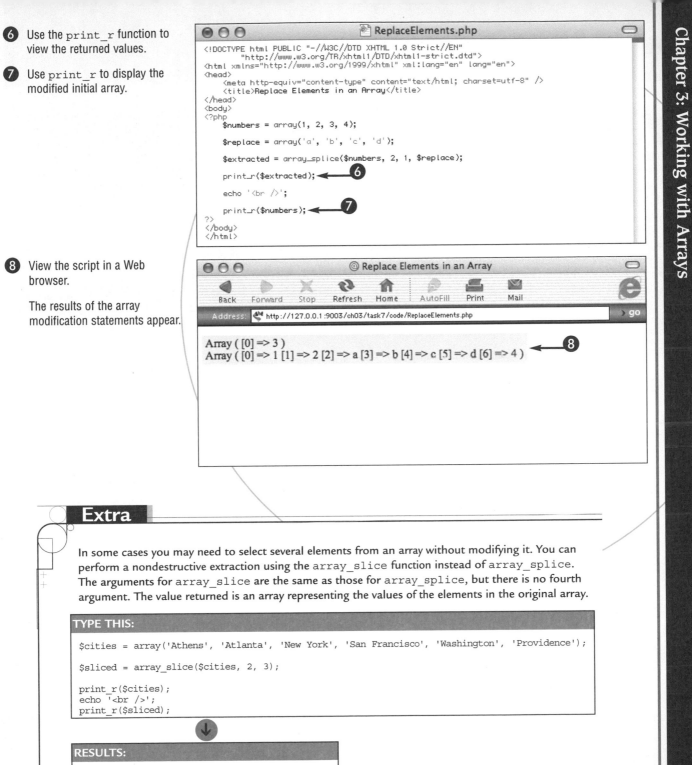

```
ReplaceElements.php

<!DOCTYPE html PUBLIC "-//W3C//DTD XHTML 1.0 Strict//EN"
        "http://www.w3.org/TR/xhtml1/DTD/xhtml1-strict.dtd">
<html xmlns="http://www.w3.org/1999/xhtml" xml:lang="en" lang="en">
<head>
    <meta http-equiv="content-type" content="text/html; charset=utf-8" />
    <title>Replace Elements in an Array</title>
</head>
<body>
<?php
    $numbers = array(1, 2, 3, 4);

    $replace = array('a', 'b', 'c', 'd');

    $extracted = array_splice($numbers, 2, 1, $replace);

    print_r($extracted);          6

    echo '<br />';

    print_r($numbers);          7
?>
</body>
</html>
```

8 View the script in a Web browser.

The results of the array modification statements appear.

```
Replace Elements in an Array

Back  Forward  Stop  Refresh  Home  AutoFill  Print  Mail

Address: http://127.0.0.1:9003/ch03/task7/code/ReplaceElements.php    go

Array ( [0] => 3 )
Array ( [0] => 1 [1] => 2 [2] => a [3] => b [4] => c [5] => d [6] => 4 )    8
```

Extra

In some cases you may need to select several elements from an array without modifying it. You can perform a nondestructive extraction using the `array_slice` function instead of `array_splice`. The arguments for `array_slice` are the same as those for `array_splice`, but there is no fourth argument. The value returned is an array representing the values of the elements in the original array.

TYPE THIS:

```
$cities = array('Athens', 'Atlanta', 'New York', 'San Francisco', 'Washington', 'Providence');

$sliced = array_slice($cities, 2, 3);

print_r($cities);
echo '<br />';
print_r($sliced);
```

RESULTS:

The browser displays the source array in its unmodified form. The `$sliced` array is printed and contains values from the `$cities` array.

Sort an Array

Y ou can use the `sort` function to sort an array, placing the elements in order from lowest to highest according to any one of three algorithms. For example, you can sort an array of prices into their numeric value or an array of names alphabetically. You can also sort an array having mixed types, but be mindful of the way PHP handles comparisons of differing types.

The `sort` function accepts two arguments. The first argument is required and represents the array you want to sort. The second represents the algorithm by which to sort. The possible values are the PHP constants `SORT_REGULAR`, `SORT_NUMERIC`, and `SORT STRING`. This argument is optional and defaults to `SORT_REGULAR` if omitted.

Specifying the sorting algorithm you want to use is useful when you need to ensure that PHP performs a particular

sorting operation. For example, the default algorithm treats numeric values as strings, ordering by each successive digit instead of the actual numeric value. For example, the numbers `1`, `4`, `58`, `23` are sorted `1`, `23`, `4`, `58`. To force PHP to sort the numbers by their actual values, you can call the `sort` function with `sort($nums, SORT_NUMERIC);`.

The sort function modifies the array on which it operates and returns `true` and `false` to represent success and failure, respectively.

The `sort` function returns values in order of lowest to highest according to the chosen algorithm. You can sort from highest to lowest using the `rsort` function. The `rsort` function operates exactly as the sort function, but arranges the elements in descending order.

Sort an Array

① Create your array, passing in a series of values.

② Call the `sort` function, passing the variable representing your array as the first argument.

③ Using the `print_r` function, display the structure and contents of your array.

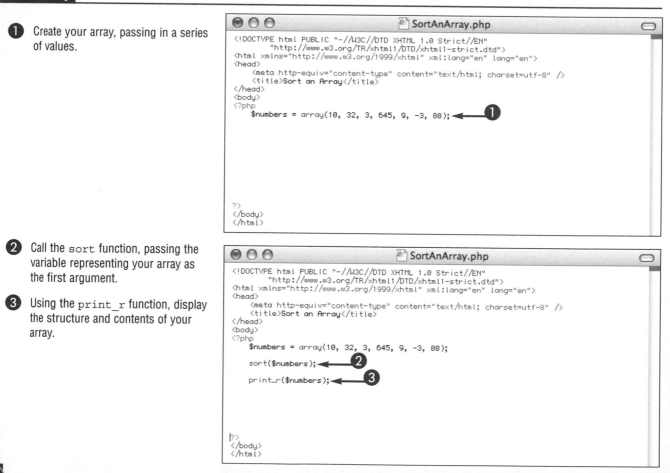

④ Call the `rsort` function, passing your array as an argument.

⑤ Use `print_r()` to display the modified initial array, now sorted in reverse order.

```
SortAnArray.php

<!DOCTYPE html PUBLIC "-//W3C//DTD XHTML 1.0 Strict//EN"
        "http://www.w3.org/TR/xhtml1/DTD/xhtml1-strict.dtd">
<html xmlns="http://www.w3.org/1999/xhtml" xml:lang="en" lang="en">
<head>
    <meta http-equiv="content-type" content="text/html; charset=utf-8" />
    <title>Sort an Array</title>
</head>
<body>
<?php
    $numbers = array(10, 32, 3, 645, 9, -3, 88);

    sort($numbers);

    print_r($numbers);

    echo '<br />';

    rsort($numbers);              ←———4

    print_r($numbers);            ←———5
?>
</body>
</html>
```

⑥ View the script in a Web browser.

The results of the array sorting statements appear.

```
@ Sort an Array

Back  Forward  Stop  Refresh  Home  AutoFill  Print  Mail

Address: http://127.0.0.1:9003/ch03/task8/code/SortAnArray.php        go

Array ( [0] => -3 [1] => 3 [2] => 9 [3] => 10 [4] => 32 [5] => 88 [6] => 645 )   ←———6
Array ( [0] => 645 [1] => 88 [2] => 32 [3] => 10 [4] => 9 [5] => 3 [6] => -3 )
```

Extra

PHP does not have a constant representing a random sorting algorithm. Instead, you can sort your array in random order using the `shuffle` function. Unlike other sorting functions, the `shuffle` function accepts only one argument: the array to be shuffled. Before calling the `shuffle` function, you should have PHP initialize its random number generator by passing a seed number to it. The `srand` function allows you to set a number as the seed used in generating random numbers with the `shuffle` and other randomization functions.

TYPE THIS:

```
srand((double) microtime() * 1000000);
$letters = array('A','B','C','D','E','F');
shuffle($letters);
print_r($letters);
```

→

RESULTS:

The browser displays the `$letters` array in its new order.

Sort an Associative Array

You can sort associative arrays in much the same way as simple numerically indexed arrays. PHP provides functions to sort associative arrays by both keys and values. To sort an associative array based on the values, keeping the key-value mappings intact, you can use the asort and arsort functions. You can sort based on the keys using ksort and krsort. The integrity between keys and values is maintained across each of these functions.

Each sorting function accepts two arguments. The first is the variable representing the array you want to sort. Remember that the array used should be associative. Optionally, you can set the algorithm to be used in the sorting operation by passing a predefined PHP constant to the function. The possible values for the second parameter are SORT_REGULAR, SORT_NUMERIC, and SORT_STRING. If the second argument is omitted, the SORT_REGULAR value is used as a default.

The asort function sorts your associative array according to the values stored in each element. The values are sorted from lowest to highest. To sort from highest to lowest you can use the arsort function.

You can sort an associative array by its keys using the ksort function. Much like the asort function, ksort sorts your array from lowest to highest. To sort by key from highest to lowest, you can use the krsort function.

Sort an Associative Array

① Create your associative array, passing in a series of values.

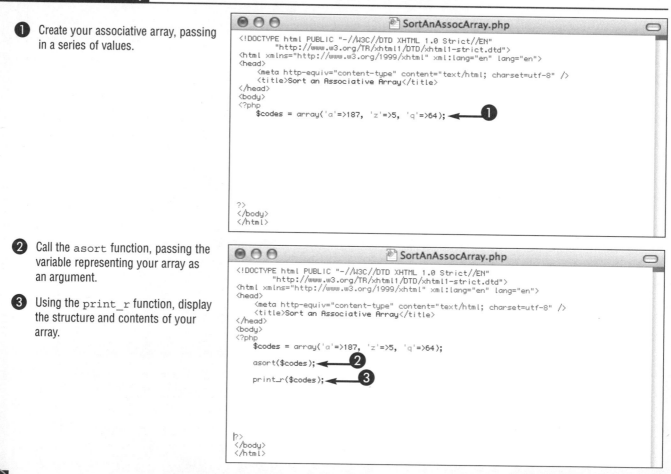

② Call the asort function, passing the variable representing your array as an argument.

③ Using the print_r function, display the structure and contents of your array.

④ Call the `ksort` function, passing your array as an argument.

⑤ Use `print_r` to display the modified initial array, now sorted by keys.

SortAnAssocArray.php

```
<!DOCTYPE html PUBLIC "-//W3C//DTD XHTML 1.0 Strict//EN"
        "http://www.w3.org/TR/xhtml1/DTD/xhtml1-strict.dtd">
<html xmlns="http://www.w3.org/1999/xhtml" xml:lang="en" lang="en">
<head>
    <meta http-equiv="content-type" content="text/html; charset=utf-8" />
    <title>Sort an Associative Array</title>
</head>
<body>
<?php
    $codes = array('a'=>187, 'z'=>5, 'q'=>64);

    asort($codes);

    print_r($codes);

    echo '<br />';

    ksort($codes);          ◄———— 4

    print_r($codes);        ◄———— 5
?>
</body>
</html>
```

⑥ View the script in a Web browser.

The results of the array sorting statements appear.

@ Sort an Associative Array

Address: http://127.0.0.1:9003/ch03/task9/code/SortAnAssocArray.php › go

Array ([z] => 5 [q] => 64 [a] => 187)   ◄———— 6
Array ([a] => 187 [q] => 64 [z] => 5)

Extra

You find that, though you can choose one of three sorting algorithms to use with your sorting functions, your sorting needs are not always met. For example, you may have a listing of numbered links with items such as `link_1.html`, `link_2.html`, and `link_13.html`. If you sort such a list using the standard sort functions, the final ordering may be `link_1.html`, `link_13.html`, and `link_2.html`. To obtain a more natural sorting, you can use the `natsort` function. Based on Martin Pool's Natural Order String Comparison algorithm, the `natsort` function accepts an array and sorts it according to the way humans tend to order strings containing numerical values. To learn more about Martin Pool's work, you can visit www.naturalordersort.org.

TYPE THIS:

```
$names = array('n1', 'n2', 'n10', 'n43', 'n3', 'n30');
natsort($names);
print_r($letters);
```

→

RESULTS:

The browser displays the `$names` array in its new order: n1, n2, n3, n10, n30, n43.

Sort Using a Custom Sort Function

PHP provides several powerful and efficient functions to use in sorting both simple and associative arrays. You may find occasions where you need to use your own algorithm in sorting data. Luckily, PHP provides a mechanism by which you can specify a function to use in sorting. Any function that accepts two arguments and returns 1, 0, or −1 can be used in custom sorting applications. You can use a custom function to sort both simple and associative arrays.

The functions used for custom sorting are usort, uasort, and uksort. All three functions accept two arguments. The first is the array you want to sort. The second is the name of the custom function to be used in the sorting.

The usort function is used in sorting numerically indexed arrays. To sort associative arrays you can use the uasort

and uksort functions to sort by values and keys, respectively.

When a custom sort function is used, elements in an array are passed to the function in pairs. The function compares the two values and depending on the specific criteria used returns a value representing the success of the comparison. The possible values are 1, 0, and −1. When a function returns 1, the first element is placed before the second in the sequence. When 0 is returned, the two values are treated as equals. A return value of −1 means that the second value is placed before the first in the array.

Unlike the other built-in sorting methods, there is no secondary version of the custom sorting functions to reverse sort. This is because the final sorting criteria are set inside the custom function.

Sort Using a Custom Sort Function

① Create an array, passing in a series of values.

```
<!DOCTYPE html PUBLIC "-//W3C//DTD XHTML 1.0 Strict//EN"
        "http://www.w3.org/TR/xhtml1/DTD/xhtml1-strict.dtd">
<html xmlns="http://www.w3.org/1999/xhtml" xml:lang="en" lang="en">
<head>
    <meta http-equiv="content-type" content="text/html; charset=utf-8" />
    <title>Sort Using a Custom Sort Function</title>
</head>
<body>
<?php
    $years = array(2002, 2004, 1977, 1492, 1905, 2001, 1979, 1958);    ←①

?>
</body>
</html>
```

② Define a custom sort function that accept two arguments and returns 1, 0, or -1.

```
<!DOCTYPE html PUBLIC "-//W3C//DTD XHTML 1.0 Strict//EN"
        "http://www.w3.org/TR/xhtml1/DTD/xhtml1-strict.dtd">
<html xmlns="http://www.w3.org/1999/xhtml" xml:lang="en" lang="en">
<head>
    <meta http-equiv="content-type" content="text/html; charset=utf-8" />
    <title>Sort Using a Custom Sort Function</title>
</head>
<body>
<?php
    $years = array(2002, 2004, 1977, 1492, 1905, 2001, 1979, 1958);

    function leapYearsFirst($a, $b){
        $aIsLeap = ($a % 4 == 0);
        $bIsLeap = ($b % 4 == 0);
        if(($aIsLeap && $bIsLeap) || (!$aIsLeap && !$bIsLeap)){
            if($a < $b) return -1;
            if($a == $b) return 0;
            if($a > $b) return 1;                                        ←②
        }else if($aIsLeap){
            return -1;
        }else if($bIsLeap){
            return 1;
        }
    }

?>
</body>
</html>
```

3 Use `usort` to have PHP sort using your custom function.

4 Pass your array as the first argument and the name of your function as the second.

5 Use `print_r` to display your sorted array.

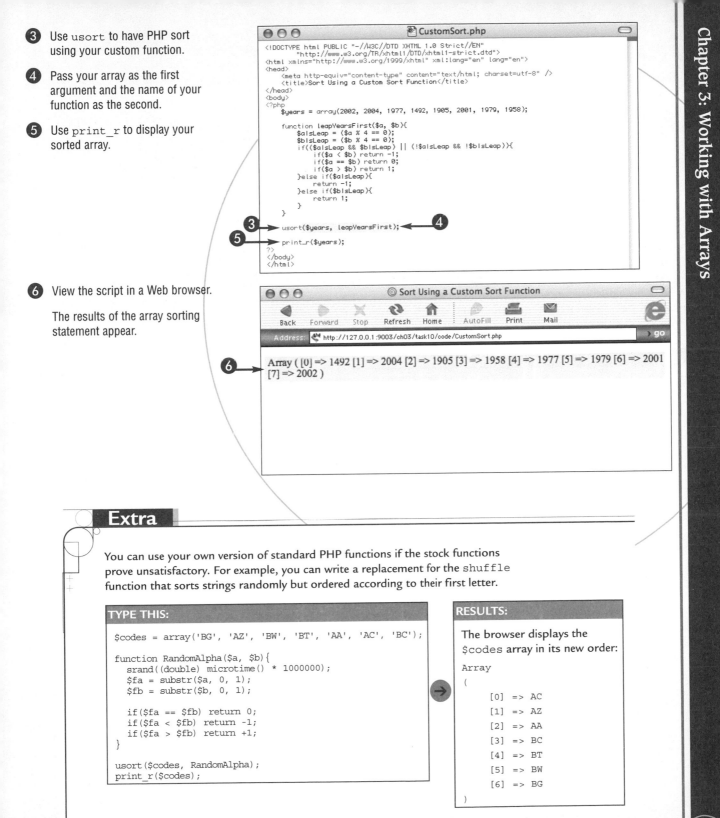

```
CustomSort.php

<!DOCTYPE html PUBLIC "-//W3C//DTD XHTML 1.0 Strict//EN"
        "http://www.w3.org/TR/xhtml1/DTD/xhtml1-strict.dtd">
<html xmlns="http://www.w3.org/1999/xhtml" xml:lang="en" lang="en">
<head>
    <meta http-equiv="content-type" content="text/html; charset=utf-8" />
    <title>Sort Using a Custom Sort Function</title>
</head>
<body>
<?php
    $years = array(2002, 2004, 1977, 1492, 1905, 2001, 1979, 1958);

    function leapYearsFirst($a, $b){
        $aIsLeap = ($a % 4 == 0);
        $bIsLeap = ($b % 4 == 0);
        if(($aIsLeap && $bIsLeap) || (!$aIsLeap && !$bIsLeap)){
            if($a < $b) return -1;
            if($a == $b) return 0;
            if($a > $b) return 1;
        }else if($aIsLeap){
            return -1;
        }else if($bIsLeap){
            return 1;
        }
    }

    usort($years, leapYearsFirst);

    print_r($years);
?>
</body>
</html>
```

6 View the script in a Web browser.

The results of the array sorting statement appear.

Address: http://127.0.0.1:9003/ch03/task10/code/CustomSort.php

Array ([0] => 1492 [1] => 2004 [2] => 1905 [3] => 1958 [4] => 1977 [5] => 1979 [6] => 2001 [7] => 2002)

Extra

You can use your own version of standard PHP functions if the stock functions prove unsatisfactory. For example, you can write a replacement for the `shuffle` function that sorts strings randomly but ordered according to their first letter.

TYPE THIS:

```
$codes = array('BG', 'AZ', 'BW', 'BT', 'AA', 'AC', 'BC');

function RandomAlpha($a, $b){
    srand((double) microtime() * 1000000);
    $fa = substr($a, 0, 1);
    $fb = substr($b, 0, 1);

    if($fa == $fb) return 0;
    if($fa < $fb) return -1;
    if($fa > $fb) return +1;
}

usort($codes, RandomAlpha);
print_r($codes);
```

RESULTS:

The browser displays the `$codes` array in its new order:

```
Array
(
    [0] => AC
    [1] => AZ
    [2] => AA
    [3] => BC
    [4] => BT
    [5] => BW
    [6] => BG
)
```

Get Information About an Array

Y ou can use several built-in PHP functions to access information about an array.

You can find the number of items in an array using the count function. The count function is commonly used in loops to help determine the number of iterations a looping structure should perform. The array_count_values function accepts an array as an argument and returns an array representing the number of times each value appears in the primary array.

You can use array_keys to extract all keys in an associative array. The array_values function is analogous and extracts all values from an associative array. Both functions return a new array. The array_values function is useful in converting an associative array into a simple array.

The array_sum function can be used to add all numeric values in an array and return the sum as a number.

Each key-value pair in an associative array can be switched using the array_flip function. In order for array_flip to function correctly, each key and value needs to be of a numeric or string data type.

Each of these functions accepts an array as a single argument. Modifications made inside the function are reflected in the target array.

Often, you need to search an array for a value to determine whether or not it is present. You can use the in_array function to perform a search. The in_array function accepts two arguments — the value for which you want to search and the target array. A Boolean value of true is returned if the value is found. A false value is returned otherwise.

Get Information About an Array

① Create an array, passing in a series of values.

```
<!DOCTYPE html PUBLIC "-//W3C//DTD XHTML 1.0 Strict//EN"
    "http://www.w3.org/TR/xhtml1/DTD/xhtml1-strict.dtd">
<html xmlns="http://www.w3.org/1999/xhtml" xml:lang="en" lang="en">
<head>
    <meta http-equiv="content-type" content="text/html; charset=utf-8" />
    <title>Get Information About an Array</title>
</head>
<body>
<?php
    $votes = array(1, 1, 2, 1, 2, 2, 2, 2, 1, 1, 2, 1, 2);    ◀——①



?>
</body>
</html>
```

② Use the count function to find the number of items in your array.

③ Use the echo statement to print the result.

```
<!DOCTYPE html PUBLIC "-//W3C//DTD XHTML 1.0 Strict//EN"
    "http://www.w3.org/TR/xhtml1/DTD/xhtml1-strict.dtd">
<html xmlns="http://www.w3.org/1999/xhtml" xml:lang="en" lang="en">
<head>
    <meta http-equiv="content-type" content="text/html; charset=utf-8" />
    <title>Get Information About an Array</title>
</head>
<body>
<?php
    $votes = array(1, 1, 2, 1, 2, 2, 2, 2, 1, 1, 2, 1, 2);

    $count = count($votes);    ◀——②

    echo "There were $count votes made.<br />";    ◀——③


?>
</body>
</html>
```

4 Call `array_count_values`, passing your array as an argument.

5 Use `print_r` to display the associative array returned by `array_count_values`.

```
000                    GetInformation.php
<!DOCTYPE html PUBLIC "-//W3C//DTD XHTML 1.0 Strict//EN"
        "http://www.w3.org/TR/xhtml1/DTD/xhtml1-strict.dtd">
<html xmlns="http://www.w3.org/1999/xhtml" xml:lang="en" lang="en">
<head>
    <meta http-equiv="content-type" content="text/html; charset=utf-8" />
    <title>Get Information About an Array</title>
</head>
<body>
<?php
    $votes = array(1, 1, 2, 1, 2, 2, 2, 2, 1, 1, 2, 1, 2);

    $count = count($votes);

    echo "There were $count votes made.<br />";

    $tally = array_count_values($votes);        ← 4

    print_r($tally);        ← 5
?>
</body>
</html>
```

6 View the script in a Web browser.

The result of the `array_count_values` call appears.

```
000            @ Get Information About an Array
Back  Forward  Stop  Refresh  Home  AutoFill  Print  Mail
Address: http://127.0.0.1:9003/ch03/task11/code/GetInformation.php    › go

There were 13 votes made.
Array ( [1] => 6 [2] => 7 )        ← 6
```

Extra

You can combine the functionality of these functions to determine complex information about arrays. For example, you can write a function to find the sum of distinct values in an array.

TYPE THIS:

```
$numbers = array(100, 230, 500, 100);

function array_sum_distinct($arr){
  $vals_count = array_count_values($arr);
  $vals = array_keys($vals_count);
  return array_sum($vals);
}

echo 'The sum is: ' . array_sum_distinct($numbers);
```

RESULTS:

The browser displays the sum of the unique values in the $numbers array. The total displayed is 830 instead of 930 because the duplicate value of 100 is not added to the sum total.

Using the List Statement

You can quickly assign semantically meaningful array names to the values in an array using the `list` statement. This makes working with array values easier than accessing values with numeric indexes because your code has descriptive variable names for values instead of relatively meaningless numbers.

The `list` statement follows an operation format that is somewhat distinct from other common PHP operations. Though the list statement is followed by parentheses, it is not really a function. Instead, it is a language construct. The `list` statement is the left-side operand in any operations in which it is used. The `list` statement accepts any number of variable names as arguments. The call to `list` is followed by a list of variable names. The assignment operator (=) and an array whose values are to be extracted follow. Each

variable name passed to the `list` statement is used to represent the values in the array in order of array index. For example, if you type `list($a, $b, $c) = array('x', 'y', 'z');`, the variable `$a` will be assigned a value of `'x'`.

When using the `list` statement you should only assign simple, numerically indexed arrays with sequential indexes beginning with zero (0). If you need to skip values in the target array, you can pass empty arguments to the `list` statement by typing only a comma instead of a variable name. For example, by typing `list(,,$third) = array('one', 'two', 'three');`, you can assign the value `'three'` to the `$third` variable.

Because the `list` statement is not a function it does not return a value.

Using the List Statement

① Create an array, passing in a series of values.

② Type `list(`, followed by a series of variables.

③ Close the statement by typing `)`.

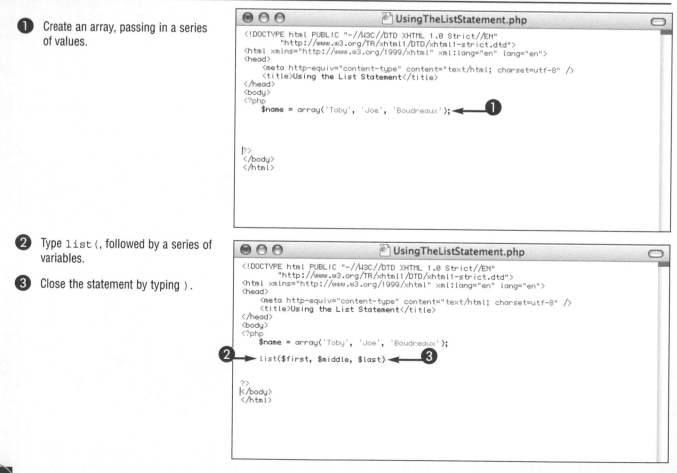

④ Type the assignment operand along with the name of your array.

⑤ Use the `echo` statement to display the variables.

```
UsingTheListStatement.php

<!DOCTYPE html PUBLIC "-//W3C//DTD XHTML 1.0 Strict//EN"
        "http://www.w3.org/TR/xhtml1/DTD/xhtml1-strict.dtd">
<html xmlns="http://www.w3.org/1999/xhtml" xml:lang="en" lang="en">
<head>
    <meta http-equiv="content-type" content="text/html; charset=utf-8" />
    <title>Using the List Statement</title>
</head>
<body>
<?php
    $name = array('Toby', 'Joe', 'Boudreaux');

    list($first, $middle, $last) = $name;          ← ④

    echo "The full name is $first $middle $last.";  ← ⑤
?>
</body>
</html>
```

⑥ View the script in a Web browser.

The values in the array are assigned to the variables used in the `list` statement.

```
Using the List Statement

Back  Forward  Stop  Refresh  Home  AutoFill  Print  Mail

Address: http://127.0.0.1:9003/ch03/task12/code/UsingTheListStatement.php      go

The full name is Toby Joe Boudreaux.  ← ⑥
```

Extra

The `list` statement is often combined with the `each` function to form the condition of a loop structure such as the `while` loop. The `each` function returns an array representing the key and value of an element in an associative array. The `each` function uses the internal array index pointer to determine which element to return. The internal pointer is then set to the next item. When the pointer moves beyond the bounds of the array, `each` returns `false`.

The array returned from `each` is in the order key, value. That is, the key is item `0` and the value is item `1`.

TYPE THIS:

```
$person = array('Name'=>'Toby', 'city'=>'New York', 'title'=>'Director of Engineering');

while(list($key, $value) = each($person)){
  echo "$key: $value<br />";
}
```

↓

RESULTS:

The browser displays the information from the `$person` array by key and value. When the last key from `$person` has been returned, the `while` loop exits.

Using the Foreach Statement

You can access elements in an array using the foreach statement. Using the foreach statement is similar to using the for or while loops when combined with commands to count and select array items.

The foreach statement allows you to automatically iterate over an array, selecting an element on each cycle. There are two formats for the foreach statement. The simpler of the two is used to select the value of the current element on each loop cycle. You create a simple foreach statement by typing foreach($myArray as $value) with any code you want to execute on each cycle enclosed in curly braces ({}).

To iterate over an associative array, extracting each key and value as distinct variables, you can use the format foreach($myArray as $key=>$value) with any code enclosed in curly braces. The $key variable is set to the key for the current array element, with the $value variable set to the element value.

As soon as the last item in the array is processed, the foreach statement ceases execution. Because the foreach statement is not a function, the $key and $value variables are accessible by other code in your PHP script. The values reflect the last element in the array.

Unlike other functions used to iterate over arrays, there is no need to call the reset function before using the foreach statement. PHP calls reset automatically before the first item of the target array is selected.

The foreach statement operates on a copy of the array, not on the array itself. It is important to remember that setting the $key or $value variable inside the body of the foreach statement has no effect on the target array.

Using the Foreach Statement

① Create an associative array, passing in a series of values.

```
000                          Foreach.php
<!DOCTYPE html PUBLIC "-//W3C//DTD XHTML 1.0 Strict//EN"
        "http://www.w3.org/TR/xhtml1/DTD/xhtml1-strict.dtd">
<html xmlns="http://www.w3.org/1999/xhtml" xml:lang="en" lang="en">
<head>
    <meta http-equiv="content-type" content="text/html; charset=utf-8" />
    <title>Using the Foreach Statement</title>
</head>
<body>
<?php
    $states = array('CA'=>'California', 'DC'=>'District of Columbia',
    'GA'=>'Georgia', 'NY'=>'New York', 'RI'=>'Rhode Island');      ← ①


?>
</body>
</html>
```

② Type foreach(.

③ Type the name of a variable to represent the element key.

④ Type the => operator.

⑤ Type the name of a variable to represent the value of the element.

```
000                          Foreach.php
<!DOCTYPE html PUBLIC "-//W3C//DTD XHTML 1.0 Strict//EN"
        "http://www.w3.org/TR/xhtml1/DTD/xhtml1-strict.dtd">
<html xmlns="http://www.w3.org/1999/xhtml" xml:lang="en" lang="en">
<head>
    <meta http-equiv="content-type" content="text/html; charset=utf-8" />
    <title>Using the Foreach Statement</title>
</head>
<body>
<?php
    $states = array('CA'=>'California', 'DC'=>'District of Columbia',
    'GA'=>'Georgia', 'NY'=>'New York', 'RI'=>'Rhode Island');

②→  foreach($states as $abbrev=>$name)

?>
</body>
</html>
                             ↑       ↑   ↑
                             ③      ④   ⑤
```

6 In the body of the foreach statement, echo the current key and value.

```
Foreach.php

<!DOCTYPE html PUBLIC "-//W3C//DTD XHTML 1.0 Strict//EN"
        "http://www.w3.org/TR/xhtml1/DTD/xhtml1-strict.dtd">
<html xmlns="http://www.w3.org/1999/xhtml" xml:lang="en" lang="en">
<head>
    <meta http-equiv="content-type" content="text/html; charset=utf-8" />
    <title>Using the Foreach Statement</title>
</head>
<body>
<?php
    $states = array('CA'=>'California', 'DC'=>'District of Columbia',
    'GA'=>'Georgia', 'NY'=>'New York', 'RI'=>'Rhode Island');

    foreach($states as $abbrev=>$name){
        echo "The abbreviation for $name is $abbrev.<br />";     ← 6
    }
?>
</body>
</html>
```

7 View the script in a Web browser.

The key and value of each element in the array are printed to the output stream.

```
Using the Foreach Statement

Back  Forward  Stop  Refresh  Home  AutoFill  Print  Mail

Address: http://127.0.0.1:9003/ch03/task13/code/Foreach.php    go

The abbreviation for California is CA.
The abbreviation for District of Columbia is DC.
The abbreviation for Georgia is GA.         ← 7
The abbreviation for New York is NY.
The abbreviation for Rhode Island is RI.
```

Extra

After passing an array to the foreach statement by reference, use the unset function to destroy the key and value variables you create. The unset function removes the value from a variable so that PHP can delete it. Clearing the key and value variables with unset helps ensure that the next time the key and value variable names are used they are not set to represent the values used in the previous foreach statement.

TYPE THIS:

```
$source = array(array('a1', 'a2'), array('b1', 'b2'), array('c1', 'c2'));

foreach($source as &$value){
  echo '(1) The value is: ' . $value . '<br />';
}

$secondary = array('l', 'm', 'n', 'o', 'p');

foreach($secondary as $value){
  echo '(2) The value is: ' . $value . '<br />';
}

print_r($source);
```

RESULTS:

The element at the second index of $source does not point to the array containing 'c1' and 'c2' as expected. Instead, the last item of the $secondary array is assigned. If unset($value) is used before the second foreach statement, the $value variable is freed and the initial $source array is not modified.

Print an Array

The value of a variable can usually be written to the output stream using a common echo or print statement. This is true of variables representing arrays, but the depth of information displayed is limited to the word Array.

To print detailed information about an array, you can use the print_r, var_dump, and var_export functions. Each of these functions accepts a variable as an argument and displays some level of detailed information about that variable.

The print_r function displays human-readable information about a variable. The print_r function accepts two arguments. The first is the variable about which information should be displayed. The second parameter is optional and tells the print_r function to return the string description instead of writing it to the output stream. The

print_r function moves the internal array element pointer to the last item in the array so it is a good practice to reset the pointer using the reset function after each print_r statement.

The var_dump function displays array information in a format similar to the print_r function. Along with keys and values, var_dump displays type information for each value. You can view information about multiple arrays with one var_dump statement by passing more than one array as arguments.

The third function you can use to print an array is var_export. This function is similar to var_dump except that the string printed by var_export is valid PHP code. Like print_r, var_export accepts an optional second argument specifying whether the function should return the description instead of writing to the output stream.

Print an Array

1 Create an array, passing in a series of values.

2 Use the print_r function to display information about the array.

```
000                    PrintAnArray.php
<!DOCTYPE html PUBLIC "-//W3C//DTD XHTML 1.0 Strict//EN"
        "http://www.w3.org/TR/xhtml1/DTD/xhtml1-strict.dtd">
<html xmlns="http://www.w3.org/1999/xhtml" xml:lang="en" lang="en">
<head>
    <meta http-equiv="content-type" content="text/html; charset=utf-8" />
    <title>Print an Array</title>
</head>
<body>
<?php
    $mixed = array('scooter'=>'Vespa', 'year'=>1977, 'apple', 'children'=>array());    1

    print_r($mixed);    2



?>
</body>
</html>
```

3 Use var_dump to display information about the array.

```
000                    PrintAnArray.php
<!DOCTYPE html PUBLIC "-//W3C//DTD XHTML 1.0 Strict//EN"
        "http://www.w3.org/TR/xhtml1/DTD/xhtml1-strict.dtd">
<html xmlns="http://www.w3.org/1999/xhtml" xml:lang="en" lang="en">
<head>
    <meta http-equiv="content-type" content="text/html; charset=utf-8" />
    <title>Print an Array</title>
</head>
<body>
<?php
    $mixed = array('scooter'=>'Vespa', 'year'=>1977, 'apple', 'children'=>array());

    print_r($mixed);

    echo '<br /><br />';

    var_dump($mixed);    3


?>
</body>
</html>
```

④ Use `var_export` to display information about the array.

```
000                    📄 PrintAnArray.php                          ⬭
<!DOCTYPE html PUBLIC "-//W3C//DTD XHTML 1.0 Strict//EN"
        "http://www.w3.org/TR/xhtml1/DTD/xhtml1-strict.dtd">
<html xmlns="http://www.w3.org/1999/xhtml" xml:lang="en" lang="en">
<head>
    <meta http-equiv="content-type" content="text/html; charset=utf-8" />
    <title>Print an Array</title>
</head>
<body>
<?php
    $mixed = array('scooter'=>'Vespa', 'year'=>1977, 'apple', 'children'=>array());

    print_r($mixed);

    echo '<br /><br />';

    var_dump($mixed);

    echo '<br /><br />';

    var_export($mixed);      ◄———— 4
?>
</body>
</html>
```

⑤ View the script in a Web browser.

Each of the functions displays information about the array differently.

```
000                    @ Print an Array                          ⬭
 ◄     ►     ✕      ↻       🏠        ✎        🖨       ✉          e
Back  Forward  Stop  Refresh  Home   AutoFill  Print    Mail
Address: 🔷 http://127.0.0.1:9003/ch03/task14/code/PrintAnArray.php      › go
```

Array ([scooter] => Vespa [year] => 1977 [0] => apple [children] => Array ( ))

array(4) { ["scooter"]=> string(5) "Vespa" ["year"]=> int(1977) [0]=> string(5) "apple"   ◄———— 5
["children"]=> array(0) { } }

array ('scooter' => 'Vespa', 'year' => 1977, 0 => 'apple', 'children' => array ( ),)

Extra

Because the output of the `var_export` function is valid PHP code representing the structure and values of a variable, you can combine it with the `eval` function to write a custom cloning function.

TYPE THIS:

```
$data = array('orange', 'banana', 'apple');

function clone_array($source){
  $arrayBody = var_export($source, true);
  eval('$newArray = ' .$arrayBody . ';');
  return $newArray;
}

$cloned = clone_array($data);

print_r($cloned);
```

→

RESULTS:

The description of the `$data` array is passed to `eval`, which executes the code. The resulting `$cloned` array is printed using `print_r`.

109

Change the Case of a String

You can change the case of a string to uppercase or lowercase using several functions provided as part of the PHP language. For example, you can use the strtolower function to change an entire string to lowercase. The strtoupper function provides the opposite functionality, changing the case of each character in a given string to uppercase.

PHP provides a function to use in changing the first letter of a string to uppercase. The ucfirst function accepts a string or variable as an argument and returns a new string with the first letter capitalized. This is useful when you try to normalize data such as names, cities, or titles of books.

If you have a string made of several words, each needing to be capitalized, you can use the ucwords function. PHP assumes that the first letter following a space, tab, or carriage return is the beginning of a new word and capitalizes it.

Each of these functions accepts the target string as an argument and performs *nondestructive* operations on it. Instead of modifying the source string, each function returns a new string. If you want to replace your source string with the new string, you can use the assignment operator in conjunction with a call to one of the functions with your source string as an argument. For example, $myString = strtolower($myString); modifies the $myString variable so that all characters are lowercase.

In some cases, you may need to perform a sequence of operations in order to normalize your strings. For example, using ucwords with a string consisting of uppercase letters yields no modifications. It is always a good practice to call strtolower first when using ucwords.

Change the Case of a String

① Create a string variable consisting of multiple words.

② Use strtolower to set all characters to lowercase.

③ Use the assignment operator (=) to modify your variable.

④ Call ucwords, passing your variable as an argument.

⑤ Use echo to display the modified string.

⑥ Display the page in your Web browser.

The string is displayed with the first letter of each word capitalized.

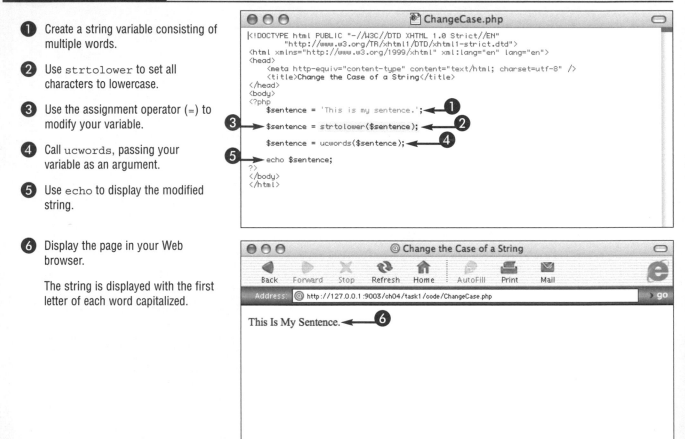

```
<!DOCTYPE html PUBLIC "-//W3C//DTD XHTML 1.0 Strict//EN"
        "http://www.w3.org/TR/xhtml1/DTD/xhtml1-strict.dtd">
<html xmlns="http://www.w3.org/1999/xhtml" xml:lang="en" lang="en">
<head>
    <meta http-equiv="content-type" content="text/html; charset=utf-8" />
    <title>Change the Case of a String</title>
</head>
<body>
<?php
    $sentence = 'This is my sentence.';
    $sentence = strtolower($sentence);

    $sentence = ucwords($sentence);

    echo $sentence;
?>
</body>
</html>
```

This Is My Sentence.

Using ASCII Values

PHP provides support for working with ASCII values. ASCII stands for American Standard Code for Information Interchange and is a system that helps standardize the values of characters for portability across computer systems and languages.

Characters stored as ASCII text are mapped to numeric character codes. The ASCII system contains 127 codes for standard characters. There is an extended ASCII set consisting of 255 character mappings. Each character has an associated ASCII value. This includes special control characters and whitespace characters such as the tab character.

To find the ASCII code for a given character, you can use the ord function. When you pass a character to the ord function, it returns the ASCII character code. This is often useful when dealing with file in/out operations, such as

writing to a file. Certain characters, such as the tab and carriage return characters often need to be encoded to ASCII prior to writing them to the output stream. If you need to write control characters such as backspace or escape, you can use the ord function to get their ASCII code to prevent the control characters from being interpreted as actual commands. To pass a control or whitespace character to the ord function, you need to use the appropriate escape sequence, such as \t for the tab character.

To convert a known ASCII code into a character, you can use the chr function. Like ord, chr accepts a single argument and returns a value. In the case of chr, you pass a numeric code representing an ASCII entry and the associated character is returned. This function is most useful when reading from an ASCII-encoded file or stream.

Using ASCII Values

① Create a variable to represent a character.

② Use ord to find the ASCII code for the given character.

③ Echo the ASCII value to the screen.

④ Using the chr function, convert the ASCII code back into a character.

⑤ Echo the original character to the screen.

⑥ Display the page in your Web browser.

The ASCII and standard versions of the character appear.

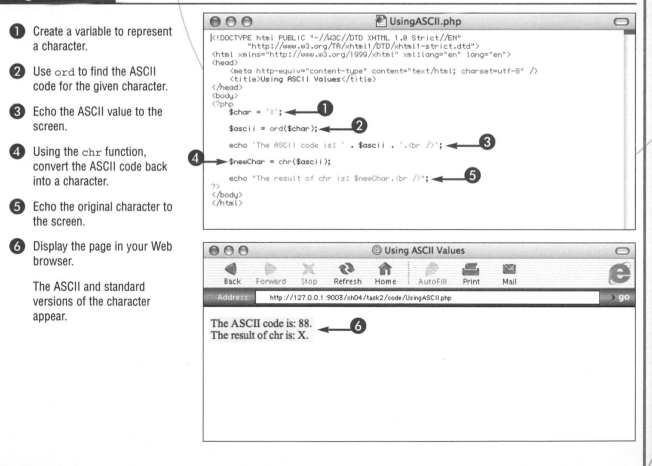

```
UsingASCII.php

<!DOCTYPE html PUBLIC "-//W3C//DTD XHTML 1.0 Strict//EN"
        "http://www.w3.org/TR/xhtml1/DTD/xhtml1-strict.dtd">
<html xmlns="http://www.w3.org/1999/xhtml" xml:lang="en" lang="en">
<head>
    <meta http-equiv="content-type" content="text/html; charset=utf-8" />
    <title>Using ASCII Values</title>
</head>
<body>
<?php
    $char = 'X';                                          ①

    $ascii = ord($char);                                  ②

    echo 'The ASCII code is: ' . $ascii . '.<br />';      ③

    $newChar = chr($ascii);                           ④

    echo "The result of chr is: $newChar.<br />";         ⑤
?>
</body>
</html>
```

```
Using ASCII Values

Back  Forward  Stop  Refresh  Home  AutoFill  Print  Mail

Address:  http://127.0.0.1:9003/ch04/task2/code/UsingASCII.php    go

The ASCII code is: 88.          ⑥
The result of chr is: X.
```

Print a Formatted String

You can use the `printf` function to create formatted strings containing variables without having to perform manual string concatenation.

The `printf` function accepts two or more arguments. The first is a string consisting of normal text along with format rules that tell PHP how to display the string.

Each additional argument is taken as a value to be substituted for a placeholder in the format string. Substitution is performed according to the order in which placeholders and arguments appear. If your format string contains more placeholders than arguments, the last argument passed is used in all remaining substitutions.

Format rules begin with the percentage symbol (`%`).

The second argument is optional. It is a sign specifier with a value of plus (+) or minus (-) that tells PHP to force a number to display its sign.

The third argument is a padding signifier. The padding signifier consists of a single quotation mark followed by the character you want to use to pad your string. The default padding character is a single space.

The fourth argument is an optional alignment signifier. The minus (-) sign forces left justification. Without this signifier the default right alignment is used.

A width signifier is the optional fifth optional argument. This specifies the minimum number of characters the conversion should use.

The sixth argument is an optional precision signifier that sets the number of digits to be used after the decimal in a floating-point number.

The last argument is required and is a signifier for the type of data to be displayed.

The `printf` function returns the length of the outputted string.

Print a Formatted String

① Create a variable containing format rules.

② Create values to be used in the `printf` operation.

③ Use the `printf` function to print the formatted string to the output stream.

PrintFormatted.php

```php
<!DOCTYPE html PUBLIC "-//W3C//DTD XHTML 1.0 Strict//EN"
    "http://www.w3.org/TR/xhtml1/DTD/xhtml1-strict.dtd">
<html xmlns="http://www.w3.org/1999/xhtml" xml:lang="en" lang="en">
<head>
    <meta http-equiv="content-type" content="text/html; charset=utf-8" />
    <title>Printing a Formatted String</title>
</head>
<body>
<?php
    $format = "There are %d monkeys in the %s.";
    $num = 10.5;
    $location = 'Toaster';

    printf($format, $num, $location);    ◄── ③
?>
</body>
</html>
```

④ View the script in a Web browser.

The formatted string appears with the variables in place of the format rules.

Printing a Formatted String

Back | Forward | Stop | Refresh | Home | AutoFill | Print | Mail

Address: http://127.0.0.1:9003/ch04/task3/code/PrintFormatted.php   › go

There are 10 monkeys in the Toaster.   ◄── ④

Extra

The possible values for the type specifier are:

%	A literal percent character — no argument is required
b	An integer, presented as a binary number
c	An integer, presented as the character with that ASCII value
d	An integer, presented as a (signed) decimal number
e	Scientific notation (for example, 1.2e+2)
u	An integer, presented as an unsigned decimal number
f	A float, presented as a floating-point number
o	An integer, presented as an octal number
s	A string
x	An integer presented as a hexadecimal number (with lowercase letters)
X	An integer presented as a hexadecimal number (with uppercase letters)

Find String Length

Y ou can use the `strlen` function to find the number of characters in a given string.

The length of a string can be useful when processing strings. For example, you may use the length to set a loop condition in order to iterate over each character in a string to perform an operation or find a value.

Finding the length of a string is most often encountered when performing validation and normalization of data submitted to your script using Web forms. It is common to require that data conform to minimum and maximum length requirements. You can find the length of a string by passing either the string or a variable representing the string to the `strlen` function. An integer representing the number of characters in the string is the return value.

Escaped characters are treated as one character by the `strlen` function. This is also true of spaces. For example, the string "Column 1\Column 2" has 17, not 14 or 18, characters. This is true of all escaped characters, including quotes, control characters, and ASCII characters. To learn more about escape sequences, you can refer to the task "Create a String Variable" in Chapter 2.

If a numeric value is passed to the `strlen` function, it is converted to a string equivalent before being processed. Decimals and other noninteger characters are counted when the value is evaluated as a string. For example, the number 3.145 is found to have five characters, not four, as you might expect.

The length of a string is also useful when performing operations with built-in PHP string manipulation functions such as `substr` and `substr_compare`.

Find String Length

① Create a string variable and assign a value.

② Type `strlen`, passing the variable to the function as an argument.

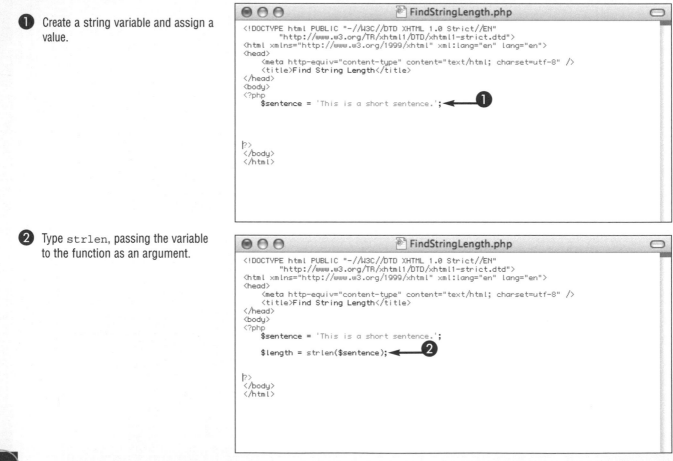

❸ Use the `echo` statement to write the length of your string to the output stream.

```
FindStringLength.php

<!DOCTYPE html PUBLIC "-//W3C//DTD XHTML 1.0 Strict//EN"
        "http://www.w3.org/TR/xhtml1/DTD/xhtml1-strict.dtd">
<html xmlns="http://www.w3.org/1999/xhtml" xml:lang="en" lang="en">
<head>
    <meta http-equiv="content-type" content="text/html; charset=utf-8" />
    <title>Find String Length</title>
</head>
<body>
<?php
    $sentence = 'This is a short sentence.';

    $length = strlen($sentence);

    echo "The length of the sentence is $length characters.<br />";     ◀──── ❸
?>
</body>
</html>
```

❹ View the script in a Web browser.

The length of the string appears.

```
                    @ Find String Length

Back   Forward   Stop   Refresh   Home   AutoFill   Print   Mail

Address:  http://127.0.0.1:9003/ch04/task4/code/FindStringLength.php        ▸ go

The length of the sentence is 25 characters.  ◀──── ❹
```

Extra

You can use the `strspn` function to determine the length of the longest portion of a string, or *substring*, that matches a given *mask*. The mask is a set of characters of which you want your substring to be composed. For example, you can search for numbers with a mask such as `0123456789`. The `strspn` function returns the length of the first portion of the target string that matches the mask. Optionally, you can pass an initial offset and a length from the offset to define a substring to which the mask should be applied.

TYPE THIS:		RESULTS:

`$target = '125000';`
`$mask = "0123456789";`
`$num = strspn($target, $mask);`
`echo "The new salary is $num figures.";`
	→	The browser displays "The new salary is 6 figures."

To find the longest portion of a string that does not match a given mask, you can use the `strcspn` function. Like `strspn`, it accepts a target string, a mask string, an optional offset, and an optional length. The return value is the length of the matching substring.

TYPE THIS:		RESULTS:

`$target = 'The new salary is 125000.';`
`$mask = "0123456789";`
`$num = strcspn($target, $mask);`
`echo $num;`
	→	The browser displays 18, which is the length of the longest portion of the string not matching the mask.

Convert a String into an Array

You can change a string into an array of characters using the `explode` function. The `explode` function accepts three arguments. The first argument is a separator by which you divide the string. Each occurrence of the separator in the source string is used as a boundary separating one substring from another. If the separator is an empty string or null value, `explode` returns false. Otherwise, each substring is pushed into an array returned by the function. The array elements are sorted in order of their occurrence in the source string. It is important to note that the separator itself is not returned in the array.

The second argument is the source string you want to transform into an array. You can pass either an explicit string or a variable representing a string. If the string does not contain any instances of the separator, `explode` returns an array containing a single element equal to the source string.

The third argument is optional and represents the maximum number of divisions the `explode` function should return. If a limit is set, the last entry in the array is the value of the remainder of the string. Keep in mind that, because no `explode` operation is performed on the remainder, any occurrences of the separator are included.

You can use the `list` and `each` statements along with `explode` to split a delimited string into individual variables. By passing the `each` function the result of an `explode` operation, you can extract values from a string. You can use the `list` statement to assign those values to distinct variables. To learn more about the `each` function and `list` statement, see the task "Using the List Statement" in Chapter 3.

Convert a String into an Array

① Create a variable representing a delimited string.

```
● ○ ○                            ConvertString.php                            ○
<!DOCTYPE html PUBLIC "-//W3C//DTD XHTML 1.0 Strict//EN"
        "http://www.w3.org/TR/xhtml1/DTD/xhtml1-strict.dtd">
<html xmlns="http://www.w3.org/1999/xhtml" xml:lang="en" lang="en">
<head>
    <meta http-equiv="content-type" content="text/html; charset=utf-8" />
    <title>Convert a String into an Array</title>
</head>
<body>
<?php
    $sentence = 'This is a short sentence.';          ◄━━ ①

?>
</body>
</html>
```

② Create a variable to represent the result of an `explode` operation.

```
● ○ ○                            ConvertString.php                            ○
<!DOCTYPE html PUBLIC "-//W3C//DTD XHTML 1.0 Strict//EN"
        "http://www.w3.org/TR/xhtml1/DTD/xhtml1-strict.dtd">
<html xmlns="http://www.w3.org/1999/xhtml" xml:lang="en" lang="en">
<head>
    <meta http-equiv="content-type" content="text/html; charset=utf-8" />
    <title>Convert a String into an Array</title>
</head>
<body>
<?php
    $sentence = 'This is a short sentence.';

    $words =  ◄━━ ②

?>
</body>
</html>
```

③ Call explode, passing the delimiter and the string as arguments.

④ Use the print_r function to view the resulting array.

```
<!DOCTYPE html PUBLIC "-//W3C//DTD XHTML 1.0 Strict//EN"
    "http://www.w3.org/TR/xhtml1/DTD/xhtml1-strict.dtd">
<html xmlns="http://www.w3.org/1999/xhtml" xml:lang="en" lang="en">
<head>
    <meta http-equiv="content-type" content="text/html; charset=utf-8" />
    <title>Convert a String into an Array</title>
</head>
<body>
<?php
    $sentence = 'This is a short sentence.';

    $words = explode(' ', $sentence);      ◄── ③

    print_r($words);     ◄── ④
?>
</body>
</html>
```

ConvertString.php

⑤ View the script in a Web browser.

The string is split into pieces based on the separator passed to explode.

Convert a String into an Array

http://127.0.0.1:9003/ch04/task5/code/ConvertString.php

Array ([0] => This [1] => is [2] => a [3] => short [4] => sentence.) ◄── ⑤

Extra

You can use the implode function to create a string from an array of values. The implode function accepts two arguments. The first is a string to be used as a delimiter between each array element in the final string. You can pass an empty string to have the array elements joined with no delimiter.

TYPE THIS:
```
$vals = array('Toby', 'Joe', 'Boudreaux';
$delim = ' ';
$name = implode($delim, $vals);
echo "The name is $name.<br />"
```

RESULTS:
The browser displays "The name is Toby Joe Boudreaux."

You can use the implode function with the explode function to replace all delimiters in a delimited string.

TYPE THIS:
```
$commaDelim = "Toby,Joe,Boudreaux";
$pipeDelim = implode('|', explode(',', $commaDelim));
echo $pipeDelim;
```

RESULTS:
The browser displays "Toby|Joe|Boudreaux"

Trim a String

Y ou can remove the leading and trailing whitespace in a string by using the trim function.

The trim function accepts the target string as an argument and returns a version with all trailing and leading whitespace characters removed. Whitespace characters are the space tab, newline, carriage return, NULL byte, and vertical tab characters.

The trim function is useful when processing data submitted through Web forms or when reading data from files and streams. In most cases, whitespace at the beginning or end of a string is meaningless and its removal will not hinder processing.

The trim function accepts an optional second argument representing characters to be trimmed. If this parameter is specified, the characters contained in the string are removed instead of the default whitespace characters. The list should

be passed as a string. To specify a range of characters, you can pass the beginning and ending characters separated by the range operator (..).

You can trim data from only the leading side with the ltrim function. The ltrim function performs a left trim. Much like the trim function, ltrim accepts a string as an argument, followed by an optional list of characters to be trimmed. The return value is a string minus any leading whitespace or special characters.

The rtrim function performs a right trim. The rtrim function is used exactly as the ltrim function. You can use ltrim and rtrim together to perform operations more complicated than trim allows. For example, you may want to trim all whitespace from the end of a string and trim all whitespace except tabs from the beginning. You can use the second argument of the ltrim function to specify all whitespace characters minus the tab character.

Trim a String

① Create a variable representing a string with leading and trailing whitespace characters.

```
TrimAString.php
<!DOCTYPE html PUBLIC "-//W3C//DTD XHTML 1.0 Strict//EN"
        "http://www.w3.org/TR/xhtml1/DTD/xhtml1-strict.dtd">
<html xmlns="http://www.w3.org/1999/xhtml" xml:lang="en" lang="en">
<head>
    <meta http-equiv="content-type" content="text/html; charset=utf-8" />
    <title>Trim a String</title>
</head>
<body>
<?php
    $sentence = "    This is a short sentence.\r\n";      ←①

?>
</body>
</html>
```

② Using ltrim, remove the whitespace from the string.

③ Use the echo statement to print the string.

```
TrimAString.php
<!DOCTYPE html PUBLIC "-//W3C//DTD XHTML 1.0 Strict//EN"
        "http://www.w3.org/TR/xhtml1/DTD/xhtml1-strict.dtd">
<html xmlns="http://www.w3.org/1999/xhtml" xml:lang="en" lang="en">
<head>
    <meta http-equiv="content-type" content="text/html; charset=utf-8" />
    <title>Trim a String</title>
</head>
<body>
<?php
    $sentence = "    This is a short sentence.\r\n";

    $sentence = ltrim($sentence);      ←②

    echo "($sentence)<br />";      ←③

?>
</body>
</html>
```

④ Using `rtrim`, remove the trailing whitespace and assign the result to your variable.

⑤ Echo the variable to see the whitespace removed.

```
<!DOCTYPE html PUBLIC "-//W3C//DTD XHTML 1.0 Strict//EN"
    "http://www.w3.org/TR/xhtml1/DTD/xhtml1-strict.dtd">
<html xmlns="http://www.w3.org/1999/xhtml" xml:lang="en" lang="en">
<head>
    <meta http-equiv="content-type" content="text/html; charset=utf-8" />
    <title>Trim a String</title>
</head>
<body>
<?php
    $sentence = "    This is a short sentence.\r\n";

    $sentence = ltrim($sentence);

    echo "($sentence)<br />";

    $sentence = rtrim($sentence);          ← ④

    echo "($sentence)";                    ← ⑤
?>
</body>
</html>
```

⑥ View the script in a Web browser.

The whitespace is removed from the string.

Address: http://127.0.0.1:9003/ch04/task6/code/TrimAString.php

(This is a short sentence.) ← ⑥
(This is a short sentence.)

Extra

You can add whitespace to a string using the `str_pad` function. While any character or data may be used in the `str_pad` function, adding whitespace characters is useful when writing strings of variable lengths to the output stream while trying to maintain a column format. The `str_pad` function has two required arguments. The first is the input string you want to pad. The second argument is the number of characters the final string should be.

Optionally, you can specify a third argument representing the string to be used to pad the input string until it reaches the specified length. By default, this value is a single-space character. The fourth argument can be one of three PHP constants representing the side or sides to which the pad data should be added to the input string. The options are `STR_PAD_RIGHT`, `STR_PAD_LEFT`, and `STR_PAD_BOTH`, representing the right, left, and both sides, respectively. The default option is `STR_PAD_RIGHT`.

TYPE THIS:

```
$input = 'Hello!';
echo str_pad($input, 20, '*', STR_PAD_BOTH);
```

RESULTS:

The browser displays
"*******Hello!*******"

Compare Strings

You can perform a case-sensitive comparison of two strings using the `strcmp` function. Each string is compared using the ASCII value of the characters of which it is composed. To learn more about ASCII, see the task "Using ASCII Values."

The `strcmp` function accepts two arguments representing the strings to be compared. It returns an integer value in one of three ranges depending on the result of the comparison. If the first string has an ASCII value less than that of the second, a number less than zero is returned. If the two strings are equal, the return value is zero. A value greater than zero is returned when the first string is greater than the second.

If one of the strings exactly matches the first characters of the other, the return value represents the number of additional characters in the longer string. If an empty string is passed as one of the two values, the number of characters in the nonempty string is returned. If the first string is the shorter or is empty, the return value is negative. If the second is shorter or empty, the return value is positive.

String comparisons are helpful when sorting strings based on their values or comparing preset values against user-submitted input. For example, you can compare a password submitted by a user against a preset password in order to grant or revoke access to parts of your site.

If you use the `strcmp` function as the condition in an `if` statement, any negative or zero value is interpreted as `false`. Positive values returned from `strcmp` are treated as `true`.

Compare Strings

① Create a variable representing a string.

② Create a second variable representing a different string value.

```
CompareStrings.php

<!DOCTYPE html PUBLIC "-//W3C//DTD XHTML 1.0 Strict//EN"
        "http://www.w3.org/TR/xhtml1/DTD/xhtml1-strict.dtd">
<html xmlns="http://www.w3.org/1999/xhtml" xml:lang="en" lang="en">
<head>
    <meta http-equiv="content-type" content="text/html; charset=utf-8" />
    <title>Trim a String</title>
</head>
<body>
<?php
    $first = 'one';        ⟵①

    $second = 'two';    ⟵②



?>
</body>
</html>
```

③ Use the `strcmp` function to compare the two variables.

```
CompareStrings.php

<!DOCTYPE html PUBLIC "-//W3C//DTD XHTML 1.0 Strict//EN"
        "http://www.w3.org/TR/xhtml1/DTD/xhtml1-strict.dtd">
<html xmlns="http://www.w3.org/1999/xhtml" xml:lang="en" lang="en">
<head>
    <meta http-equiv="content-type" content="text/html; charset=utf-8" />
    <title>Trim a String</title>
</head>
<body>
<?php
    $first = 'one';

    $second = 'two';

    $result = strcmp($first, $second);    ⟵③


?>
</body>
</html>
```

④ Use the echo statement to
print the value returned from
the function.

```
CompareStrings.php

<!DOCTYPE html PUBLIC "-//W3C//DTD XHTML 1.0 Strict//EN"
        "http://www.w3.org/TR/xhtml1/DTD/xhtml1-strict.dtd">
<html xmlns="http://www.w3.org/1999/xhtml" xml:lang="en" lang="en">
<head>
    <meta http-equiv="content-type" content="text/html; charset=utf-8" />
    <title>Trim a String</title>
</head>
<body>
<?php
    $first = 'one';

    $second = 'two';

    $result = strcmp($first, $second);

    echo "The result of the comparison was $result.<br />";   ← ④
?>
</body>
</html>
```

⑤ View the script in a Web
browser.

The numeric return value of the
strcmp function is displayed.

```
@ Compare Strings

Address: http://127.0.0.1:9003/ch04/task7/code/CompareStrings.php    go

The result of the comparison was -5.   ← ⑤
```

You can perform case-insensitive string comparisons using the strcasecmp function. The
function performs exactly as the strcmp function.

TYPE THIS:

```
$first = 'Hello!';
$second = 'HeLlO!';
if(strcasecmp($first, $second) == 0){
  echo "The strings $first and $second are
  equivalent.<br />";
}
```

RESULTS:

The browser displays "The strings Hello!
And HeLlO! are equivalent."

The strncasecmp function performs a case-insensitive comparison of two strings up to a given
number of characters. For example, you can compare only the first three letters of strings of varying
lengths. The rstrncasecmp function performs as the strcasecmp function, but accepts a third
argument representing the number of letters to use in the comparison.

TYPE THIS:

```
$first = 'Hello, Friend!';
$second = 'HeLlO!';
if(strncasecmp($first, $second, 5) == 0){
  echo "The strings $first and $second are
  equivalent.<br />";
}
```

RESULTS:

The browser displays "The strings Hello,
Friend! And HeLlO! are equivalent."

121

Access or Replace Characters by Position in a String

Y ou can access a character in a string using curly braces ({ }). By typing the name of a string variable followed by curly braces with a numeric index you can extract the character at the index as if the string were an array.

PHP provides a mechanism for finding the character at a given position in a string. Like accessing array elements using square brackets, the index is zero-based.

You can use any expression that returns a number inside the curly braces. For example, for a string variable $name you can access the last character using $name{strlen($name)-1}. Because the strlen function returns the number of characters in the $name variable, but the character indexing is a zero-based system, you must subtract 1 from the length to find the last character.

You can replace a character in a string by assigning a new value to the position the character occupies. For example, for a $name variable with a value of 'Toby Boudreaux' you can replace the first character using $name{0} = 'B'. This changes the value of the $name string to 'Boby Boudreaux.'

You can add a character to the end of a string by using an offset equal to the length of the string. To add a character to $name, you can type $name{strlen($name)} = '!', which results result in a $name variable equal to 'Boby Boudreaux!'.

It is possible to assign an offset greater than the length of a string. For a string $str with a value of 'ABC' you can add 20 spaces by typing $str{strlen($str)+20} = ' ';.

If you use a negative offset, an error appears.

Access or Replace Characters by Position in a String

① Create a variable representing a string.

② Find a character in the variable using curly braces and a numeric index.

```
AccessReplace.php
<!DOCTYPE html PUBLIC "-//W3C//DTD XHTML 1.0 Strict//EN"
        "http://www.w3.org/TR/xhtml1/DTD/xhtml1-strict.dtd">
<html xmlns="http://www.w3.org/1999/xhtml" xml:lang="en" lang="en">
<head>
    <meta http-equiv="content-type" content="text/html; charset=utf-8" />
    <title>Access or Replace Characters by Position in a String</title>
</head>
<body>
<?php
    $source = 'ABCDEFGHIJKLMNOPQRSTUVWXYZ';        ①

    $char = $source{4};        ②



?>
</body>
</html>
```

③ Print the character to the output stream.

④ Using curly braces, assign a new character for a given position.

```
AccessReplace.php
<!DOCTYPE html PUBLIC "-//W3C//DTD XHTML 1.0 Strict//EN"
        "http://www.w3.org/TR/xhtml1/DTD/xhtml1-strict.dtd">
<html xmlns="http://www.w3.org/1999/xhtml" xml:lang="en" lang="en">
<head>
    <meta http-equiv="content-type" content="text/html; charset=utf-8" />
    <title>Access or Replace Characters by Position in a String</title>
</head>
<body>
<?php
    $source = 'ABCDEFGHIJKLMNOPQRSTUVWXYZ';

    $char = $source{4};

    echo "The char at position 4 is: $char.<br />";        ③

    $source{4} = ' ';        ④

?>
</body>
</html>
```

⑤ Print the result to the output stream using `echo`.

```
                                    AccessReplace.php
<!DOCTYPE html PUBLIC "-//W3C//DTD XHTML 1.0 Strict//EN"
        "http://www.w3.org/TR/xhtml1/DTD/xhtml1-strict.dtd">
<html xmlns="http://www.w3.org/1999/xhtml" xml:lang="en" lang="en">
<head>
    <meta http-equiv="content-type" content="text/html; charset=utf-8" />
    <title>Access or Replace Characters by Position in a String</title>
</head>
<body>
<?php
    $source = 'ABCDEFGHIJKLMNOPQRSTUVWXYZ';

    $char = $source{4};

    echo "The char at position 4 is: $char.<br />";

    $source{4} = ' ';

    echo "The string is ($source).";          ← ⑤
?>
</body>
</html>
```

⑥ View the script in a Web browser.

The source string is modified.

```
                 @ Access or Replace Characters by Position in a...
  Back  Forward  Stop  Refresh  Home  AutoFill  Print  Mail
  Address:  http://127.0.0.1:9003/ch04/task8/code/AccessReplace.php        go

The char at position 4 is: E.
The string is (ABCD FGHIJKLMNOPQRSTUVWXYZ).   ← ⑥
```

Extra

You can use a counter variable in a loop to iterate over each character of a string. To replace a character in a string using curly braces, use the assignment operator (=).

TYPE THIS:

```
$source = 'ABCDEFGHIJKLMNOPQRSTUVWXYZ';
for($i=0; $i<strlen($source); $i++){
  $char = $source{$i};
  echo "The character at $i is: $char.<br />";
}
```

RESULTS:

The browser displays a message for each character in the string.

Search for a Substring or Character

Y ou can find the position of a substring using the strpos and strrpos functions.

The strpos function finds and returns the first occurrence of a substring in a given string. The strpos function accepts two required arguments. The first is the string in which PHP should search. The second is the string for which PHP should search. There is an optional third argument representing an offset to be used in the search. For example, an offset of 3 tells PHP to begin the search at the third character.

The strpos function returns a Boolean false if no occurrence of the search string is found. If the search string is found, the position of the first character of the search string inside the target string is returned. It is important to note that a value of zero (0) may be returned if the target string begins with the substring. This requires special

consideration for how the result of strpos is used, because a value of 0 can be interpreted by PHP to represent a Boolean false. For example, searching for the string "Toby" inside the target string "TobyJoe" would return a zero (0) value. It is best to test the result using if(strpos("TobyJoe", "Toby") !== false).

The strrpos function returns the position of the last occurrence of a search string in a target string. The arguments for strrpos are the same as those for strpos. There is a target string, a search string, and an optional integer offset. If the search string is found, the position of the first matching character is returned. If there is no match, a Boolean false value is returned.

To prevent confusion when using the result of strpos and strrpos in a conditional statement, you can use the === operator. Your condition might be written as if(strpos('toby', 'to') === false).

Search for a Substring or Character

① Create a variable representing a string.

② Create a second variable representing a string for which to search.

```
SearchSubstring.php
<!DOCTYPE html PUBLIC "-//W3C//DTD XHTML 1.0 Strict//EN"
        "http://www.w3.org/TR/xhtml1/DTD/xhtml1-strict.dtd">
<html xmlns="http://www.w3.org/1999/xhtml" xml:lang="en" lang="en">
<head>
    <meta http-equiv="content-type" content="text/html; charset=utf-8" />
    <title>Search for a Substring or Character</title>
</head>
<body>
<?php
    $source = 'This is the first sentence in the book.';      ①

    $search = 'the';      ②

?>
</body>
</html>
```

③ Using strpos find the first occurrence of the search string.

④ Using echo, print the value to the output stream.

```
SearchSubstring.php
<!DOCTYPE html PUBLIC "-//W3C//DTD XHTML 1.0 Strict//EN"
        "http://www.w3.org/TR/xhtml1/DTD/xhtml1-strict.dtd">
<html xmlns="http://www.w3.org/1999/xhtml" xml:lang="en" lang="en">
<head>
    <meta http-equiv="content-type" content="text/html; charset=utf-8" />
    <title>Search for a Substring or Character</title>
</head>
<body>
<?php
    $source = 'This is the first sentence in the book.';

    $search = 'the';

    $pos = strpos($source, $search);      ③

    echo "The first position is: $pos.<br />";      ④

?>
</body>
</html>
```

⑤ Use strrpos to find the last occurrence of the search string.

⑥ Using echo, print the value to the output stream.

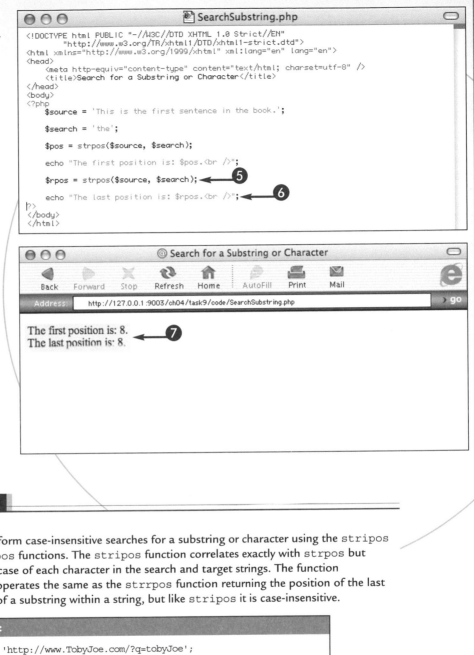

```
SearchSubstring.php
<!DOCTYPE html PUBLIC "-//W3C//DTD XHTML 1.0 Strict//EN"
        "http://www.w3.org/TR/xhtml1/DTD/xhtml1-strict.dtd">
<html xmlns="http://www.w3.org/1999/xhtml" xml:lang="en" lang="en">
<head>
    <meta http-equiv="content-type" content="text/html; charset=utf-8" />
    <title>Search for a Substring or Character</title>
</head>
<body>
<?php
    $source = 'This is the first sentence in the book.';

    $search = 'the';

    $pos = strpos($source, $search);

    echo "The first position is: $pos.<br />";

    $rpos = strpos($source, $search);        ← ⑤

    echo "The last position is: $rpos.<br />";    ← ⑥
?>
</body>
</html>
```

⑦ View the script in a Web browser.

The first and last positions of the search string are found

```
Search for a Substring or Character
Back  Forward  Stop  Refresh  Home  AutoFill  Print  Mail
Address: http://127.0.0.1:9003/ch04/task9/code/SearchSubstring.php    › go

The first position is: 8.    ← ⑦
The last position is: 8.
```

Extra

You can perform case-insensitive searches for a substring or character using the stripos and strripos functions. The stripos function correlates exactly with strpos but ignores the case of each character in the search and target strings. The function strripos operates the same as the strrpos function returning the position of the last occurrence of a substring within a string, but like stripos it is case-insensitive.

TYPE THIS:

```
$source = 'http://www.TobyJoe.com/?q=tobyJoe';
$search = 'tobyjoe';
$pos = stripos($source, $search);
$rpos = strripos($source, $search);
echo "The first occurrence is: $pos and the second is: $rpos.<br />";
```

↓

RESULTS:

The browser displays "The first occurrence is: 11 and the second is: 26."

125

Extract or Replace a Substring

Y ou can access a portion of a string, or a *substring* using the substr function.

The substr function accepts two required arguments. The first specifies the string from which the substring is extracted. The second is an integer representing the offset to be used in the extraction. To extract the entire string you can specify an offset of zero (0). To extract all but the first character, you can specify an offset of one (1).

The substr function accepts an optional third parameter specifying the length of the substring.

You can replace a substring occurrence using substr_replace. Like the substr function, you specify the range of characters in your substring by passing an offset and optional length argument. The first argument is the

source string. The second is the string value to use in the replacement operation. The third argument is the offset. The fourth is an optional value specifying the number of characters from the offset to include in the replacement.

You can replace a substring with a string of a different length. The characters making up the substring are removed before the replacement string is inserted. You can remove a portion of a string by passing an empty replacement argument to substr_replace.

If the offset passed to either of these functions is a negative number, the starting position of the substring is set to the length of the string minus the offset. When handling a negative substring offset, PHP begins counting with 1, not 0 as with other string and array index operations.

Extract or Replace a Substring

① Create a variable representing a string.

② Create a second variable representing a string to use as a replacement.

```
ExtractSubstring.php

<!DOCTYPE html PUBLIC "-//W3C//DTD XHTML 1.0 Strict//EN"
        "http://www.w3.org/TR/xhtml1/DTD/xhtml1-strict.dtd">
<html xmlns="http://www.w3.org/1999/xhtml" xml:lang="en" lang="en">
<head>
    <meta http-equiv="content-type" content="text/html; charset=utf-8" />
    <title>Extract or Replace a Substring</title>
</head>
<body>
<?php
    $source = 'My favorite food is pizza.';      ①

    $newFood = 'cake';      ②


?>
</body>
</html>
```

③ Using substr, find a substring, passing in an offset and length.

④ Echo the value of the substring.

```
ExtractSubstring.php

<!DOCTYPE html PUBLIC "-//W3C//DTD XHTML 1.0 Strict//EN"
        "http://www.w3.org/TR/xhtml1/DTD/xhtml1-strict.dtd">
<html xmlns="http://www.w3.org/1999/xhtml" xml:lang="en" lang="en">
<head>
    <meta http-equiv="content-type" content="text/html; charset=utf-8" />
    <title>Extract or Replace a Substring</title>
</head>
<body>
<?php
    $source = 'My favorite food is pizza.';

    $newFood = 'cake';

    $currentFood = substr($source, 20, 5);      ③

    echo "My favorite food was $currentFood.<br />";      ④


?>
</body>
</html>
```

⑤ Use `substr_replace` to replace the substring.

⑥ Using `echo`, print the value to the output stream.

ExtractSubstring.php

```php
<!DOCTYPE html PUBLIC "-//W3C//DTD XHTML 1.0 Strict//EN"
    "http://www.w3.org/TR/xhtml1/DTD/xhtml1-strict.dtd">
<html xmlns="http://www.w3.org/1999/xhtml" xml:lang="en" lang="en">
<head>
    <meta http-equiv="content-type" content="text/html; charset=utf-8" />
    <title>Extract or Replace a Substring</title>
</head>
<body>
<?php
    $source = 'My favorite food is pizza.';

    $newFood = 'cake';

    $currentFood = substr($source, 20, 5);

    echo "My favorite food was $currentFood.<br />";

    $source = substr_replace($source, $newFood, 20, 5);  ⑤

    echo $source;  ⑥
?>
</body>
</html>
```

⑦ View the script in a Web browser.

The results of the `substr` and `substr_replace` operations appear.

@ Extract or Replace a Substring

| Back | Forward | Stop | Refresh | Home | AutoFill | Print | Mail |

Address: http://127.0.0.1:9003/ch04/task10/code/ExtractSubstring.php › go

My favorite food was pizza. ⑦
My favorite food is cake.

Extra

You can find the number of occurrences of a substring in a string using the `substr_count` function. The `substr_count` function is case-sensitive. It accepts two arguments. The first is the target string in which PHP searches and the second is the substring for which PHP searches. The return value is an integer representing the number of occurrences. If there is no match, `substr_count` returns `false`.

TYPE THIS:

```php
$votes = '1,0,1,1,0,0,1,0,1,1,0,1,1,1,0,0';
$search = '1';
$count = substr_count($votes, $search);
echo "There were $num votes for $search.<br />";
```

RESULTS:

→ The browser displays "There were 9 votes for 1."

Replace All Instances of a Word

You can replace all instances of a word or substring in a target string using the `str_replace` function.

The `str_replace` function accepts three required arguments and an optional fourth argument. The first three represent the search value, replacement value, and search target, in that order. Each of these values can be a string, number, Boolean, or array.

The fourth argument represents the number of successful replace operations performed by the call to `str_replace`. The value is passed as a reference. This causes the value of the variable you pass to be set as soon as `str_replace` completes all operations.

The return value of `str_replace` is either a string or array depending on the type of the third argument. If the search target is an array of strings, the return value is an array of strings with all instances of the search value replaced with the replacement value.

If the search and replace values pass as arrays, each value in the search array is replaced by the value in the replacement array with a correlating index. If the replacement array has fewer values than the search array or if the search value is an array and the replacement value is not, the last replacement value is used for the remainder of the search values.

For example, you can replace all vowels in a string using `str_replace(array('a','e','i','o','u'), '*', 'Hello');`. The return value is a string with the value `'H*ll*'`.

To perform a similar operation on an array of strings, you can use `str_replace(array('a','e','i','o','u'), '*', array('Hello', 'Goodbye'));`. The value returned is an array containing `'H*ll*'` as the first element and `'G**dby*'` as the second.

Replace All Instances of a Word

① Create a variable representing a string.

② Create a second variable representing a string to use as a search value.

③ Create a variable representing a string to use as a replacement value.

```
ReplaceAll.php
<!DOCTYPE html PUBLIC "-//W3C//DTD XHTML 1.0 Strict//EN"
    "http://www.w3.org/TR/xhtml1/DTD/xhtml1-strict.dtd">
<html xmlns="http://www.w3.org/1999/xhtml" xml:lang="en" lang="en">
<head>
    <meta http-equiv="content-type" content="text/html; charset=utf-8" />
    <title>Replace All Instances of a Word</title>
</head>
<body>
<?php
    $a = 'How much wood would a woodchuck chuck if a woodchuck could chuck wood?';    ①

    $find = 'woodchuck';    ②

    $replace = 'cow';    ③


?>
</body>
</html>
```

④ Using `str_replace` to replace all occurrences of the search term with the replacement.

```
ReplaceAll.php
<!DOCTYPE html PUBLIC "-//W3C//DTD XHTML 1.0 Strict//EN"
    "http://www.w3.org/TR/xhtml1/DTD/xhtml1-strict.dtd">
<html xmlns="http://www.w3.org/1999/xhtml" xml:lang="en" lang="en">
<head>
    <meta http-equiv="content-type" content="text/html; charset=utf-8" />
    <title>Replace All Instances of a Word</title>
</head>
<body>
<?php
    $a = 'How much wood would a woodchuck chuck if a woodchuck could chuck wood?';

    $find = 'woodchuck';

    $replace = 'cow';

    $b = str_replace($find, $replace, $a);    ④

?>
</body>
</html>
```

5 Use `echo` to print the result.

```
ReplaceAll.php

<!DOCTYPE html PUBLIC "-//W3C//DTD XHTML 1.0 Strict//EN"
        "http://www.w3.org/TR/xhtml1/DTD/xhtml1-strict.dtd">
<html xmlns="http://www.w3.org/1999/xhtml" xml:lang="en" lang="en">
<head>
    <meta http-equiv="content-type" content="text/html; charset=utf-8" />
    <title>Replace All Instances of a Word</title>
</head>
<body>
<?php
    $a = 'How much wood would a woodchuck chuck if a woodchuck could chuck wood?';

    $find = 'woodchuck';

    $replace = 'cow';

    $b = str_replace($find, $replace, $a);

    echo $b;        ◀── 5
?>
</body>
</html>
```

6 View the script in a Web browser.

The result of the search-and-replace operation appears.

```
@ Replace All Instances of a Word

Back  Forward  Stop  Refresh  Home  AutoFill  Print  Mail

Address:  http://127.0.0.1:9003/ch04/task11/code/ReplaceAll.php      › go

How much wood would a cow chuck if a cow could chuck wood?  ◀── 6
```

Extra

You can perform a case-insensitive string replacement operation using `eregi_replace`.
The arguments and return values are the same as those for the `str_replace` function
but the operation ignores the case of each character in the target and search strings.

TYPE THIS:

```
$target = 'Everyone went to the sea.';
$search = 'e';
$replace = '*';
$modified = eregi_replace($search, $replace, $target);
echo $modified;
```

RESULTS:

→ The browser
displays '*v*ryon*
w*nt to th* s*a.'

Work with HTML Text

You can use the `htmlspecialchars` and `htmlentities` functions to convert special HTML characters in a given string to their encoded entity values. The character entity representing a given character begins with an ampersand (&) and is followed by a name or number for the character. The entity is terminated by a semicolon (;). For example, the character entity for a trademark is often written as `&trade;` where "trade" is the name of the entity.

When a Web browser renders an HTML document, it replaces all encoded entities with their human-readable characters or symbols. The purpose of encoding entities is that HTML requires certain characters to have a special meaning outside their character value. The ampersand with which all encoded entities begin is an example of a character given special meaning. To have a Web browser display an ampersand, you type `&amp;`.

The `htmlspecialchars` function converts the most common HTML characters to their character entity values. The `htmlspecialchars` function replaces the ampersand (&), double quote ("), single quote ('), and less than (<) and greater than (>) characters with their associated entity reference value. The arguments for the `htmlspecialchars` function are the required string to be converted, followed by an optional quote-style flag and character set name. The quote-style flag can be one of three PHP constants. The options are `ENT_COMPAT`, `ENT_QUOTES`, and `ENT_NOQUOTES`. They tell PHP to convert only double quotes, both double and single quotes, or no quotes, respectively.

You can use `htmlentities` to translate all HTML special characters to their entity references. The arguments and functionality is the same as the `htmlspecialchars` function. The return value for each function is the source string with all replacements made.

Work with HTML Text

① Create a variable representing a string containing special characters.

② Use the `echo` statement to print the variable to the output stream.

③ Using `htmlspecialchars`, replace the common characters with their entity references.

④ Display the result using the `echo` statement.

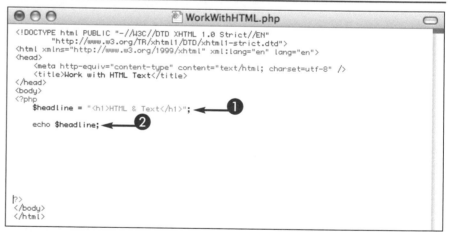

⑤ Use `htmlentities` to replace all HTML characters in the string.

⑥ Display the result with the `echo` statement.

```
WorkWithHTML.php
<!DOCTYPE html PUBLIC "-//W3C//DTD XHTML 1.0 Strict//EN"
        "http://www.w3.org/TR/xhtml1/DTD/xhtml1-strict.dtd">
<html xmlns="http://www.w3.org/1999/xhtml" xml:lang="en" lang="en">
<head>
    <meta http-equiv="content-type" content="text/html; charset=utf-8" />
    <title>Work with HTML Text</title>
</head>
<body>
<?php
    $headline = "<h1>HTML & Text</h1>";

    echo $headline;

    $h2 = htmlspecialchars($headline);

    echo "$h2<br />";

    $h3 = htmlentities($headline);          ← ⑤

    echo "$h3<br />";          ← ⑥
?>
</body>
</html>
```

⑦ View the script in a Web browser.

The string appears with each level of characters encoded.

```
Work with HTML Text
Address: http://127.0.0.1:9003/ch04/task12/code/WorkWithHTML.php
```

HTML & Text   ← ⑦

```
<h1>HTML & Text</h1>
<h1>HTML & Text</h1>
```

Extra

You can use the `strip_tags` function to remove all HTML or XML tags from a string. This is useful when extracting content from a markup document or when handling user-submitted information that contains harmful HTML. The `strip_tags` function accepts a string as an argument and returns a string with all tags removed.

TYPE THIS:

```
$html = '<p>He was <em>very</em> angry!</p>';
$content = strip_tags($html);
echo $content;
```

RESULTS:

The browserdisplays "He was very angry!"

The `nl2br` function replaces all occurrences of a newline character (`\n`) with an XHTML-compliant line-break element (`<br />`).

TYPE THIS:

```
$content = "The First Line\nGoes Above the Second";
$html = nl2br($content);
echo $content;
```

RESULTS:

The browser displays "The First Line Goes Above the Second".

Work with Unicode Text

PHP5 provides limited support for encoding data according to the Unicode specification. Unicode is a system created to map character data to numbers according to a universal specification. When transporting data from one computer system or language to another, a common system of encoding is of great benefit. Before Unicode, there were hundreds of unique and unrelated encodings. While PHP does not fully support the Unicode specification, methods are provided to allow you to encode a string into a Unicode-friendly format.

The `utf8_encode` function allows you to encode a string of characters into a series of numeric values according to the UTF-8 specification. UTF-8 stands for *UCS Transformation Format 8* and is one of many encoding schemes defined as part of the Unicode project. Encoding data as Unicode is useful when dealing with languages with special characters or when interoperating with disparate computer systems.

The `utf8_encode` function accepts a string in ISO-8859-1 format and returns a string encoded in UTF-8. To decode the string back to ISO-8859-1, you can use the `utf8_decode` function.

Due to the limited support for Unicode in PHP, you should be careful when using data returned from a `utf8_encode` operation. It is not uncommon that unmapped characters are used. The `utf8_encode` function uses a question mark (?) to signify an unknown character. This can lead to problems when inserting encoded data directly into a database, for example. To prevent data loss, it is best to check the result of `utf8_encode` against the source string using `utf8_decode`. If a decoded version of the string does not equal the original string, the encoding function may have encountered unrecognizable data.

Work with Unicode Text

1. Create a string containing special characters.

2. Using the `utf8_encode` function, convert the string to Unicode.

3. Print the resulting string using an `echo` statement.

4. Using `utf8_decode`, convert the string back to ISO-8559-1.

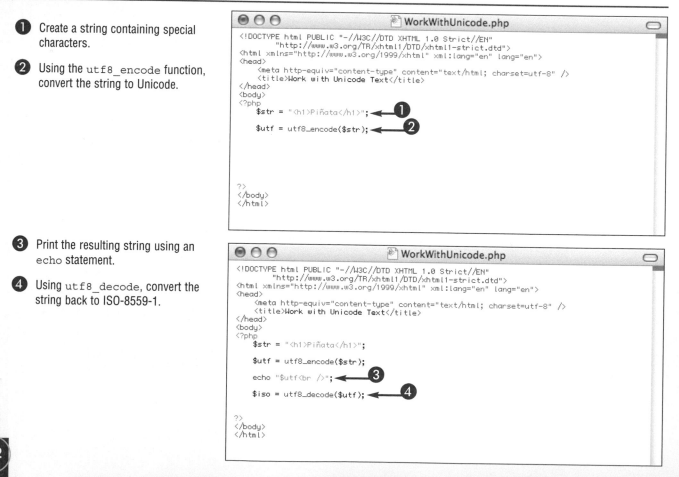

5 Print the result to the output stream using an echo statement.

```
⬤⬤⬤                    📄 WorkWithUnicode.php                         ⬭
<!DOCTYPE html PUBLIC "-//W3C//DTD XHTML 1.0 Strict//EN"
        "http://www.w3.org/TR/xhtml1/DTD/xhtml1-strict.dtd">
<html xmlns="http://www.w3.org/1999/xhtml" xml:lang="en" lang="en">
<head>
    <meta http-equiv="content-type" content="text/html; charset=utf-8" />
    <title>Work with Unicode Text</title>
</head>
<body>
<?php
    $str = "<h1>Piñata</h1>";

    $utf = utf8_encode($str);

    echo "$utf<br />";

    $iso = utf8_decode($utf);

    echo "$iso<br />";    ⬅ 5

?>
</body>
</html>
```

6 View the script in a Web browser.

The string is encoded to UTF-8 then decoded back to ISO-8559-1.

```
⬤⬤⬤                    @ Work with Unicode Text                      ⬭
 ◀      ▶     ✖      🔄      🏠      📄       🖨       ✉        e
Back  Forward Stop  Refresh  Home  AutoFill  Print   Mail
Address:    http://127.0.0.1:9003/ch04/task13/code/WorkWithUnicode.php    ▸ go


PiÃ±ata

           ⬅ 6

Piñata
```

UTF-8 encoding allows for *wide character* values to be encoded. A wide character value is a character represented with up to four bytes. To contrast, ISO-8859-1 represents all characters with a single byte. In the table below, each *b* represents a bit that can be used to store character data.

BYTES	BITS	REPRESENTATION
1	7	0bbbbbbb
2	11	110bbbbb 10bbbbbb
3	16	1110bbbb 10bbbbbb 10bbbbbb
4	21	11110bbb 10bbbbbb10bbbbbb 10bbbbbb

Introduction to Regular Expressions

Regular expressions are patterns composed of special characters that are used to perform operations on the contents of strings and other sets. You can use regular expressions to perform complex searches, audits, and modifications of your data.

You can use regular expressions to validate formatted strings such as e-mails or URLs, to extract data from log files, parse dates and times, and perform other useful text-search and text-rewrite functions.

Engines

Regular expressions are parsed and processed by a regular expression engine. PHP provides libraries for handling both PCRE regular expressions and POSIX regular expressions. PCRE stands for Perl Compatible Regular Expressions. In most cases, using PCRE regular expressions results in faster operations than when using the POSIX equivalent. The PCRE library is fairly ubiquitous which can be important when deciding which style of regular expressions you will use in a project.

Format

A regular expression is a string consisting of normal and special characters. Like common control characters, to a regular expression engine certain characters in a pattern have meaning beyond their display value. For example, the carat (^) symbol denotes the beginning of a line. The dollar sign ($) denotes the end of a line. To match all data in a single line, you can use a pattern such as ^.*$, which tells the regular expression engine to find the beginning of a line followed by any character (.) repeated any number of times (*) followed by the end of a line.

Special Characters

Each PCRE pattern must begin and end with a delimiter character. Most commonly the forward slash (/) is used. Patterns are strings and should be enclosed in double quotes when passed to an expression matching function. The POSIX-extended regular expression extension does not require that patterns be delimited by a special character. A listing of regular expression control characters follows.

CONTROL CHARACTER	DESCRIPTION
\	General-purpose escape character
^	Start of subject
^	Start of subject (or line, in multiline mode)
$	End of subject (or line, in multiline mode)
.	Match any character except newline
[	Start character class definition
]	End character class definition
|	Start of alternative branch
(	Start subpattern
)	End subpattern
?	Extends the meaning of (, also 0 or 1 quantifier, also quantifier minimizer
*	0 or more quantifier
+	1 or more quantifier
{	Start min/max quantifier
}	End min/max quantifier

Classes

You can enclose any part of a pattern in square brackets to create a *character class*. Character classes are used to group characters together as subexpressions. The control characters allowed in a character class definition are:

CONTROL CHARACTER	DESCRIPTION
\	General escape character
^	Negate the class, but only if the first character
-	Indicates character range
]	Terminates the character class

Escape Sequences

You can specify types of characters using any of several escape sequences. To search for any whitespace character you can use \s. To find a character that is anything but whitespace, you can use \S. The possible values for character types are:

ESCAPE SEQUENCE	DESCRIPTION
\d	Any decimal digit
\D	Any character that is not a decimal digit
\s	Any whitespace character
\S	Any nonwhitespace character
\w	Any word character
\W	Any nonword character

These control characters and escape sequences are the used in both the PCRE and POSIX regular expression libraries. The similarities in syntax can be demonstrated with an example. To check the validity of the structure of an e-mail address, the following PCRE pattern can be used.

```
'/^[A-z0-9_\-]+[@][A-z0-9_\-]+([.][A-z0-9_\-]+)+[A-z]{2,4}$/'
```

The POSIX version of the pattern differs only in the use of the opening and closing delimiters required by the PCRE expression.

```
^[A-z0-9_\-]+[@][A-z0-9_\-]+([.][A-z0-9_\-]+)+[A-z]{2,4}$
```

Both patterns check for a pattern of at least one number or letter followed by an @ symbol followed by at least one number, letter, underscore, or hyphen followed by a dot (.) followed by two, three, or four letters.

Find a Substring Using Regular Expressions

You can use the Perl Compatible Regular Expressions (PCRE) functions to match values in a string against a regular expression pattern. To find substrings in a string that match a given pattern you can use the preg_match function.

The preg_match function accepts two required arguments. The first is the regular expression pattern to be matched. The second is the search string to be scanned. Optionally, you can pass a third argument to represent an array to contain all matches found in the search string. If you want to find the position at which the matching substring begins, you can pass the PHP constant PREG_OFFSET_CAPTURE as a fourth argument. The fifth and final argument is an optional number representing the position at which the regular expression match begins.

If used without an array to contain matches, the preg_match function returns zero (0) or one (1) to represent no matches or one match. If the match array is specified, it is populated with a single element if a match is found. The element is itself an array containing the matching substring. If the PREG_OFFSET_CAPTURE flag is set, the element contains a second item equal to the position at which the match begins.

For a result array $matches returned from a call to preg_match with an offset capture flag specified, you may access the result with $matches[0][0] for the substring and $matches[0][1] for the position at which the substring begins. If the pattern has no matching substring, the array is empty. You can use the count function to find the number of items in the array.

Find a Substring Using Regular Expressions

① Create a variable representing a string to scan.

② Specify a regular expression pattern.

③ Type preg_match(.

④ Pass your search pattern.

⑤ Pass your target string.

⑥ Specify an array to contain the matching substring elements.

⑦ Pass the PREG_OFFSET_CAPTURE flag and close the function call with).

⑧ Use `print_r` to display the array of matches.

```
                                    📄 RegexSubstring.php
○ ○ ○
<!DOCTYPE html PUBLIC "-//W3C//DTD XHTML 1.0 Strict//EN"
        "http://www.w3.org/TR/xhtml1/DTD/xhtml1-strict.dtd">
<html xmlns="http://www.w3.org/1999/xhtml" xml:lang="en" lang="en">
<head>
        <meta http-equiv="content-type" content="text/html; charset=utf-8" />
        <title>Find a Substring Using Regular Expressions</title>
</head>
<body>
<?php
        $matches = array();

        $name = 'Toby Joe Boudreaux';

        $pattern = "/o[aeiou]/";

        preg_match($pattern, $name, $matches, PREG_OFFSET_CAPTURE);

        print_r($matches);  ←  ⑧
?>
</body>
</html>
```

⑨ View the script in a Web browser.

The first match value and associated position value appear.

```
○ ○ ○              @ Find a Substring Using Regular Expressions
   ◄       ►       ✕        ↻        🏠        AutoFill    🖨        ✉        e
  Back   Forward  Stop   Refresh    Home                 Print    Mail
  Address:     http://127.0.0.1:9003/ch04/task15/code/RegexSubstring.php          › go


  Array ( [0] => Array ( [0] => oe [1] => 6 ) )  ←  ⑨
```

Apply It

Because `preg_match` returns a zero or one on failure or success at finding a match for a given pattern, you can use the result directly as the test in a conditional statement. If a match is found, the test succeeds; otherwise it fails.

TYPE THIS:

```
$html = '<body><h1>Headline</h1></body>';
if(preg_match("/<h1>(.+)<\/h1>/", $html)){
  echo 'The html has a top-level header element.<br />';
}else{
  echo 'The html does not have a top-level header element.<br />';
}
```

→

RESULTS:

The browser displays "The html has a top-level header element."

Replace a Substring Using Regular Expressions

You can perform complex string replacements in PHP using the `preg_replace` function. The `preg_replace` function scans a target string or array of strings for any number of regular expression patterns. For each pattern match found, a corresponding replacement value or pattern is used.

The `preg_replace` function accepts three required arguments and supports an optional fourth argument. The first argument is a string or array of strings representing the regular expression patterns to use in finding matches. The second argument is a string or array of strings representing the values to use in replacement operations. Each value can be a simple string or a regular expression pattern. To learn more about using regular expression patterns as replacement parameters, see the task "Reformat a String Using Regular Expressions."

The third parameter is a string or array of strings in which you want PHP to search. The fourth argument is an optional integer representing the number of maximum matches you want to find.

The return value is either a string or an array depending on the type of the third argument. If a simple string is passed as the search subject, the return value is a string with all substrings matching patterns in the first argument replaced with their corresponding values from the second argument. If the second argument is not an array but a single element, each matching pattern in the first argument is replaced with the value of the second. If both the search and replace values are arrays, the search pattern at a given index is replaced with the replacement value at the corresponding index. If there is no replacement value at a given index in the search array, an empty string is used.

Replace a Substring Using Regular Expressions

① Create a variable representing a string to scan.

② Using an `echo` statement, print the original string.

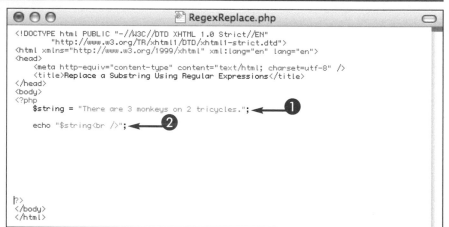

```
<!DOCTYPE html PUBLIC "-//W3C//DTD XHTML 1.0 Strict//EN"
        "http://www.w3.org/TR/xhtml1/DTD/xhtml1-strict.dtd">
<html xmlns="http://www.w3.org/1999/xhtml" xml:lang="en" lang="en">
<head>
    <meta http-equiv="content-type" content="text/html; charset=utf-8" />
    <title>Replace a Substring Using Regular Expressions</title>
</head>
<body>
<?php
    $string = "There are 3 monkeys on 2 tricycles.";     ①

    echo "$string<br />";     ②



?>
</body>
</html>
```

③ Specify a regular expression pattern or array of patterns to be used in the search.

④ Specify a string or array of strings to be used in the replacement.

```
<!DOCTYPE html PUBLIC "-//W3C//DTD XHTML 1.0 Strict//EN"
        "http://www.w3.org/TR/xhtml1/DTD/xhtml1-strict.dtd">
<html xmlns="http://www.w3.org/1999/xhtml" xml:lang="en" lang="en">
<head>
    <meta http-equiv="content-type" content="text/html; charset=utf-8" />
    <title>Replace a Substring Using Regular Expressions</title>
</head>
<body>
<?php
    $string = "There are 3 monkeys on 2 tricycles.";

    echo "$string<br />";

    $pattern = array("/1/","/2/","/3/","/4/","/5/");     ③

    $replacement = array('one', 'two', 'three', 'four', 'five');     ④


?>
</body>
</html>
```

⑤ Type preg_replace(.

⑥ Pass the search pattern value(s) as the first argument.

⑦ Pass the replacement value(s) as the second argument.

⑧ Pass the string in which you intend to search as the third argument and close the function call with).

⑨ Use an echo statement to display the result of the operation.

```
● ● ●                          📄 RegexReplace.php                              ▭
<!DOCTYPE html PUBLIC "-//W3C//DTD XHTML 1.0 Strict//EN"
        "http://www.w3.org/TR/xhtml1/DTD/xhtml1-strict.dtd">
<html xmlns="http://www.w3.org/1999/xhtml" xml:lang="en" lang="en">
<head>
    <meta http-equiv="content-type" content="text/html; charset=utf-8" />
    <title>Replace a Substring Using Regular Expressions</title>
</head>
<body>
<?php
    $string = "There are 3 monkeys on 2 tricycles.";

    echo "$string<br />";

    $pattern = array("/1/","/2/","/3/","/4/","/5/");

    $replacement = array('one', 'two', 'three', 'four', 'five');

    $string = preg_replace($pattern, $replacement, $string);   ◄── ⑧

    echo $string;
?>
</body>
</html>
```
⑤ → $string = preg_replace($pattern, ...
⑨ → echo $string;
⑥ ⑦

⑩ View the script in a Web browser.

Each matching regular expression is replaced with a corresponding string value.

```
● ● ●              @ Replace a Substring Using Regular Expressions           ▭
 ◄      ►      ✕      ↻      ⌂         ▨        🖨        ✉                  e
Back  Forward  Stop  Refresh  Home    AutoFill  Print    Mail
Address: @ http://127.0.0.1:9003/ch04/task16/code/RegexReplace.php          › go

There are 3 monkeys on 2 tricycles.              ◄── ⑩
There are three monkeys on two tricycles.
```

Extra

When using arrays as the first and second arguments, the keys are processed in the order they appear in the array. This is not necessarily the same as the numerical index order. If you use indexes to identify which pattern should be replaced by which replacement, you should call ksort on each array prior to calling preg_replace.

TYPE THIS:

```
$string = "There are 3 monkeys on 2 tricycles.";
$pattern = array();
$pattern[0] = "/1/";
$pattern[2] = "/3/";
$pattern[1] = "/2/";
$replacement = array();
$replacement[0] = 'one';
$replacement[1] = 'two';
$replacement[2] = 'three';
$string = preg_replace($pattern, $replacement, $string);
echo $string;
```

RESULTS:

→ The browser displays "There are two monkeys on three tricycles." instead of the correct version, which is "There are three monkeys on two tricycles."

Reformat a String Using Regular Expressions

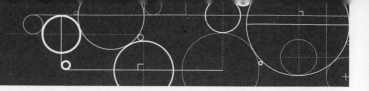

You can use the `preg_replace` function to reformat a string or substring according to a replacement pattern.

For each matching regular expression search string passed as the first argument to `preg_replace`, you can apply a corresponding regular expression format string. The format string or array of strings is passed as the second argument to the `preg_replace` function.

The third argument is the string or array of strings in which PHP searches for each value in the first argument. For each matching pattern, the corresponding format string is applied. The return value of the `preg_replace` function is either a single string or array of strings depending on the format of the search subject argument.

A replacement pattern or format pattern consists of regular character data mixed with escaped *backreference* values. A

backreference is a numerical reference representing the nth parenthesized value for a given search expression. For example, in the search expression `/(\w+)\s(\w+)\r/` you access the first word using `$1` and the second using `$2`. You can define a replacement pattern in the form of `"\$2 \$1"` to reverse the order of the words found in the first pattern.

If you define a replacement pattern consisting of a numerical backreference immediately followed by a number, you must isolate the backreference using curly braces ({}). For example, a replacement pattern defined as `"\$13"` looks for the 13th parenthesized value. To instead find the first parenthesized value and follow it with the number 3, you can use `"\${1}3"`. The curly braces tell PHP to treat the 1 as a special value while the number 3 is treated as simple character data.

Reformat a String Using Regular Expressions

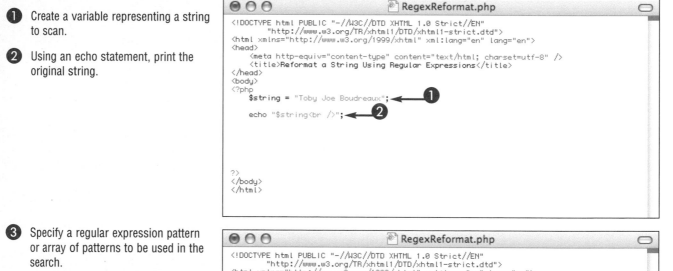

① Create a variable representing a string to scan.

② Using an echo statement, print the original string.

③ Specify a regular expression pattern or array of patterns to be used in the search.

④ Specify a replacement pattern to be used in the replace operations.

5. Type `preg_replace(`.

6. Pass the search pattern value(s) as the first argument.

7. Pass the replacement value(s) as the second argument.

8. Pass the string in which you intend to search as the third argument and close the function call with `)`.

9. Use an `echo` statement to display the result of the operation.

10. View the script in a Web browser.

   The string is reformatted according to the replacement pattern.

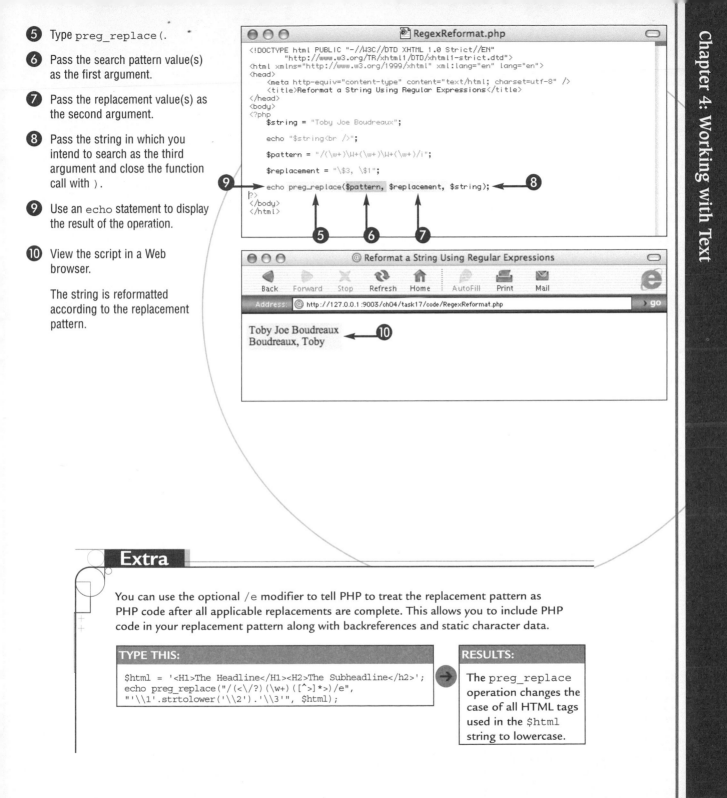

Extra

You can use the optional `/e` modifier to tell PHP to treat the replacement pattern as PHP code after all applicable replacements are complete. This allows you to include PHP code in your replacement pattern along with backreferences and static character data.

TYPE THIS:

```
$html = '<H1>The Headline</H1><H2>The Subheadline</h2>';
echo preg_replace("/(<\/?)(\w+)([^>]*>)/e",
"'\\1'.strtolower('\\2').'\\3'", $html);
```

→

RESULTS:

The `preg_replace` operation changes the case of all HTML tags used in the `$html` string to lowercase.

Create an Array of Matches Using Regular Expressions

You can search a string to find all substrings matching a regular expression pattern using the `preg_match_all` function. Like the `preg_match` function, `preg_match_all` scans a given string for substrings matching a regular expression pattern and returns the matching values as an array. The `preg_match` function stops execution when a single match is found. You can use the `preg_match_all` function to find all substrings matching your pattern. To read more about the `preg_match` function, you can refer to the task "Find a Substring Using Regular Expressions."

The `preg_match_all` function accepts three required arguments. The first is the string representing the regular expression pattern to be matched. The second argument is the string in which PHP should search for matches. The third argument is a reference to an array into which PHP pushes the matching substrings.

Optionally, you can pass additional arguments representing sorting flags and an offset position at which PHP begins the search. You can pass any combination of three sorting flags. The values are `PREG_PATTERN_ORDER`, `PREG_SET_ORDER`, and `PREG_OFFSET_CAPTURE`. The offset parameter is an integer specifying the character position at which the search for your regular expression pattern begins.

For a result array `$matches` returned from a call to `preg_match_all` with the `PREG_OFFSET_CAPTURE` flag set, you may access the result with `$matches[0][0]` for the substring and `$matches[0][1]` for the position at which the substring begins. If the pattern had no matching substring, the array is empty. You can use the `count` function to find the number of items in the array.

Create an Array of Matches Using Regular Expressions

① Create a variable representing a string to scan.

② Specify a regular expression pattern.

③ Type `preg_match_all(`.

④ Pass your search pattern.

⑤ Pass your target string.

⑥ Specify an array to contain the matching substring elements.

⑦ Pass the `PREG_OFFSET_CAPTURE` flag and close the function call with `)`.

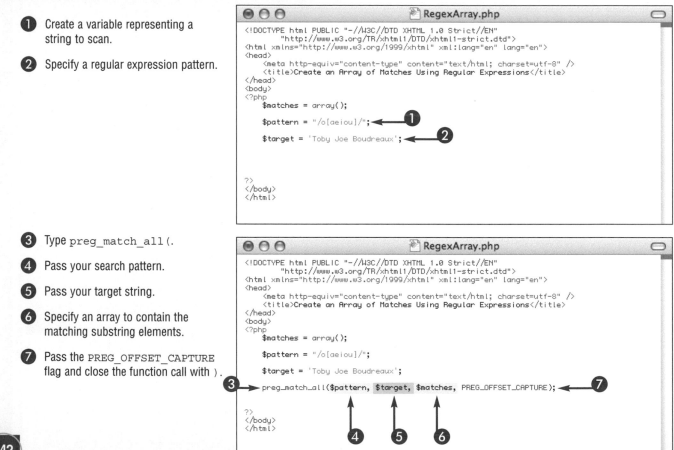

```
000                          RegexArray.php
<!DOCTYPE html PUBLIC "-//W3C//DTD XHTML 1.0 Strict//EN"
    "http://www.w3.org/TR/xhtml1/DTD/xhtml1-strict.dtd">
<html xmlns="http://www.w3.org/1999/xhtml" xml:lang="en" lang="en">
<head>
    <meta http-equiv="content-type" content="text/html; charset=utf-8" />
    <title>Create an Array of Matches Using Regular Expressions</title>
</head>
<body>
<?php
    $matches = array();

    $pattern = "/o[aeiou]/";          ①

    $target = 'Toby Joe Boudreaux';    ②


?>
</body>
</html>
```

```
000                          RegexArray.php
<!DOCTYPE html PUBLIC "-//W3C//DTD XHTML 1.0 Strict//EN"
    "http://www.w3.org/TR/xhtml1/DTD/xhtml1-strict.dtd">
<html xmlns="http://www.w3.org/1999/xhtml" xml:lang="en" lang="en">
<head>
    <meta http-equiv="content-type" content="text/html; charset=utf-8" />
    <title>Create an Array of Matches Using Regular Expressions</title>
</head>
<body>
<?php
    $matches = array();

    $pattern = "/o[aeiou]/";

    $target = 'Toby Joe Boudreaux';

③  preg_match_all($pattern, $target, $matches, PREG_OFFSET_CAPTURE);   ⑦

?>
</body>
</html>
```
④ ⑤ ⑥

⑧ Use `print_r` to display the array of matches.

```
● ● ●                    📄 RegexArray.php                              ⬤
<!DOCTYPE html PUBLIC "-//W3C//DTD XHTML 1.0 Strict//EN"
        "http://www.w3.org/TR/xhtml1/DTD/xhtml1-strict.dtd">
<html xmlns="http://www.w3.org/1999/xhtml" xml:lang="en" lang="en">
<head>
    <meta http-equiv="content-type" content="text/html; charset=utf-8" />
    <title>Create an Array of Matches Using Regular Expressions</title>
</head>
<body>
<?php
    $matches = array();

    $pattern = "/o[aeiou]/";

    $target = 'Toby Joe Boudreaux';

    preg_match_all($pattern, $target, $matches, PREG_OFFSET_CAPTURE);

    print_r($matches); ←———⑧
?>
</body>
</html>
```

⑨ View the script in a Web browser.

All matching values and associated position values appear.

```
● ● ●        @ Create an Array of Matches Using Regular Expr...        ⬤
  ◀         ▶        ✕        🔄        🏠       AutoFill    🖨        ✉           e
 Back    Forward    Stop    Refresh    Home    AutoFill   Print    Mail

Address: @ http://127.0.0.1:9003/ch04/task18/code/RegexArray.php          ⟩ go

Array ( [0] => Array ( [0] => Array ( [0] => oe [1] => 6 ) [1] => Array ( [0] => ou [1] => 10 ) )
)
```

Extra

The PREG_PATTERN_ORDER and PREG_SET_ORDER flags are used to specify the structure of the array returned from preg_match_all. For a results array $matches, setting the PREG_PATTERN_ORDER flag results in $matches[0] containing an array of full pattern matches and $matches[1] containing an array of parenthesized values. For a results array $matches, setting the PREG_SET_ORDER flag results in each element of $matches being set to an array containing the full pattern match and the parenthesized match.

TYPE THIS:

```
echo 'PREG_PATTERN_ORDER:<br />';
preg_match_all("/o([aeiou])/", "Toby Joe Boudreaux",
$matches, PREG_PATTERN_ORDER);
echo "{$matches[0][0]}, {$matches[0][1]}<br />";
echo "{$matches[1][0]}, {$matches[1][1]}<br />";
echo 'PREG_SET_ORDER:<br />';
preg_match_all("/o([aeiou])/", "Toby Joe Boudreaux",
$matches, PREG_SET_ORDER);
echo "{$matches[0][0]}, {$matches[0][1]}<br />";
echo "{$matches[1][0]}, {$matches[1][1]}<br />";
```

RESULTS:

The browser displays:

PREG_PATTERN_ORDER:

oe, ou

e, u

PREG_SET_ORDER:

oe, e

ou, u

Open or Create a File

Your applications may often require you to access text files stored on your Web server. For example, you may want to read configuration settings or write to a custom log file. Many applications do not require the robust functionality of a relational database system and can instead be built around simple text files. For example, you may want to store a list of users in a tab-delimited text file. PHP provides quick and simple methods to create, read, and write contents to files.

You can open and create files on your Web server using the fopen function. The fopen function accepts two arguments and returns a *file handle* that you can use in reading and writing to a file. You can think of a file handle as a variable representing a file on your server.

The first argument to fopen is the path to the file you want to open or create. This path should be a string and is relative not to your Web root, but to your server root. The second argument is the mode in which you want to open the file. For example, you can use the a+ access mode to open a file for reading and writing. If the file exists, the cursor is placed at the end of the file. Otherwise, the file is created. As soon as you have an active file handle, you can read data using the fread function.

The fread function accepts two arguments. The first is the active file handle from which you want to read. The second is an integer representing the number of bytes you want to read. The return value is a string representing the data read from the file.

Open or Create a File

① Create a variable to represent a file handle followed by the assignment operator (=).

② Type fopen(.

③ Pass the name of a file you want to open.

④ Pass the access mode followed by).

⑤ Create a variable to store a string of data read from the file.

⑥ Using fread, read the first 1024 bytes from your file handle.

⑦ Close the file with fclose.

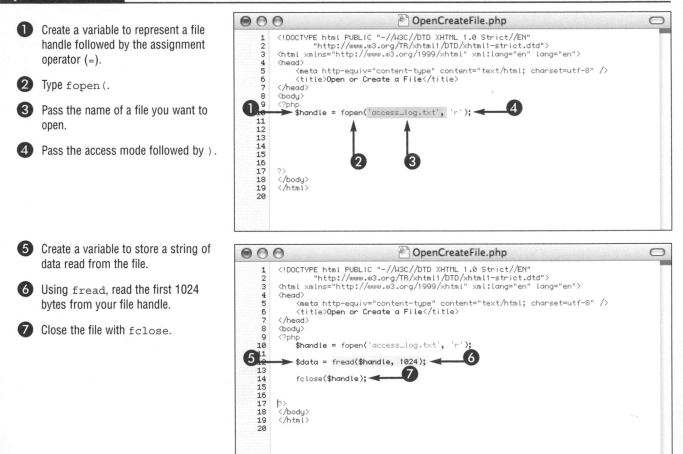

8 Echo the result to the browser.

```
1   <!DOCTYPE html PUBLIC "-//W3C//DTD XHTML 1.0 Strict//EN"
2       "http://www.w3.org/TR/xhtml1/DTD/xhtml1-strict.dtd">
3   <html xmlns="http://www.w3.org/1999/xhtml" xml:lang="en" lang="en">
4   <head>
5       <meta http-equiv="content-type" content="text/html; charset=utf-8" />
6       <title>Open or Create a File</title>
7   </head>
8   <body>
9   <?php
10      $handle = fopen('access_log.txt', 'r');
11
12      $data = fread($handle, 1024);
13
14      fclose($handle);
15
16      echo "The result of the read operation was: <br />$data";    ◄── 8
17  ?>
18  </body>
19  </html>
20
```

9 View your script in a Web browser.

The first 1024 bytes of data appear.

Open or Create a File

Address: http://127.0.0.1:9003/ch05/task1/code/OpenCreateFile.php

The result of the read operation was:
This data is contained in a file called access_log.txt.   ◄── 9

Extra

There are several possible values for the access mode argument to `fopen`. Each access mode specifies whether file creation occurs and where the cursor is placed in the opened file. The possible values for the access mode argument are:

r	Read only access. Place the cursor at the start of the file.
r+	Read and write access. Place the cursor at the start of the file.
w	Write only access. Place the cursor at the start of the file. Create the file if it does not exist.
w+	Read and write access. Place the cursor at the start of the file. Create the file if it does not exist.
a	Write only access. Place the cursor at the end of the file. Create the file if it does not exist.
a+	Read and write access. Place the cursor at the end of the file. Create the file if it does not exist.
x	Create and open for writing only. Place the cursor at the beginning of the file. If the file already exists, return `false` and throw an error.
x+	Create and open for reading and writing. Place the cursor at the beginning of the file. If the file already exists, return `false` and throw an error.

Write to a File

You can use an active file handle to write to a file using the `fwrite` function. The `fwrite` function accepts two required arguments. The first is the handle returned from a call to `fopen`. The second is a string representing the data you want to write to the file. Optionally, you can specify a third argument representing the maximum number of bytes you want to write to the file.

For example, you may have a file handle created using `fopen`, passing an access flag of `r+`. To overwrite all data in the file, you can type `fwrite` followed by the variable representing your file handle and the string representing your data as arguments.

PHP provides an alias function to `fwrite` named `fputs`. The functions are identical and interchangeable, though it is

always a good practice to choose one to maintain consistency across your applications and scripts.

Close all opened files when relevant operations are complete. You can close an opened file using `fclose`. The `fclose` function accepts a single argument representing the file handle you want to close. The `fclose` function returns a Boolean `true` on success and `false` on failure.

When attempting to open or close a file you may encounter errors. The most common errors encountered when working with files are those involving file permissions and ownership. It is good practice to test a file handle before attempting a write or close operation. You can read about setting permissions on Unix servers in the task "Set Unix File Permissions." For Windows-based servers, refer to your operating system documentation.

Write to a File

① Create a variable to represent a file handle.

② Use `fopen` to open the file.

- Be sure to choose an access mode allowing write access.

③ Create a string to represent your data.

④ Type the name of a variable, the assignment operator (=), and `fwrite`, followed by the file handle and data variable as arguments.

⑤ Close the file handle using `fclose`.

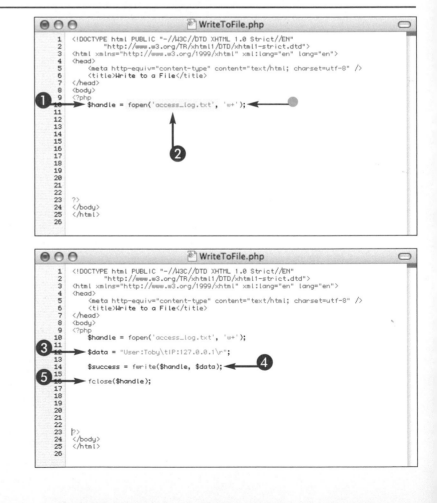

6 Echo the result of the `fwrite` operation to the output stream.

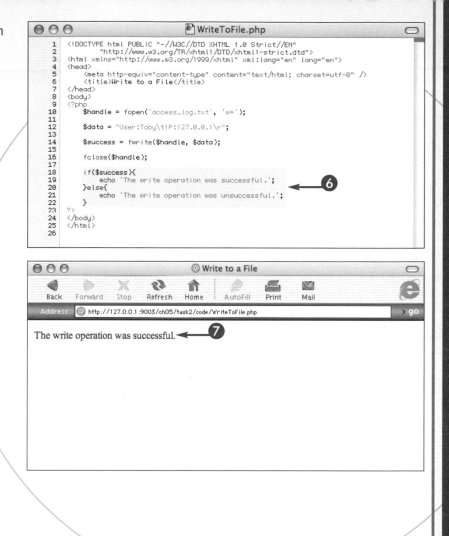

```
1   <!DOCTYPE html PUBLIC "-//W3C//DTD XHTML 1.0 Strict//EN"
2       "http://www.w3.org/TR/xhtml1/DTD/xhtml1-strict.dtd">
3   <html xmlns="http://www.w3.org/1999/xhtml" xml:lang="en" lang="en">
4   <head>
5       <meta http-equiv="content-type" content="text/html; charset=utf-8" />
6       <title>Write to a File</title>
7   </head>
8   <body>
9   <?php
10      $handle = fopen('access_log.txt', 'w+');
11
12      $data = "User:Toby\tIP:127.0.0.1\r";
13
14      $success = fwrite($handle, $data);
15
16      fclose($handle);
17
18      if($success){
19          echo 'The write operation was successful.';
20      }else{
21          echo 'The write operation was unsuccessful.';
22      }
23  ?>
24  </body>
25  </html>
26
```

WriteToFile.php

7 View your script in a Web browser.

The success or failure of the `fwrite` operation is reflected.

Write to a File

Address: http://127.0.0.1:9003/ch05/task2/code/WriteToFile.php

The write operation was successful.

Extra

You can lock files for read and/or write access while performing a sequence of operations by using the `flock` function. Using `flock` tells the operating system to restrict access to a specific file. The `flock` function accepts two required arguments. The first is the valid file handle on which you want to place a lock. The second is a flag representing the type of lock you want to create.

To prevent write operations from occurring while reading a file, you can pass the `LOCK_SH` flag as the second argument. To prevent read operations from occurring while writing to a file, you can pass the `LOCK_EX` flag.

By default, the lock is only advisory outside of the current PHP processes. This means that the actual functionality may differ based on your operating system and the other applications that are running. To have PHP try to enforce the block more strongly, you can pass a Boolean true value as the third argument.

Copy or Delete a File

Y ou can use PHP to manipulate files on your Web server. There are functions that provide platform-agnostic methods of creating, copying, deleting, and moving files.

You can use the `copy` function to copy a file to a new location. This is useful when creating backups of files before performing write operations, or when performing automated maintenance such as log file backup. The `copy` function accepts two arguments. The first is a string representing the path to the file you want to copy. The second is a string representing the location to which you want to copy the file. When successful, the copy function returns a Boolean `true` value. When an error occurs, `false` is returned.

To delete a file, you can use the `unlink` function. This function performs a platform-independent delete operation by dereferencing a file so that the operating system can overwrite the space the file occupies on the hard drive. The `unlink` function accepts a string representing the path to the file you want to delete. If the deletion is successful, `unlink` returns `true`. Otherwise, it returns `false`.

Generally, it is best to check to see if a file exists before trying to copy or delete it. You can check for a file using the `file_exists` function. The `file_exists` function accepts a string representing the path to a file. If the file exists, `file_exists` returns `true`. Otherwise, it returns `false`. You can use the call to `file_exists` as the condition in an `if` statement to prevent errors from being generated if there are typos in the file path or if the path does not exist.

Copy or Delete A File

① Use `file_exists` to check for a file.

② Type `copy(`.

③ Pass the path to the file you want to copy.

④ Pass the destination path followed by `)`.

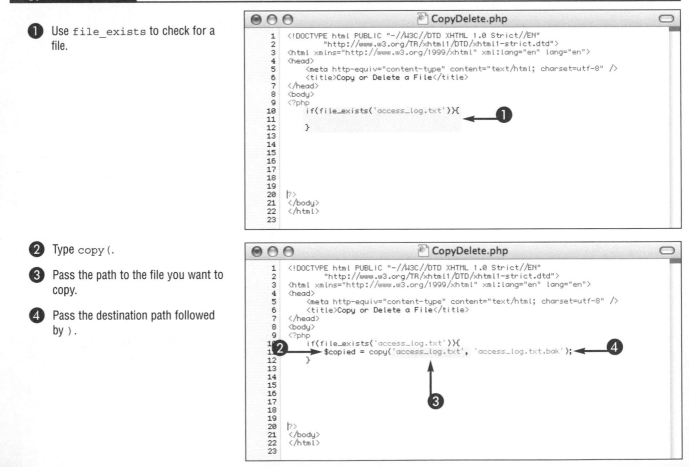

5 If the `copy` operation is successful, remove the copied file using `unlink`.

6 Use `echo` statements to verify the success of each operation.

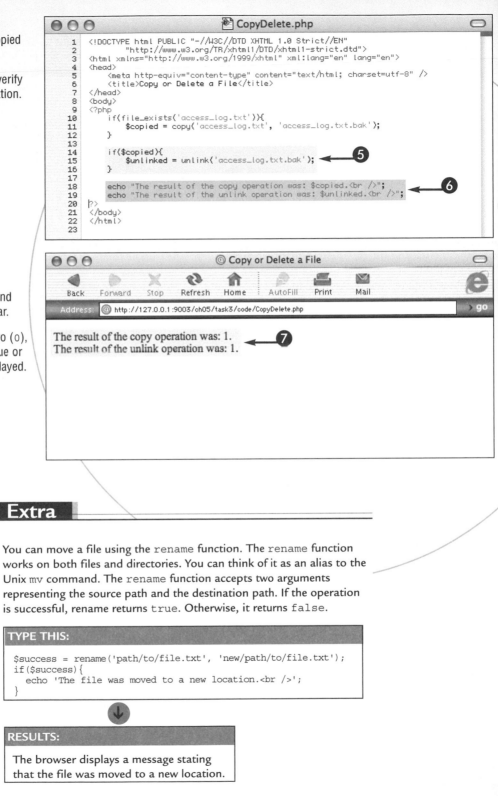

```
1    <!DOCTYPE html PUBLIC "-//W3C//DTD XHTML 1.0 Strict//EN"
2        "http://www.w3.org/TR/xhtml1/DTD/xhtml1-strict.dtd">
3    <html xmlns="http://www.w3.org/1999/xhtml" xml:lang="en" lang="en">
4    <head>
5        <meta http-equiv="content-type" content="text/html; charset=utf-8" />
6        <title>Copy or Delete a File</title>
7    </head>
8    <body>
9    <?php
10       if(file_exists('access_log.txt')){
11           $copied = copy('access_log.txt', 'access_log.txt.bak');
12       }
13
14       if($copied){
15           $unlinked = unlink('access_log.txt.bak');          ← 5
16       }
17
18       echo "The result of the copy operation was: $copied.<br />";     ← 6
19       echo "The result of the unlink operation was: $unlinked.<br />";
20    ?>
21    </body>
22    </html>
23
```

7 View your script in a Web browser.

The results of the `copy` and `unlink` operations appear.

The integer one (1) or zero (0), representing a Boolean true or false, respectively, is displayed.

Address: http://127.0.0.1:9003/ch05/task3/code/CopyDelete.php

The result of the copy operation was: 1.   ← 7
The result of the unlink operation was: 1.

Extra

You can move a file using the `rename` function. The `rename` function works on both files and directories. You can think of it as an alias to the Unix `mv` command. The `rename` function accepts two arguments representing the source path and the destination path. If the operation is successful, `rename` returns `true`. Otherwise, it returns `false`.

TYPE THIS:

```
$success = rename('path/to/file.txt', 'new/path/to/file.txt');
if($success){
   echo 'The file was moved to a new location.<br />';
}
```

RESULTS:

The browser displays a message stating that the file was moved to a new location.

Access File Attributes

You can use PHP to access various information about a file. You can access information such as the time a file was last accessed or modified, the size of the file, whether it is writeable or readable, and who owns the file.

To access the `stat` attributes for a file, you can use the `stat` and `fstat` functions. The `stat` function accepts the path to a file and returns an associative array containing a great deal of file information. Each attribute is accessible by key. The `fstat` function operates exactly as the `stat` function but accepts an open file handle instead of a string representing the path to the file about which you want to gather information.

To determine if a file is writeable, you can use the `is_writable` function. The `is_readable` function can be used to determine if a file is readable by PHP. Each of these functions accepts a string representing the path to the file in question and returns a Boolean value representing the status of the file.

You can find out whether a file at a given location is a symbolic link to another file by using `is_link`. If `is_link` returns true, you can access the linked file using `readlink`, passing the same file path you used for `is_link`.

Whenever you use functions to access information about a file, it is a good practice to call `clearstatcache()` before any other function calls are made. The `clearstatcache` function clears the results of the last `stat` call, preventing the possibility of gathering information about the wrong file.

Access File Attributes

① Use `is_readable` to check whether a file is readable.

② Use `is_writable` to check whether a file is writeable.

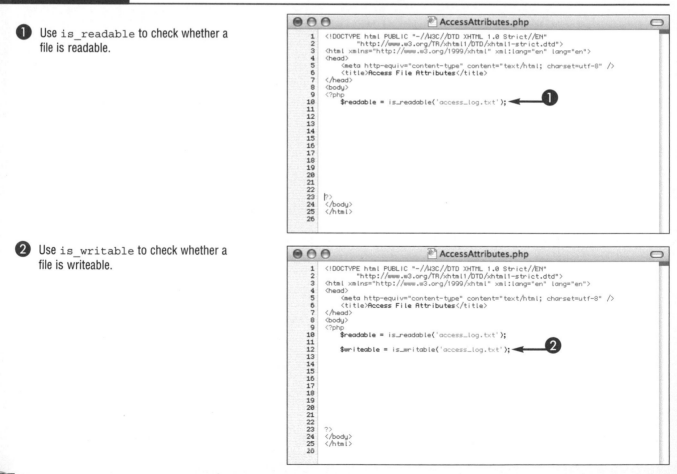

3 Use `echo` statements to verify the status of the file.

4 Call `clearstatcache()`.

5 Call `stat`, passing the file path as an argument.

6 Use `print_r` to examine the array returned.

7 View your script in a Web browser.

The attributes associated with the file appear.

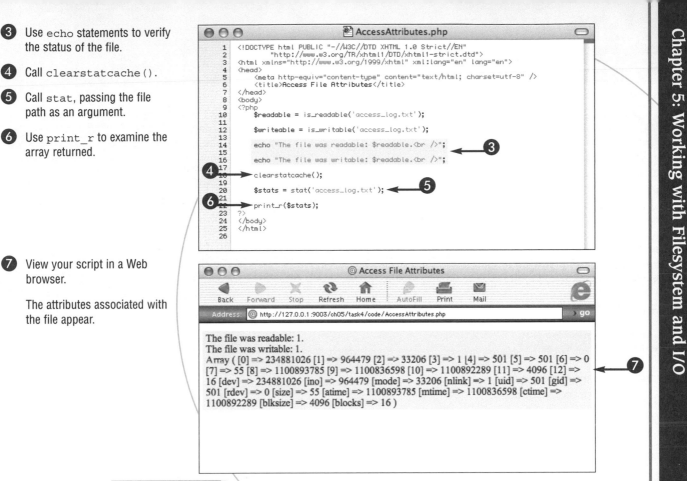

```
AccessAttributes.php
1   <!DOCTYPE html PUBLIC "-//W3C//DTD XHTML 1.0 Strict//EN"
2       "http://www.w3.org/TR/xhtml1/DTD/xhtml1-strict.dtd">
3   <html xmlns="http://www.w3.org/1999/xhtml" xml:lang="en" lang="en">
4   <head>
5       <meta http-equiv="content-type" content="text/html; charset=utf-8" />
6       <title>Access File Attributes</title>
7   </head>
8   <body>
9   <?php
10      $readable = is_readable('access_log.txt');
11
12      $writeable = is_writable('access_log.txt');
13
14      echo "The file was readable: $readable.<br />";
15
16      echo "The file was writable: $readable.<br />";
17
18      clearstatcache();
19
20      $stats = stat('access_log.txt');
21
22      print_r($stats);
23  ?>
24  </body>
25  </html>
26
```

```
Access File Attributes
Back  Forward  Stop  Refresh  Home  AutoFill  Print  Mail
Address: http://127.0.0.1:9003/ch05/task4/code/AccessAttributes.php   go

The file was readable: 1.
The file was writable: 1.
Array ( [0] => 234881026 [1] => 964479 [2] => 33206 [3] => 1 [4] => 501 [5] => 501 [6] => 0
[7] => 55 [8] => 1100893785 [9] => 1100836598 [10] => 1100892289 [11] => 4096 [12] =>
16 [dev] => 234881026 [ino] => 964479 [mode] => 33206 [nlink] => 1 [uid] => 501 [gid] =>
501 [rdev] => 0 [size] => 55 [atime] => 1100893785 [mtime] => 1100836598 [ctime] =>
1100892289 [blksize] => 4096 [blocks] => 16 )
```

Extra

The associative array returned by calls to `stat` and `fstat` contain attributes about a file. The keys and their descriptions are listed below.

dev	device number
ino	inode number
mode	inode protection mode
nlink	number of links
uid	userid of owner
gid	groupid of owner
rdev	device type, if inode device *
size	size in bytes
atime	time of last access (Unix timestamp)
mtime	time of last modification (Unix timestamp)
ctime	time of last inode change (Unix timestamp)
blksize	blocksize of filesystem IO *
blocks	number of blocks allocated

* Only valid on systems supporting the st_blksize type — other systems (i.e. Windows) return -1.

Set Unix File Permissions

You can use PHP to modify the owner and group of a file. Modifying this information allows you to reassign the user and groups of users who have access to the file. You can also change the level of access, or *permissions*, that apply to each user in relation to a given file or directory.

Each file on a Unix file system has an attribute for read, write, and execute permissions for three groups: the owner of the file, the group to which the file belongs, and all other users.

When viewing the output of an `ls` command, you can see that each file has a string representing the permissions. The permissions might be set to `--rwxr-xr-x` for a file that is writeable only by the owner but readable and executable by all. This setting can also be represented using the octal value `0755`.

You can use the `chmod` function to change the permissions of a file. The `chmod` function accepts two arguments — the path to the file and the octal value representing the desired permissions. To change the group to which a file belongs, you can use the `chgrp` function. The `chgrp` function accepts the path to the file and the name of the group as arguments. Both `chmod` and `chgrp` return `true` on success and `false` on failure.

You can use the `chown` function to change the owner of a file. The `chown` function accepts the path to the file and the name of the user to which ownership is assigned. If the operation is successful, `chown` returns `true`. Otherwise, it returns `false`.

Set Unix File Permissions

① To assign a new group to a file, type `chgrp()`.

② Between the parentheses, type the path to the file and the name of the group.

③ Use the `echo` statement to confirm the operation.

```
1   <!DOCTYPE html PUBLIC "-//W3C//DTD XHTML 1.0 Strict//EN"
2       "http://www.w3.org/TR/xhtml1/DTD/xhtml1-strict.dtd">
3   <html xmlns="http://www.w3.org/1999/xhtml" xml:lang="en" lang="en">
4   <head>
5       <meta http-equiv="content-type" content="text/html; charset=utf-8" />
6       <title>Set Unix File Permissions</title>
7   </head>
8   <body>
9   <?php
10      $group = chgrp('access_log.txt', 'www');
11
12      echo "The result of chgrp was: $group.<br />";
13
14
15
16
17
18
19
20
21  ?>
22  </body>
23  </html>
24
```

④ To change the owner of a file, type `chown()`.

⑤ Between the parentheses, type the path to the file and the name of the owner.

⑥ Use the `echo` statement to confirm the operation.

```
1   <!DOCTYPE html PUBLIC "-//W3C//DTD XHTML 1.0 Strict//EN"
2       "http://www.w3.org/TR/xhtml1/DTD/xhtml1-strict.dtd">
3   <html xmlns="http://www.w3.org/1999/xhtml" xml:lang="en" lang="en">
4   <head>
5       <meta http-equiv="content-type" content="text/html; charset=utf-8" />
6       <title>Set Unix File Permissions</title>
7   </head>
8   <body>
9   <?php
10      $group = chgrp('access_log.txt', 'www');
11
12      echo "The result of chgrp was: $group.<br />";
13
14      $owner = chown('access_log.txt', 'www');
15
16      echo "The result of chown was: $owner.<br />";
17
18
19
20
21  ?>
22  </body>
23  </html>
24
```

7 To change the permissions of a file, type `chmod()`.

8 In the parentheses, type the path to the file and the octal value to be used.

Be sure to prefix the octal value with a zero (0).

9 Use the `echo` statement to confirm the operation.

```
                                    📄 SetUnixPerms.php
 1  <!DOCTYPE html PUBLIC "-//W3C//DTD XHTML 1.0 Strict//EN"
 2       "http://www.w3.org/TR/xhtml1/DTD/xhtml1-strict.dtd">
 3  <html xmlns="http://www.w3.org/1999/xhtml" xml:lang="en" lang="en">
 4  <head>
 5      <meta http-equiv="content-type" content="text/html; charset=utf-8" />
 6      <title>Set Unix File Permissions</title>
 7  </head>
 8  <body>
 9  <?php
10      $group = chgrp('access_log.txt', 'www');
11
12      echo "The result of chgrp    : $group.<br />";
13
14      $owner = chown('access_log.txt', 'www');
15
16      echo "The result of chown was: $owner.<br />";
17
18      $perms = chmod('access_log.txt', 0755);
19
20      echo "The result of chmod was: $perms.<br />";
21  ?>
22  </body>
23  </html>
24
```

10 View your script in a Web browser.

The statements printed to the output stream confirm the success of each operation.

Note: For information about Windows permissions, refer to the task "Set File and Folder Permissions on Windows" in Chapter 1.

```
                              @ Set Unix File Permissions
 Back  Forward  Stop  Refresh  Home   AutoFill  Print  Mail
 Address: @ http://127.0.0.1:9003/ch05/task5/code/SetUnixPerms.php        › go

 The result of chgrp was: 1.
 The result of chown was: 1.     ◄— 10
 The result of chmod was: 1.
```

Extra

You can determine which octal value is needed to represent a given set of permissions.

OCTAL DIGIT	TEXT EQUIVALENT	MEANING
0	- - -	All types of access are denied
1	- - x	Execute access is allowed only
2	- w -	Write access is allowed only
3	- w x	Write and execute access are allowed
4	r - -	Read access is allowed
5	r - x	Read and execute access are allowed
6	r w -	Read and write access are allowed
7	r w x	Read, write, and execute are allowed

Work with Directories

You can use PHP to create and delete directories on your Web server. The `mkdir` function creates a new directory, while the `rmdir` function removes a directory already on the server. You may need to create temporary directories to store uploaded files or files that are being moved during automated maintenance. By using the PHP directory management functions, you can perform these tasks without having to open a shell or FTP session.

The `mkdir` function returns a Boolean value representing the success of the directory creation operation. The `mkdir` function has one required argument representing the directory you want to create. To create a directory in the same directory as your PHP script, you can pass the name of the directory. To create a directory in a different location

than your script, specify the full path. Optionally, you can pass a second argument representing an octal value for PHP to use in setting the permissions for the directory. An optional third argument represents a Boolean value that tells PHP whether to use recursive `mkdir` calls to create a nested folder. For example, you may use `mkdir('a/b/c',0755, 1);` to create a folder c inside a folder b inside a folder a.

The `rmdir` function removes a directory from the file system on the Web server. The `rmdir` function accepts a string representing the path to the directory you want to delete. In order for the `rmdir` function to succeed, the directory must be empty and PHP must have permission to delete the directory. If successful, `rmdir` returns `true`. Otherwise, it returns `false`.

Work with Directories

① Type `mkdir()` to create a new directory.

② Between the parentheses, type the path to the directory you want to create.

③ Use the `echo` statement to confirm the operation.

④ Type `mkdir()` to create a recursive directory.

⑤ Between the parentheses, type the path to the directory, the permissions mode, and the recursive flag.

⑥ Use the `echo` statement to confirm the operation.

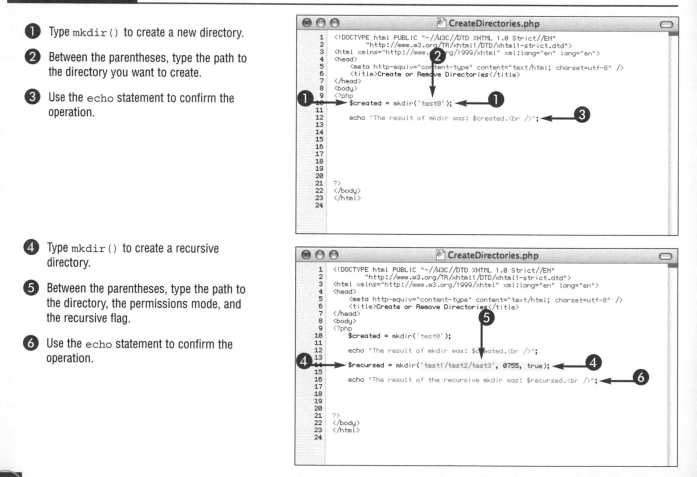

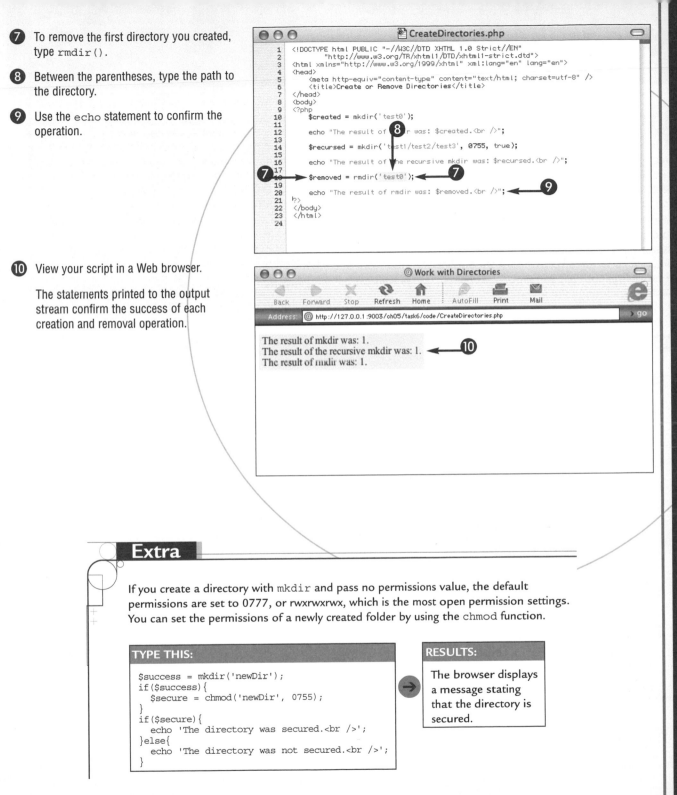

7 To remove the first directory you created, type `rmdir()`.

8 Between the parentheses, type the path to the directory.

9 Use the `echo` statement to confirm the operation.

10 View your script in a Web browser.

The statements printed to the output stream confirm the success of each creation and removal operation.

Extra

If you create a directory with `mkdir` and pass no permissions value, the default permissions are set to 0777, or rwxrwxrwx, which is the most open permission settings. You can set the permissions of a newly created folder by using the `chmod` function.

TYPE THIS:

```
$success = mkdir('newDir');
if($success){
   $secure = chmod('newDir', 0755);
}
if($secure){
   echo 'The directory was secured.<br />';
}else{
   echo 'The directory was not secured.<br />';
}
```

RESULTS:

The browser displays a message stating that the directory is secured.

Get a List of Files in a Directory

PHP provides methods for opening and reading the contents of a directory. You can use the `opendir` function to open a *directory handle* or pointer to a directory. When you have a value directory handle, you can use the `readdir` function to read the contents of the directory for which the handle was created.

The `opendir` function accepts a string representing the path to the directory you want to open. The return value is a directory handle to be used in the PHP directory management functions. If the directory does not exist or is inaccessible for permissions or other reasons, PHP throws an error. It is always good practice to use the `is_dir` function to check to see if a directory exists before trying to create a handle.

When a valid directory handle is created you can use the `readdir` function to iterate over a directory and read the name of each file in the directory. The `readdir` function accepts the handle created by `opendir` as an argument and is most commonly used in a loop structure such as a `while` loop. When the last file in a directory is read, the `readdir` function returns `false`.

You can use the `rewinddir` function to reset the internal file pointer in a given directory handle to the first file in the directory. When the read operations are complete, close the directory handle with the `closedir` function. Both the `rewinddir` and `closedir` functions accept a valid directory handle as an argument and return a Boolean value representing their success or failure.

Get a List of Files in a Directory

① Use `is_dir` to determine if your directory exists.

② Type `opendir()` to create a new directory handle.

③ Between the parentheses, type the path to the directory.

```
● ● ●                              ListFiles.php
1   <!DOCTYPE html PUBLIC "-//W3C//DTD XHTML 1.0 Strict//EN"
2       "http://www.w3.org/TR/xhtml1/DTD/xhtml1-strict.dtd">
3   <html xmlns="http://www.w3.org/1999/xhtml" xml:lang="en" lang="en">
4   <head>
5       <meta http-equiv="content-type" content="text/html; charset=utf-8" />
6       <title>Get a List of Files in a Directory</title>
7   </head>
8   <body>
9   <?php
10      if(is_dir('.')){
11          if($handle = opendir('.')){
12
13
14          }
15
16      }
17
18  ?>
19  </body>
20  </html>
21
```

④ Create a `while` loop.

⑤ For the condition, type a variable followed by the assignment operator (=) and a call to `readdir`, passing your handle as an argument.

Note: The identical comparison operator (`!==`) is used.

⑥ Use the `echo` statement to print the name of each file returned.

```
● ● ●                              ListFiles.php
1   <!DOCTYPE html PUBLIC "-//W3C//DTD XHTML 1.0 Strict//EN"
2       "http://www.w3.org/TR/xhtml1/DTD/xhtml1-strict.dtd">
3   <html xmlns="http://www.w3.org/1999/xhtml" xml:lang="en" lang="en">
4   <head>
5       <meta http-equiv="content-type" content="text/html; charset=utf-8" />
6       <title>Get a List of Files in a Directory</title>
7   </head>
8   <body>
9   <?php
10      if(is_dir('.')){
11          if($handle = opendir('.')){
12              while(false !== ($file = readdir($handle))){
13                  echo "The file name is: $file<br />";
14              }
15          }
16
17      }
18  ?>
19  </body>
20  </html>
21
```

7 Close the directory using the `closedir` function.

```
                                    ListFiles.php
1    <!DOCTYPE html PUBLIC "-//W3C//DTD XHTML 1.0 Strict//EN"
2          "http://www.w3.org/TR/xhtml1/DTD/xhtml1-strict.dtd">
3    <html xmlns="http://www.w3.org/1999/xhtml" xml:lang="en" lang="en">
4    <head>
5        <meta http-equiv="content-type" content="text/html; charset=utf-8" />
6        <title>Get a List of Files in a Directory</title>
7    </head>
8    <body>
9    <?php
10       if(is_dir('.')){
11           if($handle = opendir('.')){
12               while(false !== ($file = readdir($handle))){
13                   echo "The file name is: $file<br />";
14               }
15           }
16           closedir($handle);          ←——— 7
17       }
18   ?>
19   </body>
20   </html>
21
```

8 View your script in a Web browser.

The names of each file in the directory are printed to the output stream.

```
                        Get a List of Files in a Directory
Address: http://127.0.0.1:9003/ch05/task7/code/ListFiles.php        go

The file name is: .
The file name is: ..
The file name is: .DS_Store          ←——— 8
The file name is: ListFiles.php
```

Extra

You can use the `system` command to execute a shell command on the Web server with PHP. To list the contents of a directory in a Unix shell session, you can use the `ls --l` command. The same command can be passed to the `system` function as a string. PHP acts as the standard output for the command and prints the result to the output stream.

TYPE THIS:

```
<pre>
<?php
  system('ls --l');
?>
</pre>
```

→

RESULTS:

The browser displays a file listing all files in the directory along with information such as owner, group, and permissions.

Using Output Buffering

Y ou can use the output buffering functions in PHP to have more control of the data your scripts write to the output stream. You can control when and how your script prints output by creating an *output buffer* to capture all data that otherwise is sent directly to the user.

You can begin output buffering by using the ob_start function. When a new output buffer is created, all data that is otherwise printed is captured. The ob_start function has no required arguments but accepts three optional arguments. The first is the name of a callback function to be used in processing the data in the buffer. The function specified is called before the output is flushed to the browser. Any function set as a callback accepts and returns a string.

The second optional argument can be an integer and represents the number of bytes at which the callback function is called. If passed, this argument tells PHP to trigger the callback function on every first newline after the

given number of bytes. To bypass setting this value, you can pass null.

The third argument is a Boolean representing whether the buffer should be deleted when ob_end is called.

You can obtain the contents of the output buffer at any point using the ob_get_contents function. The ob_get_contents function accepts no arguments and returns a string representing the contents of the buffer. If there is no current buffering operation, the function returns a null value.

To send the contents of the output buffer but continue buffering new data, you can use the ob_flush function. To send the contents of the output buffer to the output stream and stop buffering, you can use ob_end_flush.

If there is any reason you need to delete the contents currently in the buffer without flushing it to the screen, you can use the ob_clean function.

Using Output Buffering

① Type ob_start() to start output buffering.

② Perform operations that print data to the output stream.

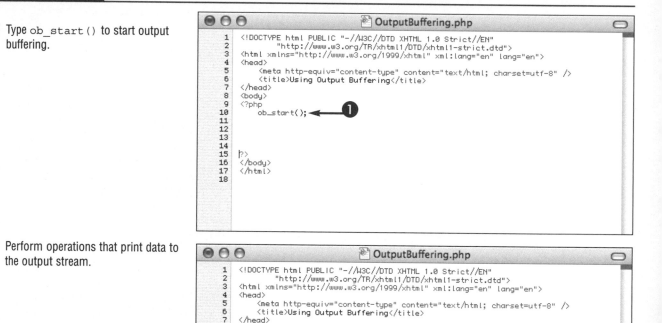

③ Print the contents of the buffer to the output stream using `ob_end_flush()`.

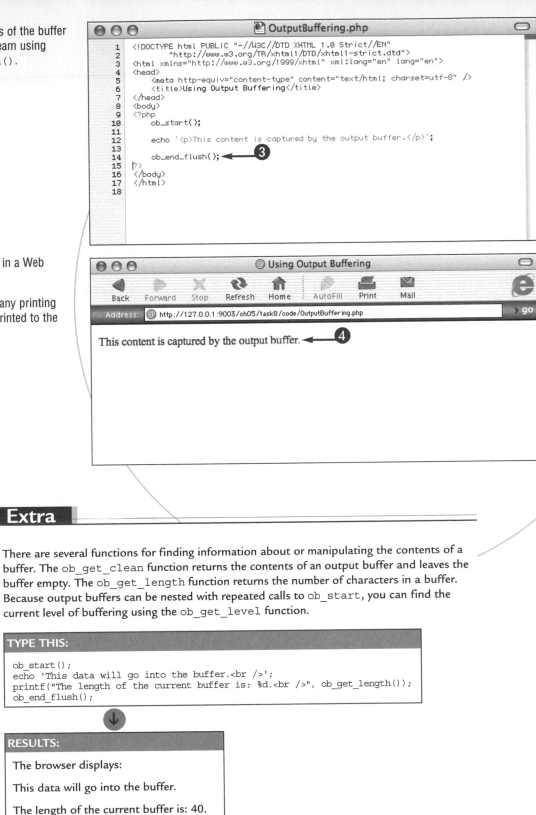

④ View your script in a Web browser.

The contents of any printing operations are printed to the output stream.

```
<!DOCTYPE html PUBLIC "-//W3C//DTD XHTML 1.0 Strict//EN"
          "http://www.w3.org/TR/xhtml1/DTD/xhtml1-strict.dtd">
<html xmlns="http://www.w3.org/1999/xhtml" xml:lang="en" lang="en">
<head>
    <meta http-equiv="content-type" content="text/html; charset=utf-8" />
    <title>Using Output Buffering</title>
</head>
<body>
<?php
    ob_start();

    echo '<p>This content is captured by the output buffer.</p>';

    ob_end_flush();
?>
</body>
</html>
```

This content is captured by the output buffer.

Extra

There are several functions for finding information about or manipulating the contents of a buffer. The `ob_get_clean` function returns the contents of an output buffer and leaves the buffer empty. The `ob_get_length` function returns the number of characters in a buffer. Because output buffers can be nested with repeated calls to `ob_start`, you can find the current level of buffering using the `ob_get_level` function.

TYPE THIS:

```
ob_start();
echo 'This data will go into the buffer.<br />';
printf("The length of the current buffer is: %d.<br />", ob_get_length());
ob_end_flush();
```

RESULTS:

The browser displays:

This data will go into the buffer.

The length of the current buffer is: 40.

159

Set Custom HTTP Headers

Y ou can use PHP to set custom HTTP headers in the response returned by the server. The `header` function allows you to pass the HTTP command you want to issue.

The `header` function accepts one required and one optional argument. The first argument is a string representing the command. For example, you can redirect users to another page using the `Location` command.

The second argument is a Boolean `true` or `false` value that tells PHP whether the `header` should overwrite any previous headers.

HTTP headers must be set before any content is written to the output stream. The easiest methods to ensure that headers are sent first are to put all calls to the `header` function at the very top of the page or to use output

buffering to capture any output until after the headers are sent. To learn more about output buffering, you can refer to the task "Using Output Buffering."

Custom HTTP headers are useful for controlling the way data is sent from the server to browsers. You can set the MIME type of the data returned by your script using the `Content-Type` header command.

You can tell browsers and proxy servers not to cache the output of your script by `Expires` and `Cache-Control` or `Pragma` commands.

HTTP Authentication functionality can be accessed using the `header` function along with the `WWW-Authorization` command and the appropriate HTTP authentication status response.

Set Custom HTTP Headers

① Type `header()`.

② In the parentheses, pass the HTTP header command you want to send.

③ Repeat Steps 1 and 2 for all additional headers.

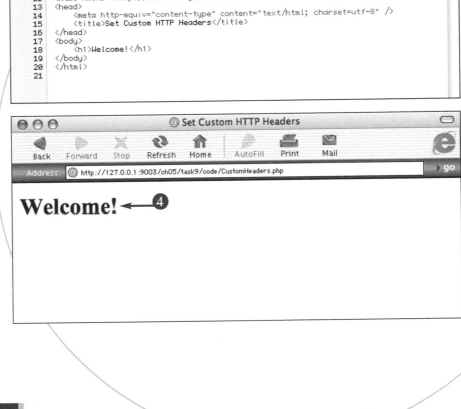

```php
<?php
    header('Expires: Mon, 26 Jul 1997 05:00:00 GMT');

    header('Last-Modified: ' . gmdate("D, d M Y H:i:s") . ' GMT');

    header('Cache-Control: no-store, no-cache, must-revalidate');

    header('Cache-Control: post-check=0, pre-check=0', false);
?>
<!DOCTYPE html PUBLIC "-//W3C//DTD XHTML 1.0 Strict//EN"
        "http://www.w3.org/TR/xhtml1/DTD/xhtml1-strict.dtd">
<html xmlns="http://www.w3.org/1999/xhtml" xml:lang="en" lang="en">
<head>
    <meta http-equiv="content-type" content="text/html; charset=utf-8" />
    <title>Set Custom HTTP Headers</title>
</head>
<body>
    <h1>Welcome!</h1>
</body>
</html>
```

④ View your script in a Web browser.

The results of any visible HTTP header commands appear.

Address: http://127.0.0.1:9003/ch05/task9/code/CustomHeaders.php

Welcome! ← ④

Extra

When conditionally using the certain commands with the header function, such as the Location command, it is desirable to halt all processing beyond the point in your script at which the header command is sent. To stop execution, you can use the exit statement immediately following the call to the header function.

TYPE THIS:

```php
<?php
$authorized = false;
if(!$authorized){
  header('Location: unauthorized.php');
  exit();
}
?>
<h1>Welcome!</h1>
```

RESULTS:

The browser redirects the user to the appropriate page, never showing the Welcome! message.

Execute Shell Commands

Y ou can use PHP to execute commands as if you were logged into a shell session on the Web server. The functions you can use to execute an external program are system, exec, shell_exec, and passthru. All four options provide access to external programs, but the results of the external operations are handled differently.

The system command accepts one required and one optional argument. The first argument is a string representing the shell command you want to execute. This value should match the command you would type were you in a shell session on the server. All flags and parameters should be included in the command.

By default, the system function prints the results of the shell command directly to the browser as ASCII text. If you want to capture this output in a variable instead of displaying it, you can pass a second argument to the

system function representing the variable to which the data should be written. If the command fails, system returns false.

The exec function accepts a shell command as the first argument. Optionally, you can pass a second argument representing an array to which each line of output from the external program is written. A variable pointer can be passed as a third parameter if you want to capture the return status of exec.

The shell_exec function accepts a single argument representing the command you want to run. The complete output, or false on error, is the return value.

The passthru function is identical to exec except that the output returned is binary instead of ASCII. This allows you to set custom content-type headers to pass images or other nontext data types to PHP from external programs.

Execute Shell Commands

① Type the name of a variable to contain the return value of a system call.

② Type system().

Note: The cd command equivalent for Windows is dir *.*.

③ Pass the command you want to execute between the parentheses.

④ Type the name of a variable to contain the output of an exec call.

⑤ Type exec().

⑥ Pass the command you want to execute between the parentheses.

⑦ Pass an array to capture the output.

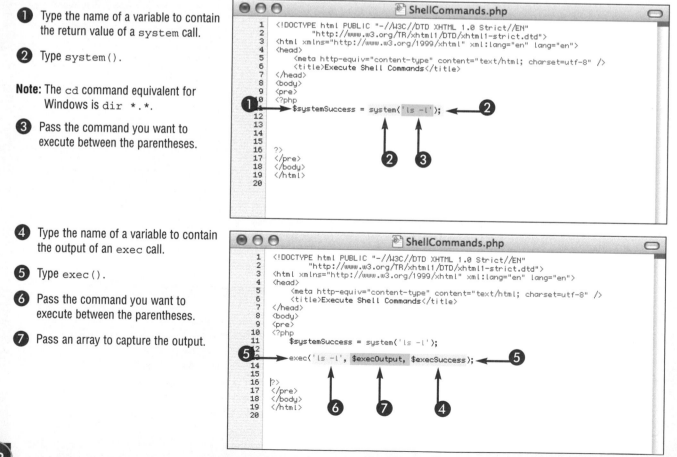

8 Use `print_r` to display the contents of the array.

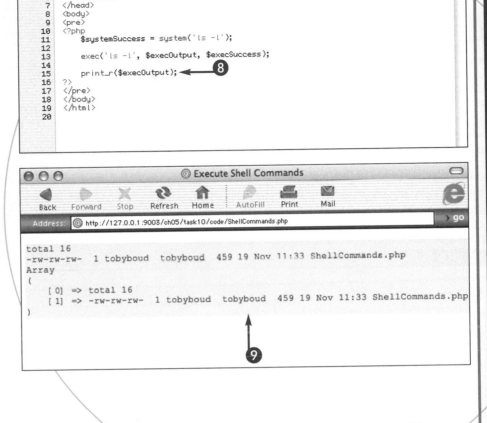

```
ShellCommands.php
1   <!DOCTYPE html PUBLIC "-//W3C//DTD XHTML 1.0 Strict//EN"
2        "http://www.w3.org/TR/xhtml1/DTD/xhtml1-strict.dtd">
3   <html xmlns="http://www.w3.org/1999/xhtml" xml:lang="en" lang="en">
4   <head>
5       <meta http-equiv="content-type" content="text/html; charset=utf-8" />
6       <title>Execute Shell Commands</title>
7   </head>
8   <body>
9   <pre>
10  <?php
11      $systemSuccess = system('ls -l');
12
13      exec('ls -l', $execOutput, $execSuccess);
14
15      print_r($execOutput);          ←  8
16  ?>
17  </pre>
18  </body>
19  </html>
20
```

9 View your script in a Web browser.

The return value of `system` is printed directly to the browser, and the value of `exec` appears as an array.

```
Execute Shell Commands

Back  Forward  Stop  Refresh  Home  AutoFill  Print  Mail

Address:  http://127.0.0.1:9003/ch05/task10/code/ShellCommands.php      go

total 16
-rw-rw-rw-  1 tobyboud   tobyboud   459 19 Nov 11:33 ShellCommands.php
Array
(
    [ 0] => total 16
    [ 1] => -rw-rw-rw-  1 tobyboud   tobyboud   459 19 Nov 11:33 ShellCommands.php
)

                                        9
```

Extra

Any time user-controlled parameters are used in executing a shell command it is vitally important to secure the command before execution. It is not difficult to take advantage of a trusting programmer and trick a system into executing malicious code. Fortunately, there are two functions provided by PHP that cleanse shell commands and arguments, preventing exploitation.

TYPE THIS:

```
$malicious = 'ls --l; cat /etc/passwd;';
system($malicious);
```

⬇

RESULTS:

The browser displays not only the results of the `ls --l` command, but the `/etc/passwd` file is also displayed, qualifying the command as a security breach.

TYPE THIS:

```
$malicious = 'ls --l; cat /etc/passwd;';
$safe = escapeshellcmd($malicious);
system($safe);
```

⬇

RESULTS:

The browser displays the error returned by the `ls` program. The error is due to the escaped second command being an unrecognized argument.

Send an E-Mail

A convenient function provided by PHP is the `mail` function. You can use the `mail` function to send an e-mail from your Web server to any number of e-mail addresses. This functionality allows you to easily build contact forms into your projects. You can also use the `mail` function to have PHP send e-mails to you when a page is accessed or when errors occur.

The `mail` function accepts three required arguments, all of which should be string values. The first is the e-mail address of the recipient of your message. The second argument is the subject of the message — that is, the copy that is displayed in the subject field of the recipient e-mail client. The third argument is the body of the message.

There are two additional optional arguments accepted by the `mail` function. The first represents any custom mail headers you want to send. These can include `From:`, `Reply-To:`,

`X-Mailer:`, `CC:`, and `BCC:` among others. Using custom headers allows you full control of the mail sent from PHP. For example, you can make it appear that a message was sent from an account on a different domain. The final argument is a string representing any commands or flags to be sent to your mail program.

For e-mail functionality to be available, PHP must have access to the `sendmail` binary on your system at the point when PHP is compiled. If your server uses another mail program, you should use its `sendmail` wrapper. PHP looks for the `sendmail` program in your environment `PATH` variable. If it is not found, the following locations are searched: `/usr/bin:/usr/sbin:/usr/etc:/etc:/usr/ucblib:/usr/lib`. It is important to note that the user that compiles PHP must have permission to access the `sendmail` binary.

Send an E-Mail

① Type `mail()`.

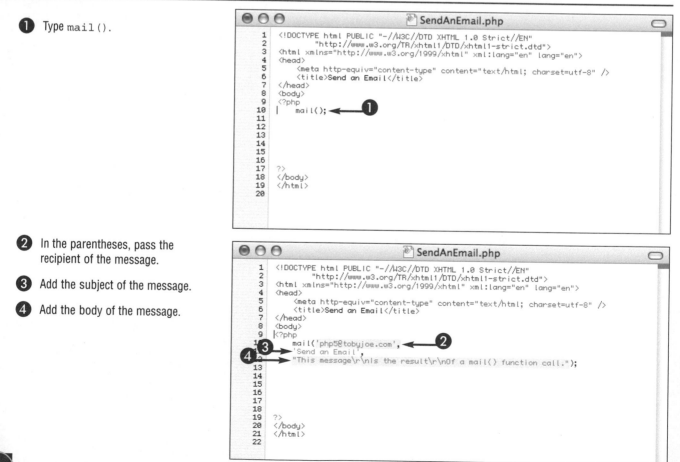

② In the parentheses, pass the recipient of the message.

③ Add the subject of the message.

④ Add the body of the message.

⑤ Add a variable to represent the success or failure of the `mail` function.

⑥ Use the `echo` statement to print a message to the output stream.

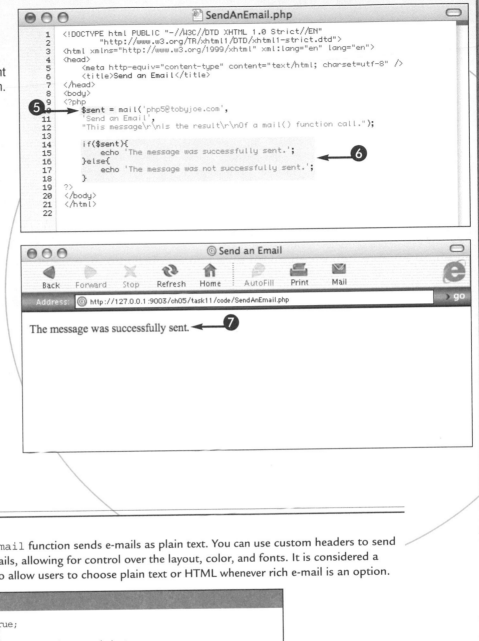

```
   SendAnEmail.php
1  <!DOCTYPE html PUBLIC "-//W3C//DTD XHTML 1.0 Strict//EN"
2       "http://www.w3.org/TR/xhtml1/DTD/xhtml1-strict.dtd">
3  <html xmlns="http://www.w3.org/1999/xhtml" xml:lang="en" lang="en">
4  <head>
5      <meta http-equiv="content-type" content="text/html; charset=utf-8" />
6      <title>Send an Email</title>
7  </head>
8  <body>
9  <?php
10     $sent = mail('php5@tobyjoe.com',
11         'Send an Email',
12         "This message\r\nIs the result\r\nOf a mail() function call.");
13
14     if($sent){
15         echo 'The message was successfully sent.';
16     }else{
17         echo 'The message was not successfully sent.';
18     }
19 ?>
20 </body>
21 </html>
22
```

⑦ View your script in a Web browser.

The browser displays the success or failure message for the `mail` function.

```
   Send an Email
Back  Forward  Stop  Refresh  Home  AutoFill  Print  Mail
Address: http://127.0.0.1:9003/ch05/task11/code/SendAnEmail.php      go

The message was successfully sent. ◄── 7
```

Extra

By default, the `mail` function sends e-mails as plain text. You can use custom headers to send rich HTML e-mails, allowing for control over the layout, color, and fonts. It is considered a good practice to allow users to choose plain text or HTML whenever rich e-mail is an option.

TYPE THIS:

```
$useHTML = true;
if($useHTML){
  $headers = "MIME-Version: 1.0\r\n";
  $headers .= "Content-type: text/html; charset=iso-8859-1\r\n";
  mail($user, $subject, $htmlBody, $headers);
}else{
  mail($user, $subject, $textBody);
}
```

↓

RESULTS:

If the `$useHTML` variable is `true`, an HTML e-mail is sent to the address represented by `$user`. Otherwise, a plain-text e-mail is sent.

Create
a Form

You can use HTML forms to collect information from users and submit it to server-side programs for processing. For example, you can create a contact form that allows users to send you e-mail without exposing your e-mail address. By using PHP to capture the information submitted by the form, you can make your sites more interactive and rich.

You can create a form using the `<form>` element. The `<form>` element exists within the `<body>` element of an HTML document. Depending on the document type declaration (DTD) you use for your document, there may be limitations and requirements on where and how the `<form>` element is created. You can refer to the documentation for your chosen DTD at the World Wide Web Consortium site at www.w3.org.

The `<form>` element has an attribute that specifies the location of the script or application that accepts and processes the data the form collects. The `action` attribute is specified in the opening `<form>` element as a quoted attribute. For example, to submit your data to a script called `sendEmail.php` you use `<form action="sendEmail.php">`.

Forms are submitted as HTTP requests. You can specify whether you want to use a POST or GET method using the `method` attribute. When using a GET method, all parameters and their values are passed as part of the URL to the form. Generally, HTTP POST requests are used to process large forms while GET requests are used to process smaller forms. To submit information to `sendEmail.php` using a GET request, your opening form tag might look like `<form action="sendEmail.php" method="get">`.

Create a Form

① Type `<form>` to open the form at the appropriate place in your document.

② Inside the opening tag, add an `action` attribute and set the value to the path of your script.

③ Add a `method` attribute and set it to `"post"` or `"get"`.

④ Type `</form>` to close the form.

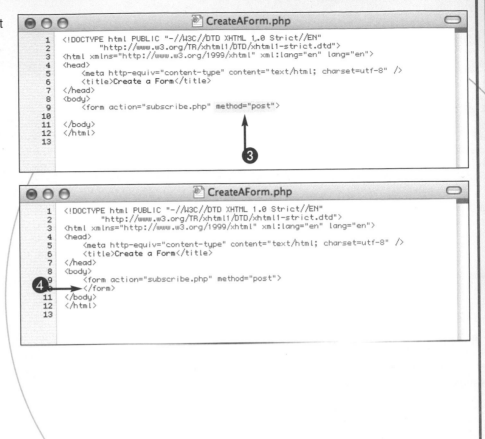

Extra

The GET method makes it easier to test and debug your scripts because you can directly manipulate the URL sent from your form to the server. For example, a form sent to a PHP script called `sendEmail.php` might have a parameter for the subject of the e-mail to be sent. The GET request might be sent as `sendEmail.php?subject=Hello!`. You could change the subject parameter manually to send a different subject without having to use the HTML form. For simple forms, the benefit may be unclear, but for more complex forms it is often useful to manipulate the query string to test various combinations of variables. Unfortunately, this also makes it easier for users to break your scripts to exploit security loopholes your program might contain. The POST method may provide a slight benefit over the GET method where security is concerned because users cannot accidentally modify or delete parameters. No matter which method is used, server-side validation of all user-submitted data is crucial for security. The minimum validation measures you should undertake are a check that all required parameters are present and that each is of the specific type required by your script.

Understanding Form Elements

Y ou can use HTML forms to capture data from users. An HTML form consists of a `<form>` element inside of which any number of child elements can be placed. You can create multiple forms in a page, but only one can be submitted by a user at a given time. Forms are submitted using either an HTTP POST or GET request. The value of each element in a form is sent to the server in a key-value pair. The key for a submitted value is the same string as the name attribute of the form element used to submit the value.

Each `<form>` element can contain any number of fields. A field element provides a point at which data may be collected. When a form is submitted to a program for processing, the `name` and `value` of each field are sent as part of the HTTP request. Depending on the `method` attribute used in the `<form>` element, these key-value pairs may be sent as a visible query string with the URL.

Common Element Attributes

Type

The `type` attribute sets the type of control to be used for an `<input>` element.

Name

The `name` attribute specifies the identifying key by which the value is passed to the script targeted by the `action` attribute of the `<form>` element.

Value

You can specify the default value of many elements using the `value` attribute. Any user-provided data is used in place of the default value.

Size

You can specify the width of an `<input>` element using the `size` attribute. This attribute may be forbidden depending on the DTD being used for the document.

Maxlength

The `maxlength` attribute is used to set the maximum number of characters the field can contain.

Common Elements

Input

You can create a simple text box using the `<input>` element with a `type` attribute set to `text`. You can set the key by which the value typed into the text box is accessed using the `name` attribute. The `value` attribute can be used to set a default value for the text field.

```
<input type="text" name="username" value="New Userv />
```

Textarea

Text input boxes that allow multiple lines of text are created using a `<textarea>` element. Like most form elements, `<textarea>` elements should have a `name` attribute to represent the key by which the element value may be accessed. There is no `value` attribute for a `<textarea>` element. Instead, the default value is set between the opening and closing tags.

```
<textarea name="bio">This is my biography. It consists of
multiple lines.</textarea>
```

Select

The `<select>` element allows you to create a method of selecting one or more of many options from a list. A browser typically renders a `<select>` element as either a drop-down list or a box with all options listed inside. This depends on the presence of the optional `multiple` attribute. Select elements contain one or more `<option>` elements.

```
<select name="interests" multiple="multiple"></select>
```

Option

The values represented by `<select>` elements are defined using `<option>` elements. Each `<select>` element can have one or more `<option>` elements, each of which should have a unique `value` attribute.

```
<select name="interests" multiple="multiple">

  <option value="cycling">Cycling</option>

  <option value="photography">Photography</option>

</select>
```

Password

You can create a field for typing sensitive data using an `<input>` element with a `type` attribute set to `password`. Browsers hide any data typed into a password field to protect it from onlookers. When contained within a form using the GET method, the data is still submitted as a visible part of the query string in the URL. If a `value` attribute is used to set the default value it should be noted that viewing the source of the HTML document could reveal sensitive information.

```
<input type="password" name="creditcardnumber" />
```

Checkbox

Checkboxes allow users to select zero, one, or more options from a group. You can create a checkbox using an `<input>` element with the `type` attribute set to `checkbox`. The `value` attribute sets the value to be passed to the server when the checkbox is checked. You can use the `checked` attribute to specify that a box should be checked by default. Like other form elements, the `name` attribute sets the name by which the server accesses your data. You can group checkboxes by adding square brackets `[]` to the end of the `name` and using the same `name` for each checkbox in the group.

```
<input type="checkbox" name="sendEmail" value="yes" />

<input type="checkbox" name="interests[]"
value="photography" checked="checked" />

<input type="checkbox" name="interests[]" value="cycling" />
```

Radio Button

Radio buttons are like checkboxes except that they allow for only one of many options to be chosen. You can use the `<input>` element to create a radio button by setting the `type` attribute to `radio`. All radio button elements that represent possible values for a given choice should have the same name attribute set. Unlike checkboxes, you do not need to add square brackets to the name of a radio button.

```
<input type="radio" name="sex" value="female" />

<input type="radio" name="sex" value="male" />
```

File Upload

A file upload element can be created using a standard `<input>` element with a `type` attribute set to `file`. A file upload element is most often displayed as a text field into which users can type the path to the file on their local filesystem. Accompanying the text field is a browse button that can be used to locate a file on a local computer to transfer it to the server. When a file upload element is used to transfer a file to Web server, the file can be accessed by the PHP script set to process the form submission using the key set as the name attribute of the `<input>` element.

```
<input type="file" name="userFile" />
```

Submit Button

All forms should have a submit button to allow a user to submit data to the program defined in the `action` attribute of the `<form>` element. You can create a submit button by setting the `type` attribute of an `<input>` element to `submit`. A `value` attribute can be used to set the display value of the submit button.

```
<input type="submit" name="save" value="Save!" />
```

Add Elements
to a Form

You can use HTML forms to collect information from visitors to a particular Web page. Each bit of information collected from a user is collected using a form element. There are elements representing small text boxes, large text boxes, checkboxes, radio buttons, and passwords, among others. To learn more about form elements, see the task "Understanding Form Elements."

Each field added to a form is represented by an element. An element is added to a page by typing the opening and closing tags for the element between the opening and closing tags for the form in which the element is contained. It is recommended (and perhaps required) that you always add tags in pairs. In other words, for every opening tag your document should have a matching closing tag or the

opening tag should be self-closing. All opened elements should be closed before the closing of their parent elements.

Some elements may contain other elements. For example, the select element can contain any number of option elements representing options to be presented to a user.

The order in which elements are arranged inside a form can be important for more than visual reasons. If you use the same value for a name attribute in multiple elements, you may find that the value of the last element in the form with that name is sent to the server. Generally, it is best that the name attribute for each element in your form be unique for all elements except grouped radio buttons and grouped checkboxes.

Add Elements to a Form

① Inside the `<form></form>` tags, type the opening tag for an element.

② Set the name attribute along with any other attributes required for the element.

③ Set the default value of the element.

④ Close the element by typing the closing tag.

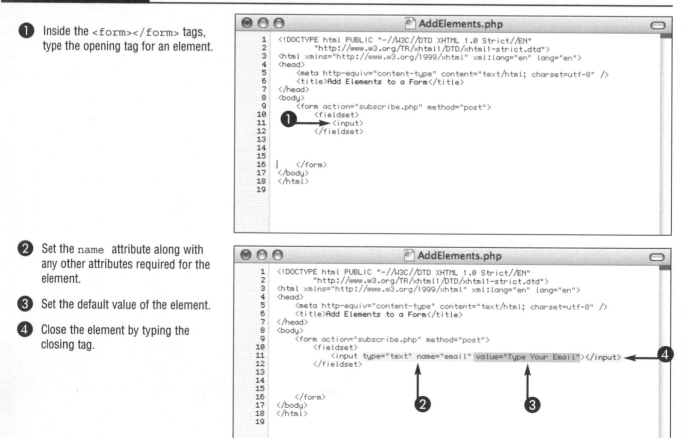

⑤ Repeat Steps 1 to 4 for any additional elements.

```
                                    AddElements.php
 1   <!DOCTYPE html PUBLIC "-//W3C//DTD XHTML 1.0 Strict//EN"
 2        "http://www.w3.org/TR/xhtml1/DTD/xhtml1-strict.dtd">
 3   <html xmlns="http://www.w3.org/1999/xhtml" xml:lang="en" lang="en">
 4   <head>
 5       <meta http-equiv="content-type" content="text/html; charset=utf-8" />
 6       <title>Add Elements to a Form</title>
 7   </head>
 8   <body>
 9       <form action="subscribe.php" method="post">
10           <fieldset>
11               <input type="text" name="email" value="Type Your Email"></input>
12           </fieldset>
13           <fieldset>
14               <input type="submit" name="submit" value="Sign Up!"></input>
15           </fieldset>
16       </form>
17   </body>
18   </html>
19
```

⑥ View the script in a Web browser.

The form is displayed with all defined form elements available as user controls.

```
                              Add Elements to a Form
  Back   Forward   Stop   Refresh   Home   AutoFill   Print   Mail
  Address:  http://127.0.0.1:9003/ch06/task3/code/AddElements.php       › go

  Type Your Email
  Sign Up!
```

Extra

Depending on the document type declaration (DTD) used in your HTML document, you may be required to enclose form elements within special `fieldset` elements. A `fieldset` groups related form fields on the page. The HTTP request sent to the server will not contain any information about `fieldset` elements used in your page.

Example:
```
<form id="userInfo" action="userInfo.php" method="get">
  <fieldset id="userNames">
    <input type="text" name="userNameFirst" id="userNameFirst" />
    <input type="text" name="userNameLast" id="userNameLast" />
  </fieldset>
</form>
```

Process Submitted Form Data

Y ou can use PHP to access data submitted by an HTML form to a script on your Web server. When a form is submitted, each named form element and its value are converted to key-value pairs and sent along as part of a POST or GET HTTP request. PHP makes it easy to look up variables and use them in your script.

When a GET request is sent to your script, all variables are accessible using the built-in `$_GET` array. The `$_GET` array is a globally accessible variable. Because the `$_GET` array is associative, each form element submitted by your Web form can be accessed by name. For example, if your GET request contains a variable named `email`, you can access it using `$_GET['email']`.

Like the `$_GET` array, PHP creates an array representing data sent using a POST request. To access variables in a POST request, you can use the `$_POST` array.

Though both the `$_GET` and `$_POST` arrays exist and are accessible in all scripts, you should check for the existence of a particular variable using a function such as `array_key_exists` or `isset` before trying to access a key. For example, you can check whether a variable named `email` exists in a POST request using `if(isset($_POST['email'])){}`. If you attempt to access an array key that does not exist, PHP throws an error.

To get a listing of all variables sent as part of a form submission, you can use the `array_keys` function. To learn more about array handling, you can refer to the task "Get Information about an Array" in Chapter 3.

Process Submitted Form Data

① Create an HTML document containing a form that uses your script as the `action` attribute.

② Set the `method` attribute of the form to GET or POST.

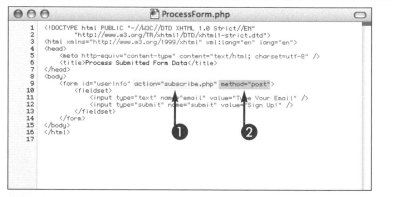

③ Create a PHP script to accept the form submission.

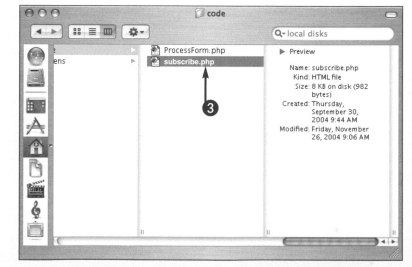

In the PHP script, use the `print_r` function to view the contents of the `$_GET` array.

⑤ Use the `print_r` function to also view the contents of the `$_POST` array.

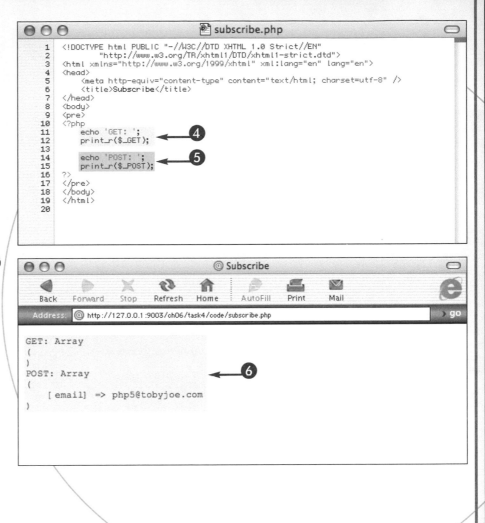

⑥ View your initial script in a Web browser and submit the form.

The browser goes to your processing script which prints the contents of the `$_GET` and `$_POST` arrays.

Extra

You can create a single processing form that handles both GET and POST requests. If you want to have the two methods handled differently, you can detect which method was used and process using a conditional statement. If the two request methods can be handled the same, you can use the `$_REQUEST` array in place of both `$_GET` and `$_POST`. The `$_REQUEST` variable allows you to access variables passed as part of the query string as well as those posted using a POST request. For example, you may have a form with an action attribute set to `userInfo.php?do=adduser` and a method attribute set to POST. While you could access the `do` parameter using the `$_GET` array and all submitted fields using the `$_POST` array, you can access both using `$_REQUEST`. Keep in mind that conflicts may occur if the same key is used in the query string and in the form. Generally, it is better to access variables using `$_GET` and `$_POST` because of the added clarity and ease in preventing naming conflicts.

Process Multiple Form Selections

Though most of the elements present in Web forms allow for single values such as a username or password, many forms allow users to choose multiple options from a list or group. While it is possible to create a variable name for each choice and pass grouped options separately, it makes maintenance and processing more difficult both because your PHP script is forced to handle multiple variables and because it needs to treat each distinct variable as part of a group. You can make multiple form selections easier to process by having your form submit the choices as an array.

You can set a `<select>` box to allow multiple selections by setting the optional `multiple` attribute. For example, you can type `<select name="interests" multiple="multiple"></select>` to create a select box that allows users to select multiple options. To have the

values passed to your PHP script as an array, you need only to add square brackets after the name of the select box. The above can be modified to `<select name="interests[]" multiple="multiple"></select>`.

When processing array values submitted to PHP, you can access the group using the `$_GET` or `$_POST` arrays. To access the above example, you can use `$_POST['interests']`. Notice that the square brackets are not used in the PHP script. The group of options is automatically converted to a native PHP array.

You can perform normal array operations on a grouped value submitted by a Web form. For example, you can use the count function to determine the number of options chosen by a user. To learn more about array handling, you can refer to Chapter 3.

Process Multiple Form Selections

① Create an HTML document containing a form.

② Set the `action` attribute to point to a PHP script that processes the file.

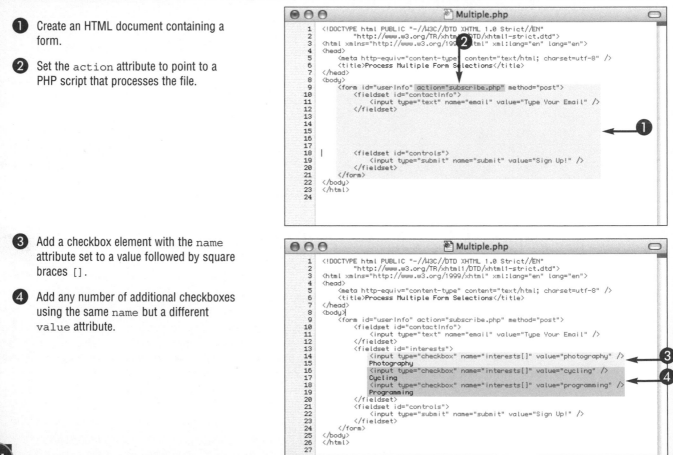

③ Add a checkbox element with the `name` attribute set to a value followed by square braces `[]`.

④ Add any number of additional checkboxes using the same `name` but a different `value` attribute.

⑤ Create a PHP script to accept the form submission.

⑥ Access the grouped parameter by name.

⑦ Use `print_r` to display the value of the grouped parameter.

 ⑤ → 📄 subscribe.php

```
1   <!DOCTYPE html PUBLIC "-//W3C//DTD XHTML 1.0 Strict//EN"
2          "http://www.w3.org/TR/xhtml1/DTD/xhtml1-strict.dtd">
3   <html xmlns="http://www.w3.org/1999/xhtml" xml:lang="en" lang="en">
4   <head>
5       <meta http-equiv="content-type" content="text/html; charset=utf-8" />
6       <title>Subscribe</title>
7   </head>
8   <body>
9   <pre>
10  <?php
11      echo 'INTERESTS: ';
12      print_r($_POST['interests']);
13  ?>
14  </pre>
15  </body>
16  </html>
17
```

⑦ (points to line 11 `echo 'INTERESTS: ';`)

⑦ (points to line 12 `print_r($_POST['interests']);`)

⑥ (points to `$_POST['interests']`)

⑧ View the form page in a Web browser and submit it.

The array structure created by the form appears.

@ Subscribe

Back Forward Stop Refresh Home AutoFill Print Mail

Address: http://127.0.0.1:9003/ch06/task5/code/subscribe.php ▸ go

```
INTERESTS: Array
(
    [0] => photography        ◄— ⑧
    [1] => programming
)
```

Extra

When treating a set of checkboxes as a group, you must set the name attribute of each checkbox to the same value. Like select boxes, you must add square brackets to the end of the value of the name attribute to tell the Web browser to treat the elements as a group and pass them to PHP as an array.

Example:
```
<form action="quiz.php?q=1" method="post">
  <p>Which of these animals is the cutest?</p>
  <fieldset>
    A. Bunny <input type="checkbox" name="answer1[]" value="a" />
    B. Lemur <input type="checkbox" name="answer1[]" value="b" />
    C. Gerbil <input type="checkbox" name="answer1[]" value="c" />
  </fieldset>
</form>
```

Create a File Upload Form

Y ou can create an HTML form that allows users to upload a file to your Web server. For example, you may want to allow users to upload photographs to a community site or submit a resume saved as a Word document or PDF. After the file has been uploaded, you can use PHP to access the file. There are functions to move, delete, open, and modify a file after it is uploaded.

Any form can be used to upload a file as long as certain conditions are met. First, the <form> tag must have the enctype attribute set to multipart/form-data. The enctype attribute tells the Web browser in which your form is displayed to encode the request it sends to the server in such a way that the server knows that there are multiple packets composing the submission. Secondly, set the

action attribute of the <form> element to post. This is due to the fact that there are practical limits on the size of HTTP GET requests and even small files are composed of relatively large amounts of data.

To create an interface control that allows users to select a file on their hard drive and upload it, you can use an <input> element with the type attribute set to file. When clicked, the button created opens a dialog box that allows users to browse their files and select a single file. To provide for multiple file uploads, simply create many file upload buttons with different names. To learn more about adding elements to a form, you can refer to the task "Add Elements to a Form."

Create a File Upload Form

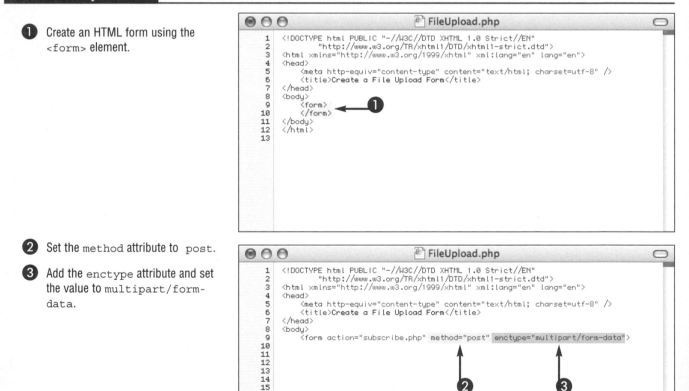

1 Create an HTML form using the <form> element.

2 Set the method attribute to post.

3 Add the enctype attribute and set the value to multipart/form-data.

④ Add a file chooser control using an `<input>` element with the `type` attribute set to `file`.

```
                          📄 FileUpload.php
1  <!DOCTYPE html PUBLIC "-//W3C//DTD XHTML 1.0 Strict//EN"
2          "http://www.w3.org/TR/xhtml1/DTD/xhtml1-strict.dtd">
3  <html xmlns="http://www.w3.org/1999/xhtml" xml:lang="en" lang="en">
4  <head>
        ─ta http-equiv="content-type" content="text/html; charset=utf-8" />
        :le>Create a File Upload Form</title>

        m action="subscribe.php" method="post" enctype="multipart/form-data">
        <fieldset id="photo">
            <input type="hidden" name="MAX_UPLOAD_SIZE" name="5000000" />
  ──▶      <input type="file" name="photo" />
        </fieldset>
        <fieldset id="controls">
            <input type="submit" name="submit" value="Upload!" />
        </fieldset>
      'orm>
        >
        >
```

```
                        @ Create a File Upload Form                    e
  ward    Stop    Refresh    Home    AutoFill    Print    Mail

http://127.0.0.1:9003/ch06/task6/code/FileUpload.php                  › go

              ( Browse... ) ◀────⑤
```

Extra

You can set a hidden form element representing the maximum size, in bytes, of a file your script will accept. This is only an advisory setting and can be easily spoofed or faked by users. The primary function of this setting is to tell browsers to warn users that a file is too large to be processed by your script. The advantage is that users will not have to wait for a large file to be transferred before being told that the file is too large. There is a setting to be used by PHP that cannot be spoofed or faked, which is essential for security.

TYPE THIS:

```
<form action="saveFile.php" enctype="multipart/form-data" method="post">
   <input type="hidden" name="MAX_FILE_SIZE" value="50000" />
   <input type="file" name="photo" />
   <input type="submit" value="submit" name="submit" />
</form>
```

RESULTS:

The browser displays a form that allows only files of less than 50,000 bytes to be uploaded to the server.

Process a File Upload

Y ou can use PHP to process a file uploaded to your Web server by an HTML form.

When the action attribute of your `<form>` is set to the name of a PHP script and the form is set to encode and upload files, PHP automatically accepts the file and saves it. The name of the saved file is initially set to a random name generated by PHP. This is a security measure that helps prevent users from uploading a dangerous script then triggering it by loading it in a Web browser.

If your form uploads a file named "photo" you can access information about it in PHP using `$_FILES['photo']`. This value represents an associative array representing information about your file. The values stored in the array are name, type, size, and the temporary name created by PHP.

To move the uploaded file from the temporary directory to which it is saved to a new location, you can use the `move_uploaded_file` function. The `move_uploaded_file` function accepts two required arguments. The first is a string representing the path to the source file. In the above example, this argument is found using `$_FILES['photo']['tmp_name']`. The second argument to the `move_uploaded_file` function is a string representing the location to which you want the file moved.

You can set ownership and permissions on the file using the `chown` and `chmod` functions. For more information about these and other file processing functions, you can refer to Chapter 5.

Process a File Upload

① Access the file information using the `$_FILES` array and the name of the uploaded file.

② Find the name used to move the file using the `tmp_name` key in the array.

③ Move the file to a new location with a new name by typing `move_uploaded_file`.

④ In parentheses, type the temporary file name, a comma, and the path to which you want to move your file.

⑤ Use the Boolean return value to display a status message.

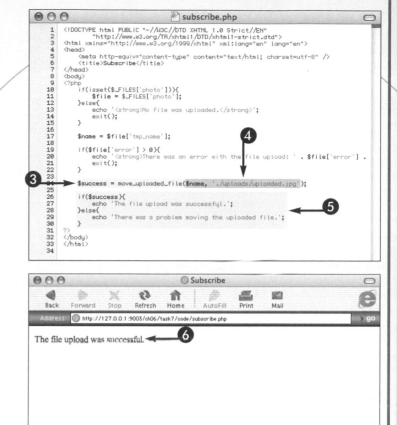

⑥ Use an HTML form to upload a file to the script.

The success or error message is displayed by the browser.

Extra

You can access any file upload errors using the $_FILES array. Like other file attributes, the error message is contained in the associative array for each uploaded file. The possible errors are listed below.

UPLOAD_ERR_OK	Value 0; There is no error
UPLOAD_ERR_INI_SIZE	Value 1; The file is larger than allowed by your PHP settings
UPLOAD_ERR_FORM_SIZE	Value 2; The file is larger than the MAX_FILE_SIZE form element allows
UPLOAD_ERR_PARTIAL	Value 3; The file was only partially uploaded
UPLOAD_ERR_NO_FILE	Value 4; No file was uploaded

Validate
User Input

All data submitted by users should be treated very carefully before being used. While client-side scripting is useful to help users complete forms, you cannot rely on JavaScript or other client-side scripting to validate user input. Many exploits exist for Web applications that casually use data submitted by users in scripts. You can use several PHP functions on the server side to confirm that user input is exactly what you and your script are expecting.

There are two approaches to validating user input. The first approach is to check each parameter to be sure that it is not missing or dangerous. You can use functions such as `isset`, `empty`, `strlen`, and `count` to verify that all expected parameters are provided and that they are not empty or less than the required length.

For each parameter you can then perform a security check. For example, you may have a text area in an HTML form

that allows users to submit comments to a weblog. You can use functions such as `striptags` to remove all HTML tags from the data. This can provide a simple safety net that might catch a great deal of problematic data.

The second approach is similar, but different. Instead of simply being sure that data is not dangerous in a given context, you can check that it is specifically what you expect. The second approach is an excellent follow-up step to the first approach.

If all required fields are submitted, you can use functions such as `is_numeric`, `is_object`, `is_string`, `is_float`, `is_bool`, `is_int`, and `is_array` to confirm that the value of each field is of the type you expect. You may also use regular expressions or other pattern matching or comparison functions to check whether each submitted value matches a form acceptable for your use.

Validate User Input

① Use `isset` to check that a parameter was passed.

② Use `empty` to verify that the value of the parameter is not blank.

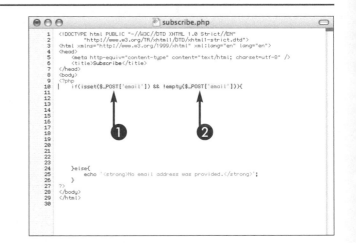

③ Use type-checking functions to verify that the value is of the correct type.

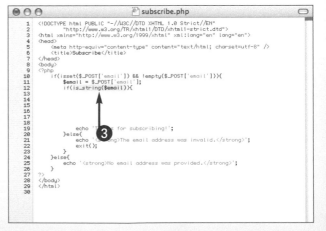

④ Perform any additional validation operations.

⑤ Act according to the result of the validation operations.

```
                                             subscribe.php
1    <!DOCTYPE html PUBLIC "-//W3C//DTD XHTML 1.0 Strict//EN"
2        "http://www.w3.org/TR/xhtml1/DTD/xhtml1-strict.dtd">
3    <html xmlns="http://www.w3.org/1999/xhtml" xml:lang="en" lang="en">
4    <head>
5        <meta http-equiv="content-type" content="text/html; charset=utf-8" />
6        <title>Subscribe</title>
7    </head>
8    <body>
9    <?php
10       if(isset($_POST['email']) && !empty($_POST['email'])){
11           $email = $_POST['email'];
12           if(is_string($email)){
13               $has_at = strpos($email, '@');          ④
14               $has_dot = strpos($email, '.');
15               if($has_at === false || $has_dot === false){
16                   echo '<strong>Improperly formatted email.</strong>';    ⑤
17                   exit();
18               }
19               echo 'Thanks for subscribing!';
20           }else{
21               echo '<strong>The email address was invalid.</strong>';
22               exit();
23           }
24       }else{
25           echo '<strong>No email address was provided.</strong>';
26       }
27   ?>
28   </body>
29   </html>
30
```

⑥ Submit an HTML form to your script.

The values are validated and the appropriate action is taken based on the result.

```
                                             Subscribe
   Back   Forward   Stop   Refresh   Home   AutoFill   Print   Mail          e
   Address:  http://127.0.0.1:9003/ch06/task8/code/subscribe.php              › go

   Improperly formatted email.  ←⑥
```

Use extreme caution when using user-submitted data in database statements or calls to external programs. This is in part because malformed data can lead to problems with your data but also because database and system commands are possible points of security failure.

SQL QUERY:

```
$query = sprintf("SELECT * FROM sometable WHERE id=%s",
$_GET['id']);
$result = mysql_query($query);
```

EXPLOIT:

If the user passes a value equivalent to the following as the value of the `id` parameter, they could trigger the deletion of your entire database table.

```
script.php?id=123;delete+from+sometable
```

Create and Read a Cookie

You can use PHP to create and read cookies. Cookies are small files stored on a viewer's computer. A cookie is associated with a given domain and may be accessed by any PHP page on that domain. Cookies allow you to persist information across visits to your site and to pages across your site. For example, you might set a cookie with a user's name and e-mail address on a login page and reuse this information on other forms on your site, reducing the amount of information a user has to type.

To create a cookie, you can use the setcookie function. The setcookie function accepts one required and five optional arguments. The first argument is a string representing the name of the cookie value you want to set.

The second argument represents the value you want to store in the cookie.

By default, a cookie is deleted when a user closes the Web browser. You can tell a cookie to persist until a given time using the third argument.

As soon as a cookie is created, you can read it using the $_COOKIE array. The name of the cookie is used as a key. For example, to read a cookie named 'user' you would use $_COOKIE['user'].

Cookies should never be used to represent user authentication or other sensitive data because users can spoof a system by manually creating cookies and accessing your site. Also, because many users reject cookies, you should never require their use. Instead, you should use cookies only as supplements that help your site function in a better or more elegant fashion. For example, PHP uses cookies to store session identifiers when possible. When cookies are rejected, PHP finds an alternate method of passing session identifiers around.

Create and Read a Cookie

① To create a cookie, type setcookie.

② In parentheses, type the name for the cookie value enclosed in quotes.

③ Type a comma and then the value you want to set to the cookie.

④ To set an expiry time, type a comma followed by the number of seconds you want to use.

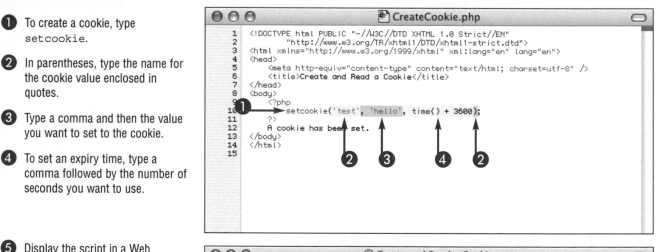

```
1  <!DOCTYPE html PUBLIC "-//W3C//DTD XHTML 1.0 Strict//EN"
2      "http://www.w3.org/TR/xhtml1/DTD/xhtml1-strict.dtd">
3  <html xmlns="http://www.w3.org/1999/xhtml" xml:lang="en" lang="en">
4  <head>
5      <meta http-equiv="content-type" content="text/html; charset=utf-8" />
6      <title>Create and Read a Cookie</title>
7  </head>
8  <body>
9      <?php
10         setcookie('test', 'hello', time() + 3600);
11     ?>
12     A cookie has been set.
13 </body>
14 </html>
15
```

⑤ Display the script in a Web browser.

The cookie is now set, assuming the browser is set to accept cookies.

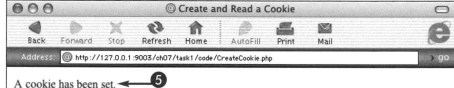

Address: http://127.0.0.1:9003/ch07/task1/code/CreateCookie.php

A cookie has been set. ◀— ⑤

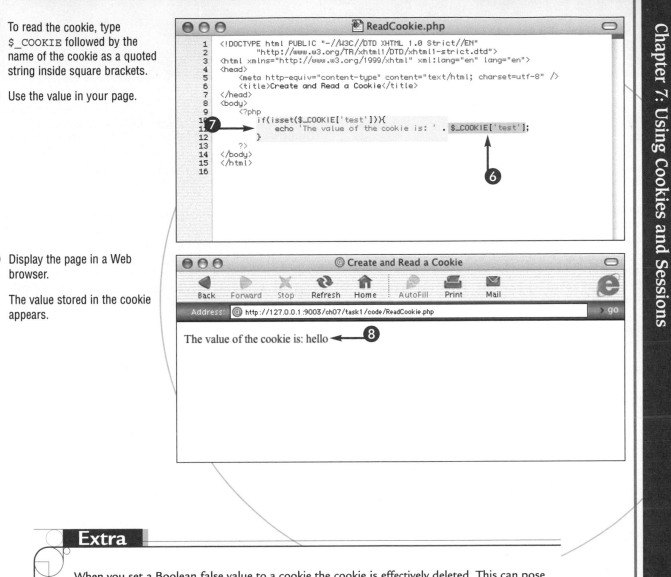

6 To read the cookie, type `$_COOKIE` followed by the name of the cookie as a quoted string inside square brackets.

7 Use the value in your page.

```
1   <!DOCTYPE html PUBLIC "-//W3C//DTD XHTML 1.0 Strict//EN"
2       "http://www.w3.org/TR/xhtml1/DTD/xhtml1-strict.dtd">
3   <html xmlns="http://www.w3.org/1999/xhtml" xml:lang="en" lang="en">
4   <head>
5       <meta http-equiv="content-type" content="text/html; charset=utf-8" />
6       <title>Create and Read a Cookie</title>
7   </head>
8   <body>
9       <?php
10          if(isset($_COOKIE['test'])){
11              echo 'The value of the cookie is: ' . $_COOKIE['test'];
12          }
13      ?>
14  </body>
15  </html>
16
```

8 Display the page in a Web browser.

The value stored in the cookie appears.

The value of the cookie is: hello

Extra

When you set a Boolean false value to a cookie the cookie is effectively deleted. This can pose an unexpected problem when using cookies to persist information across page requests. When working with objects or return values that are to be stored in cookies, you should use the numerical equivalent for each Boolean value.

The integer values 1 and 0 represent `true` and `false`, respectively.

You can use the `setrawcookie` function to set a cookie without URL encoding the value. This is useful when storing information that you do not want PHP to encode.

You can use the `header` function to set a cookie with a human-readable date instead of a number of seconds as required by the `setcookie` function.

Example:
```
header('Set-Cookie: userName=toby; expires=Saturday, 11-Dec-2004 00:00:00 GMT');
```

Delete a Cookie

You can delete a cookie before the expiration date used in its creation, or before the user closes the browser if no expiration data was set. There are several reasons for wanting to remove cookies manually. You may want to delete cookies used to store form information if a user cancels a submission process. You may want to provide a logout type of functionality that clears session identifier cookie values when a user clicks a button or link.

To delete a cookie, you can use the `setcookie` function to set a `null` value to the cookie ID as well as an expiry time in the past. You can generate a time in the past using the `time` function to generate a current timestamp in seconds and subtract a number before using it. For example, the

expression `$stamp = time() - 60;` sets the stamp to represent the moment exactly one minute before the function is called. This tells your cookie to be deleted immediately.

It is important to note that, if used at all, the path and domain values passed to the two `setcookie` statements must match.

In some cases, a Web server or Web browser may not allow you to delete a cookie before the original expiry time. It is always a good idea to set a `null` value to the cookie in the deletion statement. Additionally, you should check for `null` values wherever a cookie is accessed. Simply checking for the existence of a cookie may not be a reliable way of determining whether a given condition is true.

Delete a Cookie

 To delete a cookie, type `setcookie`.

② Type the name of the cookie you want to delete as a quoted string inside a set of parentheses.

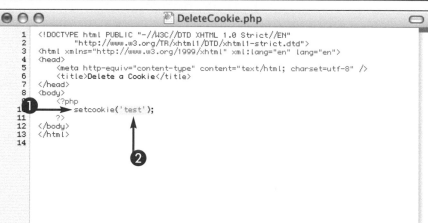

③ Type a comma followed by an empty value.

④ To set an expiry time in the past, use the `time()` function and subtract a number of seconds from the result.

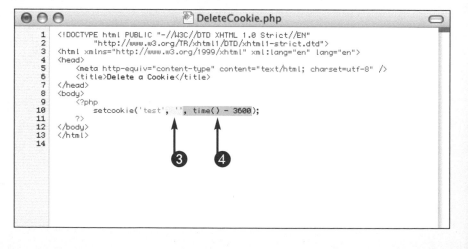

184

5 If a path was specified for the original cookie, pass the same path to the `setcookie` function call.

6 If a domain was specified for the original, pass the same domain.

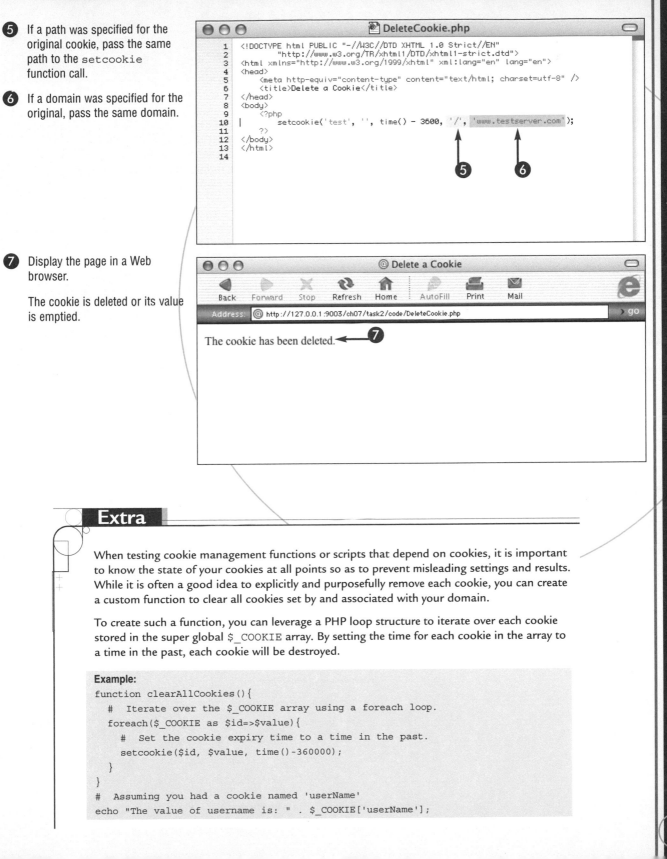

```
    🖹 DeleteCookie.php
1   <!DOCTYPE html PUBLIC "-//W3C//DTD XHTML 1.0 Strict//EN"
2           "http://www.w3.org/TR/xhtml1/DTD/xhtml1-strict.dtd">
3   <html xmlns="http://www.w3.org/1999/xhtml" xml:lang="en" lang="en">
4   <head>
5       <meta http-equiv="content-type" content="text/html; charset=utf-8" />
6       <title>Delete a Cookie</title>
7   </head>
8   <body>
9       <?php
10          setcookie('test', '', time() - 3600, '/', 'www.testserver.com');
11      ?>
12  </body>
13  </html>
14
```

7 Display the page in a Web browser.

The cookie is deleted or its value is emptied.

```
    @ Delete a Cookie
Back  Forward  Stop  Refresh  Home  AutoFill  Print  Mail
Address: @ http://127.0.0.1:9003/ch07/task2/code/DeleteCookie.php    › go

The cookie has been deleted.  ◄— 7
```

Extra

When testing cookie management functions or scripts that depend on cookies, it is important to know the state of your cookies at all points so as to prevent misleading settings and results. While it is often a good idea to explicitly and purposefully remove each cookie, you can create a custom function to clear all cookies set by and associated with your domain.

To create such a function, you can leverage a PHP loop structure to iterate over each cookie stored in the super global `$_COOKIE` array. By setting the time for each cookie in the array to a time in the past, each cookie will be destroyed.

Example:
```
function clearAllCookies(){
  #  Iterate over the $_COOKIE array using a foreach loop.
  foreach($_COOKIE as $id=>$value){
    #  Set the cookie expiry time to a time in the past.
    setcookie($id, $value, time()-360000);
  }
}
#  Assuming you had a cookie named 'userName'
echo "The value of username is: " . $_COOKIE['userName'];
```

Create a Session

When users request pages from a Web server the requests are not seen as being related. There is no persistence from one request to another. For example, you may want to allow users to customize their experience at your site by selecting a specific CSS file to be used. Due to the stateless nature of the HTTP protocol, the choice must be made on each page. To treat all page views as a related group you can create a PHP *session*.

Sessions allow you to set variables in one script and access them from another. To create a session, you can use the `session_start` function. The call to `session_start` should be the first PHP code in your page. Place it before any data, such as HTML, is written to the output stream.

Each call to `session_start` causes PHP to look up the session specified by an automatic ID assigned to each user who visits your site. If there is no ID, PHP recognizes the need to create a new session and associated ID. If `session_start` is called multiple times (due to includes, for example) in the same script, the server ignores all but the first call.

When PHP creates a new session id for a user, it writes the id to a cookie variable on the user's computer. If cookies are disabled or if the cookie from your site is blocked, PHP automatically appends the session id to each link in your page.

- call session_start() @ beg. of each page
- retrieve session vars to local vars
- check if registered b/f using.

Create a Session

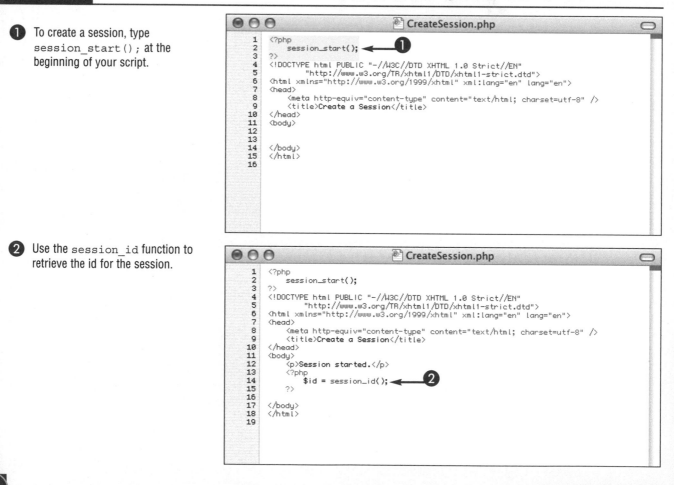

① To create a session, type `session_start();` at the beginning of your script.

```php
1  <?php
2      session_start();          ① ⟵
3  ?>
4  <!DOCTYPE html PUBLIC "-//W3C//DTD XHTML 1.0 Strict//EN"
5          "http://www.w3.org/TR/xhtml1/DTD/xhtml1-strict.dtd">
6  <html xmlns="http://www.w3.org/1999/xhtml" xml:lang="en" lang="en">
7  <head>
8      <meta http-equiv="content-type" content="text/html; charset=utf-8" />
9      <title>Create a Session</title>
10 </head>
11 <body>
12
13
14 </body>
15 </html>
16
```

② Use the `session_id` function to retrieve the id for the session.

```php
1  <?php
2      session_start();
3  ?>
4  <!DOCTYPE html PUBLIC "-//W3C//DTD XHTML 1.0 Strict//EN"
5          "http://www.w3.org/TR/xhtml1/DTD/xhtml1-strict.dtd">
6  <html xmlns="http://www.w3.org/1999/xhtml" xml:lang="en" lang="en">
7  <head>
8      <meta http-equiv="content-type" content="text/html; charset=utf-8" />
9      <title>Create a Session</title>
10 </head>
11 <body>
12     <p>Session started.</p>
13     <?php
14         $id = session_id();      ② ⟵
15     ?>
16
17 </body>
18 </html>
19
```

3 Display the session id in your script.

```
1  <?php
2      session_start();
3  ?>
4  <!DOCTYPE html PUBLIC "-//W3C//DTD XHTML 1.0 Strict//EN"
5       "http://www.w3.org/TR/xhtml1/DTD/xhtml1-strict.dtd">
6  <html xmlns="http://www.w3.org/1999/xhtml" xml:lang="en" lang="en">
7  <head>
8      <meta http-equiv="content-type" content="text/html; charset=utf-8" />
9      <title>Create a Session</title>
10 </head>
11 <body>
12     <p>Session started.</p>
13     <?php
14         $id = session_id();
15     ?>
16     <p>Session ID: <?php echo $id;?></p>   ◀── 3
17 </body>
18 </html>
19
```

CreateSession.php

4 View the script in a Web browser.

The session has been successfully started, and the value of the session id appears.

Address: http://127.0.0.1:9003/ch07/task3/code/CreateSession.php

Create a Session

Session started.

Session ID: 8457c2ecf48d57b2918a29b087627d90   ◀── 4

Extra

There are several configuration options for session management. You can modify each in the `php.ini` file on your server.

You can use the `session.save_path` configuration option to specify a directory to which you want to store session information. Depending on your server configuration, you may want to separate session files for different domains or accounts.

Example:
```
session.save_path=/home/tobyjoe/tmp/
```

You can use the `session.name` configuration option to specify a specific key to use to represent the session id assigned to each user. The default value is `PHPSESSID`.

One security issue that can arise from the default session-handling mechanism is that any user with shell access can often scan the contents of the directory set via the `session.save_path` configuration option. You can combat this type of security issue by setting the permissions for the session directory so that only the user under which PHP runs has read and write access.

Example:
```
session.name=VISITORID
```

Create and Read Session Variables

You can assign variables to a session by using the $\_SESSION$ global variable. Any value assigned to $\_SESSION$ is readable by any script served by your Web server and viewed in the same session. When a session is destroyed due to inactivity or by a call to session_destroy, the data held in the $\_SESSION$ array is deleted.

Because the $\_SESSION$ variable is an associative array, you can assign a variable to a session by typing $\_SESSION[]$ with the name of the variable between the brackets. Like all associative array keys, the name must be a string. Type the assignment operator (=) followed by the value you want to store. Any value can be stored in a session. This allows complex functionality such as storing instances of objects or multidimensional arrays.

You can also set session variables using the session_register function. The session_register function accepts two arguments. The first is a string representing the name of the variable you want to store. The second is the value you want to assign.

To access a variable in a session, you can type $\_SESSION[]$ with the name of the variable you want to access. For example, a session variable named 'isLoggedIn' can be accessed using $\_SESSION['isLoggedIn']$.

Because data is stored on the Web server and not on the user's browser, sessions provide a method of passing information across multiple pages that is more convenient and secure than using cookies or hidden form fields.

Create and Read Session Variables

① Create or continue a session using the session_start function at the top of your script.

② Set a variable by typing $\_SESSION$ followed by the name of your variable in square brackets.

③ Type the assignment operator followed by a value.

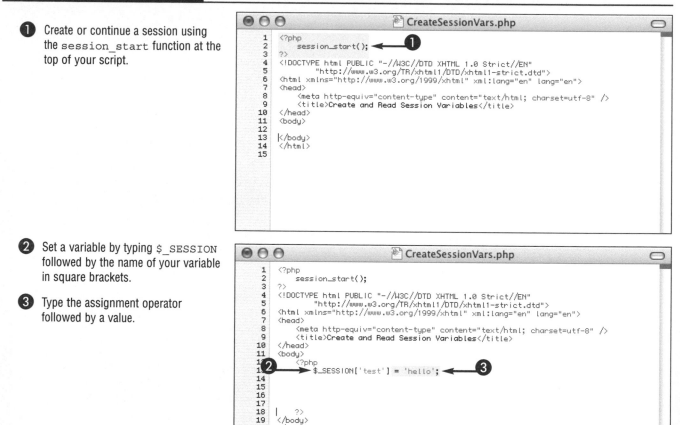

```php
<?php
    session_start();
?>
<!DOCTYPE html PUBLIC "-//W3C//DTD XHTML 1.0 Strict//EN"
        "http://www.w3.org/TR/xhtml1/DTD/xhtml1-strict.dtd">
<html xmlns="http://www.w3.org/1999/xhtml" xml:lang="en" lang="en">
<head>
    <meta http-equiv="content-type" content="text/html; charset=utf-8" />
    <title>Create and Read Session Variables</title>
</head>
<body>

</body>
</html>
```

```php
<?php
    session_start();
?>
<!DOCTYPE html PUBLIC "-//W3C//DTD XHTML 1.0 Strict//EN"
        "http://www.w3.org/TR/xhtml1/DTD/xhtml1-strict.dtd">
<html xmlns="http://www.w3.org/1999/xhtml" xml:lang="en" lang="en">
<head>
    <meta http-equiv="content-type" content="text/html; charset=utf-8" />
    <title>Create and Read Session Variables</title>
</head>
<body>
    <?php
        $_SESSION['test'] = 'hello';



    ?>
</body>
</html>
```

④ Read a session variable using the $_SESSION array along with the name of your variable.

⑤ Use the echo function to print the value to the output stream.

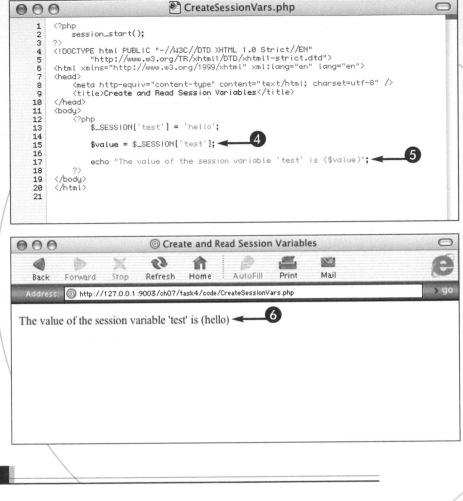

```php
1  <?php
2      session_start();
3  ?>
4  <!DOCTYPE html PUBLIC "-//W3C//DTD XHTML 1.0 Strict//EN"
5          "http://www.w3.org/TR/xhtml1/DTD/xhtml1-strict.dtd">
6  <html xmlns="http://www.w3.org/1999/xhtml" xml:lang="en" lang="en">
7  <head>
8      <meta http-equiv="content-type" content="text/html; charset=utf-8" />
9      <title>Create and Read Session Variables</title>
10 </head>
11 <body>
12     <?php
13         $_SESSION['test'] = 'hello';
14
15         $value = $_SESSION['test'];
16
17         echo "The value of the session variable 'test' is ($value)";
18     ?>
19 </body>
20 </html>
21
```

⑥ Display the script in a Web browser.

The value stored in the session appears.

Address: http://127.0.0.1:9003/ch07/task4/code/CreateSessionVars.php

The value of the session variable 'test' is (hello) ← ⑥

Extra

You can use the session_is_registered function to check for the existence of a session variable before attempting to access it. If you attempt to access a variable in the session that has not been set, PHP will throw an error. As with all variables and array keys, it is important to ensure that they exist before using them in your script.

The absence or presence of a particular session variable may be sufficient to determine important information such as the login status of a particular user or the completion of a given step in a multi-step process.

Example:
```
#  Check for the existence of the variable.
#  If set, show the user preferences.
if(session_is_registered('userID')){
  $userID = $_SESSION['userID'];
  showPreferences($userID);
#  If not set, show the user a login form and exit the script.
}else{
  showLoginForm();
  exit();
}
```

Save Session Data to a File

Session data persists on the Web server for as long as a session remains active. When a session expires or is forcibly deleted, the data with which it is associated is destroyed. You can take a snapshot of a session at a particular moment using the session_encode function. The session_encode function returns an encoded string representing the session including all variables. The current session id is not stored in the encoded session. This allows you to assign the session data to a new session at a later point. A useful application of session_encode is to provide a debugging mechanism that allows developers to replicate the state of a user session at the point that an error occurred. If a user submits a bug report, you can store the session information in a file that a developer can access when the bug is investigated.

Most often, session_encode is used in conjunction with a database or file system to store the data for future use or examination. Because the encoded session is a simple string, you can easily perform other operations with it such as e-mailing the data to an administrator.

To store the data returned by session_encode in a file, you can use functions such as fopen, fwrite, and fclose to create a file handle, write to a file, and close the handle. To learn more about filesystem operations, you can refer to Chapter 5.

To learn about restoring a session from encoded session data, you can refer to the task "Access Saved Session Data."

Save Session Data to a File

① Create a session and use it to store variables.

② Open a file pointer using fopen.

③ Type session_encode() to serialize the session data as a string and assign it to a variable.

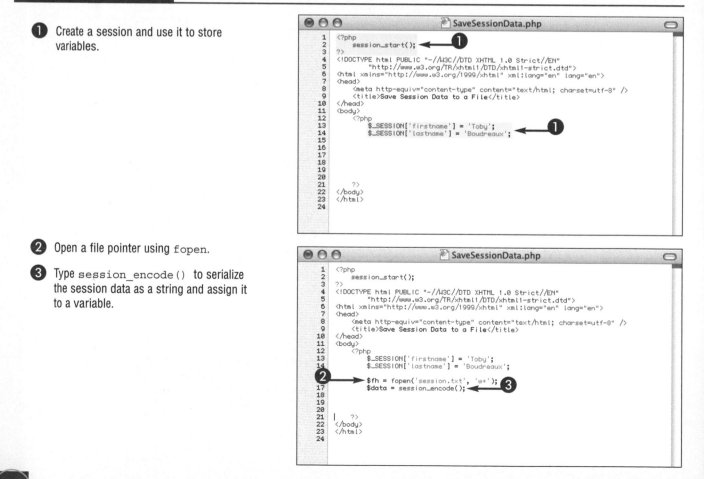

④ Use `fwrite` to write the encoded data to the file.

⑤ Close the file using `fclose`.

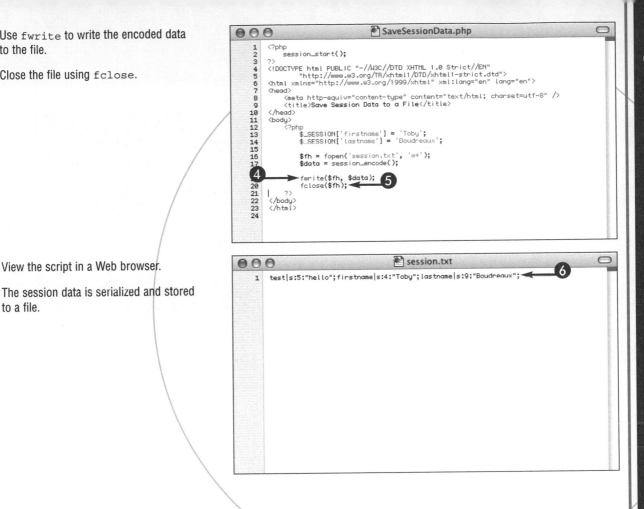

```php
<?php
    session_start();
?>
<!DOCTYPE html PUBLIC "-//W3C//DTD XHTML 1.0 Strict//EN"
    "http://www.w3.org/TR/xhtml1/DTD/xhtml1-strict.dtd">
<html xmlns="http://www.w3.org/1999/xhtml" xml:lang="en" lang="en">
<head>
    <meta http-equiv="content-type" content="text/html; charset=utf-8" />
    <title>Save Session Data to a File</title>
</head>
<body>
    <?php
        $_SESSION['firstname'] = 'Toby';
        $_SESSION['lastname'] = 'Boudreaux';

        $fh = fopen('session.txt', 'w+');
        $data = session_encode();

        fwrite($fh, $data);
        fclose($fh);
    ?>
</body>
</html>
```

⑥ View the script in a Web browser.

The session data is serialized and stored to a file.

session.txt
```
test|s:5:"hello";firstname|s:4:"Toby";lastname|s:9:"Boudreaux";
```

Extra

If you want to prevent saved encoded session data from being overwritten on successive visits to your site you can open the file in which the data is saved using a mode that appends data. This allows you to have a single file that contains many serialized sessions associated with a particular user in order of their occurrence.

While the file system is sufficient when handling relatively small amounts of data, if you end up storing large volumes of data you should use a database. Databases allow you to search and sort information while providing efficient methods of accessing partial data. An additional benefit to using databases to store session information is that multiple servers can access the same database when operating in a multi-server architecture. This can be helpful during development, as well. Additionally, you can create management or analytic tools on a separate machine residing within an intranet or otherwise protected from outside access.

Access Saved Session Data

Y ou can use PHP to replace a current session with encoded session data. For example, when a user visits your site and uses a login form to create a session, your scripts can look up a saved representation of his or her most recent session and restore it to the user's current session. This could help place a user at a particular point in a process that may be only partially completed, such as a step in a survey or test. It is common for many sites that users fail to complete registration forms that are comprised of multiple pages on their first attempt. By leveraging cookies and saved sessions you can help restore a previous registration, providing added usability to your site.

If you save an encoded session to a file or database you can read the data as a string and pass it to the session_decode function. The session_decode function takes a serialized string and deserializes it so that it can be used in a script.

The session_decode function accepts one argument representing the encoded session you want to replace into the current script context.

When using session_decode, ensure that a session has been created. You can create a session using the session_start function. Any call to session_start must be placed before all other code and data in your file. If you call session_start after data has been written to the output stream, PHP will throw a fatal error. For more about starting sessions, see "Create a Session."

To read a saved session from a file, you can use the fopen, fread, and fclose functions to open a file handle, read data from a file, and close the handle, respectively. For more about filesystem manipulation and file handling, see Chapter 5.

Access Saved Session Data

1 Use the fopen function to open the file in which you stored your session information.

2 Access the data in the file using the fread function.

```php
<?php
    session_start();
?>
<!DOCTYPE html PUBLIC "-//W3C//DTD XHTML 1.0 Strict//EN"
    "http://www.w3.org/TR/xhtml1/DTD/xhtml1-strict.dtd">
<html xmlns="http://www.w3.org/1999/xhtml" xml:lang="en" lang="en">
<head>
    <meta http-equiv="content-type" content="text/html; charset=utf-8" />
    <title>Access Saved Session Data</title>
</head>
<body>
    <?php
        $fp = fopen('session.txt', 'r');
        $data = fread($fp, 4096);


    ?>
</body>
</html>
```

3 Pass the retrieved data to the session_decode function.

```php
<?php
    session_start();
?>
<!DOCTYPE html PUBLIC "-//W3C//DTD XHTML 1.0 Strict//EN"
    "http://www.w3.org/TR/xhtml1/DTD/xhtml1-strict.dtd">
<html xmlns="http://www.w3.org/1999/xhtml" xml:lang="en" lang="en">
<head>
    <meta http-equiv="content-type" content="text/html; charset=utf-8" />
    <title>Access Saved Session Data</title>
</head>
<body>
    <?php
        $fp = fopen('session.txt', 'r');
        $data = fread($fp, 4096);

        session_decode($data);

    ?>
</body>
</html>
```

④ Use the `print_r` function to view the variables in the `$_SESSION` array.

```
                          AccessSessionData.php
1   <?php
2       session_start();
3   ?>
4   <!DOCTYPE html PUBLIC "-//W3C//DTD XHTML 1.0 Strict//EN"
5       "http://www.w3.org/TR/xhtml1/DTD/xhtml1-strict.dtd">
6   <html xmlns="http://www.w3.org/1999/xhtml" xml:lang="en" lang="en">
7   <head>
8       <meta http-equiv="content-type" content="text/html; charset=utf-8" />
9       <title>Access Saved Session Data</title>
10  </head>
11  <body>
12      <?php
13          $fp = fopen('session.txt', 'r');
14          $data = fread($fp, 4096);
15
16          session_decode($data);
17          print_r($_SESSION);
18      ?>
19  </body>
20  </html>
21
```

⑤ View your script in a Web browser.

The stored session data is restored and printed to the browser.

```
                          @ Access Saved Session Data
  Back  Forward  Stop  Refresh  Home   AutoFill   Print   Mail
  Address:  @ http://127.0.0.1:9003/ch07/task6/code/AccessSessionData.php          › go

Array ( [test] => hello [firstname] => Toby [lastname] => Boudreaux )  ◄─── ⑤
```

Extra

The data stored in a file using `session_encode` is formatted in a human-readable fashion. Because the information follows a clear format it is possible to use the data in non-PHP applications, or to manually read or modify it. Including the information as part of a debugging process can be a great help in attempting to replicate the conditions under which a given bug or error presented itself.

When reading session information using the `fopen`, `fread`, and `fclose` functions, it is important to pay attention to file system permissions.

You can use regular expressions to analyze the serialized data returned by the `session_encode` function. While it is certainly faster to use the PHP `session_decode` function, in some cases you will want to perform custom processing or manage very large strings of encoded data according to the contents. It can be more efficient to use a regular expression to scan the serialized data for certain values before decoding the entire string into an object in memory. Typically, it is best practice to rely upon the native PHP functions provided for these tasks.

Introduction to Object-Oriented Programming

The most difficult part of computer programming is not remembering the syntax and functions inherent to each language. The biggest challenge in learning to program is reconciling the way we think about the world outside of the computer with the way we have to think of our programs. Many programming languages function as little more than simple, direct sets of human-readable instructions with which we can control our machines. PHP, like C++, Objective-C, Java, and others before it, provides a way of modeling our programs after the real world. By providing a method of describing computer instructions in terms of the world around us, object-oriented programming allows us to think of code the way we think of animals, objects, and ourselves.

Objects

The most important concept of object-oriented programming is that of objects. Objects might be best described as discrete containers for information. Alternately, you can think of objects as functional representations of real-world items. Usually, objects provide methods of extracting and altering certain bits of information. For example, your television contains all sorts of proprietary information — both structural and functional. One bit of functional information is the current channel being processed and displayed. You have the ability to alter this information, or extract it, using a remote control or other interface. You never know about the internal processes triggered by sending the instruction to change the channel. This type of function encapsulation is often referred to as "black box" programming.

Instantiation

Objects are created, or *instantiated*, from a class definition. You can think of a class as a blueprint or archetype from which tangible instances are created. In PHP, you create an instance of a class using the new keyword. For example, an instance of a class named Cat can be created by typing `$myCat = new Cat();`.

Object Members

Objects are composed of both variables and functions. When a function is part of an object it is called a *method*. Variables and methods can belong to any of three scopes. Access scoping specifies which objects can access a variable or method in another object.

Granularity

You can design objects according to finer and finer levels of granularity by *subclassing* one object class from another. For example, the Cat class might inherit properties and functionality from a more general Animal class. By following a granular model, you can provide functionality across many similar types of object in a consistent and efficient manner. Each subclass overrides or adds properties and functionality to that it inherits.

Object-oriented programming provides a scalable method of developing projects using a vocabulary that parallels the real world.

Changes
in PHP 5

PHP 4 provided simple and limited support for object-oriented programming. Essentially, the object orientation consisted of a few syntactical additions that allowed developers to treat associative arrays as objects. Beneath the additions to the language the underlying mechanics were still treating objects as nothing more than associative arrays. Private variables

and methods were not a possibility in PHP 4, nor were other core object-oriented features. The OO features in PHP 5 have been rewritten in a way that allows for robust support for features present in all true OO languages. It is now possible to distinguish between private, protected, and public variables and methods, providing true encapsulation.

Passing Objects

In PHP 4, objects are passed around by value, not by reference. This means that when a variable is passed to a function, it is first converted into its associated value. In some cases the functional impact is not terribly large, such as in a function accepting a number and printing it to the output stream. In cases where an object needs to be modified or compared, the impact can be quite severe. When porting scripts from PHP 4 to PHP 5, you should take care to check all circumstances and conditions to ensure that your code has been fully audited for lost references or other unexpected functionality where object pointers are concerned.

Interfaces

PHP 5 provides the ability to declare interfaces to be implemented by classes. An interface is essentially a contract specifying a list of methods that all implementing classes must declare.

Static

You can use the new *static* keyword to specify static class methods and variables. Static methods and variables differ from instance methods and variables in that they are called on the class, not instances of the class. This allows you to implement Singleton design patterns and build utility classes in a fashion similar to those used in other languages.

Generally, the changes to PHP 5 lie heavily in the object-oriented features.

Exceptions

Exception handling is a welcome addition to PHP 5. With PHP 4, problematic behavior had to be found using conditional tests and handled using chained callback methods or other inconsistent functionality. Exceptions are types of objects that provide a wrapper for messages that can be passed around or *thrown* by problematic code. The calling statements can *catch* the exception and choose whether and how the application should proceed.

Overloading

Overloading is a feature of PHP 5 that allows for dynamic function calls and variable access. Using the built-in class methods, `__call`, `__get`, and `__set`, you can filter attempts to access and mutate variables and call unknown methods to a general function that can act accordingly.

Define a Class

Classes are like blueprints in that they define the structure, properties, and functionality of a certain type of object. Each object instantiated from a class definition is an *instance* of that class. Instances share the same structure and functionality, but their internal data values may be entirely different. In most cases, the initial state of each instance of a class that is created is a perfect match for every other instance at its initial state.

You might have a class to represent a point in two-dimensional space. The properties inherent in the class would be the position of the point on each the x and y axes. Most commonly, properties are marked as *private*, which means that only methods of the instance in question can access them. External objects access the properties using *accessor* and *mutator* methods to read and modify properties, respectively.

You can create a class using the *class* keyword. Each class definition is delimited by curly braces ({}) and contains method definitions and variable declarations. After the *class* keyword, you must type the name of the class. The standard naming convention is to choose a name that signifies the object you want to describe and capitalize the first letter. Good class names are User, Page, RequestProcessor, and ItalicsTextDecorator. If your class is a subclass of another class, you follow the class name with the *extends* keyword followed by the name of the superclass. To learn more about subclassing, please refer to the task "Extend a Class."

After the name of the class and any subclassing notation, open the class definition by typing an opening curly brace, {. Close the class definition by typing a closing curly brace, }.

Define a Class

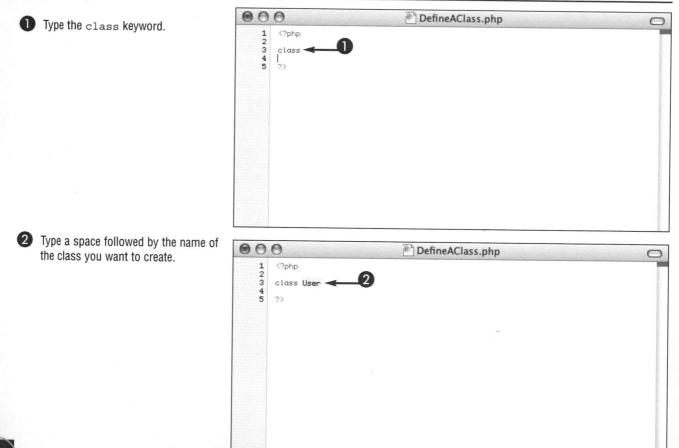

① Type the **class** keyword.

② Type a space followed by the name of the class you want to create.

3 Type an opening curly brace ({) to open the class definition block.

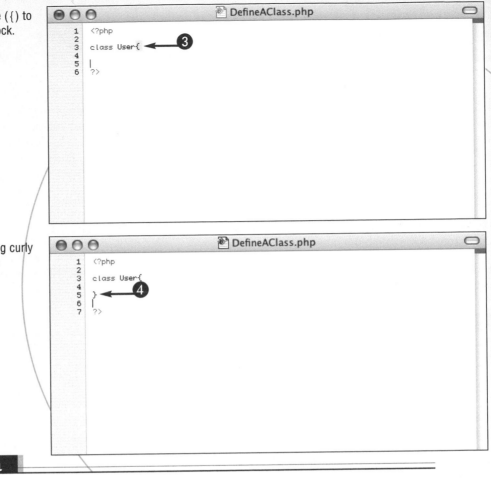

4 On a new line, type a closing curly brace (}) to close the class definition block.

The class is defined.

Extra

You can create a class that itself cannot be instantiated by declaring the class *abstract*. An abstract class is a class that must be subclassed in order to have an instance created. This is useful when you wish to specify a core object from which many other objects should inherit functionality but when you do not want the core object to be used due, for example, to its being too vague and abstract. All methods declared in an abstract class must be themselves marked abstract and can contain no implementation details.

Example:
```
abstract class Animal{
  abstract private function live();
  abstract public function die();
}

class Cat extends Animal{
  private $alive;
  private function live(){
    $this->alive = true;
  }
  public function die(){
    $this->alive = false;
  }
}
```

Create Class Constructors and Destructors

Y ou can create constructors and destructors for a class. Constructors and destructors are functions that are automatically called at the point of instantiation and deletion, respectively. A constructor can be used to set the initial value of variables, open database connections or file handles, create sockets, or perform almost any other functionality. Most typically, constructors perform automatic maintenance functionality such as setting private variables and logging status information for debugging and tracking purposes.

You can create a constructor by overriding the public __construct function inherent — if not explicitly defined — in each class definition. The __construct function can accept any number of arguments of any type but cannot

return a value or be marked with an access level other than public. You never have to call __construct explicitly. Instead, it is called automatically when resources are allocated to your new object instance.

The __destruct function is much like __construct, except that it is called immediately before resources for your object are deallocated. Most commonly, destructor functions are used to free memory and close sockets and other connections. In PHP, memory management is handled for you, so there is no need to worry about memory leaks and other problems that often occur in C++ applications, for example. Instead, you can use the __destruct function to close your database connections and perform logging functionality.

Create Class Constructors and Destructors

① Open your class definition.

② Create a constructor by defining a public function named __construct.

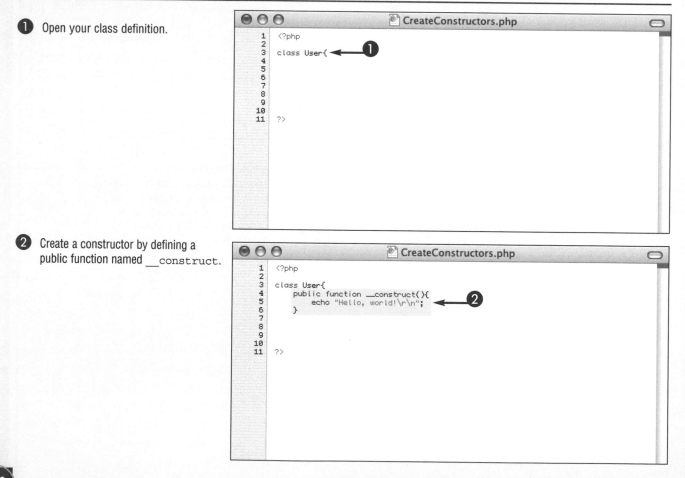

3 Create a destructor by defining a function named __destruct.

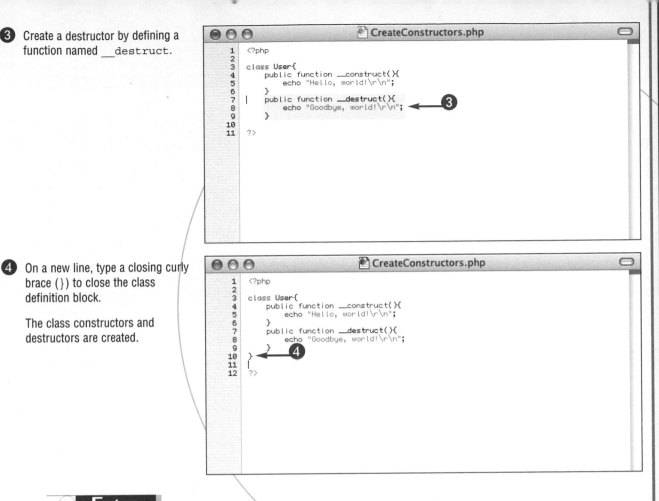

```php
<?php

class User{
    public function __construct(){
        echo "Hello, world!\r\n";
    }
    public function __destruct(){
        echo "Goodbye, world!\r\n";
    }

?>
```

4 On a new line, type a closing curly brace (}) to close the class definition block.

The class constructors and destructors are created.

```php
<?php

class User{
    public function __construct(){
        echo "Hello, world!\r\n";
    }
    public function __destruct(){
        echo "Goodbye, world!\r\n";
    }
}

?>
```

Extra

An interesting use for constructors and destructors is to create data objects that restore and save themselves on instantiation and destruction. For example, you might create a User object that uses its constructor to read information from a database based on a user id. When you delete the User instance, you can use the destructor function to save any unsaved information to the database.

Example:

```php
class User{
    private $unsaved;
    private $user_id;
    private $user_name;
    public function __construct($user_id){
        // use the userID to query the database here
        $this->user_id = $user_id;
        $this->user_name = $result['username'];
    }
    public function setUserName($user_name){
        $this->user_name = $user_name;
        $this->unsaved = true;
    }
    public function save(){
        // connect to the database and update
        $this->unsaved = false;
    }
    public function __destruct(){
        if($this->unsaved){
            $this->save();
        }
    }
}
```

Define a Method

Methods are functions that are part of an object. While you can think of functions as general-purpose machines into which you feed things and out of which you retrieve results, a method is a specialized version of the same within a given object context. Methods can be marked as accessible only within an object, only within an object subclass hierarchy, or accessible to any external sources.

Typically, methods are commands — ways of telling an object to perform one of its core processes. For example, a `Cat` object might have methods to eat and sleep. The naming convention for methods should always be semantically useful. For the eat functionality, your method would be `eat($food)`. For sleep, you might have `sleep($hours)`.

You can define a method for a class by creating a function inside the class definition. To create a private method that only the class methods can access, preface the function definition with the private keyword. The default access scope for methods is public — that is, any object may call the method directly. It is a good idea to explicitly use the public keyword to mark public functions as such to limit confusion and maintain ease in forward compatibility.

A special scope is the protected access scope. When a method is marked as protected, only classes in the same inheritance tree can access the method. For example, a subclass can call a protected method of its parent class.

Methods can accept any number of arguments, but care should be taken when trying to use global variables inside of a method. It is generally best practice to pass all variables to a method as parameters.

Define a Method

① Inside of a class definition, create a function.

Any calls to object methods or variables should be prefaced with the `$this` keyword and the pointer notation `->`.

② Mark the method as public with the public keyword.

```php
<?php

class Person{
    public function setName($name){
        echo "The name passed was $name.\r\n";
    }
}

?>
```

③ Create another method, marking it private with the private keyword.

```php
<?php

class Person{
    public function setName($name){
        echo "The name passed was $name.\r\n";
    }
    private function readDiary(){
        echo "I am reading my diary.\r\n";
    }
}

?>
```

④ Create an instance of your class using the new keyword.

⑤ Type code that calls each of the two methods.

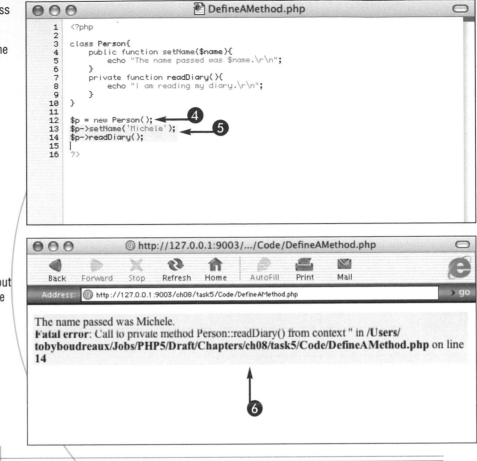

```php
<?php

class Person{
    public function setName($name){
        echo "The name passed was $name.\r\n";
    }
    private function readDiary(){
        echo "I am reading my diary.\r\n";
    }
}

$p = new Person();
$p->setName('Michele');
$p->readDiary();

?>
```

⑥ View the script in a Web browser.

The public method is called, but the attempt to access a private method triggers an error.

The name passed was Michele.
Fatal error: Call to private method Person::readDiary() from context " in **/Users/tobyboudreaux/Jobs/PHP5/Draft/Chapters/ch08/task5/Code/DefineAMethod.php** on line **14**

Extra

In cases where you want to provide limited public access to a method, you can create a public method that acts as a filtering delegate for a private method. For example, you may have a UserLog class with a log() method. You can use the instanceof keyword to test that the calling class is in fact a User object. While it would be possible to simply use a conditional test and call the logging code directly, it is often useful to abstract it into a separate function so that it may be used by other methods in your class.

Example:
```
class UserLog{
  public __constructor(){
    $this->doLog('UserLog instance created.');
  }
  public function log($caller, $message){
    if($caller instanceof User){
      // do logging
      $this->doLog($message);
    }
  }
  private function doLog($message){
    // logging implementation here
  }
}
```

Clone an Object

You can specify behavior to be performed when an object is copied by overloading the __clone method inherent to each object.

Cloning an instance of an object provides a way of creating a snapshot of the object at a given moment. This is good when implementing rollback or undo functionality and when otherwise implementing the Memento design pattern.

The __clone function is a public function that can be called directly as an instance method on the object you want to duplicate. Unlike the constructor function __construct, the __clone method will return a new object instance matching the current, possibly modified, instance instead of the default instance created by using the new keyword.

For example, you may have a Person object with private variables representing name, age, and other properties. When the constructor is called, the age variable may be set to zero to represent that the object is new. When you want to clone the Person object, you want all of the traits to be carried over to the new instance, but you may want to reset the age to zero.

To invoke the cloning mechanism, you use the clone keyword. You can create an instance $b, which is a clone of instance $a using $b = clone $a;.

The __clone method of $b is called after the clone is made. This flow allows you to only override the cloned values of properties you want to override while providing built-in cloning of all others.

Clone an Object

① Inside of a class definition, create member variables with accessor and mutator methods.

② Create a public function named __clone.

Explicitly reset any variables you do not want to have cloned.

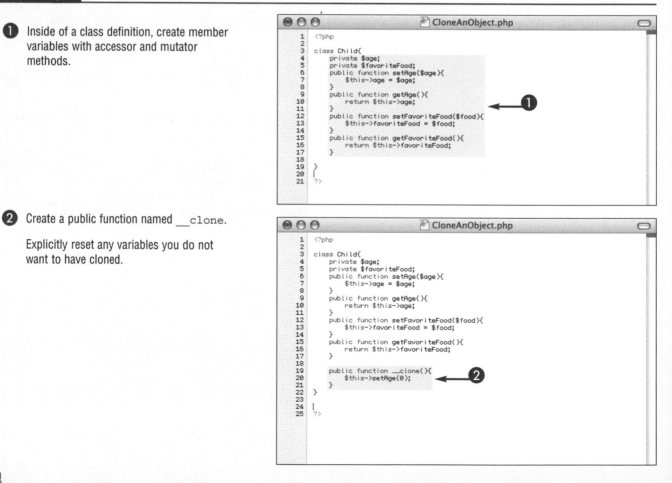

③ Create an instance of your cloneable class using the `new` keyword.

④ Set values using the mutators.

⑤ Use the `clone` keyword to create a clone.

⑥ Use the accessor methods to check the values in the cloned object.

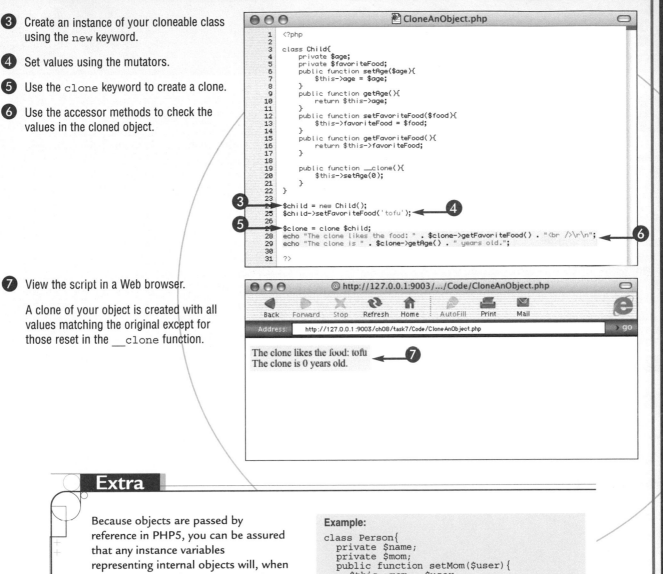

```php
<?php

class Child{
    private $age;
    private $favoriteFood;
    public function setAge($age){
        $this->age = $age;
    }
    public function getAge(){
        return $this->age;
    }
    public function setFavoriteFood($food){
        $this->favoriteFood = $food;
    }
    public function getFavoriteFood(){
        return $this->favoriteFood;
    }

    public function __clone(){
        $this->setAge(0);
    }
}

$child = new Child();
$child->setFavoriteFood('tofu');

$clone = clone $child;
echo "The clone likes the food: " . $clone->getFavoriteFood() . "<br />\r\n";
echo "The clone is " . $clone->getAge() . " years old.";

?>
```

⑦ View the script in a Web browser.

A clone of your object is created with all values matching the original except for those reset in the `__clone` function.

The clone likes the food: tofu
The clone is 0 years old.

Extra

Because objects are passed by reference in PHP5, you can be assured that any instance variables representing internal objects will, when cloned, point to the same external object. For example, if you use an injection method to set a database handle in instances of objects that interact with a database, you can be assured that any cloned objects will use the same database handle.

Example:
```php
class Person{
  private $name;
  private $mom;
  public function setMom($user){
    $this->mom = $user;
  }
  public function getMom(){
    return $this->mom;
  }
  public function setName($name){
    $this->name = $name;
  }
  public function getName(){
    return $this->name;
  }
}
$mom = new Person();
$mom->setName('Shelly');
$child = new Person();
$child->setName('Noah');
$child->setMom($mom);
$clone = clone $child;
echo "The mother of the clone is:
" . $clone->getMom()->getName();
```

Create Private and Static Members

By default, class methods are accessible to any calling object in your script. As long as the pointer to your instance is valid, any function or object may call any of its public methods. You can restrict access to a method by declaring it private. These two access scopes may also be applied to instance variables. By creating a private member variable, you restrict direct access to it. Restricting access to a member variable is a key concept in object-oriented programming. While not required, providing accessor and mutator methods for all variables is a best practice because it provides a layer of separation between the data and the means of access. Typical accessors are named according to a pattern such as `getNAME` where `NAME` is the name of the variable. Mutator methods are named similarly, using a `setNAME` pattern.

To mark a variable as private, simply specify the private keyword before the name of the variable in the class definition. Thus marked, a private variable may be accessed only by methods of the class in which it is defined.

Static variables are those that are defined in the class definition and are thereafter immutable or unchangeable. You can think of static variables as class constants. Static members are accessed not by way of class instances, but by class definitions. For example, you may have a class that supplies Decorator pattern functionality for string values. If the class is called `EmphasisHTMLDecorator` and has variables for the opening and closing tags to be wrapped around a string, you can access the information using `EmphasisHTMLDecorator::openingTag` and `EmphasisHTMLDecorator::closingTag`.

The double-colon operator (`::`) is used to access a static variable or method of a class. It is important to note that the `$this` keyword is not allowed inside of a static method, as `$this` is created in an *instance* of a class. Instead, the `self` keyword is allowed.

Create Private and Static Members

① Inside of a class definition, create a member variable using the `static` keyword.

② Assign a value to the static variable.

③ Repeat Steps 1 and 2 for any additional static members.

```
PrivateStatic.php

1   <?php
2
3   class EmphasisHTMLDecorator{
4       static $openingTag = '<em>';
5       static $closingTag = '</em>';
6   }
7
8   ?>
```

④ Type code that is specific to instances of your class versus static members.

- You can access the static members from within your instance members using the `self::$NAME` notation.

⑤ Create an instance of your class.

```
PrivateStatic.php

1   <?php
2
3   class EmphasisHTMLDecorator{
4       static $openingTag = '<em>';
5       static $closingTag = '</em>';
6       private $string;
7       public function __construct($string){
8           $this->string = $string;
9       }
10      public function getString(){
11          return self::$openingTag . $this->string . self::$closingTag;
12      }
13  }
14
15  $html = 'Hello, world!';
16  $em = new EmphasisHTMLDecorator($html);
17
18  ?>
```

6 Access the static members from outside of the instance using the `CLASSNAME::$NAME` notation.

```php
<?php

class EmphasisHTMLDecorator{
    static $openingTag = '<em>';
    static $closingTag = '</em>';
    private $string;
    public function __construct($string){
        $this->string = $string;
    }
    public function getString(){
        return self::$openingTag . $this->string . self::$closingTag;
    }
}

$html = 'Hello, world!';
$em = new EmphasisHTMLDecorator($html);

echo 'The opening tag is: ' . htmlspecialchars(EmphasisHTMLDecorator::$openingTag);

?>
```

PrivateStatic.php

7 View the script in a Web browser.

The static member is accessible to both the instance and external functions and objects.

@ http://127.0.0.1:9003/.../Code/PrivateStatic.php

Address: http://127.0.0.1:9003/ch08/task8/Code/PrivateStatic.php

The opening tag is: <em> ◄── **7**

Extra

You can create entire static classes by declaring all class methods and members as static. This is most often done for utility classes that do not in themselves represent a type of object but allow for grouped utility behavior. For example, you may have a `Math` static class with methods for finding square roots, prime numbers, and so on. There would be no need to have multiple instances of such a class floating around your application because there would be no per-instance deviation from the class definition itself. Instead, by using a static class, you provide a portable grouping of related functionality.

TYPE THIS:

```php
static class Math{
  public static function sqrt($num){
    return sqrt($num);
  }
  public static function abs($num){
    return abs($num);
  }
}
echo "The absolute representation of -12 is:
" . Math::abs(-12);
```

RESULT:

The absolute representation of –12 is: 12

Extend a Class

You can create classes at finer and finer levels of granularity by subclassing, or extending classes to add specific functionality. By extending a class, you inherit all of its functionality and properties, but have the opportunity to add your own or modify those that have been inherited. When a class inherits from another class, the inheriting class is the *subclass* and the source class is the *superclass*.

You can extend a class by using the `extends` keyword along with the name of the class from which you want to inherit properties. Class inheritance can extend for as far as you want, but generally there are only a few layers of granularity.

An example of an inheritance chain might be `Pug` extends `Dog` extends `Animal`. The `Animal` class holds properties and methods applicable to *all* animals. Any properties or additional methods that apply exclusively, yet universally, to dogs are added or changed in the `Dog` subclass. The same applies for the `Pug` subclass of `Dog`.

To overload a method inherited by a parent class, you can simply redefine the same method with the same name. If you want to simply add functionality to a method inherited from a parent class, you can use the parent keyword to invoke the parent method in a static context. For example, to add to the functionality in the parent `__construct` function, you can call `parent::__construct();` followed by your own code.

Extend a Class

① Define a class to represent a type of object.

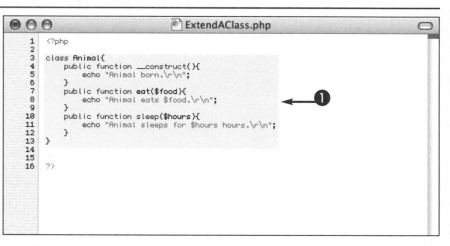

② Create a new class of finer granularity that is of the type defined in the first class.

③ Use the `extends` keyword followed by the name of the first class to add the new class to the inheritance chain.

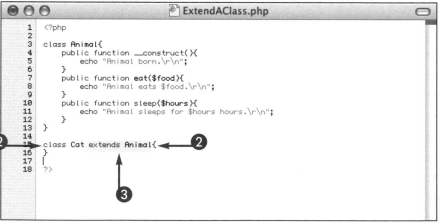

④ Overload a method inherited from the parent class by creating your own version of the function.

- You can call the parent method before your own code if you want to add to the method instead of overriding it.

⑤ Create an instance of the subclass and call an inherited method.

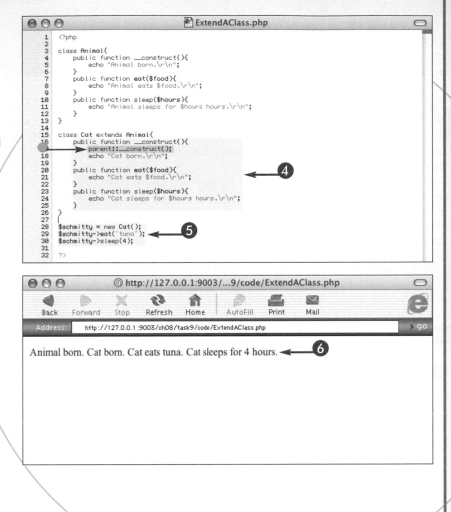

⑥ View the script in a Web browser.

The subclass instance calls the method it inherited from its parent class.

Extra

You can create a class that can never be instantiated but instead functions as a general template representing qualities of a type of object. Creating a class to represent an object type that is extremely general is called creating an *abstract* class. You can create an abstract class using the abstract keyword before the class definition. Any class marked as abstract cannot be instantiated directly. Instead, abstract classes must be subclasses and instances of the subclass are created. Any method in an abstract class must be declared abstract itself using the abstract keyword in the function definition. Additionally, abstract class methods are not implemented — that is, there is no code composing the method body.

TYPE THIS:

```
abstract class Thing{
    abstract public function be();
}
$t = new Thing();
```

RESULT:

An error is thrown when trying to instantiate an abstract class.

207

Work with External Data in Classes

You can access external data and functions in your classes. This includes calling functions, accessing global variables, and accessing class definitions for instantiating new objects or accessing static variables and methods.

When a function is called without the `$this` keyword and object access (`->`) operator, the scope is assumed to be global. Any data returned from a global function is accessible locally. You can pass local variables to a global function for manipulation. To call a global function from within a class, just type the name of the function.

You can access classes by class name from within a class. For example, you may have a `Person` class that creates a new `Child` person using `$child = new Child();`.

To access static methods and variables of an external class you can use the name of the class followed by the `::` operator. As with function calls, any return values are accessible within the scope of your class.

Constants, when defined, may be accessed by name alone. To access a variable in the global scope from within class methods, preface the variable name with the `global` keyword.

Generally, it is bad practice to directly access external data from within a class, because classes should be portable and fairly abstract.

Work with External Data in Classes

① Define a class to represent a type of object.

② Create a function in the global scope.

③ Create a method of your class with the same name as the function in the global scope.

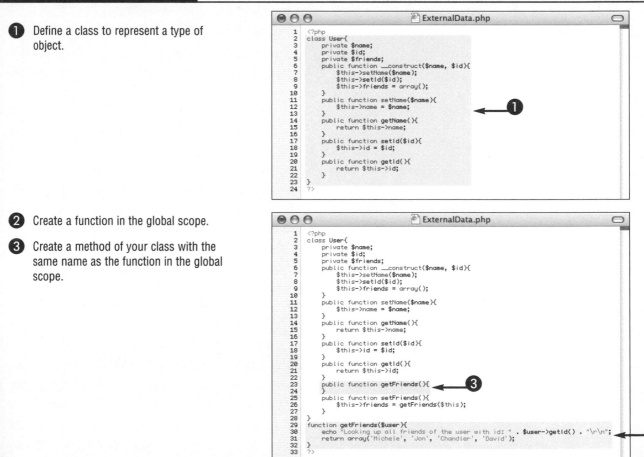

④ Type code in your class to call the global function.

⑤ Type code to call the class method.

● Be sure to preface the method call with `$this->` to denote local scoping.

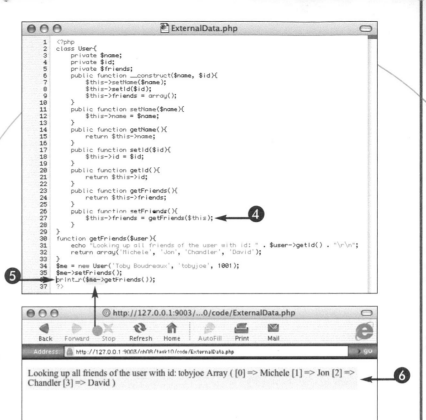

```php
<?php
class User{
    private $name;
    private $id;
    private $friends;
    public function __construct($name, $id){
        $this->setName($name);
        $this->setId($id);
        $this->friends = array();
    }
    public function setName($name){
        $this->name = $name;
    }
    public function getName(){
        return $this->name;
    }
    public function setId($id){
        $this->id = $id;
    }
    public function getId(){
        return $this->id;
    }
    public function getFriends(){
        return $this->friends;
    }
    public function setFriends(){
        $this->friends = getFriends($this);          ④
    }
}
function getFriends($user){
    echo "Looking up all friends of the user with id: " . $user->getId() . "\r\n";
    return array('Michele', 'Jon', 'Chandler', 'David');
}
$me = new User('Toby Boudreaux', 'tobyjoe', 1001);
$me->setFriends();                    ⑤
print_r($me->getFriends());
?>
```

⑥ View the script in a Web browser.

Both the global function and the class method are called at the appropriate times.

Looking up all friends of the user with id: tobyjoe Array ([0] => Michele [1] => Jon [2] => Chandler [3] => David)   ⑥

Extra

You can follow a design pattern called Dependency Injection to keep your classes as abstract and portable as possible. A design pattern is a way of handling and solving a common problem. The Dependency Injection pattern is a way of structuring classes so that they allow external configuration of variables, classes, and objects on which your class depends. The configuration happens either through the class constructor or by accessor and mutator methods.

Example:
```php
class HomeTheater{
  private $display;
  private $mediaPlayer;
  public function __construct(){
    $this->display = new LCDTV();
    $this->mediaPlayer = new DVDPlayer();
  }
}
// Dependency Injection pattern:
class HomeTheater{
  private $display;
  private $mediaPlayer;
  public function __construct($display, $mediaPlayer){
    $this->display = $display;
    $this->mediaPlayer = $mediaPlayer;
  }
}
$ht = new HomeTheater(new HDTV(), new DVR());
```

Access Information About an Object

PHP provides several functions that allow you to find information about an object. For example, you can use functions to determine the class of which an object is an instance.

The `class_exists` function accepts a string representing a class name. If a class by a given name exists, the function returns a Boolean `true`. Otherwise, it returns false. A similar function exists for finding interfaces called `interface_exists`.

You can obtain a list of all class methods using the `get_class_methods` function. The `get_class_methods` function accepts a string representing the name of a class and returns an array of strings representing the method names.

The `get_declared_classes` and `get_declared_interfaces` functions return arrays representing the names of all classes and all interfaces, respectively, declared in the scope of the current script.

To determine whether a class has a parent class, you can take one of two approaches. The `get_parent_class` function returns the name of the parent class for a class. If the class passed to the `get_parent_class` function has no subclass, the return value is empty. Alternately, you can use the `is_subclass_of` function to determine whether a class is a subclass of another class.

The `method_exists` function accepts an object pointer and method name and returns `true` if a method by that name exists for the object, `false` otherwise.

Access Information About an Object

① Define a class to represent a type of object.

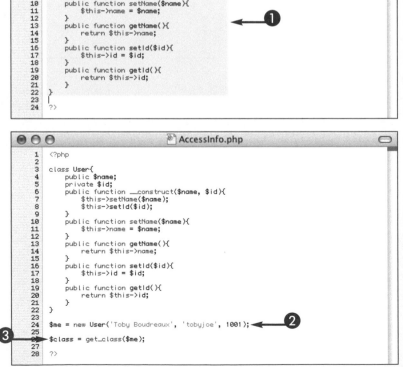

② Create an instance of your object.

③ Use the `get_class` function to get the class associated from which your instance was instantiated.

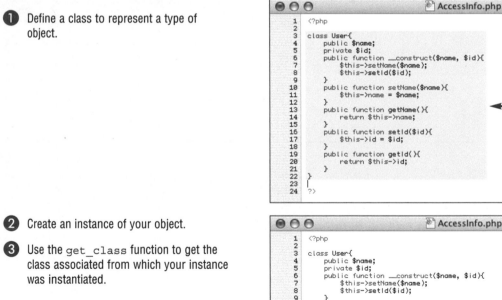

④ Get a list of the methods in your class using the `get_class_methods` function.

⑤ Get a list of your class variables using the `get_class_vars` function.

⑥ Use the `print_r` function to list the methods and the variables.

```php
<?php

class User{
    public $name;
    private $id;
    public function __construct($name, $id){
        $this->setName($name);
        $this->setId($id);
    }
    public function setName($name){
        $this->name = $name;
    }
    public function getName(){
        return $this->name;
    }
    public function setId($id){
        $this->id = $id;
    }
    public function getId(){
        return $this->id;
    }
}

$me = new User('Toby Boudreaux', 'tobyjoe', 1001);

$class = get_class($me);

echo "Class: $class";

echo '<br /><br />Methods: <br />';
print_r(get_class_methods($class));

echo '<br /><br />Vars: <br />';
print_r(get_class_vars($class));

?>
```

⑦ View the script in a Web browser.

The class methods and variables are found and displayed.

```
Class: User

Methods:
Array ( [0] => __construct [1] => setName [2] => getName [3] => setId [4] => getId )

Vars:
Array ( [name] => [id] => )
```

Address: http://127.0.0.1:9003/ch08/task11/code/AccessInfo.php

---

Extra

You can use the `get_object_vars` function to get the current values for each variable in your object. This differs from `get_class_vars` in that it does not return the default values as specified in the class definition. Instead, it displays the values in the current object. The instance variables must be in the public scope for the `get_object_vars` function to be read.

TYPE THIS:

```php
class CalendarDate{
  public $year=1970;
  public $month=01;
  public $day=01;
  public function __construct($y=null,
$m=null, $d=null){
    $this->year = ($y) ? $y : $this->year;
    $this->month = ($m) ? $m : $this->month;
    $this->day = ($d) ? $d : $this->day;
  }
}
$c = new CalendarDate(1977, 12, 11);
print_r(get_class_vars('CalendarDate'));
print_r(get_object_vars($c));
```

RESULT:

```
Array
(
    [year] => 1970
    [month] => 1
    [day] => 1
)
Array
(
    [year] => 1977
    [month] => 12
    [day] => 11
)
```

Check for Classes and Methods

You can use PHP to obtain a listing of classes in the current script scope. The get_declared_classes function returns an array with the names of all classes to which your script has access. Obtaining a listing of all possible classes is useful when debugging complex modular applications of which you may or may not know the current state. A listing of available classes can point to conflicts or missing libraries and modules.

When scanning the output of a call to get_declared_classes, you see classes that are core to the PHP language library as well as many support classes that comprise components in your application. By keeping yourself aware of the classes in the current scope, you can help prevent the types of conflicts that arise due to a lack of namespaces.

You can use the class_exists function to determine whether a class by a given name exists. This is useful in modules that might need to instantiate classes included from other files. If PHP is told to instantiate an undefined class an error is thrown. By first checking for the existence of a class with class_exists you can throw an error or exception instead of having the runtime engine find an error.

The method_exists function is useful when calling a method on an object that is of an unknown class. Generally, you know the methods associated with your classes, but in some cases an object may be created by an intermediary process or object, such as when using the Factory design pattern.

Check for Classes and Methods

1 Define a class to represent a type of object.

```php
<?php

class User{
    public $name;
    private $id;
    public function __construct($name, $id){
        $this->setName($name);
        $this->setId($id);
    }
    public function setName($name){
        $this->name = $name;
    }
    public function getName(){
        return $this->name;
    }
    public function setId($id){
        $this->id = $id;
    }
    public function getId(){
        return $this->id;
    }
}

?>
```

2 Create an instance of your object.

3 Use the get_declared_classes function to get a listing of all classes defined in the current scope.

```php
<?php

class User{
    public $name;
    private $id;
    public function __construct($name, $id){
        $this->setName($name);
        $this->setId($id);
    }
    public function setName($name){
        $this->name = $name;
    }
    public function getName(){
        return $this->name;
    }
    public function setId($id){
        $this->id = $id;
    }
    public function getId(){
        return $this->id;
    }
}

$me = new User('Toby Boudreaux', 'tobyjoe', 1001);

$classes = get_declared_classes();

?>
```

④ Get a list of the methods in your class using the `get_class_methods` function.

⑤ Use the `print_r` function to list the methods and the classes.

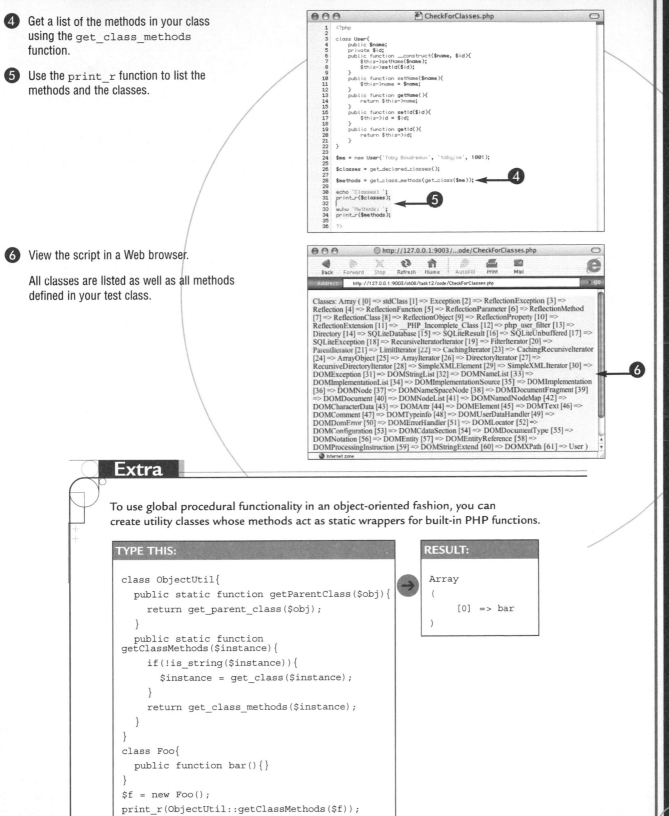

```php
<?php

class User{
    public $name;
    private $id;
    public function __construct($name, $id){
        $this->setName($name);
        $this->setId($id);
    }
    public function setName($name){
        $this->name = $name;
    }
    public function getName(){
        return $this->name;
    }
    public function setId($id){
        $this->id = $id;
    }
    public function getId(){
        return $this->id;
    }
}

$me = new User('Toby Boudreaux', 'tobyjoe', 1001);

$classes = get_declared_classes();

$methods = get_class_methods(get_class($me));

echo 'Classes: ';
print_r($classes);

echo 'Methods: ';
print_r($methods);

?>
```

⑥ View the script in a Web browser.

All classes are listed as well as all methods defined in your test class.

Classes: Array ([0] => stdClass [1] => Exception [2] => ReflectionException [3] => Reflection [4] => ReflectionFunction [5] => ReflectionParameter [6] => ReflectionMethod [7] => ReflectionClass [8] => ReflectionObject [9] => ReflectionProperty [10] => ReflectionExtension [11] => __PHP_Incomplete_Class [12] => php_user_filter [13] => Directory [14] => SQLiteDatabase [15] => SQLiteResult [16] => SQLiteUnbuffered [17] => SQLiteException [18] => RecursiveIteratorIterator [19] => FilterIterator [20] => ParentIterator [21] => LimitIterator [22] => CachingIterator [23] => CachingRecursiveIterator [24] => ArrayObject [25] => ArrayIterator [26] => DirectoryIterator [27] => RecursiveDirectoryIterator [28] => SimpleXMLElement [29] => SimpleXMLIterator [30] => DOMException [31] => DOMStringList [32] => DOMNameList [33] => DOMImplementationList [34] => DOMImplementationSource [35] => DOMImplementation [36] => DOMNode [37] => DOMNameSpaceNode [38] => DOMDocumentFragment [39] => DOMDocument [40] => DOMNodeList [41] => DOMNamedNodeMap [42] => DOMCharacterData [43] => DOMAttr [44] => DOMElement [45] => DOMText [46] => DOMComment [47] => DOMTypeinfo [48] => DOMUserDataHandler [49] => DOMDomError [50] => DOMErrorHandler [51] => DOMLocator [52] => DOMConfiguration [53] => DOMCdataSection [54] => DOMDocumentType [55] => DOMNotation [56] => DOMEntity [57] => DOMEntityReference [58] => DOMProcessingInstruction [59] => DOMStringExtend [60] => DOMXPath [61] => User)

Extra

To use global procedural functionality in an object-oriented fashion, you can create utility classes whose methods act as static wrappers for built-in PHP functions.

TYPE THIS:

```php
class ObjectUtil{
  public static function getParentClass($obj){
    return get_parent_class($obj);
  }
  public static function
getClassMethods($instance){
    if(!is_string($instance)){
      $instance = get_class($instance);
    }
    return get_class_methods($instance);
  }
}
class Foo{
  public function bar(){}
}
$f = new Foo();
print_r(ObjectUtil::getClassMethods($f));
```

RESULT:

```
Array
(
    [0] => bar
)
```

Using Object Serialization

Y ou can serialize objects using the `serialize` function. Serialization is a way of taking an object in its current state and encoding it so that it can be saved and restored at a later point. You can also pass serialized objects through sockets, files, and sessions or store them in databases.

The `serialize` function accepts a single argument representing the value to be serialized. When serializing an object you pass the variable representing the pointer to the object instance. The return value of the serialize function is a string.

Each object in PHP has a native function called `__sleep` that is called when an object is serialized. You can overload the `__sleep` method to perform any additional functionality you need such as closing a database connection or file handle, logging, or performing any other utility functionality you need.

You can restore an object that has been serialized by passing the serialized string representation of the object to the `unserialize` function. When restoring an object using `unserialize`, you must be sure that the original class definition for your object is available in the current script scope.

When `unserialize` is called on a serialized object, the `__wakeup` method is called. Like `__sleep`, the `__wakeup` method is built in to each class and may be selectively overloaded in your own classes. Common functionality for the `__wakeup` function is restoring database connections or file handles and logging activity. You may also want to have an object act in a self-aware fashion so that it checks its environment when restored.

Using Object Serialization

① Define a class to represent a type of object.

```php
<?php

class User{
    private $name;
    private $id;
    public function __construct($name, $id){
        $this->setName($name);
        $this->setId($id);
    }
    public function setName($name){
        $this->name = $name;
    }
    public function getName(){
        return $this->name;
    }
    public function setId($id){
        $this->id = $id;
    }
    public function getId(){
        return $this->id;
    }
}

?>
```
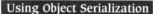

② Create an instance of your object.

③ Serialize the object by typing the name of a variable to represent your serialized data.

④ Type the assignment operator followed by a call to `serialize` with your object instance in parentheses.

```php
<?php

class User{
    private $name;
    private $id;
    public function __construct($name, $id){
        $this->setName($name);
        $this->setId($id);
    }
    public function setName($name){
        $this->name = $name;
    }
    public function getName(){
        return $this->name;
    }
    public function setId($id){
        $this->id = $id;
    }
    public function getId(){
        return $this->id;
    }
}

$me = new User('Toby Boudreaux', 'tobyjoe', 1001);

$serialized = serialize($me);

?>
```

5 Print the serialized representation of your object to the output stream.

6 Use the `unserialize` function to restore your serialized object.

7 Use `print_r` to display the structure of your object.

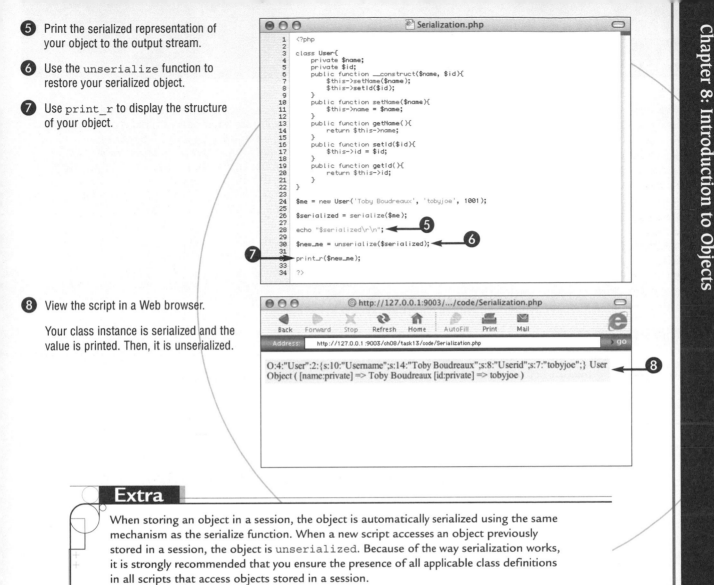

```php
<?php

class User{
    private $name;
    private $id;
    public function __construct($name, $id){
        $this->setName($name);
        $this->setId($id);
    }
    public function setName($name){
        $this->name = $name;
    }
    public function getName(){
        return $this->name;
    }
    public function setId($id){
        $this->id = $id;
    }
    public function getId(){
        return $this->id;
    }
}

$me = new User('Toby Boudreaux', 'tobyjoe', 1001);

$serialized = serialize($me);

echo "$serialized\r\n";

$new_me = unserialize($serialized);

print_r($new_me);

?>
```

8 View the script in a Web browser.

Your class instance is serialized and the value is printed. Then, it is unserialized.

O:4:"User":2:{s:10:"Username";s:14:"Toby Boudreaux";s:8:"Userid";s:7:"tobyjoe";} User Object ([name:private] => Toby Boudreaux [id:private] => tobyjoe)

Extra

When storing an object in a session, the object is automatically serialized using the same mechanism as the serialize function. When a new script accesses an object previously stored in a session, the object is unserialized. Because of the way serialization works, it is strongly recommended that you ensure the presence of all applicable class definitions in all scripts that access objects stored in a session.

TYPE THIS:

```php
session_start();
class Foo{
  private $bar = 'bat';
  public function __sleep(){
    echo "Foo serialized.<br />";
    return array('bar');
  }
  public function __wakeup(){
    echo "Foo unserialized.<br />";
  }
}
$f = new Foo();
$_SESSION['myFoo'] = $f;
```

RESULT:

→

```
Foo serialized.
```

Using Class Autoloading

PHP 5 provides a very useful interceptor function called __autoload that is called whenever an attempt is made to instantiate an unknown class.

The __autoload function is defined in the global scope and accepts as a single argument the string representing the class name.

The most common usage of autoloading is to take the name of the class for which the __autoload function is called and look for a file matching that class name and, if found, including it. For example, if the class for which you are looking is called User you might try to include User.class.php by way of the __autoload function.

You can add additional functionality to an __autoload function definition for your script. For example, you can

add logging or debugging functionality to build a record of attempts to call undeclared classes. This type of report is very useful when refactoring and debugging your code. Though the __autoload function can be used to get around occasional errors until the point at which they can be repaired, it is generally considered poor form to rely heavily and exclusively on this type of functionality instead of being careful to include classes explicitly.

Understanding the use of autoloading is important because many applications and frameworks you will encounter will use it as a mechanism for locating class files. Because PHP is an interpreted language, the source of any applications or frameworks you use is available for audits and, in some cases, modification.

Using Class Autoloading

① Create an __autoload function to catch undeclared class instantiation calls.

② Use the function to load your class and perform any additional functionality.

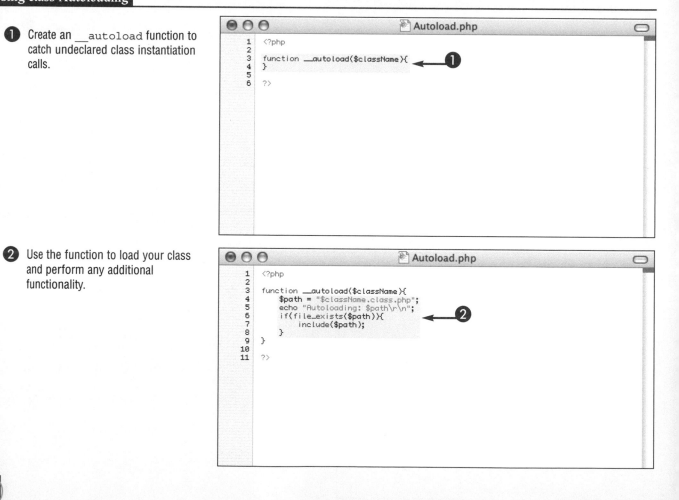

③ Attempt to instantiate an undeclared class.

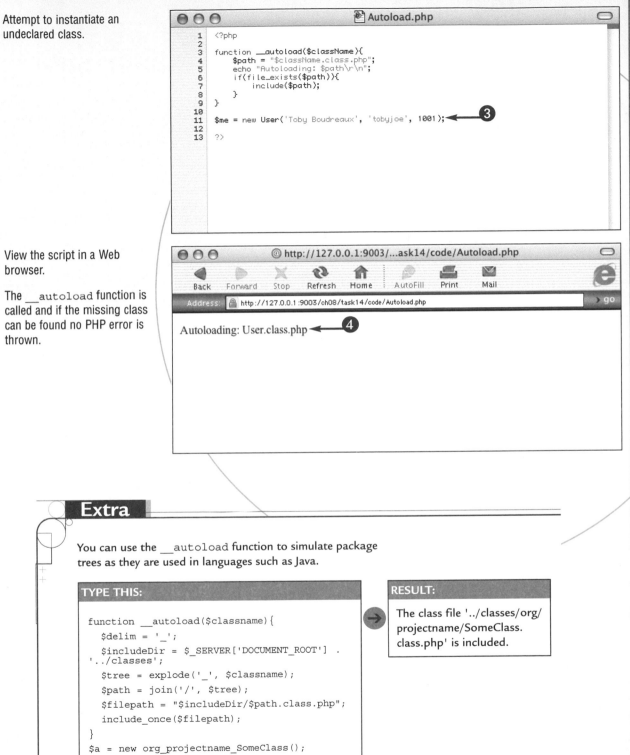

```php
<?php

function __autoload($className){
    $path = "$className.class.php";
    echo "Autoloading: $path\r\n";
    if(file_exists($path)){
        include($path);
    }
}

$me = new User('Toby Boudreaux', 'tobyjoe', 1001); ◄── ③

?>
```

④ View the script in a Web browser.

The __autoload function is called and if the missing class can be found no PHP error is thrown.

@ http://127.0.0.1:9003/...ask14/code/Autoload.php

Address: http://127.0.0.1:9003/ch08/task14/code/Autoload.php

Autoloading: User.class.php ◄── ④

Extra

You can use the __autoload function to simulate package trees as they are used in languages such as Java.

TYPE THIS:

```php
function __autoload($classname){
  $delim = '_';
  $includeDir = $_SERVER['DOCUMENT_ROOT'] .
'../classes';
  $tree = explode('_', $classname);
  $path = join('/', $tree);
  $filepath = "$includeDir/$path.class.php";
  include_once($filepath);
}
$a = new org_projectname_SomeClass();
```

RESULT:

The class file '../classes/org/projectname/SomeClass.class.php' is included.

Overload an Object Method

When an attempt is made to access an undeclared property of an object, an error is thrown.

You can intercept calls to access and mutate unknown properties using the __get and __set class methods that are built into each class created in PHP 5. By defining your own __get and __set methods in your classes, you can specify custom functionality to be performed when a property is accessed.

The __get method accepts a string representing the name of the property being accessed. You can perform actions as simple as delegating a call to a getter, or accessor, function or returning the value being sought directly from the __get method.

Alternately, you can perform complex functionality such as looking up values in databases or hooking in to logging or debugging mechanisms.

The __set method accepts two arguments. The first is a string representing the name of the property you want to set. The second is the value the property should represent when the function has been processed.

You can use the __get and __set methods to selectively access private variables without the need for a specialized getter or setter method for each property. For example, you may want to create a variable in your class that you want external objects to be able to read but not write. You can accomplish this by defining the __get method so that it returns the value of any private variable and defining the __set method to do nothing. When your property is accessed through $obj->property syntax, the __get or __set method is called.

Overload an Object Method

① Create a class with private members defined.

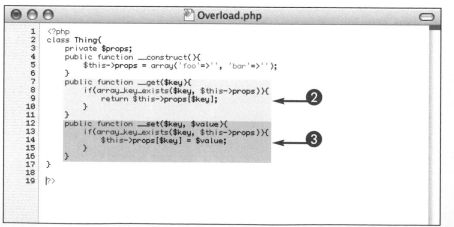

② Create a __get method that returns the value of your variable.

③ Create a __set method that sets the value of your variable.

④ Create an instance of your object.

⑤ Assign a value directly.

⑥ Retrieve a value directly and print the value.

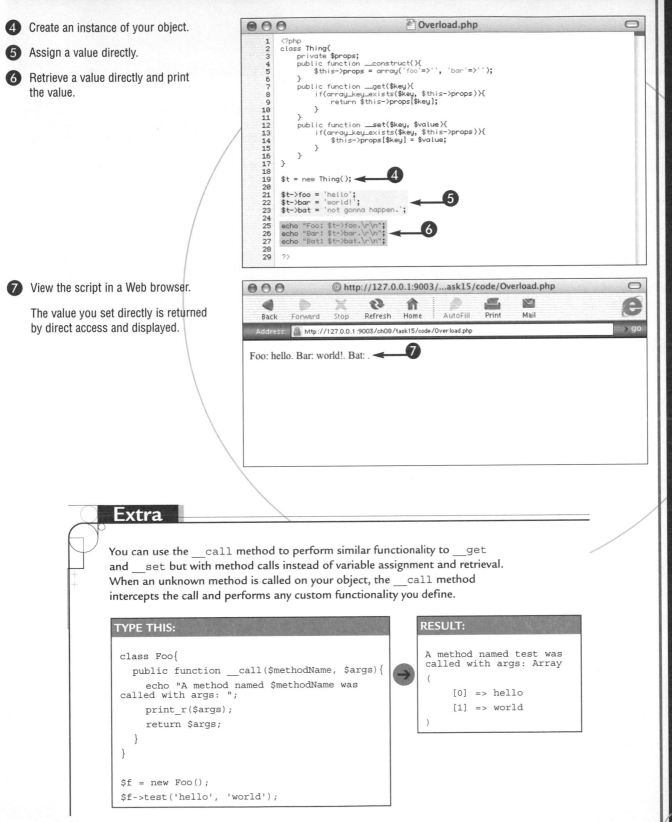

```php
<?php
class Thing{
    private $props;
    public function __construct(){
        $this->props = array('foo'=>'', 'bar'=>'');
    }
    public function __get($key){
        if(array_key_exists($key, $this->props)){
            return $this->props[$key];
        }
    }
    public function __set($key, $value){
        if(array_key_exists($key, $this->props)){
            $this->props[$key] = $value;
        }
    }
}

$t = new Thing();                              ⟵ ④

$t->foo = 'hello';
$t->bar = 'world!';                            ⟵ ⑤
$t->bat = 'not gonna happen.';

echo "Foo: $t->foo.\r\n";
echo "Bar: $t->bar.\r\n";                      ⟵ ⑥
echo "Bat: $t->bat.\r\n";

?>
```

⑦ View the script in a Web browser.

The value you set directly is returned by direct access and displayed.

Address: http://127.0.0.1:9003/ch08/task15/code/Overload.php

Foo: hello. Bar: world!. Bat: . ⟵ ⑦

Extra

You can use the __call method to perform similar functionality to __get and __set but with method calls instead of variable assignment and retrieval. When an unknown method is called on your object, the __call method intercepts the call and performs any custom functionality you define.

TYPE THIS:

```php
class Foo{
    public function __call($methodName, $args){
        echo "A method named $methodName was
called with args: ";
        print_r($args);
        return $args;
    }
}

$f = new Foo();
$f->test('hello', 'world');
```

RESULT:

```
A method named test was
called with args: Array
(
    [0] => hello
    [1] => world
)
```

Using Iterators

Y ou can create objects to iterate over an object by leveraging the `Iterator` and `IteratorAggregate` interfaces in your classes.

You can create your iterator by defining a class that implements the `Iterator` interface. The `Iterator` interface is comprised of the following methods: `rewind()`, `next()`, `current()`, `hasMore()`, `key()`, `valid()`, and a constructor that accepts an object or collection to be targeted by the iterator.

Any collection or object that implements the `IteratorAggregate` interface can be accessed through an iterator that conforms to the `Iterator` interface.

The `IteratorAggregate` interface is comprised of a single method named `getIterator()` that returns an iterator for your object.

Iterators are useful because they allow a level of reusability and abstraction to the common task of moving through a collection of objects, one object at a time, until each has been evaluated or processed. While similar functionality can be implemented directly using `foreach` loops and other looping constructs, the Iterator design pattern allows for the internal structure of your collection and the methods used to select items to change without impacting the application code that needs to evaluate each item.

Another benefit is that you can swap iterators for other iterators and collections for other collections because the public interfaces `Iterator` and `IteratorAggregate` remain consistent across all implementing classes.

Using Iterators

① Create a class that implements the `Iterator` interface.

- The class should have a constructor that accepts an object over which it will iterate.

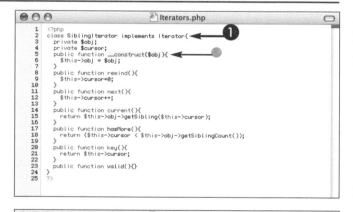

② Create a class representing your collection.

- Be sure to implement the `IteratorAggregate` interface, including the `getIterator()` method.

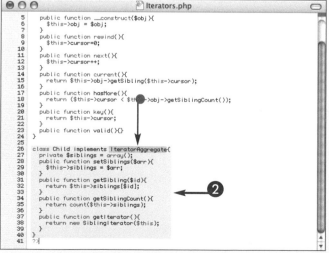

③ Type code that utilizes the Iterator to select items.

```
17    public function hasMore(){
18        return ($this->cursor < $this->obj->getSiblingCount());
19    }
20    public function key(){
21        return $this->cursor;
22    }
23    public function valid(){}
24 }
25
26 class Child implements IteratorAggregate{
27    private $siblings = array();
28    public function setSiblings($arr){
29        $this->siblings = $arr;
30    }
31    public function getSibling($id){
32        return $this->siblings[$id];
33    }
34    public function getSiblingCount(){
35        return count($this->siblings);
36    }
37    public function getIterator(){
38        return new SiblingIterator($this);
39    }
40 }
41
42 $c = new Child();
43 $c->setSiblings(array('Ryan', 'Rob', 'Michele'));
44 $it = $c->getIterator();
45
46 $it->rewind();
47 while($it->hasMore()){
48    $s = $it->current();
49    echo "$s<br />\r\n";
50    $it->next();
51 }
52
53 ?>
```

④ View the script in a Web browser.

Each item in your collection is selected using the Iterator.

Ryan
Rob
Michele

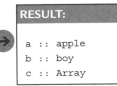

Apply It

You can use `foreach` loops to iterate over the public values in an object. By default, all public values are accessed using this message. This may be useful in many cases, but in others you may want to iterate over some properties and not others or over a collection represented by a single property in your object.

TYPE THIS:

```
class Foo{
  public $a = 'apple';
  public $b = 'boy';
  public $c = array('x'=>'one', 'y'=>'two');
}
$f = new Foo();
foreach($f as $k=>$v){
  echo "$k :: $v\r\n";
}
```

RESULT:

```
a :: apple
b :: boy
c :: Array
```

Introduction to Databases

You can use all of the applications you develop with PHP to access, evaluate, and manipulate information of some sort. For the purpose of your operations, the data is stored in volatile memory. This provides quick access to the objects your script creates. As soon as your script terminates, the data is deleted from memory. If your application crashes or if there is a power loss, the data is lost forever. You can use a database to store information permanently, providing access whenever you need it.

Databases

A database is an application or repository used to store and retrieve data. A database can be as simple as a single text or XML file with entries in a proprietary format that has meaning to your application, or it can be as complex as a large commercial relational database balanced across a network of servers. No single database is inherently better than others universally. For some purposes, using flat files can be the better choice.

Relational Data

In Web application development, you most often encounter relational databases. A relational database stores data in *tables* that can be imagined as grids or spreadsheets. Data is stored in columns and rows. Columns represent a type of value and rows represent individual records. A record is a single entry representing a discrete set of information.

When distinct tables have columns whose types and values overlap they can be linked by cross-referencing. Any time a column in one table is used to reference a column in another table, the tables are said to be relational. By creating relationships between data in separate tables, you can help ensure that your data is normalized and reduce redundancy.

In many cases, you may want to store objects in a database. While databases that specialize in object storage exist, you most often encounter relational databases. Because the data in relational databases is two-dimensional, it is necessary to *flatten* objects to reduce multidimensional structures to a two dimensional structure used by most database engines before storing them. Creating a framework that provides object persistence is a large undertaking. There are several projects in development that can leverage the object-oriented abilities of PHP 5 against a relational database. For simple applications, you can develop specialized adapters to translate an object of a given type into a database table or tables.

You can access your data from within PHP by creating a connection to the database. As soon as you have established a connection, you seek out data by issuing queries. You can create queries in most relational databases using the ANSI Standard Query Language (SQL). SQL is a simple standard consisting of commands such as SELECT, UPDATE, INSERT, and DELETE.

Relational database management systems (RDBMS) such as MySQL and MSSQL provide support for SQL with many additional, proprietary properties and functionality.

Design a Database

When faced with the necessity of creating a database, the challenges of designing a set of tables that provide flexibility and extensibility can be quite daunting. Though possible to restructure a database after it has been in use, the better option is to plan for most — if not all — possible uses and design a system that provides flexibility.

Forward Thinking

Though it is possible to create a generic database table and modify it as your needs grow, it is almost inevitable that you will reach a point where the data is too disorganized to use with any efficiency. To avoid the pitfalls of poor design, evaluate your needs early.

Ask the following questions:

- What data should the database store?
- What methods of access will be used?
- Who are the users and what are their roles?
- What privileges do users require?
- How should the data in the database be separated and grouped?
- Are there certain types of data or records that are accessed more often than others?
- What data groups relate to each other and what are the dependencies?
- What measures should be taken to ensure accurate and consistent data?

The First Normal Form

As soon as these questions are answered you can move toward designing and *normalizing* your database. Normalization is the process of forcing a database to conform to three fairly simple rules. Each rule is referred to as a *normal form*.

The first normal form requires that all data be broken into logical groups with one field being a unique primary key or identifier. A table in a database represents each grouping. The only fields entered into this group are those that depend on the primary key for meaning. For example, you may have a table called person with fields such as person_id, person_firstname, and person_lastname, person_employer, person_city, person_parent.

The Second Normal Form

The second normal form requires that a table conform to the first normal form and that all data related to a table, but not dependent on the primary key, be stored in secondary tables, which themselves follow the first normal form. For example, your person table can conform to the second normal form if the person_employer and person_city fields are removed. Neither a city nor an employer depends on the person. Instead, you may create a location table with columns such as location_zip, location_city, and location_state. Additionally, you can create an employer's table with employer_id and employer_name.

The Third Normal Form

The third normal form specifies that a table conform to the second normal form and that all non-key fields are independent of all other non-key fields.

Database Design Software

There are many software packages that prove useful in designing relational databases. Some, such as Microsoft's Visio, are commercial applications. Others, such as the open source Dia application are either free or inexpensive. Very often, database design and diagramming applications can create the code necessary to create your databases on the database server.

Choose a Database Server

There are several relational database management systems (RDBMS) that you can use with PHP. When choosing an RDBMS, consider several factors such as your budget, the volume of information you need to store, and the types of access needed. Another consideration is the scalability of the database in question and whether factors such as load balancing are applicable to your system.

When developing applications for clients, you may want to consider factors outside the scope of the features of a particular system. For example, the popularity of MySQL may mean that your client will have an easier time finding developers to maintain or repurpose data at a later date.

Commercial database systems most often come bundled with customer service and support, which may be another important consideration when evaluating the needs of your application.

Generally, the databases mentioned here are somewhat interchangeable as long as certain considerations are made. Through careful design and with the help of some of the administration tools provided with each, you can maintain a data source that can grow with your application or organization without overspending or overcomplicating your IT systems.

MySQL

The most popular database used to serve content on the Web with PHP is MySQL. The MySQL RDBMS is stable, fast, and efficient. The database system runs on Unix and Linux platforms, as well as Windows and Mac OS X. MySQL is easy to install and administer and is often the first RDBMS with which Web developers have experience. MySQL is an open-source software project, which means there is no cost for using it with most applications. For more information about MySQL you can refer to the MySQL Web site at www.mysql.com.

PostgreSQL

Much like MySQL, the PostgreSQL RDBMS is an open-source system deployed on a large number of sites running on Unix and Linux servers. Generally, PostgreSQL is considered to have more features than MySQL, but the stability and ubiquity of MySQL often makes it a better choice for many applications.

SQLite

PHP 5 includes a bundled embedded database called SQLite. The SQLite database is SQL-compliant and runs twice as fast as MySQL. The limitations of SQLite are mostly in scalability. For simple usage in cases where MySQL or PostgreSQL are not available, the use of SQLite should be considered. The source for SQLite is in the public domain and there are no limitations on the usage. Read more about SQLite at www.sqlite.org.

Oracle

Oracle is an incredibly powerful and rich commercial database system. Most commonly used on large corporate networks and Web sites, Oracle supports advanced security and provides a highly scalable solution. The administration and management tools provided with Oracle are quite powerful. Oracle is available for Unix/Linux and Windows systems. To learn more about Oracle, refer to www.oracle.com.

Microsoft SQL Server

The dominant database offering from Microsoft is Microsoft SQL Server, often referred to as MSSQL. MSSQL is a proven, enterprise-level database server comparable only to Oracle in features, scalability, and management. MSSQL runs only on the Windows operating system and requires a commercial license for use. To read more about MSSQL, please refer to www.microsoft.com/sql.

Introduction to Structured Query Language (SQL)

Relational databases store information and allow for great flexibility in selecting data according to given criteria. The Structured Query Language, or SQL, is an ANSI standard language used to communicate with your database server.

With SQL, you can select information from any number of tables in your database. The relational nature of a relational database means that data is broken into logical

groupings — represented by database tables — with data linked by virtue of *foreign keys* or overlapping fields between multiple tables. For example, you may have a table called `employer` with an `employer_id` field, and a table called employee with an `employer_id` field. When the `employer_id` field in each table matches, the tables are considered related. The `employer_id` fields are considered the foreign keys in the relationship.

Select

You can use a SELECT statement to ask for data from a table. SELECT statements tell the database to retrieve information from any number of tables and return it as a *result set*.

Syntax:
```
SELECT [fields] FROM [tables];
```

Optionally, you can specify conditions on which fields will be returned. To specify a condition, you can use the WHERE clause.

Syntax:
```
SELECT [fields] FROM [tables] WHERE [condition];
```

The condition must evaluate to a Boolean true or false value. You may have a SELECT statement that selects employees for a given employer.

Syntax:
```
SELECT employee.*, employer.employer_name
FROM employee, employer WHERE
employer.employer_id-1001 AND
employee.employer_id=employer.employer_id;
```

Properties of tables (columns) that should be selected are denoted by the table name, a dot (.) and the name of the property. The asterisk (*) after the table name means that all fields should be selected from the table. The above query returns all information about employees plus the employer name for a given company whose id in the database is 1001.

Insert

You can use the INSERT statement to add a record to a table in a database. The INSERT statement uses the INTO clause to specify the name of the table into which you want the data inserted.

Example:
```
INSERT INTO employees (employee_firstname,
employee_lastname, employer_id) VALUES
('Toby', 'Boudreaux', 1001);
```

Update

You can use the UPDATE statement to update an existing record in a database. The UPDATE statement is always used with a conditional WHERE clause. The WHERE clause specifies the record to be updated. For example, you can use the WHERE clause to specify the `employer_id` and update the employers table.

Example:
```
UPDATE employers SET employer_name =
'Michele Howley, Inc' WHERE employer_id =
1001;
```

Delete

You can use the DELETE statement to remove a record already in a database. If no WHERE clause is used, all records will be removed from the tables specified. You should take great care in using the DELETE statement and even greater care in which users have DELETE privileges. To delete all employees not named Toby you specify a WHERE clause that tests the `employee_firstname` field of the employee table.

Example:
```
DELETE FROM employee WHERE employee_firstname != 'Toby';
```

Using a Database Client

Most of the relational database management systems (RDBMS) you encounter are built using a client/server architecture. The database software runs on a server and applications are treated as clients that connect to the server to perform operations on the data. Most often, you can connect to a database using a client application that resides on the same machine as the server or on your own machine.

To connect to MySQL, you can use the `mysql` client application. To connect to the `mysql` client, open a terminal session with a computer running the MySQL server application. Most often, this is your Web server, but in some cases a dedicated database machine runs the database software. After you activate a server shell session, type `mysql` to attempt to connect to the server. Depending on the configuration, you may have to use the `-u` and `-p` flags to specify your username and that a password should be used for the connection. Ask the server administrator for any usernames and passwords needed.

If the `mysql` client application starts, you are given a `mysql>` prompt. Interaction with the server consists of typing commands. Use a semicolon to terminate each command. You can type multiline statements as long as no unescaped semicolon characters are a part of the statement. You can view databases using the `SHOW DATABASES;` command.

To use a given database, type the `USE` statement followed by the database name and a semicolon. For example, to connect to a database named `company_directory`, you would type `USE company_directory;` and then press the Enter key.

As soon as you specify a database, you can use the Structured Query Language (SQL) to perform operations. To learn more about SQL, please refer to the task "Introduction to Structured Query Language (SQL)."

Using a Database Client

① Locate and start the client application for your chosen database management system.

```
● ● ●                Terminal — mysql — 102x30
[tj-ibook:~] tobyboud% mysql -u root -p  ◄——————①
Enter password:
Welcome to the MySQL monitor.  Commands end with ; or \g.
Your MySQL connection id is 1 to server version: 4.0.15

Type 'help;' or '\h' for help. Type '\c' to clear the buffer.

mysql> █
```

② Display a list of databases on your server by typing `SHOW DATABASES;` and then pressing Enter.

The list of databases is printed to the client application.

```
● ● ●                Terminal — mysql — 102x30
[tj-ibook:~] tobyboud% mysql -u root -p
Enter password:
Welcome to the MySQL monitor.  Commands end with ; or \g.
Your MySQL connection id is 5 to server version: 4.0.15

Type 'help;' or '\h' for help. Type '\c' to clear the buffer.

mysql> show databases;
+-----------+
| Database  |
+-----------+
| mysql     |            ◄——————②
| test      |
+-----------+
2 rows in set (0.01 sec)

mysql> █
```

③ Select a database to use by typing USE, the name of the database, a semicolon, and then pressing Enter.

The client application reflects the database selection.

```
● ● ●                    Terminal — mysql — 102x30
[tj-ibook:~] tobyboud% mysql -u root -p
Enter password:
Welcome to the MySQL monitor.  Commands end with ; or \g.
Your MySQL connection id is 5 to server version: 4.0.15

Type 'help;' or '\h' for help. Type '\c' to clear the buffer.

mysql> show databases;
+----------+
| Database |
+----------+
| mysql    |
| test     |
+----------+
2 rows in set (0.01 sec)

mysql> use mysql;          ◄——— ③
Reading table information for completion of table and column names
You can turn off this feature to get a quicker startup with -A

Database changed
mysql> █
```

④ Type SHOW TABLES; to view a listing of tables in the database, and press Enter.

A listing of all tables in the chosen database appears in the client application.

```
● ● ●                    Terminal — mysql — 102x30
Type 'help;' or '\h' for help. Type '\c' to clear the buffer.

mysql> show databases;
+----------+
| Database |
+----------+
| mysql    |
| test     |
+----------+
2 rows in set (0.01 sec)

mysql> use mysql;
Reading table information for completion of table and column names
You can turn off this feature to get a quicker startup with -A

Database changed
mysql> show tables;        ◄——— ④
+----------------+
| Tables_in_mysql |
+----------------+
| columns_priv   |
| db             |
| func           |
| host           |
| tables_priv    |
| user           |
+----------------+
6 rows in set (0.00 sec)

mysql> █
```

Extra

There are several standalone and Web-based client applications that can be used to manage and interact with your chosen database management system. Check the documentation and support sites for your chosen database vendor to learn about management options.

To access a database server from a remote computer, you must connect to the server through a local area network (LAN) or over the Internet. This happens most often when the database software runs on a dedicated database machine. In order to connect, you need to know the address of the machine on which the database software is running. Additionally, you need an account with which you can create a connection. This information can be provided by the database administrator (DBA) who controls the database server.

Generally, it is easier to type SQL queries in a text editor and then cut and paste them into your database client than it is to type them directly. When typing directly into a client, it is much more difficult to debug and modify SQL statements than when doing so externally.

Introduction
to SQLite

The SQLite database is an embedded database that implements a large subset of the SQL 92 standard. Benefits of the SQLite engine are that the entire database engine and the interface used to interact with the engine are combined in a single library. This makes it very easy to bundle SQLite with distributed applications. In the case of Web applications, SQLite is bundled with PHP 5 and will almost always be available.

Benefits

The most noticeable benefit to SQLite over other database management systems such as MySQL is the performance speed. SQLite operates at speeds that are often many times faster than other common engines. This, combined with the ubiquity of SQLite, makes it a system that must be considered when deciding on the data storage systems to be used in each application you develop.

Interoperability

You can use SQLite in combination with other database engines. For example, you might choose to use SQLite for configuration information, MySQL for large content storage, and PostgreSQL for transactional operations such as a storefront module.

Speed

The speed with which SQLite operates can be attributed to the combined database engine and interface. Unlike other systems, SQLite does not require a strict separation of client and server. Additionally, the SQLite system is highly tuned for speed.

Simple Storage

Data in the SQLite system is stored in simple files that negate the need for complicated administration settings. The simple files that store data are controlled by standard file system permissions, meaning there is very little to the administrative side of database management.

Because each database is represented by a single file, databases are inherently portable across SQLite systems. By moving a database file to a different SQLite installation, you can easily duplicate or migrate your data sources. Load balancing is made easier by this property as well.

Embedded Server

Because the SQLite engine is embedded, it does not run as a separate server and there is no dedicated server daemon running all the time. This frees up processing resources for other applications running on your server.

Installation

Installation of the SQLite engine is simple due to the library being bundled with the default PHP 5 install package. Instead of having to manage SQLite as a separate installation and linking to it when PHP is compiled, you need only to activate the module when you configure PHP 5 for installation. On Unix systems, you can set the directive telling PHP to use SQLite by passing the `-with-sqlite` flag to the configure command before installation.

You can build PHP 5 against an external installation of SQLite by passing the path to your SQLite install to PHP 5 through the `-with-sqlite=/path/to/sqlite/lib` directive to the configure script. This can be useful if you have a preexisting instance of SQLite on your system.

Introduction to MySQLi

The MySQL library has been an integral part of PHP development for quite some time. As both PHP and MySQL have matured, the library has expanded and evolved to take advantage of new features and enhancements in each technology. With the release of MySQL 4.1 and PHP 5, the PHP development team decided to rewrite the MySQL library to take advantage of new features without having to maintain strict backward-compatibility with deprecated technologies.

The name MySQLi can mean MySQL Interface, MySQL Improved, or MySQL Incomplete according to the support documentation. The general consensus is that the library is a solid improvement over the previous ext/mysql library. MySQLi is covered later in this chapter, in the tasks "Create a MySQLi Connection" and "Create a MySQLi Prepared Statement."

Features

MySQLi provides several new features. One of the most important is the inclusion of a functionality wrapper class that allows developers to choose whether they want to manage connections to MySQL with procedural methods as they have done thus far or use an object-oriented approach.

The mysqli class allows you not only the ability to instantiate a manageable object used as a MySQL controller, but also the ability to subclass the object to provide custom functionality. Additionally, you can pass around and serialize the mysqli instances, helping to ensure that your model layer conforms to the same object-oriented design as the rest of your system.

Prepared Statements

Another important feature of the MySQLi library is the inclusion of prepared statements. Prepared statements are part of the newest release of MySQL and are accessible through the MySQLi library. Prepared statements allow you to create a query statement once and execute it many times with varying parameters. By leveraging the automatic value assignment functionality provided by prepared statements you benefit from enhanced speed and security in addition to an ease of management that is almost exclusive of the act of building ad hoc statements inline.

Prepared Statement Performance

Prepared statements offer a performance increase for a few reasons. The first is that the query only has to be parsed once by the database server. When a statement is initially prepared, the query is loaded and parsed once. If there are errors in the syntax of the query due either to the statements and clauses chosen or problems with values, an appropriate error is thrown. If the query checks out, it is cached on the server and used with dynamic values assigned via a client application such as PHP.

Another performance enhancement is the use of a new binary protocol that avoids the slow and tedious process of converting all queries into string values before passing them across the network to the database server that then has to decode the strings into the appropriate data types.

Prepared Statement Security

The security benefits of prepared statements are significant. Because the query logic and parameters are separated and assigned by way of native assignment methods, common security exploits such as SQL Injections are all but eliminated. Additionally, this separation also allows a developer to protect SQL statements from less-privileged developers by using an SQL *phrasebook* or external storage mechanism for SQL statements. Because most phrasebooks are simple text or PHP files, they can be stored in locations protected by file-system permissions, allowing PHP to access them but not the prying eyes of others.

Create an SQLite Database

You can create an SQLite database using PHP. The function `sqlite_open` is used to create a database connection. The function accepts one required and two optional arguments. The first argument is a string representing the database file you want to open. Most often, the database file extension is .sqlite. For example, to connect to an SQLite database named "preferences" you might use a statement such as `sqlite_open ("preferences.sqlite");`.

If the database file you request does not exist, the SQLite engine attempts to create the database.

The second argument to `sqlite_open` is optional and represents the Unix permissions mode with which you want to open the file. The default is the octal value `0666`, which is also the recommended mode to use if you need to pass a third argument to the `sqlite_open` function. The third argument represents an optional error message to be returned if the database cannot be opened or created.

The `sqlite_open` function returns a database handle if the function is successful. If there is an error, the `sqlite_open` function returns a Boolean `false` value.

You can create an in-memory database by passing the string `:memory:` to the `sqlite_open` function. This is useful if you want to create a temporary database for the purpose of altering a database structure or performing data cache functionality to optimize complicated database interaction.

Because a memory database exists in volatile memory and is owned by the script in which it is created, the memory is freed and the database destroyed at the completion of the script. If you are using a memory database to alter the structure of a file-based database, be sure to implement some sort of rollback functionality so that errors in processing will not destroy your only data source. For example, do not delete the original database until a new one has been successfully created using a memory database.

Create an SQLite Database

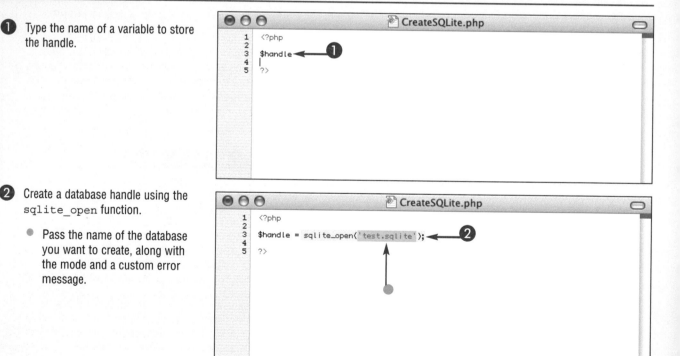

① Type the name of a variable to store the handle.

② Create a database handle using the `sqlite_open` function.

● Pass the name of the database you want to create, along with the mode and a custom error message.

3 Use a conditional test to check the validity of the handle. If there is an error, report as much through the output stream.

CreateSQLite.php

```php
1   <?php
2
3   $handle = sqlite_open('test.sqlite');
4
5   if($handle == false){
6       echo 'There was a problem creating the SQLite database.';
7       exit();
8   }
9
10  echo 'Database created.';
11
12  ?>
```

3

4 View your script in a Web browser.

The database is successfully created or, in the case of an error, the custom error message appears.

@ http://127.0.0.1:9003/...3/code/CreateSQLite.php

Back Forward Stop Refresh Home AutoFill Print Mail

Address: @ http://127.0.0.1:9003/ch10/task3/code/CreateSQLite.php   › go

Database created. ◄—— **4**

Extra

The SQLite database engine relies on system-level file-locking mechanisms in order to read from and write to the database files. Without proper file locking, data integrity cannot be ensured and many types of errors can result when simultaneous access occurs. When using the `fork()` system call, close the handle to an SQLite database file before making the call and reopen the database handle, if needed, in the child or parent process resulting from the `fork()` call.

You can create a persistent connection to a commonly used SQLite database using the `sqlite_popen` function. The `sqlite_popen` function has the same signature and return value as the `sqlite_open` function but leverages the PHP persistence functionality to maintain an open handle to the database. When called, `sqlite_popen` looks first for an open handle for the given database file. If found, the open handle is returned. Otherwise, a new handle is created and returned.

Example:
```
$handle = sqlite_popen('mydb.sqlite');
```

Add Records to an SQLite Database

You can add records to an SQLite database using an SQL INSERT statement.

The INSERT statement tells an SQL-compliant database engine to create a record in a given table and assigns values to each column in the new row. The syntax of the INSERT statement can conform to one of two major forms. The first allows you to simply insert values into a new row, passing each value explicitly to the INSERT statement. This form allows two syntactical formats. If you insert values into every column in the table, you can use the format:

```
INSERT INTO table-name VALUES (value1,
value2, ...);
```

In cases where you are not inserting an explicit value into every row, such as when using an automatically incrementing identifier column, you must specify the columns into which you intend to insert data. The order

and number of values passed must match the order and number of columns listed. The format for such a query is:

```
INSERT INTO table-name (column1, column2,
...) VALUES (value1, value2, ...);
```

The second major form an INSERT statement can take uses a SELECT statement to determine the values to be used in the creation of the new record. You can, for example, select data from many tables to determine calculated values to be inserted into a separate table for quicker reference or complex sorting. The format of the second major form is:

```
INSERT INTO table-name [(column-list)]
(SELECT (values) FROM table-name);
```

Queries are executed using the sqlite_query function. The sqlite_query function accepts two required arguments that may appear in any order. The arguments are a string representing the SQL query you want to execute and the database resource handle returned by sqlite_open or sqlite_popen.

Add Records to an SQLite Database

① Create a database handle using the sqlite_open function.

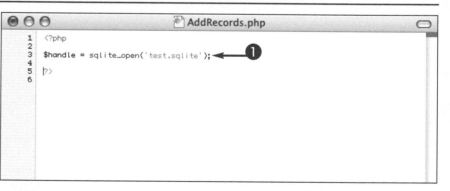

② Create a string variable to represent your query.

③ Type an INSERT statement as the value of the query string.

4 Type the name of a result identifier variable to represent the result of your INSERT statement.

5 Use the sqlite_query function to execute the INSERT statement.

6 Test the result success and print a message reflecting the status of the insertion.

```
AddRecords.php

1   <?php
2
3   $handle = sqlite_open('test.sqlite');
4
5   if($handle == false){
6       echo 'There was a problem creating the SQLite database.';
7       exit();
8   }
9
10  $query = 'INSERT INTO users (name, password) VALUES ("tobyjoe", "php")';
11
4→  $result = sqlite_query($handle, $query);    ←5
13
6
14  echo ($result) ? "Success - record added.\r\n" : "Failure - record not added.\r\n";
15
16  ?>
17
```

7 View your script in a Web browser.

If the INSERT statement is successful, the result handle test is true and your success message is printed.

If the result handle test is false, an error message is printed.

```
http://127.0.0.1:9003/...sk4/code/AddRecords.php

Back  Forward  Stop  Refresh  Home  AutoFill  Print  Mail

Address:  http://127.0.0.1:9003/ch10/task4/code/AddRecords.php      go

Success - record added.  ←7
```

Extra

You can use the ON CONFLICT clause to specify behavior that should occur when a conflict happens in your query. For example, if you attempt to insert data into a table that includes an already-used primary key, a conflict arises due to primary key columns requiring distinct values in each record. You can leverage the ON CONFLICT clause in your INSERT statement to tell SQLite to replace the existing record with the new record if a conflict occurs.

Example:
```
$handle = sqlite_open('mydb.sqlite');
$query = "INSERT OR REPLACE INTO my_table (id, name) VALUES (1, 'Toby');
$result = sqlite_query($handle, $query);
```

Retrieve Records from an SQLite Database

The most common database functionality is reading information that has been previously stored. You can use PHP and the SQLite extension to retrieve records from an SQLite database.

Record retrieval is performed with an SQL SELECT statement. The SELECT statement allows for many forms and is used to leverage SQL JOIN and UNION statements to combine data from several tables into one result set. Conditional selection is performed using the WHERE clause. You can group record sets by given column values using the GROUP BY clause and limit the number of records returned using the LIMIT and OFFSET clauses.

Generally, the SELECT statement is the richest and most dynamic statement in the SQL language. More information about the intricacies of the SQLite SELECT statement can be found at www.sqlite.org/lang.html#select.

The sqlite_query function can be used to execute a SELECT statement. It should be noted that a result set returned from a call to sqlite_query contains all records returned by the query. When accessing very large sets of records, it can be more efficient to select records progressively through the result set. To leverage unbuffered result sets, you can substitute the sqlite_unbuffered_query function for the sqlite_query function.

To access individual records in a result set, you can use the sqlite_fetch_single function in combination with the sqlite_has_more function to iterate over the record set, retrieving one record at a time.

You can retrieve all records returned as an array of arrays using the sqlite_fetch_all function. Generally, it is best to iterate over a record set, retrieving each record individually, as the sqlite_fetch_all function does not inherently provide iteration methods.

Retrieve Records from an SQLite Database

① Create a database handle using the sqlite_open function.

```
1   <?php
2
3   $handle = sqlite_open('test.sqlite');
4
5   ?>
6
```

② Create a string variable to represent your query.

③ Type a SELECT statement as the value of the query string.

④ Type the name of a result identifier variable to represent the result of your SELECT statement.

```
1   <?php
2
3   $handle = sqlite_open('test.sqlite');
4
5   if($handle == false){
6       echo 'There was a problem creating the SQLite database.';
7       exit();
8   }
9
10  $query = 'SELECT * FROM users';
11
12  $result
13  |
14  ?>
15
```

⑤ Use the `sqlite_query` function to execute the `SELECT` statement.

⑥ Use the `sqlite_has_more` function as the condition in a `while` loop to iterate over the result set.

⑦ Retrieve each record using the `sqlite_fetch_single` function and display it using a `print_r` statement.

```php
<?php

$handle = sqlite_open('test.sqlite');

if($handle == false){
    echo 'There was a problem creating the SQLite database.';
    exit();
}

$query = 'SELECT * FROM users';

$result = sqlite_query($handle, $query);       ⟵ ⑤

while(sqlite_has_more($result)){               ⑥
    $row = sqlite_fetch_single($result);       ⟵ ⑦
    print_r($row);
}                                              ⑥
|
?>
```
RetrieveRecords.php

⑧ View your script in a Web browser.

A record set is returned from the query and each record is printed to the output stream.

@ http://127.0.0.1:9003/...ode/RetrieveRecords.php

Address: @ http://127.0.0.1:9003/ch10/task5/code/RetrieveRecords.php   go

tobyjoe ⟵ ⑧

Extra

You can move through a result set using the data-seeking functions `sqlite_prev`, `sqlite_current`, `sqlite_next`, `sqlite_has_prev`, and `sqlite_rewind`. These functions are useful when iterating backward and forward over a record set or when reusing the same result set in multiple processing functions. It is generally best practice to rewind using the `sqlite_rewind` function before calling `sqlite_fetch_single` or using any of the iteration functions.

Example:
```
$handle = sqlite_open('mydb.sqlite');
$query = "SELECT * FROM mytable";
$result = sqlite_query($handle, $query);
sqlite_rewinde($result);
while(sqlite_has_more($result)){
  $row = sqlite_fetch_single($result);
  print_r($row);
}
```

Create an SQLite Function

Y ou can create a user-defined function (UDF) to be used in your SQLite queries. For example, you might create a function to reverse the order of a string or to encrypt data using the MD5 algorithm before selecting it.

To create a UDF, you can simply create any function that accepts zero or more arguments and returns a scalar value recognized by SQLite.

Setting a UDF to be recognized by SQLite can be accomplished using the `sqlite_create_function` function. The first argument for `sqlite_create_function` is the database handle returned by a call to `sqlite_open` or `sqlite_popen`. The second parameter to `sqlite_create_function` is the name you want to use

within your SQLite queries to access your custom function. The third argument is a string representing the name of the UDF to be called when the second argument is used in a query. The last argument is optional and represents the number of arguments your custom function accepts. If your function requires a specific number of arguments, it is best to specify this optional parameter.

When a UDF is called from an SQLite query, the external function set with `sqlite_create_function` is called. This callback mechanism will call the function, passing along any values specified in the query. The result returned from the callback is used as the value for the field specified in the query.

Create an SQLite Function

① Create a custom function to be set as an SQLite UDF.

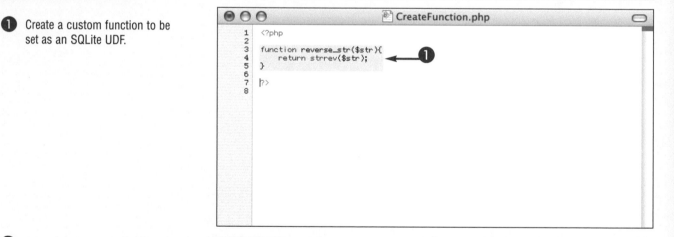

```php
<?php

function reverse_str($str){
    return strrev($str);
}

?>
```

② Use the `sqlite_create_function` function to set the database handle, function name, callback name, and number of arguments for your UDF.

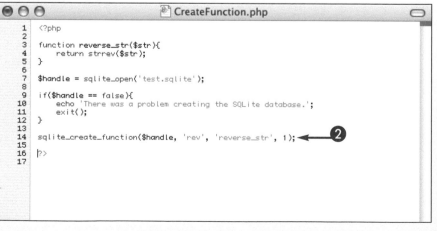

```php
<?php

function reverse_str($str){
    return strrev($str);
}

$handle = sqlite_open('test.sqlite');

if($handle == false){
    echo 'There was a problem creating the SQLite database.';
    exit();
}

sqlite_create_function($handle, 'rev', 'reverse_str', 1);

?>
```

3 Create a query that calls the UDF by name.

4 Execute the query using the `sqlite_query` function.

5 Iterate over the result set, displaying each record using the `print_r` function.

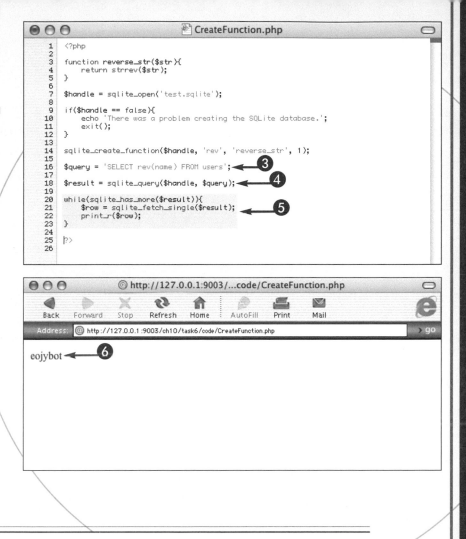

```php
<?php

function reverse_str($str){
    return strrev($str);
}

$handle = sqlite_open('test.sqlite');

if($handle == false){
    echo 'There was a problem creating the SQLite database.';
    exit();
}

sqlite_create_function($handle, 'rev', 'reverse_str', 1);

$query = 'SELECT rev(name) FROM users';       ◄—— 3

$result = sqlite_query($handle, $query);       ◄—— 4

while(sqlite_has_more($result)){
    $row = sqlite_fetch_single($result);       ◄—— 5
    print_r($row);
}

?>
```

6 View your script in a Web browser.

The custom UDF is called for each record returned as part of the result set.

Address: http://127.0.0.1:9003/ch10/task6/code/CreateFunction.php

eojybot ◄—— 6

Extra

You can create custom aggregation functionality to be used in SQLite queries. For example, you can create a function that finds the longest string value across all records in a record set. Custom aggregate functionality is defined by creating two custom functions. The first is the step function — that is, the function to be called on each record set. This function should return a value that is used by a combined aggregation function that can compare the return values of each step function call and act accordingly.

Example:
```php
function max_length_step($context, $value){
    $len = strlen($value);
    $context = ($len > $context) ? $len : $context;
}
function max_length_finalize($context){
    return $context;
}
sqlite_create_aggregate($handle, 'max_length', 'max_length_step',
'max_length_finalize');
$query = 'SELECT max_length($username) FROM user';
```

Connect to MySQL Server

The combination of MySQL and PHP is well established and ubiquitous in Web development. Part of the reason for this pairing is that the MySQL library for PHP is excellent and quite simple to use. Connecting to MySQL from PHP is a simple and essential step in storing, searching, and retrieving your database content.

The first step in using a MySQL database in your PHP application is to connect to the MySQL database server. To connect to MySQL, you must have the address of the MySQL server as well as valid account information with sufficient privileges.

The `mysql_connect` function creates a connection to a MySQL server and returns a database resource handle that can be used in further MySQL operations. The `mysql_connect` function accepts five optional parameters. If no parameters are specified, defaults are used. The first argument is a string representing the address of the server. The default address is assumed to be `localhost:3306`.

The second argument to `mysql_connect` is a string representing the username with which to connect. If no username parameter is passed, the name of the system user that owns the PHP process is used.

The third argument is the password for the username specified. If no password is specified, it is assumed that no password is necessary for the given username and an empty value is used.

If a second call to `mysql_connect` is made with the same parameters within the same script, the default behavior is to find and return the database handle generated by the first connection call. To override this functionality, you can pass a fourth argument that is a Boolean specifying whether or not to create a new link.

The final argument to `mysql_connect` represents flags for the PHP MySQL client that connects to the database. The value of this argument can be any combination of the default constants `MYSQL_CLIENT_COMPRESS`, `MYSQL_CLIENT_IGNORE_SPACE`, or `MYSQL_CLIENT_INTERACTIVE`.

Connect to MySQL Server

① Create a variable to store the database resource handle returned by `mysql_connect`.

② Type `mysql_connect`.

③ In parentheses, pass the server name, username, and password to use in the connection.

You can also specify the fourth and fifth optional arguments for the connection.

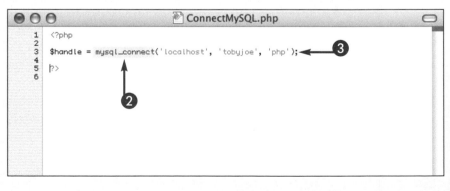

238

④ Check the value of the resource handle returned and print a message reflecting the success or failure of the attempt to connect.

⑤ Close your MySQL database connection using the `mysql_close` function.

ConnectMySQL.php

```
1  <?php
2
3  $handle = mysql_connect('localhost', 'tobyjoe', 'php');
4
5  echo ($handle) ? "Connected to MySQL.\r\n" : "Could not connect to MySQL.\r\n";
6
7  mysql_close($handle);
8
9  ?>
10
```

④ ⑤

⑥ View your script in a Web browser.

A connection to the specified MySQL server is created and a message is displayed based on the success or failure of the connection parameters.

@ http://127.0.0.1:9003/...7/code/ConnectMySQL.php

Back Forward Stop Refresh Home AutoFill Print Mail

Address: @ http://127.0.0.1:9003/ch10/task7/code/ConnectMySQL.php   go

Connected to MySQL. ◄ ⑥

Extra

You can create a persistent MySQL connection by using the `mysql_pconnect` function instead of `mysql_connect`. The `mysql_pconnect` function accepts the same arguments as `mysql_connect` except for the fourth argument, which specifies that a new link should be created. This is because the goal of `mysql_pconnect` is to create a MySQL server connection that is reusable across your scripts.

Example:
```
$server = 'localhost';
$user = 'anon_web_user';
$pass = 'somepass';
$handle = mysql_pconnect($server, $user, $pass);
if($handle == false){
  die('No database connection available: ' . mysql_error());
}
```

Add Records to a MySQL Database

Each entry in a database table is called a *record*. You can add records to a MySQL database using the SQL INSERT statement.

The INSERT statement tells an SQL-compliant database engine to create a record in a given table and assign values to each column in the new record.

The syntax of the INSERT statement can conform to one of two major forms. The first form allows you to simply insert values into a new record, passing each value explicitly to the INSERT statement. This form allows two syntactical formats. If you are inserting values into every column in the table, you can use the format:

```
INSERT INTO table-name VALUES (value1,
value2, ...);
```

In cases where you are not inserting an explicit value into every row, such as when using an automatically incrementing identifier column, you must specify the columns into which you do intend to insert data. The order and number of values passed must match the order and number of columns listed. The format for such a query is:

```
INSERT INTO table-name (column1, column2,
...) VALUES (value1, value2, ...);
```

The second major form an INSERT statement can take uses a SELECT statement to determine the values to be used in the creation of the new record. This is known as an INSERT-SELECT statement and allows you to create dynamic value sets and store them in an aggregate table. The format of the second major form is:

```
INSERT INTO table-name [(column-list)]
(SELECT (values) FROM table-name);
```

Queries are executed using the mysql_query function. The mysql_query function accepts one required and one optional argument. The first argument is a string representing the SQL query to be used in interaction with the database server. The second is the resource link identifier returned by a call to mysql_connect or mysql_pconnect. If no link identifier is passed, the last opened link is used. If there is no available link, an automatic connection is attempted using default values. It is best practice to always pass the second argument to ensure transactional integrity.

Add Records to a MySQL Database

① Create a variable to store the database resource handle returned by mysql_connect.

② Connect using mysql_connect.

③ Select a database using mysql_select_db.

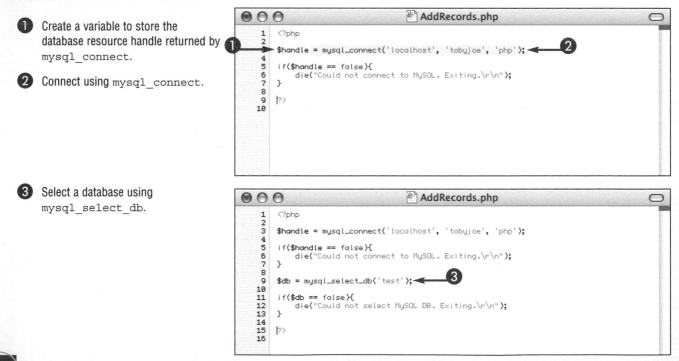

4 Create an SQL query using an INSERT statement.

5 Use mysql_query to execute the SQL query.

6 Test the result of the query operation and perform an appropriate action to reflect the success.

7 Close your MySQL database connection using the mysql_close function.

8 View your script in a Web browser.

Records are inserted into your database.

```php
<?php

$handle = mysql_connect('localhost', 'tobyjoe', 'php');

if($handle == false){
    die("Could not connect to MySQL. Exiting.\r\n");
}

$db = mysql_select_db('test');

if($db == false){
    die("Could not select MySQL DB. Exiting.\r\n");
}

$query = 'INSERT INTO user (user_name, user_password) VALUES ("toby", PASSWORD("php")

$result = mysql_query($query, $handle);

echo ($result) ? "Insert was successful.\r\n" : "Insert was unsuccessful.\r\n";

mysql_close($handle);

?>
```

AddRecords.php

http://127.0.0.1:9003/...sk8/code/AddRecords.php

Back Forward Stop Refresh Home AutoFill Print Mail

Address: http://127.0.0.1:9003/ch10/task8/code/AddRecords.php

Insert was successful. **8**

Extra

The values returned by mysql_query depend on the type of SQL statement passed to the MySQL server. For SELECT, SHOW, DESCRIBE, and EXPLAIN statements, the mysql_query function returns a result set resource identifier on success and a Boolean false on error.

When executing an UPDATE, DELETE, DROP, ALTER, or other types of SQL statements, the function returns a Boolean true value on success and false on error.

The mysql_connect function may return false if the query fails due to syntax or permission errors.

You can use the mysql_num_rows function to find the number of rows returned by a SELECT statement. The mysql_affected_rows function returns the number of rows affected by a DELETE, INSERT, REPLACE, or UPDATE statement.

TYPE THIS:

```php
// for a table with 10 records.
$result = mysql_query('SELECT * FROM table', $handle);
$num = mysql_num_rows($result);
echo "The SELECT statement returned $num rows.";

$result = mysql_query('UPDATE table SET
some_column="some_value"', $handle);
$num = mysql_affected_rows($result);
echo "The UPDATE statement changed $num rows.";
```

RESULT:

```
The SELECT statement returned 10 rows.
The UPDATE statement changed 10 rows.
```

Select Records from a MySQL Database

Y ou can select records in a MySQL database using the SQL SELECT statement.

In its simplest form, the SELECT statement retrieves every value from a given table. You can specify that all values be selected by using an asterisk (*) wildcard character instead of an explicit list of columns. For example, to select all columns and records in a table news you use SELECT * FROM news;.

The power of a relational database comes in the way tables can relate to one another. There are several methods of selecting data from multiple tables based on any number of conditional statements. To learn about joining data from various tables, you can refer to the MySQL manual at http://dev.mysql.com/doc/ as well as many other online resources.

A given SELECT query is executed using the mysql_query function. The mysql_query function accepts one required

and one optional argument. The first, required argument is a string representing the query to be executed. The second argument is the database resource link identifier created by a call to mysql_connect or mysql_pconnect.

The mysql_query function returns a result set resource identifier when used with a successful SELECT query. You can iterate over a result set using the mysql_fetch_array or mysql_fetch_object functions combined with mysql_num_rows.

When executing a SELECT query that returns a large number of rows, you can use mysql_unbuffered_query in place of mysql_query. The mysql_unbuffered_query function will not buffer all records in memory but instead provides a handle for selectively seeking individual records. The unbuffered version can be integral to saving memory for large result sets.

Select Records from a MySQL Database

① Create a variable to store the database resource handle returned by mysql_connect.

② Connect using mysql_connect.

```
SelectRecords.php
1   <?php
2
3   $handle = mysql_connect('localhost', 'tobyjoe', 'php');
4
5   if($handle == false){
6       die("Could not connect to MySQL. Exiting.\r\n");
7   }
8
9   ?>
10
```

③ Select a database using mysql_select_db.

```
SelectRecords.php
1   <?php
2
3   $handle = mysql_connect('localhost', 'tobyjoe', 'php');
4
5   if($handle == false){
6       die("Could not connect to MySQL. Exiting.\r\n");
7   }
8
9   $db = mysql_select_db('test');
10
11  if($db == false){
12      die("Could not select MySQL DB. Exiting.\r\n");
13  }
14
15  ?>
16
```

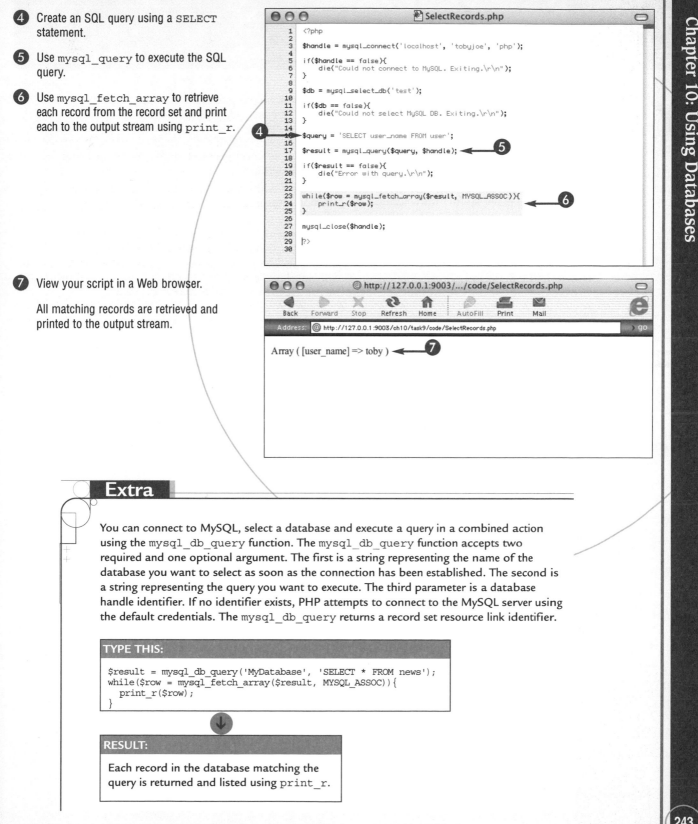

4 Create an SQL query using a SELECT statement.

5 Use mysql_query to execute the SQL query.

6 Use mysql_fetch_array to retrieve each record from the record set and print each to the output stream using print_r.

7 View your script in a Web browser.

All matching records are retrieved and printed to the output stream.

Extra

You can connect to MySQL, select a database and execute a query in a combined action using the mysql_db_query function. The mysql_db_query function accepts two required and one optional argument. The first is a string representing the name of the database you want to select as soon as the connection has been established. The second is a string representing the query you want to execute. The third parameter is a database handle identifier. If no identifier exists, PHP attempts to connect to the MySQL server using the default credentials. The mysql_db_query returns a record set resource link identifier.

TYPE THIS:

```
$result = mysql_db_query('MyDatabase', 'SELECT * FROM news');
while($row = mysql_fetch_array($result, MYSQL_ASSOC)){
   print_r($row);
}
```

RESULT:

Each record in the database matching the query is returned and listed using print_r.

243

Update Records in a MySQL Database

You can update records in a MySQL database using an SQL UPDATE statement. The UPDATE statement follows the format:

```
UPDATE table-name SET column-name = value;
```

Optionally, you can specify a WHERE clause to limit the scope of the records being updated. Without a WHERE clause, every record in your table is updated so that the column specified by *column-name* is universally set to the value represented by *value*. For example, to update all records in a table *user* to deactivate users named "Toby" you might create a query such as:

```
UPDATE user SET active=0 WHERE
name_first='Toby';
```

An UPDATE statement is executed using the mysql_query function. The mysql_query function accepts one required and two optional arguments. The first argument is the query to be executed. The second is the database handle resource identifier returned from a call to mysql_connect or mysql_pconnect. If the second argument is omitted, PHP attempts to connect to the MySQL server using the default credentials.

When used with an UPDATE statement, the mysql_query function returns a Boolean true on success and false on failure.

You can use the mysql_affected_rows function to determine the number of rows affected by the UPDATE statement. The mysql_affected_rows function accepts the database handle used to execute the query and returns an integer representing the affected row count.

Update Records in a MySQL Database

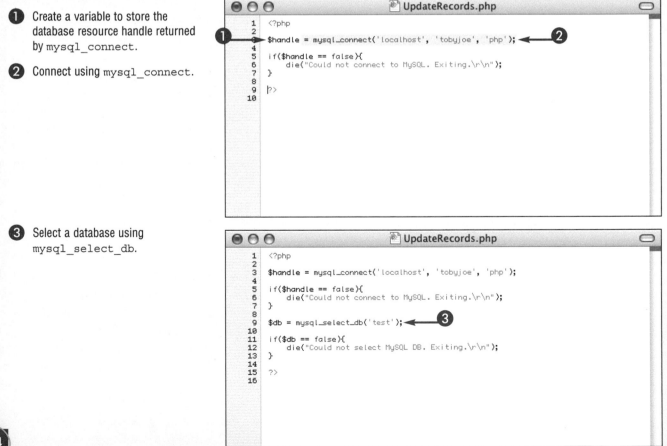

① Create a variable to store the database resource handle returned by mysql_connect.

② Connect using mysql_connect.

```php
<?php

$handle = mysql_connect('localhost', 'tobyjoe', 'php');

if($handle == false){
    die("Could not connect to MySQL. Exiting.\r\n");
}

?>
```

③ Select a database using mysql_select_db.

```php
<?php

$handle = mysql_connect('localhost', 'tobyjoe', 'php');

if($handle == false){
    die("Could not connect to MySQL. Exiting.\r\n");
}

$db = mysql_select_db('test');

if($db == false){
    die("Could not select MySQL DB. Exiting.\r\n");
}

?>
```

④ Create an SQL query using an UPDATE statement.

⑤ Execute the query using mysql_query.

⑥ Determine the number of affected rows using the mysql_affected_rows function and print the result to the output stream.

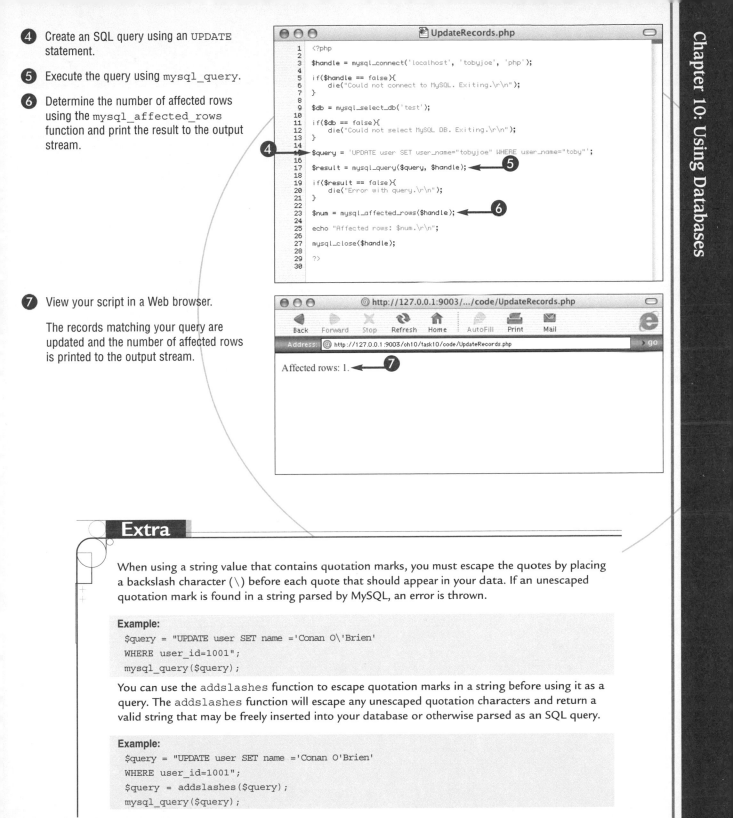

```php
<?php

$handle = mysql_connect('localhost', 'tobyjoe', 'php');

if($handle == false){
    die("Could not connect to MySQL. Exiting.\r\n");
}

$db = mysql_select_db('test');

if($db == false){
    die("Could not select MySQL DB. Exiting.\r\n");
}

$query = 'UPDATE user SET user_name="tobyjoe" WHERE user_name="toby"';

$result = mysql_query($query, $handle);

if($result == false){
    die("Error with query.\r\n");
}

$num = mysql_affected_rows($handle);

echo "Affected rows: $num.\r\n";

mysql_close($handle);

?>
```

⑦ View your script in a Web browser.

The records matching your query are updated and the number of affected rows is printed to the output stream.

Affected rows: 1. ⑦

Extra

When using a string value that contains quotation marks, you must escape the quotes by placing a backslash character (\) before each quote that should appear in your data. If an unescaped quotation mark is found in a string parsed by MySQL, an error is thrown.

Example:
```
$query = "UPDATE user SET name ='Conan O\'Brien'
WHERE user_id=1001";
mysql_query($query);
```

You can use the addslashes function to escape quotation marks in a string before using it as a query. The addslashes function will escape any unescaped quotation characters and return a valid string that may be freely inserted into your database or otherwise parsed as an SQL query.

Example:
```
$query = "UPDATE user SET name ='Conan O'Brien'
WHERE user_id=1001";
$query = addslashes($query);
mysql_query($query);
```

245

Delete Records from a MySQL Database

When working with MySQL, you often need to delete one or more records from a table in a given database. If the account with which you connect to the MySQL server has permission to delete data, you can perform deletion using an SQL DELETE statement.

The DELETE statement syntax follows the form DELETE FROM table-name WHERE condition;.

If you execute a DELETE statement without a conditional WHERE clause, all data in the table specified by *table-name* is deleted. Because of the delicate nature of SQL DELETE statement execution, take great care to prevent accidental or malicious data deletion. In most cases, use a separate database user to establish connections for destructive functionality such as executing DELETE statements. Using an account with read-only access for general-purpose data access drastically reduces the chance of unwanted data deletion.

A DELETE statement can be executed using the mysql_query function. The mysql_query function accepts one required and one optional argument. The first argument is a string representing the query you want to execute on the MySQL server. The second argument is the database handle resource identifier returned from a call to a connection function such as mysql_connect or mysql_pconnect.

When a DELETE operation is successful the mysql_query function returns a Boolean true value. If there is an error in the execution of the statement, such as when invalid syntax is used or the account with which the connection is made does not have data deletion privileges, the mysql_query function returns false.

You can determine the number of rows deleted by the execution of a DELETE query using the mysql_affected_rows function.

Delete Records from a MySQL Database

① Create a variable to store the database resource handle returned by mysql_connect.

② Connect using mysql_connect.

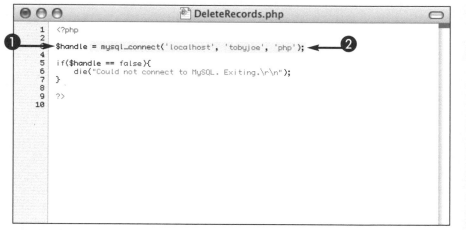

```php
1   <?php
2
3   $handle = mysql_connect('localhost', 'tobyjoe', 'php');
4
5   if($handle == false){
6       die("Could not connect to MySQL. Exiting.\r\n");
7   }
8
9   ?>
10
```

③ Select a database using mysql_select_db.

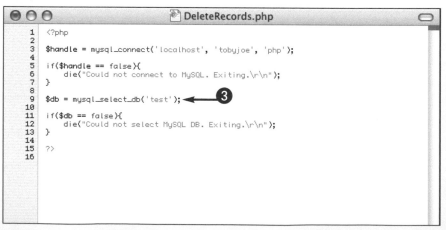

```php
1    <?php
2
3    $handle = mysql_connect('localhost', 'tobyjoe', 'php');
4
5    if($handle == false){
6        die("Could not connect to MySQL. Exiting.\r\n");
7    }
8
9    $db = mysql_select_db('test');
10
11   if($db == false){
12       die("Could not select MySQL DB. Exiting.\r\n");
13   }
14
15   ?>
16
```

④ Create an SQL query using a DELETE statement.

⑤ Execute the query using mysql_query.

⑥ Determine the number of affected rows using the mysql_affected_rows function and print the result to the output stream.

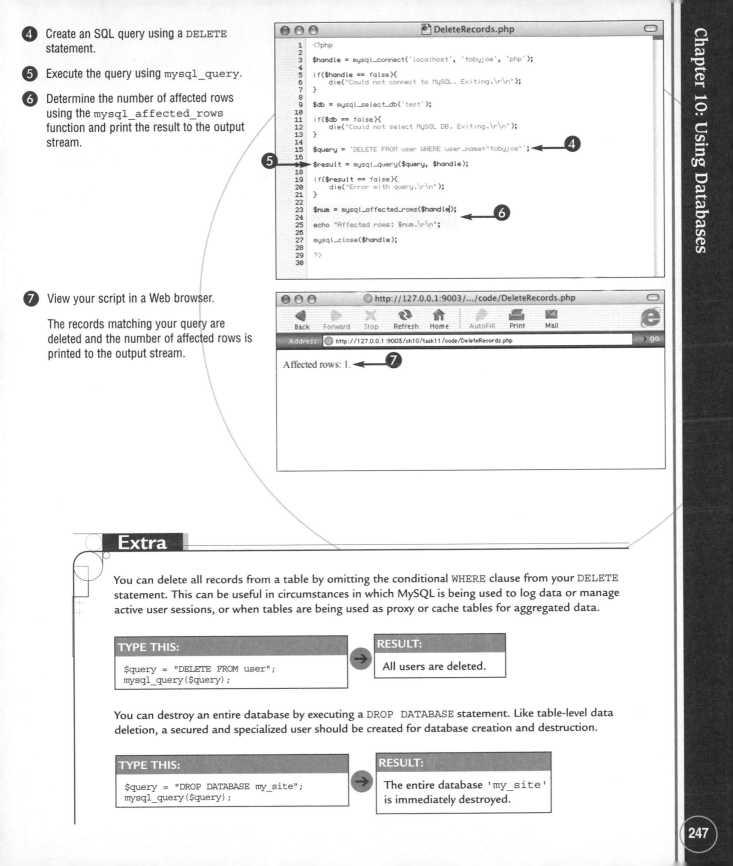

```php
<?php

$handle = mysql_connect('localhost', 'tobyjoe', 'php');

if($handle == false){
    die("Could not connect to MySQL. Exiting.\r\n");
}

$db = mysql_select_db('test');

if($db == false){
    die("Could not select MySQL DB. Exiting.\r\n");
}

$query = 'DELETE FROM user WHERE user_name="tobyjoe"';          ◀── ④

$result = mysql_query($query, $handle);    ⑤

if($result == false){
    die("Error with query.\r\n");
}

$num = mysql_affected_rows($handle);          ◀── ⑥

echo "Affected rows: $num.\r\n";

mysql_close($handle);

?>
```

⑦ View your script in a Web browser.

The records matching your query are deleted and the number of affected rows is printed to the output stream.

@ http://127.0.0.1:9003/.../code/DeleteRecords.php

Address: http://127.0.0.1:9003/ch10/task11/code/DeleteRecords.php

Affected rows: 1. ◀── ⑦

Extra

You can delete all records from a table by omitting the conditional WHERE clause from your DELETE statement. This can be useful in circumstances in which MySQL is being used to log data or manage active user sessions, or when tables are being used as proxy or cache tables for aggregated data.

TYPE THIS:

```
$query = "DELETE FROM user";
mysql_query($query);
```

RESULT:

All users are deleted.

You can destroy an entire database by executing a DROP DATABASE statement. Like table-level data deletion, a secured and specialized user should be created for database creation and destruction.

TYPE THIS:

```
$query = "DROP DATABASE my_site";
mysql_query($query);
```

RESULT:

The entire database 'my_site' is immediately destroyed.

Retrieve Records as an Associative Array

After a successful record set is retrieved by a call to the `mysql_query` function with a valid `SELECT` statement, you can iterate over the records of which the record set is comprised, fetching each as an associative array.

Because arrays are used for so many purposes in PHP, it can be useful to retrieve a record as an array and use it in various contexts and operations. You can use the `mysql_fetch_assoc` function to retrieve a single record as an array.

With an associative array a key that can be thought of as a unique name for a given element accesses a value. For example, an associative array representing a person might have keys such as `name`, `age`, `height`, `weight`, and `eye_color`. Each of these keys can be used to access its associated value using array notation. For an array named

user you can access the eye color using `$color = $user['eye_color'];`.

The keys used in the associative array may or may not match the names of columns in the tables from which you selected the data. The default behavior is to use the column names as keys, but you may override this behavior by specifying names for values in your SQL query using the `AS` modifier. For example, to select the column `eye_color` from a user table with the name `eyes` your `SELECT` statement might be written as:

`SELECT eye_color AS eyes FROM user;`

The `mysql_fetch_assoc` function accepts the record set identifier returned by a call to a function such as `mysql_query`. You can use the `mysql_fetch_assoc` function in a `while` loop to iterate over each record in a given record set.

Retrieve Records as an Associative Array

① Create a variable to store the database resource handle returned by `mysql_connect`.

② Connect using `mysql_connect`.

```php
<?php

$handle = mysql_connect('localhost', 'tobyjoe', 'php');

if($handle == false){
    die("Could not connect to MySQL. Exiting.\r\n");
}

?>
```

③ Select a database using `mysql_select_db`.

```php
<?php

$handle = mysql_connect('localhost', 'tobyjoe', 'php');

if($handle == false){
    die("Could not connect to MySQL. Exiting.\r\n");
}

$db = mysql_select_db('test');

if($db == false){
    die("Could not select MySQL DB. Exiting.\r\n");
}

?>
```

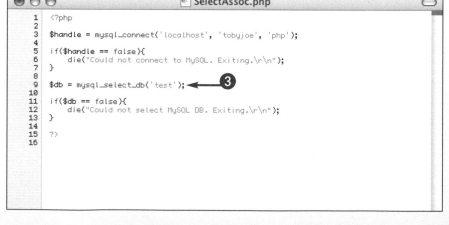

④ Create an SQL query using a SELECT statement.

⑤ Execute the query using mysql_query.

⑥ Create a while loop using an assignment statement combined with mysql_fetch_assoc to select each record in your record set.

The loop terminates when the mysql_fetch_assoc function returns a Boolean false at the end of the record set.

⑦ Print each associative array using the print_r function.

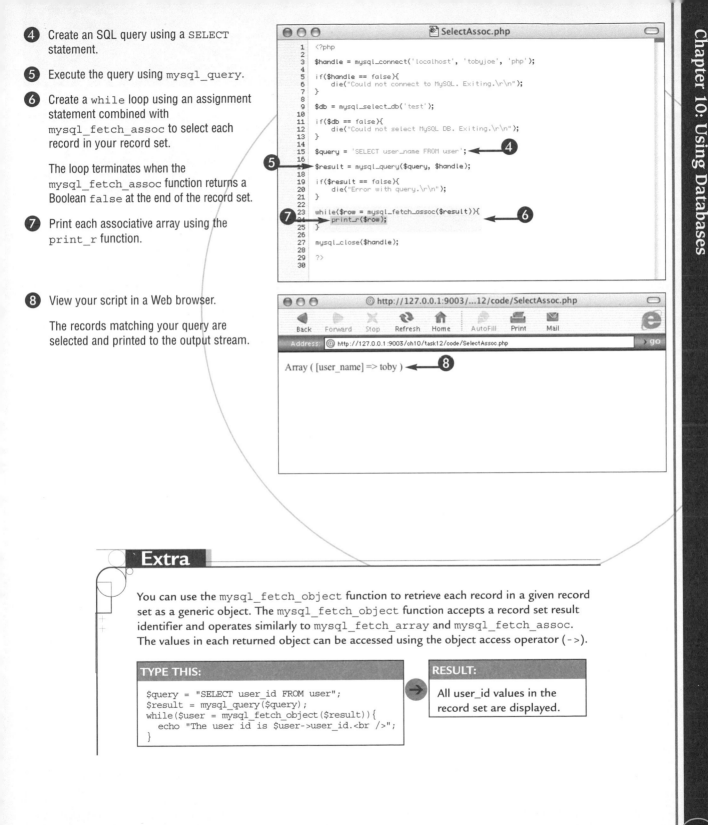

```php
<?php

$handle = mysql_connect('localhost', 'tobyjoe', 'php');

if($handle == false){
    die("Could not connect to MySQL. Exiting.\r\n");
}

$db = mysql_select_db('test');

if($db == false){
    die("Could not select MySQL DB. Exiting.\r\n");
}

$query = 'SELECT user_name FROM user';        ◄── ④

$result = mysql_query($query, $handle);        ◄── ⑤

if($result == false){
    die("Error with query.\r\n");
}

while($row = mysql_fetch_assoc($result)){       ◄── ⑥
    print_r($row);                              ◄── ⑦
}

mysql_close($handle);

?>
```

⑧ View your script in a Web browser.

The records matching your query are selected and printed to the output stream.

Array ([user_name] => toby)   ◄── ⑧

Extra

You can use the mysql_fetch_object function to retrieve each record in a given record set as a generic object. The mysql_fetch_object function accepts a record set result identifier and operates similarly to mysql_fetch_array and mysql_fetch_assoc. The values in each returned object can be accessed using the object access operator (->).

TYPE THIS:

```php
$query = "SELECT user_id FROM user";
$result = mysql_query($query);
while($user = mysql_fetch_object($result)){
    echo "The user id is $user->user_id.<br />";
}
```

RESULT:

All user_id values in the record set are displayed.

Retrieve Records from Multiple Tables in a MySQL Database

The true power of a relational database such as MySQL comes from the ability to create functional relationships between disparate sets of data. Most commonly shared keys, known as *foreign keys*, represent relationships. For example, you may have a database used in an online portfolio displaying development projects performed for various clients. In a properly normalized database, you may have a table representing clients called *client* and a table representing projects called *project*. If a business rule is in place stating that projects may be associated with only one client, your project table would have a column called `client_id` that maps to the unique identifier for each record in your client table.

You can select the client and project information from these two tables in one joined query using a conditional `WHERE` clause. The value of the `client_id` field in each project

record can be used to determine whether a project should be listed for a given client.

A query to select the contact name and all project information for a client named "Wiley" might be written as:

```
SELECT client.client_contact, project.* FROM
client, project WHERE client.client_id =
project.client_id AND
client.client_name='Wiley';.
```

Simple multitable data selection queries such as the previous example are known as `EQUI-JOIN` queries. These joins are useful when a one-to-one or one-to-many relationship exists between the sets of data targeted by your query.

More complex data joins such as `LEFT JOIN` and `RIGHT JOIN` can be studied at the MySQL documentation site hosted at http://dev.mysql.com/doc/.

Retrieve Records from Multiple Tables in a MySQL Database

① Create a variable to store the database resource handle returned by `mysql_connect`.

② Connect using `mysql_connect`.

③ Select a database using `mysql_select_db`.

```php
<?php

$handle = mysql_connect('localhost', 'tobyjoe', 'php');

if($handle == false){
    die("Could not connect to MySQL. Exiting.\r\n");
}

$db = mysql_select_db('test');

if($db == false){
    die("Could not select MySQL DB. Exiting.\r\n");
}
?>
```

④ Create an SQL query using a `SELECT` statement that targets multiple tables with associated foreign key values.

● Use the `WHERE` clause to conditionally select records from the tables.

```php
<?php

$handle = mysql_connect('localhost', 'tobyjoe', 'php');

if($handle == false){
    die("Could not connect to MySQL. Exiting.\r\n");
}

$db = mysql_select_db('test');

if($db == false){
    die("Could not select MySQL DB. Exiting.\r\n");
}

$query = 'SELECT user.user_name, employer.employer_name FROM user,
        employer WHERE user.employer_id = employer.employer_id';

?>
```

⑤ Execute the query using `mysql_query`.

⑥ Iterate over each record and print each using the `print_r` function.

```php
<?php

$handle = mysql_connect('localhost', 'tobyjoe', 'php');

if($handle == false){
    die("Could not connect to MySQL. Exiting.\r\n");
}

$db = mysql_select_db('test');

if($db == false){
    die("Could not select MySQL DB. Exiting.\r\n");
}

$query = 'SELECT user.user_name, employer.employer_name FROM user,
            employer WHERE user.employer_id = employer.employer_id';

$result = mysql_query($query, $handle);

if($result == false){
    die("Error with query.\r\n");
}

while($row = mysql_fetch_assoc($result)){
    print_r($row);
}

mysql_close($handle);

?>
```

⑦ View your script in a Web browser.

The records matching your query are selected and printed to the output stream.

Array ([user_name] => toby [employer_name] => Horn Group)

Extra

While many normalized systems are designed in a way that uses common naming to make foreign key relationships clearly visible, data tables are often brought into a database from other sources and the relationship is not clearly visible. A foreign key column is not required to share the same name as the column in another table or table that it references.

You can join more than two tables with an `EQUI-JOIN` query as easily as you can with two. By listing each table and the values you want to retrieve in the `SELECT` statement and being careful to filter values in the `WHERE` clause, you can join any number of tables.

Example:
```
$query = "SELECT topic.topic_title, thread.thread_title,
thread.owner_id, user.user_name FROM topic, thread, user
WHERE topic.topic_id=1001 AND thread.topic_id=topic.topic_id
AND user.user_id=thread.owner_id";
```

Get Information About Fields in a MySQL Table

The `mysql_list_fields` function can be used to select a listing of the fields in a MySQL database table. You may need to know the column names and data types for administrative purposes or when building a database management tool. The `mysql_list_fields` function accepts three arguments. The first represents the name of the database in which the target table is defined. The second argument is a string representing the name of the table about which you want to glean information. The third argument is a database handle resource identifier returned by a call to a connection function such as `mysql_connect` or `mysql_pconnect`. If the function is successful, it returns a resource identifier representing a standard MySQL record.

You can find the number of fields in a given table using the `mysql_num_fields` function. The `mysql_num_fields` function accepts the resource identifier returned by the `mysql_list_fields` function. You can use the integer

returned by the `mysql_num_fields` function in iterative loops in which you select each field in a given table.

As soon as you have a valid resource identifier returned by the `mysql_list_fields` function you can use functions such as `mysql_field_name` and `mysql_field_type` to determine more detailed information about a given field. The `mysql_field_len` function is used to retrieve the maximum length of data a given field can contain.

You can use the `mysql_field_flags` function to retrieve additional information about a field.

Each of these functions accepts two arguments. The first argument is the resource identifier returned by the call to `mysql_list_fields`. The second is the numerical offset position of the field you want to analyze within the fields table. The offset position begins at zero (0), as with standard PHP arrays. It is important to use the `mysql_num_fields` function to ensure that no attempts are made to access fields at an offset position outside of the actual available range.

Get Information About Fields in a MySQL Table

① Create a variable to store the database resource handle returned by `mysql_connect`.

② Connect using `mysql_connect`.

③ Select a database using `mysql_select_db`.

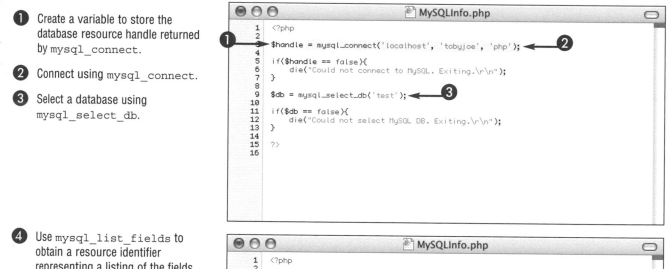

```php
<?php

$handle = mysql_connect('localhost', 'tobyjoe', 'php');

if($handle == false){
    die("Could not connect to MySQL. Exiting.\r\n");
}

$db = mysql_select_db('test');

if($db == false){
    die("Could not select MySQL DB. Exiting.\r\n");
}

?>
```

④ Use `mysql_list_fields` to obtain a resource identifier representing a listing of the fields in a table.

```php
<?php

$handle = mysql_connect('localhost', 'tobyjoe', 'php');

if($handle == false){
    die("Could not connect to MySQL. Exiting.\r\n");
}

$db = mysql_select_db('test');

if($db == false){
    die("Could not select MySQL DB. Exiting.\r\n");
}

$result = mysql_list_fields('test', 'user', $handle);

?>
```

5 Use the resource identifier in functions such as `mysql_field_name` and `mysql_field_type` to obtain details about a field.

```
MySQLInfo.php
1   <?php
2
3   $handle = mysql_connect('localhost', 'tobyjoe', 'php');
4
5   if($handle == false){
6       die("Could not connect to MySQL. Exiting.\r\n");
7   }
8
9   $db = mysql_select_db('test');
10
11  if($db == false){
12      die("Could not select MySQL DB. Exiting.\r\n");
13  }
14
15  $result = mysql_list_fields('test', 'user', $handle);
16
17  if($result == false){
18      die("Error with fields listing.\r\n");
19  }
20
21  echo 'Name: ' . mysql_field_name($result, 0) . "<br />\r\n";   ← 5
22  echo 'Type: ' . mysql_field_type($result, 0) . "\r\n";
23
24  mysql_close($handle);
25
26  ?>
27
```

6 View your script in a Web browser.

Specific information about the fields in your target table is returned.

```
@ http://127.0.0.1:9003/...sk14/code/MySQLInfo.php
Back  Forward  Stop  Refresh  Home  AutoFill  Print  Mail
Address: @ http://127.0.0.1:9003/ch10/task14/code/MySQLInfo.php        ) go

Name: user_name    ← 6
Type: string
```

Extra

You can obtain a listing of databases on your server using the `mysql_list_dbs` function. The `mysql_list_dbs` function accepts a database connection handle as an argument and returns a standard MySQL record set with each record representing a database on the system.

Example:
```
$result = mysql_list_dbs($connection);
$pos = 0;
$num = mysql_num_rows($result);
while($pos<$num){
  echo mysql_db_name($result, $pos);
  $pos++;
}
```

The `mysql_list_tables` function can be used to display a listing of all tables in a given database.

Example:
```
$result = mysql_list_tables('my_database');
$pos = 0;
$num = mysql_num_rows($result);
while($pos<$num){
  echo mysql_tablename($result, $pos);
  $pos++;
}
```

Using a Form to Modify a Record

You can create a simple HTML form to be used in executing database queries. Forms provide familiar and simple interfaces to server processing duties of any type. By pairing a form with the built-in PHP MySQL functions, you can perform full administration of your database through your browser.

The first step in creating a form to be used for MySQL administration is to secure the location from which the form is served. Exposing a form with the ability to alter data in a database can be quite dangerous. There are several methods you can use to secure the form, such as HTTP authentication through the Apache Web server.

A form can be created using the HTML `<form>` element. Each `<form>` element must have an associated action attribute. The action attribute should contain the path to a script on your Web server that performs the processing of the data submitted through the form. In this case, the data is an SQL query string.

The space into which you type your SQL query can be created using a `<textarea>` element. A `<textarea>` can accept a string of any length and submit it to the server script specified in the action attribute of the `<form>` element.

For a `<textarea>` element with a name attribute of `query` your PHP script should perform, at the most essential level, the function of calling `mysql_query` with the `$_REQUEST['query']` property.

Because of an exploit known as "SQL Injection" you should take great care in validating any form input to be used in sensitive functionality such as executing queries. The simplest way to ensure that no malicious data is used in a query is to use the `mysql_escape_string` function combined with `str_replace` to remove any semicolon characters, which can be used to attack a database.

When a query is deemed safe, you can use it in a query and report the results to the output stream to reflect the changes committed by the action.

Using a Form to Modify a Record

① Create an HTML form with the action attribute set to the current script name.

② Create a `<textarea>` element in your form, along with a submit button.

③ Open a block of PHP code for processing the submitted data.

④ Preprocess the variable representing the query submitted to the script.

⑤ Use `mysql_query` to execute the query.

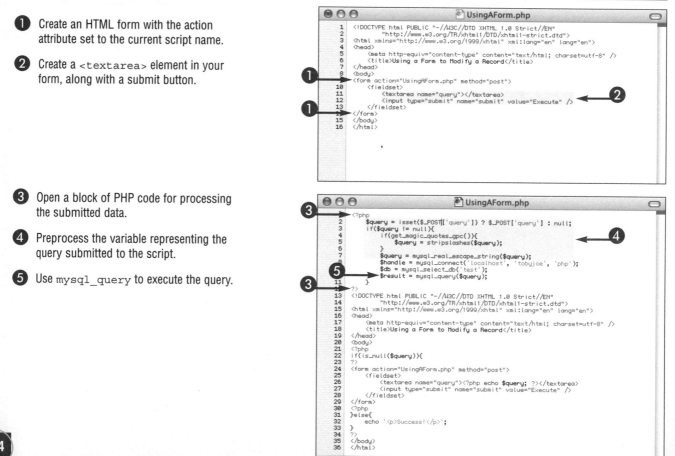

6 View your script in a Web browser and type an SQL query into the text area.

```
DELETE * FROM user;          [Execute]  ← 6
```

7 Submit the form to the Web server.

When the data is submitted to the PHP script, the query is executed.

Success! ← 7

Extra

Prevention of SQL Injection exploits should always be a high priority for developers creating applications that interact with databases. There are several ways to cleanse data that has been submitted by users. The two approaches to validating data can be described as the *negative* and *affirmative* approaches. The negative approach is generally weaker than its counterpart. By checking simply that a value is *not* what you *do not* want it to be, you are performing a negative validation. The dangerous part of this is that you may not be aware of all dangerous conditions and may fail to filter for certain data values.

The affirmative method is to ensure that the data submitted is *exactly* what you expect it to be. For example, you may want to check that an id value is numeric using the `is_numeric` function combined with a check to see that it is within an allowable range. This approach is always safer because there is never a space for unexpected data values in the queries you build and execute.

Create a MySQLi Connection

You have a choice of two approaches to creating a MySQLi connection in PHP 5. You can use a procedural approach such as that supported by earlier versions of PHP and the ext/mysql library for MySQL versions prior to MySQL 4.1. The familiarity and procedural nature is provided in order to help developers port existing database management and abstraction libraries to a version that can connect to the newer version of MySQL.

PHP 5 also provides an object wrapper for all of the functionality provided in the MySQLi procedural library. By using an object-oriented approach to database connectivity you can take advantage of the benefits of objects such as subclassing and serialization.

The mysqli_connect function is used to create a connection to a MySQL database and provide a usable database handle resource identifier. The mysqli_connection function accepts six optional arguments representing the name of the server, the name of the user with which the connection should be created, the user's password, the name of the database on which to operate, the port number, and a string representing the socket or named pipe over which the connection should be made. If any of these arguments are omitted, default values are used.

To create a connection using the object-oriented method, you can instantiate a mysqli object with the same set of arguments passed through the constructor. The value returned from the constructor is a mysqli instance with a valid connection handle or appropriate errors.

Create a MySQLi Connection

① Type the name of a variable to store your mysqli instance.

② Type the assignment operator followed by the new keyword and the mysqli constructor.

- Be sure to pass any values you want to provide for the connection.

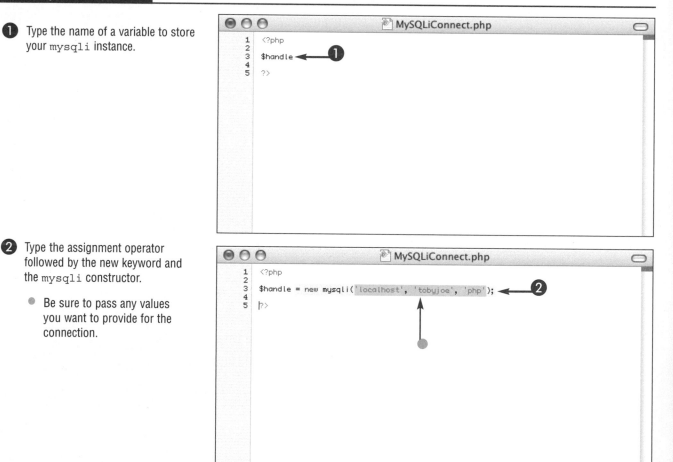

③ Use the `mysqli_connect _errno()` function to retrieve any connection errors that may occur.

④ If there were errors, print a message to the output stream; otherwise, print a success message and close the connection.

```php
<?php

$handle = new mysqli('localhost', 'tobyjoe', 'php');

if($e = mysqli_connect_errno()){
    echo "There was an error: $e.\r\n";
}else{
    echo 'Successful connection.';
}

?>
```

⑤ View the script in a Web browser.

The connection is created and an appropriate status message is printed.

```
http://127.0.0.1:9003/ch10/task17/code/MySQLiConnect.php
```

Successful connection. ◄ ⑤

Extra

To create a MySQLi connection through the procedural method you can use the `mysqli_connect` function. The `mysqli_connect` function returns a resource identifier for a database handle, or a Boolean `false`.

Example:
```php
$handle = mysqli_connect('localhost', 'user', 'pass');
if($handle == false){
  printf("Connection to mysqli failed: %s\n", mysqli_connect_error());
  exit();
}
printf("The host information is: %s\n", mysqli_get_host_info($link));
mysqli_close($link);
```

257

Create a MySQLi Prepared Statement

Y ou can use prepared statements to create safe, efficient, and reusable SQL query statements in your PHP application. Prepared statements are created using the `mysqli_prepare` procedural function or the prepare method of a `mysqli` object instance.

The `mysqli_prepare` function accepts two required arguments. The first is a resource handle representing a MySQL database connection link. The second is a string representing the query you want to use in the prepared statement. The query can contain any number of question mark (?) characters that act as placeholders for values to be assigned dynamically to the query at a later point. The placeholder markers are allowed at only certain places in a query. For example, they are allowed in the VALUES()

listing in an INSERT statement or the comparison portion of a WHERE clause. You cannot use dynamic markers in place of identifying values, such as table or column names.

The `mysqli_stmt_bind_param` function allows you to bind values of given types to dynamic markers in a prepared statement. The `mysql_stmt_bind_param` function accepts a variable number of parameters. The first is a string representing the types of values to be assigned to the markers. Each character in the string represents a data type for each marker.

Each value passed after the first argument represents the actual value to be assigned. The return value for `mysqli_stmt_bind_param` is a Boolean true on success and false on failure.

Create a MySQLi Prepared Statement

① Create a new `mysqli` instance.

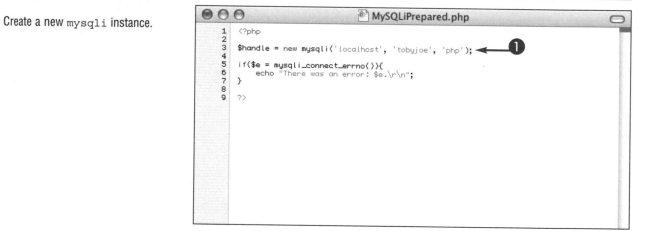

```php
<?php

$handle = new mysqli('localhost', 'tobyjoe', 'php');

if($e = mysqli_connect_errno()){
    echo "There was an error: $e.\r\n";
}

?>
```

② Create a string to represent your query.

● Use question mark (?) characters in place of your dynamic values.

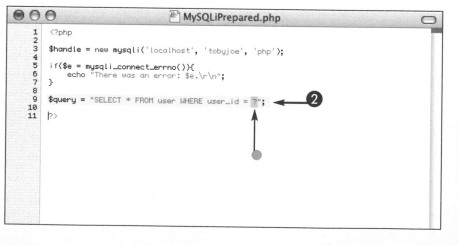

```php
<?php

$handle = new mysqli('localhost', 'tobyjoe', 'php');

if($e = mysqli_connect_errno()){
    echo "There was an error: $e.\r\n";
}

$query = "SELECT * FROM user WHERE user_id = ?";

?>
```

③ Type mysqli_prepare with your query variable in parentheses.

④ Bind parameters to your prepared statement using the mysqli_stmt_bind_param function.

⑤ Test the return value of the mysqli_stmt_bind_param function to ensure a successful statement preparation.

The statement is prepared.

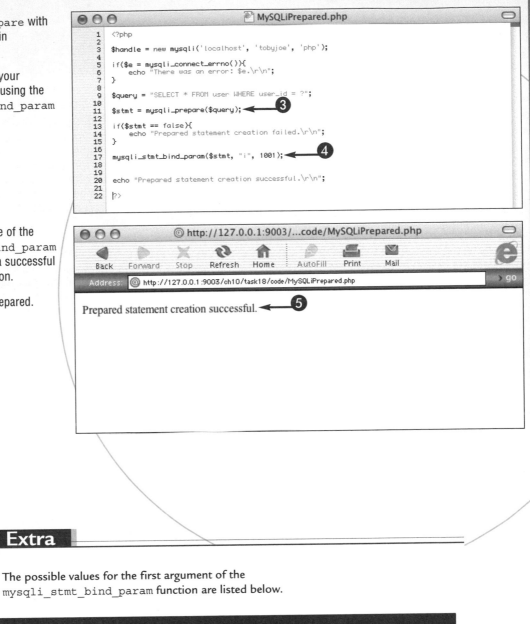

```php
<?php

$handle = new mysqli('localhost', 'tobyjoe', 'php');

if($e = mysqli_connect_errno()){
    echo "There was an error: $e.\r\n";
}

$query = "SELECT * FROM user WHERE user_id = ?";

$stmt = mysqli_prepare($query);

if($stmt == false){
    echo "Prepared statement creation failed.\r\n";
}

mysqli_stmt_bind_param($stmt, "i", 1001);


echo "Prepared statement creation successful.\r\n";

?>
```

Prepared statement creation successful.

Extra

The possible values for the first argument of the mysqli_stmt_bind_param function are listed below.

CONTROL SEQUENCE	DESCRIPTION
i	The corresponding value is an integer.
d	The corresponding value is a double.
s	The corresponding value is a string.
b	The corresponding value is a blob and will be sent in packages.

If the blob is larger than the allowable package size, you have to specify *b* for the type and use the mysqli_stmt_send_long_data function to send the data in packages.

Change PHP's Error-Reporting Level

Errors that occur during the execution of a PHP script are most often reported by writing them to the output stream. This usually means that the error messaging is displayed in the Web browser used to access the offending script. The information displayed in some error messages can reveal sensitive information, such as the structure of your Web site or information about the database. You can change the way PHP reports errors by modifying the error reporting level in the settings for your script.

Errors are grouped into types in PHP. There are simple and common errors such as improper syntax, accessing undeclared variables, and mathematical problems such as divide-by-zero errors. An additional level of severity includes calling functions with the wrong number of arguments. The most serious errors halt execution of your script. These are

called *fatal errors* and occur when required files cannot be found or when PHP encounters an internal error.

You can use the `error_reporting` function to specify which errors PHP should report. The error-reporting level is specified using predefined system constants. Generally, the level of error reporting on your development server differs from the level on your production server. The constants you can use to set error-reporting levels are `E_NOTICE`, `E_WARNING`, `E_ERROR`, `E_ALL`, and `E_STRICT`.

You can pass one or more of these constants to the `error_reporting` function to set the mode under which your script is parsed. To set multiple error-reporting levels, you can compound the values represented by the constants using the bitwise OR operator (|). For example, you can set all running errors and notices to be displayed using `error_reporting(E_ERROR|E_WARNING|E_PARSE|E_NOTICE);`.

Change PHP's Error-Reporting Level

① Type code that will generate an error.

② Change the error-reporting level by typing `error_reporting();`.

③ Inside the parentheses, set the level using system constants.

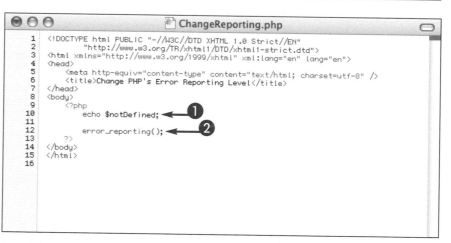

④ Compound multiple error reporting levels using the bitwise OR operator (|) between different constants.

```
1   <!DOCTYPE html PUBLIC "-//W3C//DTD XHTML 1.0 Strict//EN"
2       "http://www.w3.org/TR/xhtml1/DTD/xhtml1-strict.dtd">
3   <html xmlns="http://www.w3.org/1999/xhtml" xml:lang="en" lang="en">
4   <head>
5       <meta http-equiv="content-type" content="text/html; charset=utf-8" />
6       <title>Change PHP's Error Reporting Level</title>
7   </head>
8   <body>
9       <?php
10          echo $notDefined;
11
12          error_reporting(E_ERROR | E_WARNING | E_PARSE | E_NOTICE);
13      ?>
14  </body>
15  </html>
16
```

⑤ View the script in a Web browser.

The errors that appear reflect the levels set by the `error_reporting` function.

Notice: Undefined variable: notDefined in **/Users/tobyboudreaux/Jobs/PHP5/Draft/Chapters/ch11/task1/code/ChangeReporting.php** on line **10**

Extra

There are several error-reporting-level constants you can use to set a custom error-reporting level in your script.

MODE	DESCRIPTION
E_ERROR	Fatal run-time errors
E_WARNING	Nonfatal run-time warnings
E_PARSE	Compile-time parse errors such as bad syntax
E_NOTICE	Run-time notices, possible errors
E_CORE_ERROR	Fatal core PHP errors
E_CORE_WARNING	Nonfatal core PHP warnings
E_COMPILE_ERROR	Fatal compile-time errors reported by the Zend engine
E_COMPILE_WARNING	Nonfatal warnings reported by the Zend engine
E_USER_ERROR	User-generated error thrown by the trigger_error() function
E_USER_WARNING	User-generated warning message thrown by the trigger_error() function
E_USER_NOTICE	User-generated notice message thrown by the trigger_error() function
E_ALL	All errors and warnings, as supported, except of level E_STRICT
E_STRICT	Run-time notices. PHP will suggest possible changes to reduce notices thrown

Create a Custom Error Handler

There are many reasons that errors occur in PHP scripts. Most commonly the causes are syntax errors, attempts to access undefined variables or properties, or mathematical problems such as attempts to divide by zero. When an error occurs, you can have PHP use a custom error-handling function you create instead of the internal mechanisms enabled by default.

Using a custom error-handling function allows you to control and leverage the error-reporting functionality provided by PHP. You can define a custom function that is called whenever an error is encountered. The operations the function performs can be defined using the full power of PHP. You can choose to do something as simple as displaying a single message for all errors to performing complex database logging and e-mail messaging whenever an error occurs. Though the possibilities are endless,

generally you define a function to accomplish two tasks: perform or prevent message display and somehow notify the site administrator of the errors. There are a variety of approaches to accomplish these two core goals.

To set a custom error-handler function you can use the `set_error_handler` function. The `set_error_handler` has a single required argument representing the name of the function to be used in handling errors. Optionally, you can pass a list of the errors to which the function's use should be limited. By default, all errors are handled using your function.

Your custom function should accept four arguments: the PHP error number, the PHP error description, the name of the file in which the error occurred, and the line number of the offending line.

Create a Custom Error Handler

① Create a custom function to handle errors.

Be sure to define four arguments to accept the error information PHP passes to your function.

```
1  <!DOCTYPE html PUBLIC "-//W3C//DTD XHTML 1.0 Strict//EN"
2      "http://www.w3.org/TR/xhtml1/DTD/xhtml1-strict.dtd">
3  <html xmlns="http://www.w3.org/1999/xhtml" xml:lang="en" lang="en">
4  <head>
5      <meta http-equiv="content-type" content="text/html; charset=utf-8" />
6      <title>Create a Custom Error Handler</title>
7  </head>
8  <body>
9      <?php
10         function handleErrors($e_code, $e_desc, $e_file, $e_line){
11             echo "<ul>
12             <li>Error code: $e_code</li>
13             <li>Error description: $e_desc</li>
14             <li>Error file: $e_file</li>
15             <li>Error line: $e_line</li>
16             </ul>";
17         }
18
19
20
21
22     ?>
23  </body>
24  </html>
25
```

② Type `set_error_handler`.

③ In parentheses, type the name of your function as a string.

```
1  <!DOCTYPE html PUBLIC "-//W3C//DTD XHTML 1.0 Strict//EN"
2      "http://www.w3.org/TR/xhtml1/DTD/xhtml1-strict.dtd">
3  <html xmlns="http://www.w3.org/1999/xhtml" xml:lang="en" lang="en">
4  <head>
5      <meta http-equiv="content-type" content="text/html; charset=utf-8" />
6      <title>Create a Custom Error Handler</title>
7  </head>
8  <body>
9      <?php
10         function handleErrors($e_code, $e_desc, $e_file, $e_line){
11             echo "<ul>
12             <li>Error code: $e_code</li>
13             <li>Error description: $e_desc</li>
14             <li>Error file: $e_file</li>
15             <li>Error line: $e_line</li>
16             </ul>";
17         }
18
19         set_error_handler('handleErrors');
20
21
22     ?>
23  </body>
24  </html>
25
```

4 Type code that generates an error.

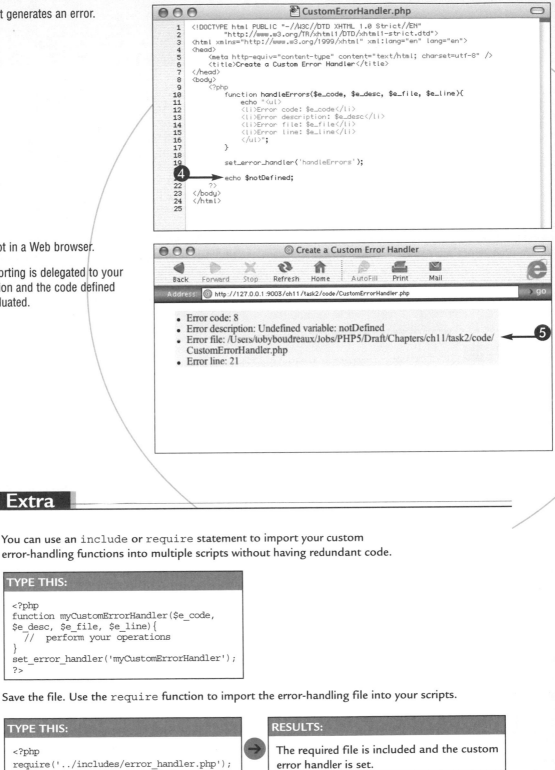

```
CustomErrorHandler.php
1   <!DOCTYPE html PUBLIC "-//W3C//DTD XHTML 1.0 Strict//EN"
2       "http://www.w3.org/TR/xhtml1/DTD/xhtml1-strict.dtd">
3   <html xmlns="http://www.w3.org/1999/xhtml" xml:lang="en" lang="en">
4   <head>
5       <meta http-equiv="content-type" content="text/html; charset=utf-8" />
6       <title>Create a Custom Error Handler</title>
7   </head>
8   <body>
9       <?php
10          function handleErrors($e_code, $e_desc, $e_file, $e_line){
11              echo "<ul>
12              <li>Error code: $e_code</li>
13              <li>Error description: $e_desc</li>
14              <li>Error file: $e_file</li>
15              <li>Error line: $e_line</li>
16              </ul>";
17          }
18
19          set_error_handler('handleErrors');
20
21          echo $notDefined;
22      ?>
23  </body>
24  </html>
25
```

5 View the script in a Web browser.

The error reporting is delegated to your custom function and the code defined therein is evaluated.

```
Create a Custom Error Handler
Back   Forward   Stop   Refresh   Home   AutoFill   Print   Mail
Address: http://127.0.0.1:9003/ch11/task2/code/CustomErrorHandler.php   go
```

- Error code: 8
- Error description: Undefined variable: notDefined
- Error file: /Users/tobyboudreaux/Jobs/PHP5/Draft/Chapters/ch11/task2/code/CustomErrorHandler.php
- Error line: 21

Extra

You can use an `include` or `require` statement to import your custom error-handling functions into multiple scripts without having redundant code.

TYPE THIS:

```php
<?php
function myCustomErrorHandler($e_code,
$e_desc, $e_file, $e_line){
    //  perform your operations
}
set_error_handler('myCustomErrorHandler');
?>
```

Save the file. Use the `require` function to import the error-handling file into your scripts.

TYPE THIS:

```php
<?php
require('../includes/error_handler.php');
    // continue with your code here
?>
```

RESULTS:

The required file is included and the custom error handler is set.

Log Errors to a File

When PHP encounters a problematic statement or operation in a script, error messages are produced and handled with either stock or custom error-handling functionality. In addition to the custom functionality you can perform by setting custom error-handling functions, you can have PHP log all errors to a file on your server.

Saving error information in a file is important because it provides a PHP-independent method of learning about errors. If, for example, a rare bug presents itself and errors are reported to your browser, you may lose the information by accidentally closing the window. By logging to a file on your server you can be sure that the data is recorded for later analysis. Additionally, by logging errors to a file you can have all user errors recorded in one location. This allows you to analyze errors that may be due to temporal issues such as traffic or periodically unavailable resources.

You can edit your `php.ini` configuration file to have PHP enable error logging and to set the location of the file to which errors should be reported. The `log_errors` directive, when set to a value of `"On"` causes the PHP engine to turn on error-logging mechanisms. The location of the target file is set using the `error_log` directive in the configuration file. If the target file does not exist, PHP attempts to create the file when the first error occurs. To learn more about the PHP configuration file, see the task "Configure PHP" in Chapter 1.

To log an error to the log file, you can use the `error_log` function. The `error_log` function accepts two arguments. The first is the message you wish to be written to the file. The second is an integer representing how the error message is stored. To have your message logged to the file specified in the `error_log` directive in the `php.ini` file, you must pass a value of zero (0) to this function.

Log Errors to a File

① In your `php.ini` file, assign the `log_errors` directive a value of `"On"`.

② Use the `error_log` directive to specify the path to a file you want to use in logging the file.

Be sure the location you select is writable by PHP.

③ In your script, find the point at which you want to log an error. Type `error_log`.

④ In parentheses, type the string value you want to store followed by a comma and a zero (0).

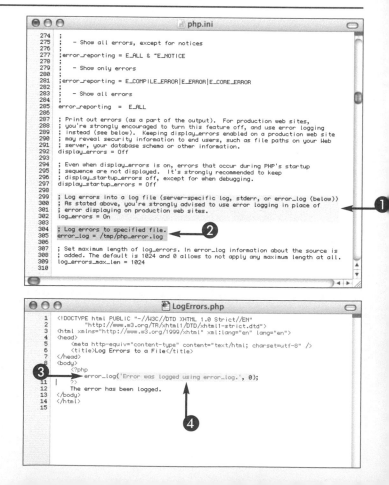

5 View the script in a Web browser.

The error generated by your script is written to the log file.

○○○　　　　　　　　　　@ Log Errors to a File　　　　　　　　　○

| Back | Forward | Stop | Refresh | Home | AutoFill | Print | Mail |

Address: @ http://127.0.0.1:9003/ch11/task3/code/LogErrors.php　　　› go

The error has been logged. ◄─── 5

6 Open the log file specified by the `error_log` directive in your `php.ini` file.

The message you passed to the `error_log` function, as well as the date and time, are written to the file.

○○○　　　　　　　　　　php_error.log　　　　　　　　　　○

1　　[11-Dec-2004 12:00:00] Error was logged using error_log. ◄─── 6

Extra

The `error_log` function accepts a second argument specifying the type of logging mechanism to be used to log the message passed as the first argument. The possible values are listed below.

CODE	DESCRIPTION
0	The message is sent to PHP's system logger, using the operating system's system-logging mechanism or a file, depending on what the `error_log` configuration directive is set to. This is the default option.
1	The message is sent by e-mail to the address in the destination parameter. This is the only message type where the fourth parameter representing headers is used. This message type uses the same internal function as the mail function.
2	The message is sent through the PHP debugging connection. This option is only available if remote debugging has been enabled. In this case, the destination parameter specifies the host name or IP address and optionally, port number, of the socket receiving the debug information.
3	The message is appended to the file destination.

Send Errors to an E-Mail Address

Y ou can use PHP to send reports of errors that occur in your scripts to an e-mail address. This can be very helpful if you want to be notified immediately of errors. While periodically scanning server logs is often sufficient to detect bugs and other errors in your scripts, prompt action is often necessary when problems are encountered in mission-critical applications. You can leverage the error_log function to send an e-mail to a specified address.

The error_log function passes a message to the internal PHP error-reporting mechanisms. There are two arguments for the error_log function. The first is a string representing the message you want to report. The second is an integer representing the type of error reporting that should take place. You can specify options for logging

messages to a text file, for example. To learn more about the options available for the error_log function, please refer to the previous task, "Log Errors to a File." The second argument must use the value one (1) to tell PHP to send the error report via e-mail.

While it is not required, you can specify the use of custom e-mail message headers when PHP reports an error. E-mail message headers contain information such as the reply-to address, the subject line, the sender address and name, and date the message was sent. For example, you could use the From: header to specify an identity from which your message was sent. Doing so enables your recipients to easily filter the messages sent from the PHP server. You can also use the subject line to mention light information about the error being reported. A brief summary is useful for deciding which errors are important.

Send Errors to an E-Mail Address

① Type error_log.

② In parentheses, type the message you want to e-mail.

③ To specify that the error should be reported using e-mail, type a comma (,) followed by a one (1).

④ Type a comma followed by the e-mail address to which you want to send the message.

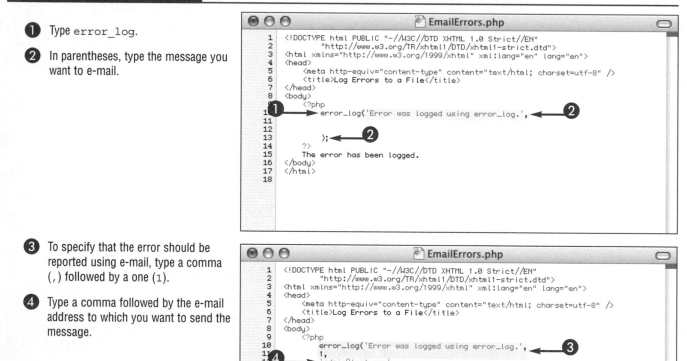

⑤ Specify custom header information by typing a comma followed by a string containing header information.

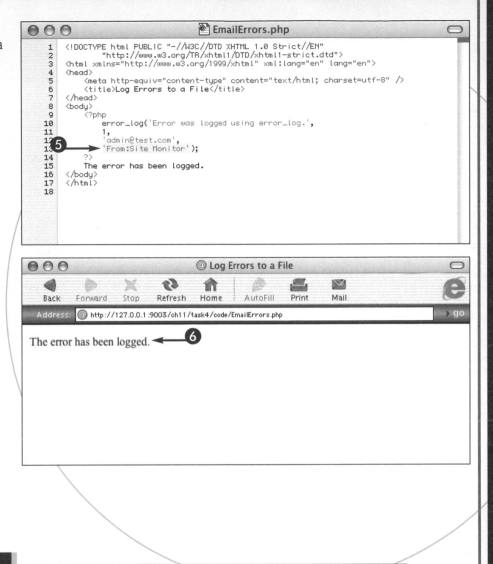

```
                                    EmailErrors.php
1    <!DOCTYPE html PUBLIC "-//W3C//DTD XHTML 1.0 Strict//EN"
2         "http://www.w3.org/TR/xhtml1/DTD/xhtml1-strict.dtd">
3    <html xmlns="http://www.w3.org/1999/xhtml" xml:lang="en" lang="en">
4    <head>
5        <meta http-equiv="content-type" content="text/html; charset=utf-8" />
6        <title>Log Errors to a File</title>
7    </head>
8    <body>
9        <?php
10           error_log('Error was logged using error_log.',
11           1,
12           'admin@test.com',
13           'From:Site Monitor');
14       ?>
15       The error has been logged.
16   </body>
17   </html>
18
```

⑥ View the script in a Web browser.

The error message is reported via e-mail.

```
                                    Log Errors to a File
Back  Forward  Stop  Refresh  Home  AutoFill  Print  Mail
Address:  http://127.0.0.1:9003/ch11/task4/code/EmailErrors.php            go

The error has been logged.  ← 6
```

Extra

To use the `error_log` function to successfully send an error report by e-mail your server must be configured properly. First and foremost, your PHP installation must be configured to work with a mail server such as sendmail. The same configuration options necessary for the PHP `mail` function are used by the `error_log` function. To inspect the settings, locate and open your `php.ini` file in a text editor. The configuration option upon which successful e-mail functionality depends is under the `[mail function]` section heading. Check that the `sendmail_path` directive is set to the correct path to your sendmail installation.

On a Windows system, you must use the `SMTP` directive instead of the `sendmail_path` directive. The `SMTP` directive should be the name of a valid SMTP server that accepts mail relays from your Web server.

Embed Debugging Messages in HTML Comments

For the purposes of quick and easy debugging you can leverage HTML comments to enclose meaningful output from your PHP scripts. While you should never use this approach to display sensitive information, you can safely output benchmarking or access time information, among many other types of data, and it is only visible to those who view the source of the document generated by your script.

To embed debugging messages in HTML comments you simply need to place opening and closing comment delimiters around PHP statements that print information to the output stream. For example, you can mark the time at which your script begins to be processed using the `microtime` function. To do so, you can open the HTML comment block by typing `<!--`. The `microtime` function returns a timestamp representing the current time of the

server on which your script is being processed. You can print the value returned by the `microtime` function by typing `<?php=microtime()?>`.

You can close the HTML comment block by typing `-->`.

By performing the same steps at the end of your file you can determine how long the processing of your script takes.

Any information may be displayed in HTML comments, but be careful not to print a closing comment delimiter by mistake. Doing so closes the comment statement early and presents unwanted data to the end user.

To view the values printed in HTML comments, you can choose to view the source of your document from within your Web browser.

Though quite helpful at times, it is best practice not to heavily use this method of debugging on your production server.

Embed Debugging Messages in HTML Comments

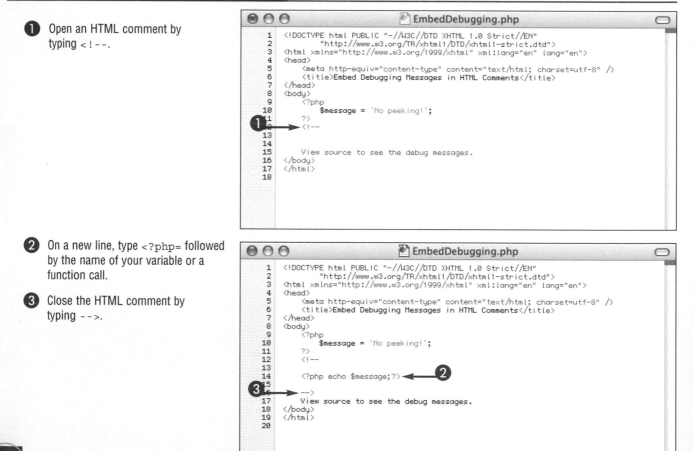

1 Open an HTML comment by typing `<!--`.

2 On a new line, type `<?php=` followed by the name of your variable or a function call.

3 Close the HTML comment by typing `-->`.

4 View your script in a Web browser.

The debugging message is not displayed.

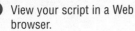

```
000        @ Embed Debugging Messages in HTML Comments          ⬤
 ◀         ▶       ✕       ↻       🏠       ✎       🖨       ✉          e
Back    Forward   Stop   Refresh   Home   AutoFill   Print   Mail
Address: @ http://127.0.0.1:9003/ch11/task5/code/EmbedDebugging.php      › go

View source to see the debug messages. ◀————— 4
```

5 View the source of the document being displayed in your Web browser.

The debugging statements are embedded between HTML comments and visible in the source of the page.

```
000          HTML: Embed Debugging Messages in HTML Comments
<!DOCTYPE html PUBLIC "-//W3C//DTD XHTML 1.0 Strict//EN"
         "http://www.w3.org/TR/xhtml1/DTD/xhtml1-strict.dtd">
<html xmlns="http://www.w3.org/1999/xhtml" xml:lang="en" lang="en">
<head>
 <meta http-equiv="content-type" content="text/html; charset=utf-8" />
 <title>Embed Debugging Messages in HTML Comments</title>
</head>
<body>
  <!--

No peeking!         ◀————— 5
 -->
 View source to see the debug messages.
</body>
</html>
```

Apply It

You can view the source code of a PHP script in the same browser window as the output of a script. The `show_source` function displays a syntax-highlighted version of the source of a PHP script. To use `show_source`, you can pass a string representing the script whose source you want to show. You can have a script display its own source by passing its name. As always, take great care to prevent sensitive information from being displayed. Generally, this function should never be used on a production server.

TYPE THIS:

```
<html xmlns="http://www.w3.org/1999/xhtml"
xml:lang="en" lang="en">
<head>
  <title>Change the Case of a String</title>
</head>
<body>
<h1>Source:</h1>
<?php show_source('test.php'); ?>
</body>
</html>
```

→

RESULTS:

```
Source:
<html xmlns="http://www.w3.org/1999/xhtml"
xml:lang="en" lang="en">
<head>
   <title>Change the Case of a String</title>
</head>
<body>
<h1>Source:</h1>
<?php show_source('test.php'); ?>
</body>
</html>
```

Using Try...Catch Statements

Much like the custom error-handler functionality provided through the `set_error_handler` function, you can use `try...catch` statements to generate and respond to custom errors generated by your application. Custom errors are referred to in many programming languages — including PHP — as *exceptions*.

When an object method or function encounters a circumstance you consider problematic, you can use the `throw` statement to generate an exception to be handled by the calling statement. To throw an exception, you use the `throw` statement along with a new `Exception` object or `Exception` subclass object.

When an exception is thrown by a function or object method, the code block that called the function should handle, or *catch* the exception. When an exception is caught, processing resumes. The `catch` block of an exception-handling statement is a great place to leverage debugging functionality. For example, you can log error statements to a file or send an e-mail to the site manager.

To use exception handling, type `try{` followed by a line break and the code that may throw an exception. After the code block terminates, type `}catch(){}`. In the parentheses, type the name of the `Exception` or `Exception` subclass you want to catch and the name of a variable to represent the exception. For example, to catch an `Exception` subclass `TestException`, your catch block can be written as `catch(TestException $e)`.

You can use multiple catch statements in your exception-handling blocks. By specifying a different `Exception` subclass in each catch block, the handler can find the appropriate block of code to execute. Though you can catch all exceptions with one catch statement by specifying the `Exception` class from which all custom exceptions are derived, it is generally best to look for an exception of a specific type. When catching multiple types, any use of the `Exception` super class should be the last catch block to prevent unreachable code.

Using Try...Catch Statements

① Open an exception-handling block by typing `try{`.

② On a new line, type code that throws a new `Exception` or `Exception` subclass.

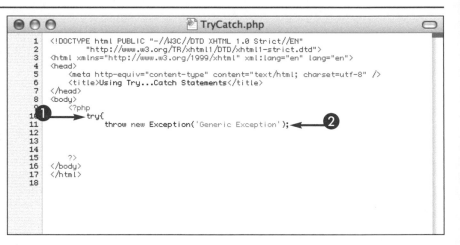

③ Create a `catch` statement by typing `catch` with the type of your exception and a variable name between parentheses.

④ Type code to catch your exception and perform any necessary processing.

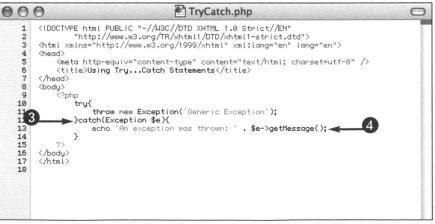

⑤ Repeat Steps 3 and 4 for any custom Exception subclasses you want to catch.

⑥ Close the exception-handling block by typing }.

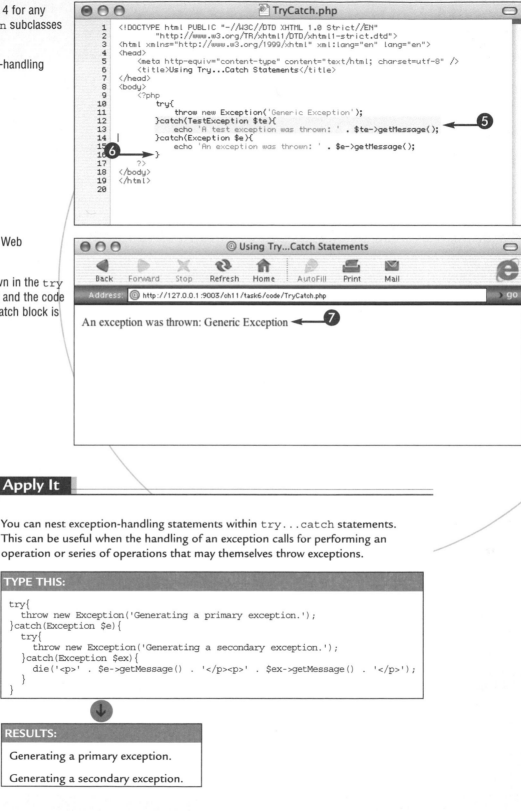

```
1    <!DOCTYPE html PUBLIC "-//W3C//DTD XHTML 1.0 Strict//EN"
2        "http://www.w3.org/TR/xhtml1/DTD/xhtml1-strict.dtd">
3    <html xmlns="http://www.w3.org/1999/xhtml" xml:lang="en" lang="en">
4    <head>
5        <meta http-equiv="content-type" content="text/html; charset=utf-8" />
6        <title>Using Try...Catch Statements</title>
7    </head>
8    <body>
9        <?php
10           try{
11               throw new Exception('Generic Exception');
12           }catch(TestException $te){
13               echo 'A test exception was thrown: ' . $te->getMessage();
14           }catch(Exception $e){
15               echo 'An exception was thrown: ' . $e->getMessage();
16           }
17        ?>
18    </body>
19    </html>
20
```

⑦ View the script in a Web browser.

The exception thrown in the try statement is caught and the code in the appropriate catch block is processed.

Address: http://127.0.0.1:9003/ch11/task6/code/TryCatch.php

An exception was thrown: Generic Exception ◄── ⑦

Apply It

You can nest exception-handling statements within try...catch statements. This can be useful when the handling of an exception calls for performing an operation or series of operations that may themselves throw exceptions.

TYPE THIS:

```
try{
  throw new Exception('Generating a primary exception.');
}catch(Exception $e){
  try{
    throw new Exception('Generating a secondary exception.');
  }catch(Exception $ex){
    die('<p>' . $e->getMessage() . '</p><p>' . $ex->getMessage() . '</p>');
  }
}
```

RESULTS:

Generating a primary exception.

Generating a secondary exception.

Introduction to XML

ou can use eXtensible Markup Language (XML) to describe, or *mark up*, data. XML allows for a human-readable, portable data format.

Tags

XML uses *tags* like those in HTML to describe data. The newest markup language for Web pages is XHTML, which is like HTML but based on XML. Each tag is enclosed in angle brackets (`<>`). When a pair of tags is used, the portion of the document from the opening tag to the closing tag is known as an *element*.

XML Rules

Nesting Elements

All opened tags must be closed. If an empty tag is defined, it must either be followed immediately by a matching closing tag or be written as a self-closing tag using a forward slash before the closing bracket, such as the line break `<br />` in XHTML. All elements must be correctly nested. Because you can place elements inside other elements, each nesting must be closed before its parent nesting. The first structure is invalid; the second, valid:

```
<children>
    <child>
        <name>toby</name>
  </children>
    </child>

<children>
    <child>
        <name>toby</name>
    </child>
</children>
```

Attributes

The opening tag of each XML element can contain any number of attributes, as in HTML. Each attribute must be a matched key-value pair, the value enclosed in quotation marks. Unmatched attributes — that is, those without an equals sign (=) and quoted value — are illegal in XML.

Encoding

Characters must be encoded according to a character-encoding scheme. This means that you have to choose the scheme by which single characters will be encoded as bytes. Different countries, languages, and locales often use different character sets, so know the anticipated uses of your XML.

Naming Elements

The name of an XML tag can be anything, as long as there are no spaces or special characters such as punctuation marks. Because developers define XML tags they are best given meaningful names. For example, the title of your document might be marked with matching `<title>` and `</title>` tags.

Document Type Definition (DTD)

The extensibility of an XML document is functionally limited by a supplementary file known as a Document Type Definition (DTD). A DTD specifies the allowable elements in any XML document with which it is associated.

XML in PHP 5

PHP 5 provides full XML processing abilities, including a full rewrite of many of the XML-related technologies from PHP 4. Dependable XML support in PHP 5 helps PHP to better fit into larger systems due to the portable nature of XML as both data and object access via technologies such as SOAP.

Document Object Model (DOM)

When an XML document is parsed using certain technologies, it can be accessed by way of a Document Object Model (DOM). A DOM document provides a traversable, object-oriented structural representation of your document, providing means of accessing individual elements, values, and attributes represented by an XML document.

Introduction to DOM XML

The Document Object Model (DOM) is an object-oriented representation of an XML document. DOM is a World Wide Web Consortium (W3C) standard that allows the traversal and modification of XML documents. The structure of a DOM document is a tree composed of nodes. The document itself acts as the top-level node with all other XML elements registered as child nodes. Any node in a DOM document can contain child nodes. Nodes contain attributes, text, and other nodes. Attributes for a given node are accessible by key.

NODE TYPE	EXAMPLE
Document Type	`<!DOCTYPE library SYSTEM "library.dtd">`
Processing Instruction	`<?xml version="1.0" encoding="utf-8" ?>`
Element	`<book id="1001"><author>Chandler McWilliams</author></book>`
Attribute	`id="1001"`
Text	Chandler McWilliams

The PHP DOMDocument object provides methods for looking up nodes by name or through XPath. XPath is an expression language used to specify the path or to execute a dynamic expression to find elements in a DOM tree. For example, you can find all nodes with a given attribute name, or all title attributes of all book nodes in an XML file representing a library. You can think of XPath as an SQL-like language for querying XML data.

The DOM XML package in PHP 5 consists of several classes, many of which are described below.

DOMDocument

You can use the DOMDocument class to load and parse an XML file or a string of XML data into a DOM tree. The DOMDocument provides the interface for moving through the object representation of the loaded data.

DOMNode

The DOMNode class is the base class from which most DOM classes are derived. By subclassing from DOMNode, classes such as DOMDocument, DOMElement, and DOMProcessingInstruction inherit common structural functionality such as the ability to contain other nodes, to compare nodes, and to replace and remove child nodes.

DOMElement

The DOMElement class is a subclass of DOMNode. Child nodes of a DOMElement are themselves DOMElement instances and are accessible with methods such as `getElementsByTagName`. Additionally, the DOMElement class provides an interface for accessing element attributes.

DOMCharacterData

The DOMCharacterData class is used to represent character data within a DOMNode or DOMNode subclass instance. Methods are provided for adding, modifying, and removing character data.

DOMDocumentType

The DOMDocumentType class is a subclass of DOMNode that contains information about the Document Type by which the XML data represented by the current DOMDocument object was defined.

DOMEntity

The DOMEntity class is a subclass of DOMNode and represents a known XML entity, whether parsed or unparsed. Properties of DOMEntity represent the stated encoding, actual encoding, version, system id, public id, and notation name.

DOMXPath

The DOMXPath class is used to instantiate an XPath evaluator for a given DOMDocument object. Methods are provided to register a namespace in which an XPath query is executed along with methods to query and evaluate XPath expressions.

DOMProcessingInstruction

A processing instruction is an XML element that provides instructions to a processor, such as the PHP processor. The DOMProcessingInstruction class is a subclass of DOMNode that provides a wrapper for processing instructions.

DOMText

The DOMText class provides a representation of textual data found in a DOMNode. Methods are provided to determine whether whitespace characters are contained within the text and to split the text into two elements at a given character offset. The `wholeText` property is used to retrieve the textual value of a DOMText instance.

Parse a File Using SimpleXML

The SimpleXML extension that ships with PHP 5 provides a new way of working with XML in PHP. The goal of the extension is to provide a simple means of accessing XML data through a standard, object-oriented interface. The SimpleXML extension provides support for iteration through common PHP loop constructs such as `foreach` and `while` loops.

As the name implies, the SimpleXML extension is simple. The list of methods available for working with the extension is quite small, but the functionality is flexible and powerful. For example, you can perform XPath lookups, delete from and add to the document structure, and open and save files.

To parse a file using SimpleXML, you can use the `simplexml_load_file` function. The `simplexml_load_file` function accepts one required and many optional arguments. The first argument is a string

representing the path to the file you want to open and parse. The file should be a valid XML file. No DTD is required to work with the SimpleXML extension, though best practice is to have a DTD for every document type. The second argument to the `simple_xml_load_file` function is a string representing the name of a custom `SimpleXMLElement` subclass. If this parameter is omitted, the base `SimpleXMLElement` class is used. In addition to these parameters, you can pass any special arguments for the libxml library on which the SimpleXML extension is based.

The `simplexml_load_file` function returns an object of the class `SimpleXMLElement`, or an applicable subclass as specified by the second argument. If there are errors during processing, such as a file access error or a malformed document error, the `simplexml_load_file` function returns false.

Parse a File Using SimpleXML

① Type the name of a variable to represent your `SimpleXMLElement` object.

```
1  <?php
2
3  $xml
4
5  ?>
```

② Type the assignment operator (=) followed by `simplexml_load_file`.

③ Pass the path to a valid XML file as a string in parentheses.

```
1  <?php
2
3  $xml = simplexml_load_file('test.xml');
4  |
5  ?>
```

4 Use the object access operator
(->) to retrieve elements by
name.

Each sibling element is contained
in an array and can be iterated
using a foreach loop.

5 Print the value of each element
to the output stream.

```
000                          ParseSimpleXML.php
 1   <?php
 2
 3   $xml = simplexml_load_file('test.xml');
 4
 5   echo '<ul>';
 6   foreach($xml->book as $book){          ←4
 7       echo '<li>' . $book['title'] . '</li>';   ←5
 8   }
 9   echo '</ul>';
10
11   ?>
```

6 View your script in a Web
browser.

The file is parsed and each
element selected in the loop is
processed.

```
000          @ http://127.0.0.1:9003/...code/ParseSimpleXML.php

  Back   Forward   Stop   Refresh   Home   AutoFill   Print   Mail

 Address: @ http://127.0.0.1:9003/ch12/task2/code/ParseSimpleXML.php        › go

   • The Gay Science
   • Thus Spoke Zarathustra
   • Capital                    ←6
   • Moses and Monotheism
```

Extra

You can use the optional second argument to simplexml_load_file to instantiate
a custom SimpleXMLElement subclass with additional or overloaded functionality.
For example, you can create a subclass that prevents users from accessing the asXML
method of each SimpleXMLElement object for security or other reasons.

Example:
```
class UserXML extends SimpleXMLElement{
  public function asXML(){
    return 'No access as XML allowed.';
  }
}
$x = simplexml_load_file('simplexml.xml', 'UserXML');
echo 'XML is: ' . $x->asXML() . "\r\n";
```

Write to a File Using SimpleXML

Y ou can use the `asXML` method of a `SimpleXMLElement` object to retrieve a string representation of the object. An XML representation is useful for many purposes, such as storing a modified XML object in a database or a session, or passing it to a DOM or other XML library function.

You can open and parse an XML file or string using the `simplexml_load_file` or `simplexml_load_string` functions, respectively. As soon as the XML file is in memory, you can perform operations to modify the structure and value of your data through the `SimpleXMLElement` object representing it.

You can use standard file I/O operations to create a file handle to be used in writing a serialized representation of

your XML object to your hard drive. The `fopen` function accepts the name of a file and an access mode code and returns a handle you can use in other file access operations. The `fwrite` function can be used to save a string of data to the file handle.

To retrieve a serialized representation of your `SimpleXMLElement` instance, you can use the `asXML` method of the object returned by `simplexml_load_file` or `simplexml_load_string`.

When all write operations have been completed, you can close the file handle using the `fclose` function. You can read more about filesystem reading and writing in Chapter 5.

Write to a File Using SimpleXML

1 Type the name of a variable to represent your `SimpleXMLElement` object.

2 Type the assignment operator (=) followed by `simplexml_load_file`.

3 Pass the path to a valid XML file as a string in parentheses.

```php
<?php

$xml = simplexml_load_file('test.xml');

?>
```

4 Create a file handle using the `fopen` function.

5 Create a string representation of the XML object using the `asXML` method of the `SimpleXMLElement` instance.

6 Write the string to the file handle using `fwrite`.

```php
<?php

$xml = simplexml_load_file('test.xml');

$handle = fopen('output.xml', 'w+');

$data = $xml->asXML();

$result = fwrite($handle, $data);

if($result){
    echo 'Success!';
}else{
    echo 'Failure.';
}

?>
```

7 Close the file handle using `fclose`.

```php
<?php

$xml = simplexml_load_file('test.xml');

$handle = fopen('output.xml', 'w+');

$data = $xml->asXML();

$result = fwrite($handle, $data);

if($result){
    echo 'Success!';
}else{
    echo 'Failure.';
}

fclose($handle);  ◄——7

?>
```

WriteSimpleXML.php

8 View your script in a Web browser.

The file is opened and parsed, and then written to a different file.

http://127.0.0.1:9003/...code/WriteSimpleXML.php

Address: http://127.0.0.1:9003/ch12/task3/code/WriteSimpleXML.php

Success! ◄——8

Extra

You can convert SimpleXML documents to DOM objects using the `dom_import_simplexml` function, passing a valid `SimpleXMLElement` or `SimpleXMLElement` subclass. The return value is a `DOMDocument` instance.

Example:
```php
$sxe = simplexml_load_file('mydata.xml');
$dom = dom_import_simplexml($sxe);
```

You can perform the opposite transformation using the `simplexml_import_dom` function, which accepts a `DOMDocument` object or subclass and returns a valid `SimpleXMLElement` object.

Example:
```php
$dom = new DOMDocument();
$dom->load('mydata.xml');
$sxe = simplexml_import_dom($dom);
```

Parse a File Using SAX

S AX stands for Simple API for XML and is a method of parsing XML files using callbacks to support event-level functionality. With SAX parsing you can create special functions to be called on events such as elements opening, character data being found in an element, and elements closing.

You can use the `xml_parser_create` function to create a new SAX processor. The `xml_parser_create` function accepts a single optional parameter representing the character encoding to be used by the parser.

You can specify a function, or callback, to be called for any of three events. The first is the element-opening event, which is triggered whenever an XML element is found. The second is the element-closing event that is called whenever an XML element ending is found. The character data

handler is triggered when CDATA is found in the XML elements.

With each of these callbacks, contextual parameters are passed to the appropriate callbacks.

To register element opening and closing callbacks, you can use the `xml_set_element_handler` function. The `xml_set_element_handler` function accepts three arguments — your SAX parser instance, a string representing the opening handler function name, and a string representing the closing handler function name.

You can register a character data handler using the `xml_set_character_data_handler` function.

Finally, you can use the `xml_parse` function to begin the parsing process for a given parser and string of data.

Parse a File Using SAX

① Create a string of XML data.

② Create a SAX parser instance using `xml_parser_create`.

③ Create callback functions for the opening and closing element tag events.

④ Use the `xml_set_element_handler` function to map the functions to the callback events.

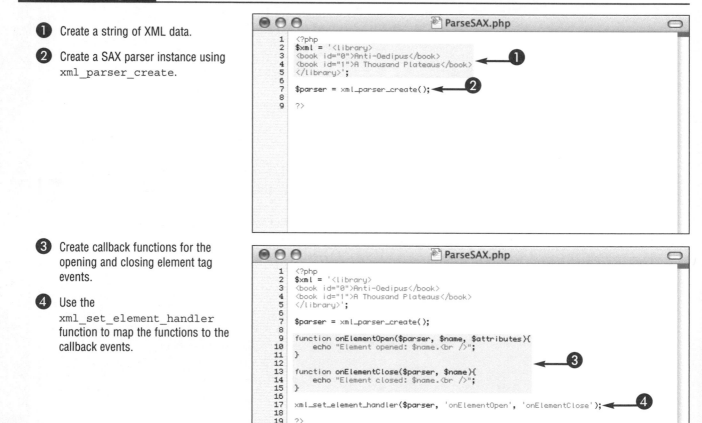

⑤ Call the `xml_parse` function, passing your parser and XML string.

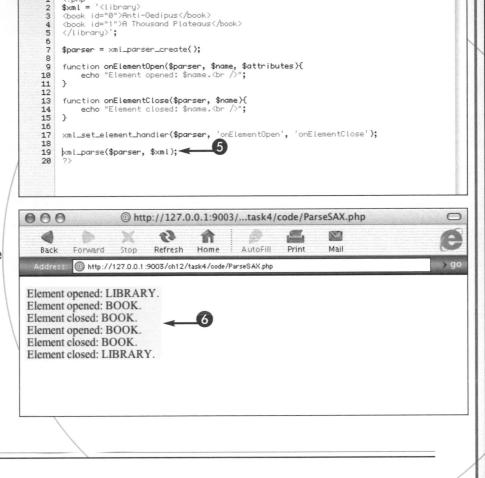

```
      ParseSAX.php
1   <?php
2   $xml = '<library>
3   <book id="0">Anti-Oedipus</book>
4   <book id="1">A Thousand Plateaus</book>
5   </library>';
6
7   $parser = xml_parser_create( );
8
9   function onElementOpen($parser, $name, $attributes ){
10      echo "Element opened: $name.<br />";
11  }
12
13  function onElementClose($parser, $name ){
14      echo "Element closed: $name.<br />";
15  }
16
17  xml_set_element_handler($parser, 'onElementOpen', 'onElementClose' );
18
19  xml_parse($parser, $xml);                    ⑤
20  ?>
```

⑥ View your script in a Web browser.

The XML file is parsed, with the appropriate callback functions being called.

```
        @ http://127.0.0.1:9003/...task4/code/ParseSAX.php
  ◀        ▶        ✖        ↻        🏠        📄        🖨        ✉
 Back   Forward   Stop   Refresh   Home   AutoFill   Print   Mail          e

Address:  @ http://127.0.0.1:9003/ch12/task4/code/ParseSAX.php          › go

Element opened: LIBRARY.
Element opened: BOOK.
Element closed: BOOK.
Element opened: BOOK.          ⑥
Element closed: BOOK.
Element closed: LIBRARY.
```

Extra

You can use SAX parsers in conjunction with other XML handling functionality. For example, you might use a SAX parser to preprocess XML data before being converted into a DOMDocument object for further processing.

You can wrap SAX functionality into a class to provide an object-oriented interface to SAX functionality.

Example:
```
class SAXOjbect{
  private $processor;
  private $success=false;
  public function __construct($encoding=null){
    $this->processor = xml_create($encoding);
    xml_set_element_handler($this->processor,
      $this->elementOpened,
      $this->elementClosed);
  }
  public function parse($data, $is_final=false){
    $this->success = xml_parse($this->processor, $data, $is_final);
  }
}
```

Parse a File Using DOM

Y ou can create an instance of a DOMDocument or DOMDocument subclass to parse an XML file into a traversable DOM structure.

You can create a DOMDocument instance using the new keyword. After a DOMDocument has been instantiated, you can use the load method to load an external XML file and have it automatically parsed into the DOMDocument instance.

The load method accepts a single required argument representing the path to the XML file you want to parse. The load method returns a Boolean true if the file is found, loaded, and parsed. If there is an error, the load method returns false.

You can call the load method statically using DOMDocument::load('file.xml');. Doing so creates a new DOMDocument instance and load the specified file.

After the DOMDocument object has been loaded, you can use methods such as getElementsByTagName and getElementById to retrieve lists of elements or individual elements contained by the DOMDocument instance. The getElementsByTagName method accepts a string representing the name of the element types to be retrieved. The return value is a DOMNodeList, which is a collection supporting iteration through standard loop structures.

The getElementById method requires that your document conform to a given DTD that specifies an element attribute of type ID for the element in question. You can use the DOMDocument validateOnParse property to ensure that the document is validated before trying to access an element id. Additionally, you can manually call the validate method of the DOMDocument object after the load method has completed to ensure that no id-related errors will be thrown.

Parse a File Using DOM

① Create a new DOMDocument instance using the new keyword and the DOMDocument class name.

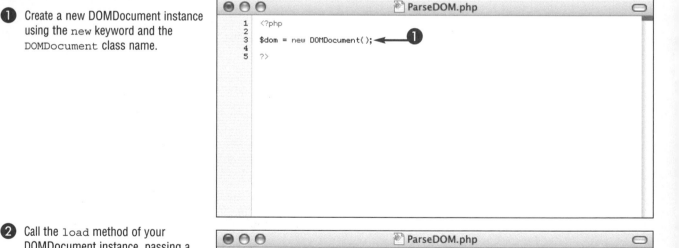

② Call the load method of your DOMDocument instance, passing a string representing the XML file you want to load.

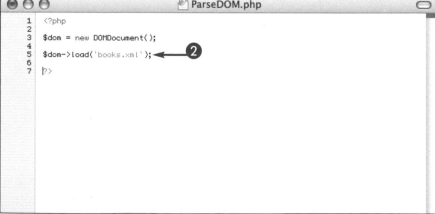

③ Use `getElementsByTagName` to retrieve a DOMNodeList collection of all elements with a specified tag.

④ Iterate over the collection using a standard `foreach` loop structure.

⑤ Print an attribute to the output stream to verify that the correct elements are parsed.

```php
<?php

$dom = new DOMDocument();

$dom->load('books.xml');

$books = $dom->getElementsByTagName('book');     ◀—— ③

foreach($books as $book){                          ◀—— ④
    echo 'Found a book titled: ' . $book->getAttribute('title') . '<br />';   ◀—— ⑤
}                                                  ◀—— ④

?>
```

⑥ View your script in a Web browser.

The XML file is loaded and parsed and all matching elements are printed.

Address: http://127.0.0.1:9003/ch12/task6/code/ParseDOM.php

Found a book titled: The Gay Science
Found a book titled: Thus Spoke Zarathustra   ◀—— ⑥
Found a book titled: Capital
Found a book titled: Moses and Monotheism

Apply It

You can subclass the DOMDocument object to create an object for a specific type of XML file, such as an application configuration file.

Example:
```php
class AppConfig extends DOMDocument{
  public static USER_TAG = 'user';
  public function __construct(){
    $this->preserveWhiteSpace = FALSE;
  }
  public function getUsers(){
    return $this->getElementsByTagName(AppConfig::USER_TAG);
  }
}
```

Write a File Using DOM

The PHP DOMDocument class is used to load, parse, and modify an XML document. You can also create a DOMDocument without loading a file, instead using methods to create new nodes and append them to your document.

The DOMDocument `createElement` method can be used to create a new DOMElement instance. The method accepts one required and one optional argument. The first is a string representing the name of the tag to be used in defining the new element. The second is a string representing the value to be set for the element after the element has been created.

When the `createElement` method is called and executes successfully, a new DOMElement instance is returned. If there is an error in the method call, a Boolean `false` value is returned. It is important to note that the DOMElement

instance created by the `createElement` method is not appended to the DOMDocument instance by which the call is made. To append the element, you must call the `appendChild` method of a DOMNode.

After modifications have been made and you are ready to store your XML in a standard XML file, you can use the DOMDocument `save` method. The `save` method accepts a string representing the name of the file to which the data should be saved. If the `save` method is successful, the number of bytes written to the hard drive is returned. If there is an error, such as a permission error, a Boolean `false` is returned.

Saving a DOMDocument does not destroy the document. For this reason, a DOMDocument can be saved progressively or saved prior to possibly destructive operations.

Write a File Using DOM

① Create a new DOMDocument instance using the `new` keyword and the DOMDocument class name.

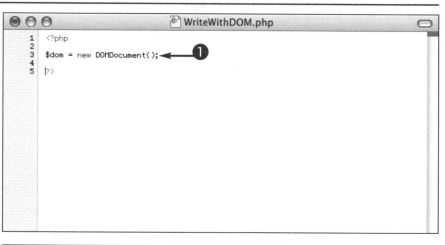

② Use the `createElement` method to create an element.

Pass the name of the tag to be used as a string argument.

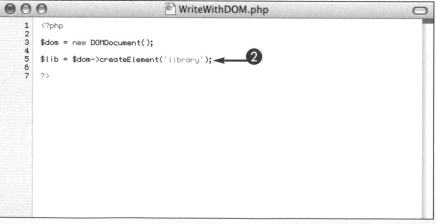

③ Use the `appendChild` method to add the new element to your document.

④ Use the DOMDocument `save` method to save the XML document to the hard drive.

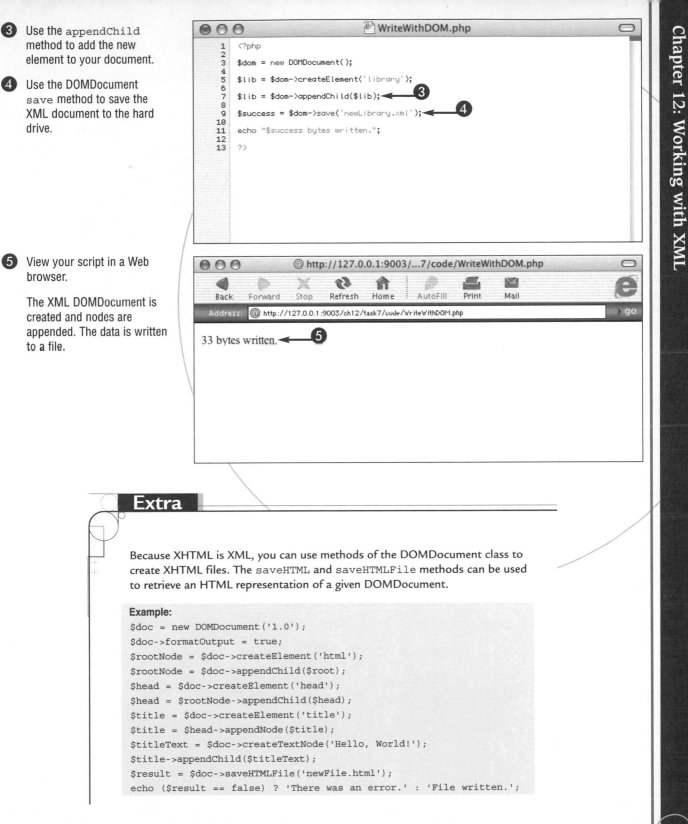

```php
<?php

$dom = new DOMDocument( );

$lib = $dom->createElement('library');

$lib = $dom->appendChild($lib);          ③

$success = $dom->save('newLibrary.xml');   ④

echo "$success bytes written.";

?>
```

⑤ View your script in a Web browser.

The XML DOMDocument is created and nodes are appended. The data is written to a file.

33 bytes written.   ⑤

Extra

Because XHTML is XML, you can use methods of the DOMDocument class to create XHTML files. The `saveHTML` and `saveHTMLFile` methods can be used to retrieve an HTML representation of a given DOMDocument.

Example:
```php
$doc = new DOMDocument('1.0');
$doc->formatOutput = true;
$rootNode = $doc->createElement('html');
$rootNode = $doc->appendChild($root);
$head = $doc->createElement('head');
$head = $rootNode->appendChild($head);
$title = $doc->createElement('title');
$title = $head->appendNode($title);
$titleText = $doc->createTextNode('Hello, World!');
$title->appendChild($titleText);
$result = $doc->saveHTMLFile('newFile.html');
echo ($result == false) ? 'There was an error.' : 'File written.';
```

Parse HTML Using DOM

When using a modern Document Type Definition (DTD) and following the rules of XHTML, your Web pages are inherently valid XML documents. Often, though, we have to handle legacy systems or those that are not well built and rely on older, messier HTML syntax.

When our documents are marked up using an XML-based language, performing operations on the files is quite simple because we can use any of a multitude of XML-related technologies to load, parse, modify, and save our documents.

Unfortunately, the rules by which many HTML documents have been structured are so flexible or so frequently broken that automating processing is an impressive undertaking. Luckily, PHP 5 provides the DOMDocument object that has convenient methods for processing not only valid XML and XHTML documents but poorly-formed HTML as well.

You can load a string of HTML into a DOMDocument using the loadHTML method. The loadHTML method accepts a single argument representing the string of HTML source code you want to process. The return value for the loadHTML method is a Boolean value representing the success of the load and parse operation.

After the DOMDocument has loaded, you can manipulate nodes in your DOM tree using the standard DOM methods such as createElement, appendChild, and getElementsByTagName.

The saveHTML method can be used to dump a current representation of your DOMDocument object to a string using HTML syntax instead of the XML syntax generated when using saveXML. To save a string to an HTML file, you can use the saveHTMLFile method. When using the saveHTMLFile method, you specify a string representing the path to a file. The method returns a Boolean false on error and the number of bytes written to file on success.

Parse HTML Using DOM

① Create a new DOMDocument instance using the new keyword and the DOMDocument class name.

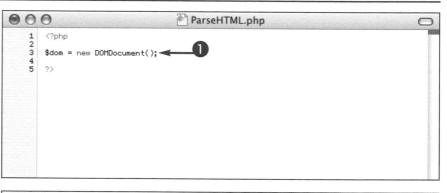

② Use the loadHTMLFile method to load an HTML file from your server.

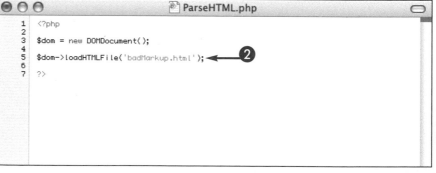

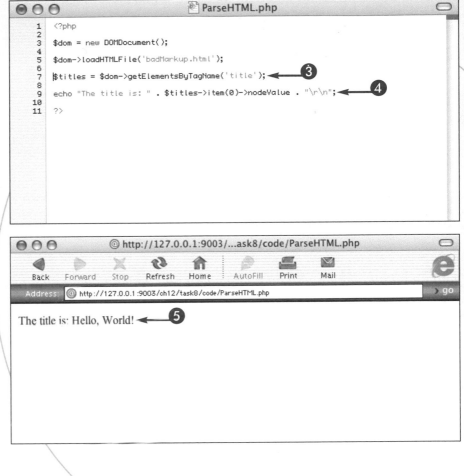

③ Locate the title of the document using `getElementsByTagName`, passing `'title'` as the search value.

④ Locate the first element in the list and print the value to the output stream.

⑤ View your script in a Web browser.

The XML DOMDocument is created and an HTML file is loaded and parsed. The title element is found and printed to the screen.

ParseHTML.php

```php
1  <?php
2
3  $dom = new DOMDocument();
4
5  $dom->loadHTMLFile('badMarkup.html');
6
7  $titles = $dom->getElementsByTagName('title');  ③
8
9  echo "The title is: " . $titles->item(0)->nodeValue . "\r\n";  ④
10
11 ?>
```

`@ http://127.0.0.1:9003/...ask8/code/ParseHTML.php`

Address: `@ http://127.0.0.1:9003/ch12/task8/code/ParseHTML.php`

The title is: Hello, World! ⑤

Extra

You can use the HTML support in the DOMDocument object to load a fairly well-formed HTML document and perform actions such as closing `<br>` tags and quoting attributes automatically. By loading an HTML string or file and using the `saveXML` method, you can have the HTML file converted to valid XML. It is important to note that the document must nest tags correctly and not use illegal characters in tags or attributes. The DOMDocument cannot clean up all poorly formed HTML, but can assist in cleaning up tag case, unclosed tags, unquoted attributes, and lacking DTDs.

TYPE THIS:

```php
$dom = new DOMDocument();

$dom-
>loadHTML('<html><head><title>
hello</title>

<body>line1<p>line2</body></
html>');
echo $dom->saveXML();
```

RESULT:

```
<?xml version="1.0" standalone="yes"?>

<!DOCTYPE html PUBLIC "-//W3C//DTD HTML
4.0 Transitional//EN" "http://www.w3.org/
TR/REC-html40/loose.dtd">

<html><head><title>hello</title></head>
<body><p>line1</p><p>line2</p></body>
</html>
```

Using XPath

XPath is a query language used to seek elements in a DOM. You can think of XPath as something similar to SQL, but for XML. Like SQL, you can perform simple straight value selections, or leverage the more complex and powerful expression evaluation functionality to perform complex searches. For example, you can find all elements with a `class` attribute matching a certain value.

To perform an XPath lookup you must first create a DOMDocument object. You can read more about creating a DOMDocument object in the task "Parse a File Using DOM."

After you have a DOMDocument object, you must create a new DOMXPath or DOMXPath subclass instance. This is accomplished using the `new` keyword. The constructor for the DOMXPath class accepts a single required argument representing a DOMDocument or DOMDocument subclass instance.

You can execute a query using the `query` method of the DOMXPath object. The `query` method accepts one required

and one optional argument. The required argument is a string representing the XPath expression to be evaluated. The second argument is a DOMNode instance representing a node within the DOMDocument object to be used as the relative point of reference. In absence of the second argument, the expression passed to the `query` method is executed relative to the root node in the DOMDocument.

XPath expression syntax is quite robust. In its simplest form, it allows you to drill down into a DOM tree using path separators in much the same way you specify paths to files in a file system. For example, you might find all third-level nodes using an expression such as `/level1/level2/level3`.

You can use XPath to look up attributes, the position of elements in their parent node, properties of nodes such as the length of their name or the number of child nodes they contain, and much more. For more information about the XPath query language, you can refer to the World Wide Web Consortium page on XPath at www.w3.org/TR/xpath.

Using XPath

① Create a new DOMDocument instance using the `new` keyword and the `DOMDocument` class name.

② Load XML data using the `load` method.

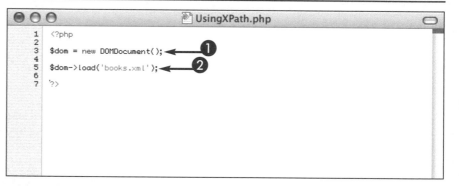

③ Create an instance of the DOMXPath class using the `new` keyword.

- Pass your instance of the DOMDocument class to the constructor.

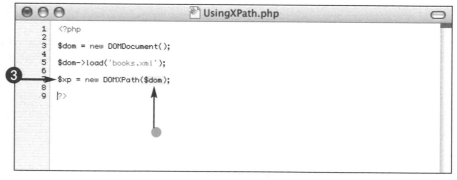

④ Use the `query` method of the DOMXPath object to retrieve a set of nodes.

⑤ Use a `foreach` loop and the `echo` statement to display the values returned by your query.

```php
UsingXPath.php
1   <?php
2
3   $dom = new DOMDocument();
4
5   $dom->load('books.xml');
6
7   $xp = new DOMXPath($dom);
8
9   $result = $xp->query('/library/book[@authorid=1001]');   ◄── 4
10
11  foreach($result as $book){
12      echo "Found a book with the title: " . $book->getAttribute('title') . "<br />";
13  }
14
15  ?>
```
⑤

⑥ View your script in a Web browser.

The XPath expression executed on the DOMDocument object returns any matching nodes.

```
@ http://127.0.0.1:9003/...sk9/code/UsingXPath.php

Back  Forward  Stop  Refresh  Home  AutoFill  Print  Mail

Address: @ http://127.0.0.1:9003/ch12/task9/code/UsingXPath.php   › go

Found a book with the title: The Gay Science      ◄── 6
Found a book with the title: Thus Spoke Zarathustra
```

Extra

You can use the DOMXPath `evaluate` method to execute an expression and return a typed value representing the result of the expression. The `evaluate` method differs from the `query` method in that the `query` method returns a DOMNodeList containing any values matching a query, or no values if there is no match. The DOMXPath `evaluate` method is useful when you want to leverage XPath functions, such as the `count` function. As of the writing of this book, the `evaluate` method is still in development, but it has been added as part of the DOMXPath API and will be available in an upcoming update.

TYPE THIS:

```
// assuming a valid DOMDocument object $dom
$xp = new DOMXPath($dom);
$num = $xp->evaluate('count(/library/book)');
echo "There are $num books in the library.";
```

→

RESULT:

```
There are 4 books
in the library.
```

Introduction to SOAP

imple Object Access Protocol (SOAP) is a standard used to allow disparate applications to communicate using XML-based messaging. Most commonly, SOAP messages are used when communicating with Web services running on remote servers. A Web service is an application that uses standard Web protocols such as HTTP to provide a point of access for other applications. Typically, a Web service provides a specific type of functionality or access to a particular application.

SOAP is covered in the tasks "Create a SOAP Client" and "Create a SOAP Server."

Purpose

SOAP was created to provide a standard way for applications running on separate servers to communicate despite differences in language or toolkit. By leveraging the portability and descriptive nature of XML combined with the architecture of Web services, the Simple Object Access Protocol allows a client application to connect to a remote Web service and request that methods be invoked with sets of well-formed and expected parameters. If a Web service recognizes and approves a given SOAP request, it performs any necessary processing and replies with a SOAP response. The client application parses the SOAP response to obtain return values and processing results.

Extensibility

The power of SOAP comes in its simplicity and extensibility. Because a SOAP request is nothing more than XML, plain text nodes are used to send data from a client to a server. The SOAP message may be comprised of any legal XML statements as long as the request conforms to the SOAP Document Type Definition. This means that one Web service might allow for methods to be invoked by name while another might rely on an expression or might automatically perform operations based on the content of the SOAP request.

Portability

The platform and language independence of SOAP provides the ability to swap frameworks, toolkits, and even languages without altering the interapplication communication protocol with which a system is developed. As long as your Web services accept a given SOAP message and reply with an accepted response, each component in the system can remain unaware of the nature and composition of other components.

Native Programming

The PHP 5 SOAP extension is the first attempt to implement native SOAP support for PHP in the C programming language in which PHP is written. Prior to PHP 5, the SOAP support was written in PHP. This fact meant that the speed with which SOAP-related processing was performed was less than optimal. Currently, the PHP 5 SOAP extension is marked as experimental, which means that caution should be taken in relying on the extension in production on mission-critical applications and services.

Using SOAP

You can create your own SOAP server and client instances in PHP. The `SoapClient` and `SoapServer` classes can be used to create instances of both client and server components. You can also subclass the `SoapClient` and `SoapServer` classes to provide your own custom functionality. To learn more about creating a SOAP client, you can refer to the task "Create a SOAP Client." Information on creating a SOAP server can be found in the task "Create a SOAP Server."

Introduction to XSLT

Extensible Stylesheet Language Transformations (XSLT) is a powerful technology used to transform XML documents into other formats. XSLT is part of a family of technologies used to specify stylesheets for XML documents. XSLT is a functional language that tells XSLT processors how transformations of XML documents should occur. XSLT is itself XML.

XSLT is covered in the task "Transform an XML File Using XSLT."

Uses

XSLT can be used to transform an XML document into a different format. You can transform an XML document so that it conforms to a different DTD than that by which it was defined. A common use for XSLT is to generate an XHTML document from XML data. You can also use XSLT to transform an XML file into a non-XML format. For example, you can use XSL to create PHP code from an XML document.

Presentation Layer

The place of XSLT in a PHP application is on the presentation layer. The robust expression engine of XSLT combined with XPath queries can be used to perform presentation logic that would otherwise require embedded PHP. The separation of application and presentation logic is important for security and efficiency as well as scalability. Due to the power of PHP, allowing for embedded scripting in the presentation layer can expose sensitive information to developers whose main responsibility is not developing the business layer. By removing any bindings with PHP from the presentation layer you help decouple presentation from business logic. Such a multitiered structure allows for future repurposing of the presentation layer or for flexibility in adding new presentation options as requirements change and technology evolves.

Templates

XSL templates are defined using the `xsl` namespace. Each XSL file is a valid XML document and acts as a stylesheet. The root node of each XSL document is an `<xsl:stylesheet>` node.

You can define XSL templates using `<xsl:template>` nodes. Each template node has a match attribute that specifies an XPath expression to be used in matching elements from your XML data to the template rule. Any XSL function nodes present within a template node tell the XSLT processor to perform some function with the data matching that node. For example, you can use the `<xsl:value-of>` node to print the value of a given XML element from your source data or from an XSL variable or expression.

You can recursively apply template matching within a given template using the `<xsl:apply-templates>` element. The recursive matching ability of XSLT is one of the strengths that make XSLT such a powerful functional language.

Looping

The `<xsl:for-each>` element provides a useful loop mechanism much like the PHP `foreach` loop structure. Because of these types of functional elements, it is entirely possible to develop your entire presentation layer using only XSLT, leaving PHP for the business logic layer and increasing the scalability and portability of your application design.

More about the XSLT language can be found at www.w3.org/TR/xslt.

Create a SOAP Client

You can create a SOAP client application to act as an endpoint in a SOAP-based Web service exchange.

When creating a SOAP client, the first step is to gather and analyze information about the SOAP server with which your client application will communicate. Because SOAP allows for messages and structured parameters to be sent from one application to another but does not itself define either the server or the client, you must take care to ensure that your client conforms to the expectations of the server.

- The essential information for creating a SOAP client is:
- The name of the method you want to call on the server
- The endpoint URL of the Web service with which you will communicate
- The SOAPAction header value for the method you want to invoke

- The namespace URI for the method you want to invoke
- The names and types of any input and output parameters accepted and provided by the server

You can use this information to create a SOAP client. A new `SoapClient` instance can be created using the `new` keyword. The `SoapClient` constructor accepts one required and one optional argument. The first argument is the URI of the Web Service Definition Language (WSDL) file to be used in defining the actions of the client. If no WSDL file URI is given, you must pass null as the first argument and provide an associative array of options for the client.

When working in WSDL-mode, you can call methods directly on the SoapClient instance as long as they have been defined in the WSDL file. When no WSDL file has been provided, you must use the `SoapClient __call` method.

Create a SOAP Client

① Create a new SoapClient instance using the `new` keyword.

② Pass the URI to a WSDL file in the constructor.

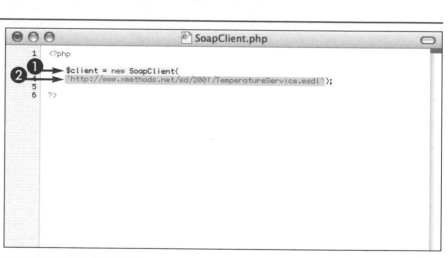

③ Call a method as defined by the WSDL file, passing any required argument as you would to an object method or function.

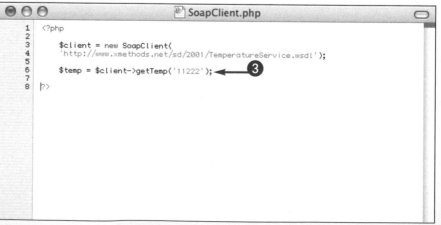

④ Test the return value to determine the success of the method invocation.

```php
1   <?php
2
3       $client = new SoapClient(
4           'http://www.xmethods.net/sd/2001/TemperatureService.wsdl' );
5
6       $temp = $client->getTemp( '11222' );
7
8       echo "The temperature in Brooklyn is: $temp.";        ← 4
9   ?>
```

SoapClient.php

⑤ View your script in a Web browser.

The SOAP client is created and a method is called on a remote SOAP server.

@ http://127.0.0.1:9003/...k11/code/SoapClient.php

Back   Forward   Stop   Refresh   Home   AutoFill   Print   Mail

Address: @ http://127.0.0.1:9003/ch12/task11/code/SoapClient.php   › go

The temperature in Brooklyn is: 43. ← 5

Extra

When working in the recommended WSDL mode, you can use a SoapClient instance to retrieve information about the SOAP server with which it communicates. The __getFunctions method returns a listing of functions accessible on the server. You can get a listing of data types for the server using the __getTypes method of the SoapClient class.

Example:
```php
$client = new SoapClient($myWSDLURI);
$functions = $client->__getFunctions();
$types = $client->__getTypes();
echo 'The functions provided by the server are: ';
print_r($functions);
echo 'The types used with the server are: ';
print_r($types);
```

Create a SOAP Server

Y ou can use PHP to create a Web service using SOAP. The SoapServer class provides functionality for handling a SOAP request and sending back a SOAP response.

The first step in creating a SOAP server is to decide what functionality it provides and determine the names of methods and structure of arguments for each method. You can use a WSDL file to define your SOAP server. WSDL is an XML-based standard used in defining the functionality of Web services. By using WSDL, clients and servers can automatically configure themselves to interact. A WSDL is therefore similar to an interface in object-oriented programming in that it acts as a contract of sorts, enabling disparate objects to interact.

After a WSDL file has been defined for your Web service, you can create an instance of the SoapServer class using the new keyword. The SoapServer constructor accepts the URI for your WSDL file as an argument. After your SoapServer instance has been created, you can use the addFunction method to map one or more functions to your SoapServer instance. Any function registered with the addFunction method is mapped to a corresponding method defined in the WSDL file.

To have your SoapServer instance handle a request, you can invoke the handle method. The handle method accepts no arguments and returns no value, instead acting as a purely functional action trigger.

Create a SOAP Server

① Create a new SoapServer instance using the new keyword.

② Pass the URI to a WSDL file in the constructor.

③ Define a function that corresponds with a message defined in the WSDL file.

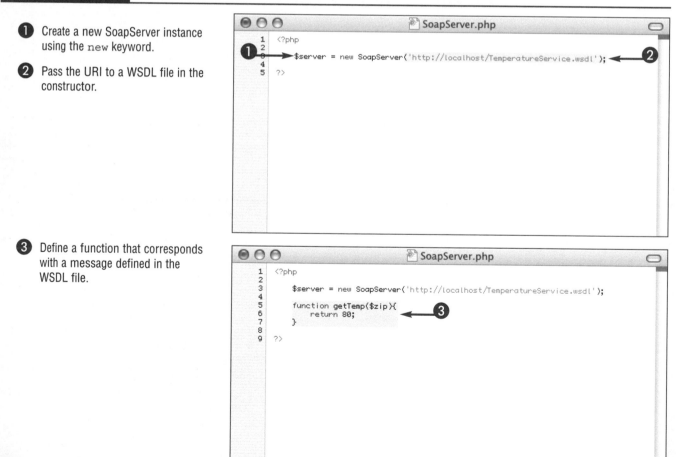

```php
<?php

    $server = new SoapServer('http://localhost/TemperatureService.wsdl');

?>
```

```php
<?php


    $server = new SoapServer('http://localhost/TemperatureService.wsdl');

    function getTemp($zip){
        return 80;
    }

?>
```

④ Use the `addFunction` method to register a function with the SoapServer instance.

⑤ Call the `handle` method of the SoapServer instance to have the server process a SOAP request.

The SOAP server is instantiated and will handle a valid SOAP request.

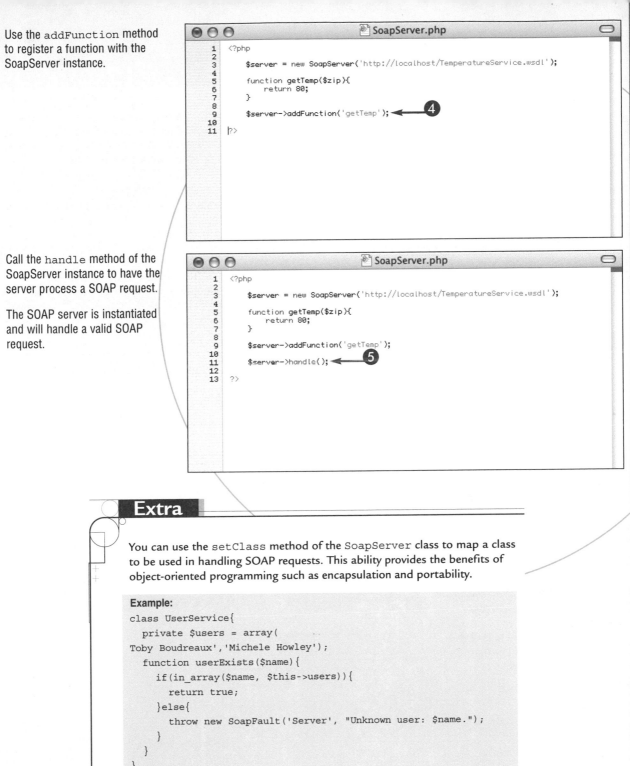

```
                                    SoapServer.php
1    <?php
2
3        $server = new SoapServer('http://localhost/TemperatureService.wsdl');
4
5        function getTemp($zip){
6            return 80;
7        }
8
9        $server->addFunction('getTemp');        ◄——— ④
10
11   ?>
```

```
                                    SoapServer.php
1    <?php
2
3        $server = new SoapServer('http://localhost/TemperatureService.wsdl');
4
5        function getTemp($zip){
6            return 80;
7        }
8
9        $server->addFunction('getTemp');
10
11       $server->handle();        ◄——— ⑤
12
13   ?>
```

Extra

You can use the `setClass` method of the `SoapServer` class to map a class to be used in handling SOAP requests. This ability provides the benefits of object-oriented programming such as encapsulation and portability.

Example:
```
class UserService{
   private $users = array(
Toby Boudreaux','Michele Howley');
   function userExists($name){
      if(in_array($name, $this->users)){
        return true;
      }else{
        throw new SoapFault('Server', "Unknown user: $name.");
      }
   }
}
$server = new SoapServer($myWSDLURI);
$server->setClass('UserService');
$server->handle();
```

Transform an XML File Using XSLT

XSLT is used to transform XML data from one format to another. You can use XSLT to perform data maintenance, enhance SOAP-based Web services, output Web pages for different client formats, and generate SVG graphics or PDF files, among many other things.

You can create an XSLT processor by instantiating the XSLTProcessor class. The importStylesheet method of the XSLTProcessor class is used to set an XSL stylesheet for the transformation. The importStylesheet method accepts a DOMDocument instance representing a loaded XSLT stylesheet.

You can set any transformation parameters using the setParameter method. The setParameter method accepts three arguments. The first is a namespace URI. You can

apply a parameter to the root namespace by passing an empty string for this value. The second argument is a string representing the key by which your parameter is accessed. The third argument is the value that is assigned to the given key.

There are three options for executing an XSLT transformation, each with a corresponding method of the XSLTProcessor object. The transformToXML method can be used to perform a transformation and return a string of XML data representing the result. Alternately, you can use the transformToURI method to write the result of the transformation to a file. Finally, you can use the transformToDoc method to transform the document and return an instance of the DOMDocument class representing the result.

Transform an XML File Using XSLT

① Create a DOMDocument instance to represent your XML data.

② Use the `load` method to load the XML data into the DOMDocument object.

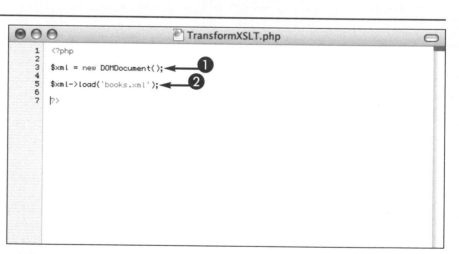

③ Create a DOMDocument instance to represent your XSLT stylesheet.

④ Use the `load` method to load the XSLT stylesheet data into the DOMDocument object.

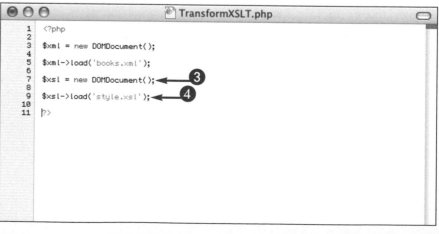

⑤ Create an instance of the XSLTProcessor class.

⑥ Use the `importStylesheet` method to assign your stylesheet DOMDocument instance to the processor.

⑦ Use the `transformToXML` method to transform your data object according to the rules of your XSL styesheet.

⑧ Print the result to the output stream.

⑨ View your script in a Web browser.

The XML data is transformed according to the XSLT stylesheet rules.

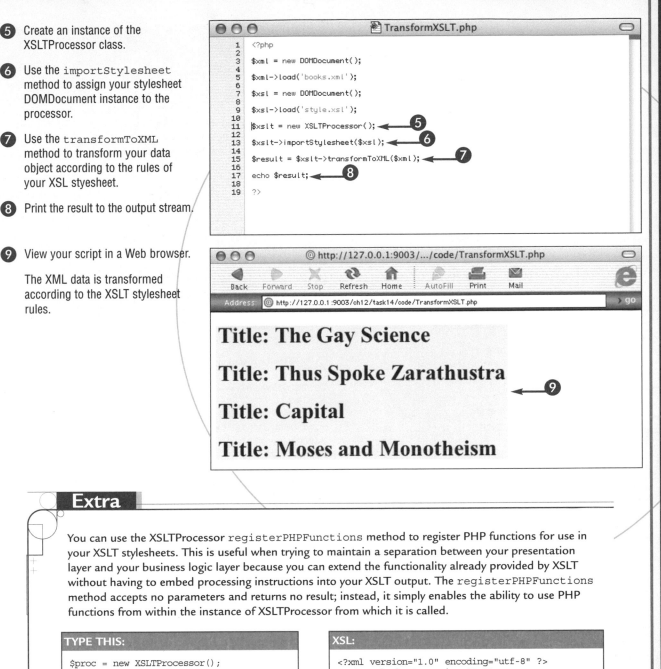

```php
1  <?php
2
3  $xml = new DOMDocument();
4
5  $xml->load('books.xml');
6
7  $xsl = new DOMDocument();
8
9  $xsl->load('style.xsl');
10
11 $xslt = new XSLTProcessor();          ← ⑤
12
13 $xslt->importStylesheet($xsl);        ← ⑥
14
15 $result = $xslt->transformToXML($xml); ← ⑦
16
17 echo $result;  ⑧
18
19 ?>
```

Title: The Gay Science

Title: Thus Spoke Zarathustra

Title: Capital

Title: Moses and Monotheism

Extra

You can use the XSLTProcessor `registerPHPFunctions` method to register PHP functions for use in your XSLT stylesheets. This is useful when trying to maintain a separation between your presentation layer and your business logic layer because you can extend the functionality already provided by XSLT without having to embed processing instructions into your XSLT output. The `registerPHPFunctions` method accepts no parameters and returns no result; instead, it simply enables the ability to use PHP functions from within the instance of XSLTProcessor from which it is called.

TYPE THIS:

```php
$proc = new XSLTProcessor();
$data = new DOMDocument();
$data->loadXML('<root></root>');
$style = new DOMDocument();
$style->load('style.xsl');
$proc->registerPHPFunctions();
$proc->importStylesheet($style);
$result = $proc->transformToXML($data);
```

XSL:

```xml
<?xml version="1.0" encoding="utf-8" ?>
<xsl:stylesheet version="1.0"
xmlns:xsl="http://www.w3.org/1999/XSL/Transform"
xmlns:php="http://php.net/xsl">
<xsl:template match="/">
  <xsl:value-of select="php:function('time')" />
</xsl:template>
</xsl:stylesheet>
```

RESULT:

```
The current time is displayed.
```

INDEX

Symbols

( ) (parentheses)
  in conditional statements, 50
  order of operations, 44, 49
:: (colons), object-oriented programming, 204–205
. (dot), concatenation operator, 44
.= (dot equal sign) concatenation-assignment operator, 46
& (ampersand)
  HTML entities, 130
  variable names, 64
&& (ampersands), logical operator, 46
* (asterisk)
  multiplication operator, 44
  wildcard character, 242
*= (asterisk equal sign) multiplication-assignment operator, 45
\ (backslash), escape character, 245
$ (dollar sign), variable names, 64, 68
$value-- (dollar sign...), postdecrement operator, 45
$value++ (dollar sign...), postincrement operator, 45
" (double quote), in string variables, 40
= (equal sign)
  assignment operator, 38, 45
  setting directives, 26
== (equal signs), comparison operator, 47
=== (equal signs), comparison operator, 47
!= (exclamation equal sign), comparison operator, 47
!== (exclamation equal signs), comparison operator, 47
! (exclamation point), logical operator, 47
(hashmark), comment delimiter, 37
< (left angle bracket), comparison operator, 47
<= (left angle bracket equal), comparison operator, 47
<%...%> (left angle bracket percent...), ASP-style PHP delimiters, 35
<?...?> (left angle bracket question mark...), PHP delimiters, 35
<<< (left angle brackets), heredoc delimiter, 41
- (minus sign), subtraction operator, 44
-= (minus equal sign) subtraction-assignment operator, 45
--$value (minus signs...), predecrement operator, 45
% (percent sign), modulus operator, 44
%= (percent equal sign) modulo-assignment operator, 46
+ (plus sign), addition operator, 44
++$value (plus signs...), preincrement operator, 45
+= (plus equal sign) addition-assignment operator, 45
? (question mark)
  ternary operator, 50
  Unicode text, 132
> (right angle bracket), comparison operator, 47
>= (right angle bracket equal), comparison operator, 47
' (single quote), in string variables, 40
/ (slash), division operator, 44
/*...*/ (slash asterisk...), comment delimiter, 36

// (slashes), comment delimiter, 36
_ (underscore), in function names, 58
|| (vertical bars), logical operator, 46
{ } (braces)
  class names, 196
  in functions, 58
  if statements, 50
  string operations, 122–123
  switch statements, 52
  while loops, 54
[ ] (square brackets), and arrays, 84
/= (slash equal sign) division-assignment operator, 46
; (semicolon)
  comment delimiter, 26
  heredoc delimiter, 41
  HTML entities, 130
  removing from database records, 254

A

abstract classes, 197, 207, 209
abstract keyword, 207
access level. See permissions
accessor methods, 196
addFunction method, 292–293
adding database records, 232–233, 240–241
Administrator accounts, 9
affirmative validation approach, 255
ampersand (&)
  HTML entities, 130
  variable names, 64
ampersands (&&), logical operator, 46
and operator, 46
Apache
  Custom install, 5
  downloading, 4
  End User License Agreement (EULA), 4
  installation location, 6
  installing, 4–7, 20–21
  shortcut commands, 7
  starting/stopping, 7, 21
  switching versions, 21
  technical support, 5
  testing, 6
  Typical install, 5
apache -k shutdown command, 7
apachectl command, 21
arguments, passing to functions, 62–65
arithmetic operators, 44
array function, 84–85, 86–87
array_flip function, 102–103

INDEX

INDEX

INDEX

INDEX

INDEX